The EOKA Cause

The EOKA Cause

Nationalism and the Failure of Cypriot Enosis

Andrew R. Novo

BLOOMSBURY ACADEMIC
LONDON • NEW YORK • OXFORD • NEW DELHI • SYDNEY

BLOOMSBURY ACADEMIC
Bloomsbury Publishing Plc
50 Bedford Square, London, WC1B 3DP, UK
1385 Broadway, New York, NY 10018, USA
29 Earlsfort Terrace, Dublin 2, Ireland

BLOOMSBURY, BLOOMSBURY ACADEMIC and the Diana logo
are trademarks of Bloomsbury Publishing Plc

First published in Great Britain 2021
This paperback edition published in 2022

Copyright © Andrew R. Novo, 2021

Andrew R. Novo has asserted his right under the Copyright, Designs and
Patents Act, 1988, to be identified as Author of this work.

For legal purposes the Acknowledgements on p. viii constitute an extension
of this copyright page.

Series design by Adriana Brioso
Cover image: Prisoners of war in Camp Kokkinotrimithia in Cyprus.
(© Jack Esten/Picture Post/Getty Images)

All rights reserved. No part of this publication may be reproduced or transmitted
in any form or by any means, electronic or mechanical, including photocopying,
recording, or any information storage or retrieval system, without prior
permission in writing from the publishers.

Bloomsbury Publishing Plc does not have any control over, or responsibility for, any
third-party websites referred to or in this book. All internet addresses given in this
book were correct at the time of going to press. The author and publisher regret any
inconvenience caused if addresses have changed or sites have ceased to exist,
but can accept no responsibility for any such changes.

A catalogue record for this book is available from the British Library.

A catalog record for this book is available from the Library of Congress.

ISBN: HB: 978-1-8386-0650-3
PB: 978-0-7556-3534-4
ePDF: 978-1-8386-0651-0
eBook: 978-1-8386-0652-7

Typeset by Deanta Global Publishing Services, Chennai, India

To find out more about our authors and books visit www.bloomsbury.com and
sign up for our newsletters

To Yiannis and Natalie, my two most valuable guides through this long and challenging process.
'More is thy due than more than all can pay.'

Contents

Acknowledgements		viii
Introduction		1
1	*Terra irredenta*: Duelling nationalisms	7
2	Imperial constitution: Rejection and radicalization	21
3	'This sacred goal': Communists, churchmen and the struggle for the nationalist narrative	31
4	Taking up arms: The continuation of politics through force	45
5	Deepening divides: Political and ethnic fractures	55
6	A time to talk: The Harding-Makarios negotiations	65
7	'To destroy EOKA and re-establish law and order'	85
8	False dawn: The failed road to peace	109
9	On all fronts: EOKA, TMT and the threat of civil war	129
10	End game: Killing a dream	149
Conclusion		167
Notes		173
Bibliography		204
Index		214

Acknowledgements

Anyone who has written a book knows that it is a long and arduous process. The process for this work began during my DPhil research at Oxford in 2007. During the years since then, I have been fortunate to benefit from the support of many people who helped make this book possible.

I am especially grateful to Gernot Klantschnig and Chieh Huang who opened their home and kitchen to me for long stretches of time during my Oxford research. Special thanks and heartfelt gratitude are due to Mrs Juliet Campbell, who hosted me at her lovely Oxford home and offered me the unpublished memoirs of Sir Alec Bishop.

I must thank Amin Aladin, Yiannis Katsarakis and Domenico Trotta, who hosted me in London at various times during seemingly innumerable trips to the National Archives, sparing me many hours on the train. Thanks are also due to Michael Jago for inspiring me to continue my studies at Oxford.

I am especially indebted to Sir Hew Strachan for his tireless efforts as my supervisor during my DPhil and his continued friendship and professional guidance. He is truly a gracious gentleman and mentor.

I am also thankful to the hard-working and helpful staff at a number of archives: the National Archives (London), the National Archives (College Park), the National Archives (Nicosia), the Imperial War Museum Archives (London), the Archives of Archbishopric of Cyprus (Nicosia) and the Archives of the Council of History Memory of the 1955–1959 EOKA Struggle (SIMAE) (Nicosia).

I am grateful to the highly professional team of editors and publishers at I.B. Tauris and Bloomsbury: Nayiri Kendir, Giles Herman, Leela Ulganathan and Dhanuja Ravi for their hard work and for their continued support in bringing this work to publication.

Finally, I am eternally grateful to my family. In particular, I must thank my parents for their unflinching emotional, physical and financial support. I must thank my sons, Stephanos and Marcos, for their kindness and the joy they bring. I must thank my mother-in-law, Yianna, whose cooking kept me going during many months of fieldwork in Cyprus. And I must thank my father-in-law, Yiannis, and my wife, Natalie, for their extraordinary help in securing and conducting interviews, translating old documents, and opening many doors that would otherwise have been closed to me. This book is dedicated to them.

Introduction

No issue has played a greater role in defining the modern history of Cyprus than the cause of Cypriot unification (*enosis*)[1] with Greece. Like many political causes, in the abstract, it is neither good nor bad. Supporters of *enosis* once considered it, and some still do consider it, a natural resolution of the essential 'Greekness' of the majority of Cypriots. Opponents often argue that it undermines the multicultural nature of Cyprus. In their view, *enosis*, as a concept, leaves Turkish-Cypriots either with no place on an island that is equally theirs or in the reduced status of second-class citizens. Both of these nationalistic views suffer from the myopia imposed by chauvinism and a selective understanding of citizenship, nationality and history.

On 1 April 1955, a segment of pro-*enosis* supporters calling themselves the National Organization of Cypriot Fighters (EOKA)[2] launched an armed struggle against British security forces. They were no more than a few dozen in number; later in the conflict, the number of sworn EOKA members would peak at approximately 300. Nevertheless, at the height of operations, 35,000 British troops along with 5,000 policemen drawn from Cyprus and across the empire were deployed to establish and keep order on an island with only half a million inhabitants.

EOKA's goal of *enosis* was distinctive among the insurgencies of the post–Cold War period. In an age when most resistance movements fought for independence, EOKA sought to unify Cyprus with an existing nation – Greece. This was not the only peculiar feature of violence in Cyprus. Contrary to the left-wing politics which inspired much anti-colonial sentiment globally, the struggle in Cyprus was spearheaded by nationalists from the right wing and championed by the Orthodox Church. Within Cyprus, both the Greek-Cypriot majority and the Turkish-Cypriot minority had sovereign states protecting and advocating their interests in the international community. Elements within the Greek government, both officially and unofficially, supported the cause of *enosis* – though more hesitantly than Greek-Cypriot nationalists desired and more cautiously than either the British or Turkish governments wanted to admit. Support from policymakers in Athens was critical in sparking and maintaining the insurgency, although they eventually proved more open to compromise than the Greek-Cypriots who initiated and carried out the campaign. The Turkish government was also an essential player. Due to its desire to protect both the Turkish-Cypriot minority and its strategic interests in Cyprus, Ankara opposed *enosis*. By 1958, Turkey was actively training and supplying a Turkish-Cypriot militant group – the Turkish Resistance Organisation (TMT)[3] – and it was feared that Greece and Turkey were on the verge of war.

Cyprus was also viewed as essential to British regional interests. Britain's withdrawal from the Indian subcontinent and Palestine after the Second World War was fundamental to a repositioning of British power. Within some circles, there were hopes that a post-war empire could be reinvigorated by focusing on territories in Asia, Africa and the Middle East. British imperialism was also adopting greater flexibility, exerting its influence through economics, military partnerships and political relationships rather than the traditional means of direct political control.[4] Cyprus was seen as a keystone to these policies. As the Middle East military headquarters from 1954, the island was a crucial component in Britain's regional posture. Troops based in Cyprus supported British interests in Jordan, Iraq and the Suez Canal. Because of these factors, events on the island affected broader alliance structures and influenced British policy throughout the region.[5]

For these reasons, the focus of this book is both local and international. It explores dynamics among and within the Greek-Cypriot and Turkish-Cypriot communities analysing the components of nationalism and ethnic conflict at play on the island. It lays out the inception and ideology of the *enosis* movement, and the nature of the British response at both the military level and the political level. Utilizing recently declassified British security documents, primary Greek-language sources from EOKA's members and interviews with key participants in conjunction with literature on both counter-insurgency and the end of the British Empire, it explores the cause of *enosis* from a multitude of perspectives. The goal is to understand why the pursuit of this objective led to violence and how the ideologies both supporting and opposing it within the broader Cypriot community (Greek-Cypriots and Turkish-Cypriots) – and within the Greek-Cypriot community specifically – determined the course of the struggle. While the compromised outcome of Cypriot independence has been studied extensively, this book also hopes to provide a brief analysis of how the peculiar factors enumerated here continue to influence conflict in Cyprus today.

On a more theoretical level, this book looks to uncover the close relationship between violence and political action. At the same time, precisely because tensions in Cyprus were inescapably linked to the broader region, the book delves into the dynamics of British, Greek and Turkish relations, with their concomitant influence on international affairs. It seeks to weave the domestic account into the international narrative by demonstrating how the relatively minor conflict in Cyprus had implications for key Cold War relationships far beyond the island.

Chronologically, Cyprus fits within a string of anti-colonial struggles against British power during the 1940s and 1950s. These conflicts include the operations of Jewish nationalists in Mandate Palestine, communist forces in Malaya and the Mau Mau Uprising in Kenya. As part of this broader discourse, Cyprus, like Palestine, Malaya and Kenya, has been the subject of serious scholarly work from several perspectives.[6] Robert Holland's excellent book *Britain and the Revolt in Cyprus 1954–1959* (1998), as the title suggests, is focused on British perspective towards events in Cyprus in tandem with domestic British politics. David French's more recent book, *Fighting EOKA* (2015), is similarly Anglo-centric, with a focus on the military aspects of the struggle, particularly analysing it as a counter-insurgency campaign.[7] Other works such as Stephen Xydis's *Cyprus: Conflict and Conciliation, 1954–1958* (1967) or Andreas Varnavas's *A History of the Liberation Struggle of EOKA (1955–1959)* (2004) focus on developments in Cyprus and in Greece. Xydis's later work *Reluctant Republic*

(1973) follows the intricate diplomacy between Greece and Turkey between 1958 and 1960 that established the modern Republic of Cyprus. Hatzivassiliou (2002) presents an analysis of the first nine decades of 'the Cyprus question'.

Complementing these works is a wealth of recent scholarship on the various nationalisms at play in Greece, Turkey and Cyprus and their influence on conflict in Cyprus. Ioannis Stefanidis's *Isle of Discord: Nationalism, Imperialism and the Making of the Cyprus Problem* (1999) is a seminal contribution followed, chronologically, by Morag (2004), Dietzel and Makrides (2009), Gates (2013), and Kitromilides (2013). The goal of *The EOKA Cause* is to unify these different streams with an analysis of the implications of violence in Cyprus on the broader region and global politics. This is important precisely because these geopolitical issues exerted such a powerful influence on events in Cyprus and, in turn, were significantly influenced by them.

At the same time, three core considerations of the British colonial power shaped the strategic environment: the global, the regional and the local. Globally, the imperatives of Cold War policy dictated the need to defend Europe from the threat of the Soviet Union through a strong NATO. Regionally, Britain hoped to maintain its influence and power projection capabilities in the Middle East and ensure the continued cooperation between Greece and Turkey. Locally, changes in the Cypriot status quo threatened law and order on the island. As events in the late 1940s and early 1950s increased the importance of Cyprus to British policymakers, the desire to put an end to British rule among Greek-Cypriots also grew in intensity, thus paving the way for a showdown.

While British policymakers were constrained by considerations along these three axes, the Greek-Cypriot nationalists who championed *enosis* had their own weaknesses. Although their cause had broad support within their own community – from both the left and right – it was opposed by both Turkey and Turkish-Cypriots with near unanimity. Greek-Cypriot leaders failed to acknowledge the real and substantive opposition from Turkey for *enosis* and underestimated or ignored the anti-*enosis* sentiment among the Turkish-Cypriot community. In choosing to pursue their goal through violence, Greek-Cypriot leaders did not calculate the unrest which violence would spark with the Turkish-Cypriot community and were ill-prepared for both the local and international ramifications of such a confrontation. Among EOKA and its supporters there was an unrealistic expectation that Turkey would remain sidelined in any dispute regarding Cyprus. At the same time, the broad-based rhetorical and emotional support for *enosis* among Greek-Cypriots did not translate to universal support for EOKA's tactics. Over the course of the struggle, divisions *within* the Greek-Cypriot community over the violence and the methods of EOKA would open additional fissures in the island's political life.

On the international level, Greek-Cypriot nationalists exerted a great deal of pressure on Greece to support their cause. But here too, they miscalculated. Exhausted from its experiences of the Second World War, the German occupation and its own civil war, Greece was not in a position to support new disruptions domestically or internationally. Greece was hesitant to upset its close relations with Britain. Later, the government in Athens came to view the cause of Cypriot *enosis* as a threat to the

Greek minority in Istanbul and its own relations with Turkey. These larger political issues of Greek-Turkish relations were never adequately accounted for by the Greek-Cypriot nationalists, who continued to pressure Greece for more support than it could reasonably be expected to give.

In the end, the cause of *enosis* was hamstrung both by local conditions and by the international climate – a resolution short of the stated cause of unification was agreed. This new arrangement was inherently unstable and created, in Xydis's memorable formulation, a 'reluctant republic'.[8] The Cypriot republic proved not only reluctant but also unstable. The jagged wounds of political divisions, intercommunal violence, constitutional collapse, coup, invasion and occupation remain unhealed. Through Cypriot society more broadly, the bad blood left behind by the unresolved legacy of the *enosis* struggle – and the violence which followed it – endures.

The regional influences and enduring implications of the struggle in Cyprus are powerful reasons to present the story of the cause of Cypriot *enosis* comprehensively and in its own right. When treated as case study or footnote for broader arguments about British decolonization, as in David French's *The British Way in Counter-Insurgency, 1945–1967*, operations in Cyprus have become par for the course of 'dirty' colonial counter-insurgency campaigns where the doctrine of 'minimal force' was only minimally applied and the notion of 'hearts and minds' was little more than window dressing for repression.[9] French's arguments build on existing critiques of British counter-insurgency approaches. John Newsinger's *British Counterinsurgency: From Palestine to Northern Ireland* (2002), for example, condemned the brutal means of repression used in various campaigns.[10] David Anderson presents a similar picture in the edited volume, *Policing and Decolonisation: Politics, Nationalism, and the Police, 1917–65* (1992). In his analysis on Cyprus, Anderson focuses on the role of law enforcement in the counter-insurgency campaign, particularly the difficulty in recruiting and maintaining loyal Greek-Cypriot officers. He is concerned with the social aspect of the police force and the ethnic tensions caused by employing Turkish-Cypriots and Greek-Cypriots to police a Greek-Cypriot nationalist movement. Such a focus is commensurate with Anderson's major work *Histories of the Hanged* (2005), a comprehensive and bitterly critical account of British policy towards the Mau Mau Uprising in Kenya. Like Kenya, Anderson sees Cyprus as 'a dirty war'.[11] Interpretations like those of French and Anderson are meant not only to expose the facts of British excesses but also to oppose the views articulated by authors such as Thomas Mockaitis (1990) who argue that Britain developed a largely successful model of counter-insurgency characterized by the doctrine of 'minimum force'. In this interpretation, 'minimal force' was the result of humanitarian impulses, respect for the law and practical considerations of intelligence gathering. It had a parallel in the efforts directed to winning 'hearts and minds'.[12]

The debate over whether the campaign in Cyprus was a 'dirty war', a successful implementation of 'minimal force' or a failure due to insufficient brutality is tangential to the core issues which defined the course of the struggle. The situation in Cyprus was more complex than any of those descriptions suggest. It was defined by larger factors than debates about counter-insurgency tactics. Cyprus was not a 'clean' war by any means, although it is reasonable to ask if any war has ever been so. In Cyprus, British forces used brutality and torture, abnegated numerous civil liberties, imprisoned thousands, executed those convicted of capital violations of emergency decrees and deployed tens of thousands of soldiers and policemen to combat EOKA. These actions, however, do not negate the fact that the British were confronted with lethal and widespread violence on the part of EOKA. In addition to protests and strikes, EOKA guerrilla teams ambushed British soldiers. EOKA gunmen shot down policemen and, most controversially, targeted Greek-Cypriots (in the police force and civilians) who they considered 'traitors' to the cause.

In formulating a response, British forces were also in a delicate situation within Cyprus and internationally. In Cyprus, they were soon forced to combat radical Turkish nationalists and attempted to contain violence *between* Greek- and Turkish-Cypriots. They attempted to maintain their interest in the island, but also sought to prevent war between Greece and Turkey – NATO allies since 1952. Lessons from other counter-insurgency campaigns were applied in Cyprus, but their application took a back seat to realities on the ground and their efficacy was circumscribed by the dynamics of international diplomacy and the realities of British grand strategy.

The Cyprus campaign took place not only in the context of other counter-insurgencies but also in the broader framework of a massive reappraisal of Britain's strategic position in the wake of the Second World War. During this period, the British Empire was changing, and refocusing itself on Africa, the Middle East and Southeast Asia while reducing the size of its army. Since its withdrawal from the Indian subcontinent, British policymakers worked to develop a new paradigm of British power through economic bonds, military cooperation, political influence and a special relationship with the United States.

These are some of the many layers to the conflict in Cyprus which this book will illuminate. The struggle in Cyprus, its causes, conduct and conclusion, have not only defined the island's post-colonial history but also shaped the broader history of the region. Like many colonial conflicts its incomplete resolution led not to a durable peace but to an enduring period of civil strife. This violence culminated in the Turkish invasion of Cyprus in 1974. Turkey's continued occupation of the northern third of Cyprus remains 'one of the most intractable questions in contemporary international relations'.[13] The dispute continues to influence relations among Turkey, Greece, Cyprus, the United States and the European Union. Today, it casts a shadow on Turkey's EU accession bid and Cyprus's own attempts to exploit the hydrocarbon wealth in its territorial waters.

Many ingredients shaped the emergency in Cyprus: nationalism, ethnic conflict, international diplomacy, decolonization and grand strategy. Much was at stake for the British in Cyprus and the campaign against *enosis* reflected this. At the same time, the deal that finally ended the violence did not satisfy the aspirations of Greek-Cypriot nationalists. Cyprus did not join the Greek state. British policymakers accepted independence for much of the island while retaining sovereign base areas. As in many other colonies, Britain's withdrawal was earlier than London had hoped, but later and less comprehensive than anti-colonialist forces would have liked. This denouement was largely the result of the successes and failures on the ground and the realities of the international political scene. In a world of continued intercommunal violence, where geopolitics retains its enduring salience, where the lines between terrorism and insurgency are increasingly vague, where communism is no longer the primary mover of insurgent movements and where ethnic conflict and renewed violence in the name of nationalism seems omnipresent, it is worth giving Cyprus a more comprehensive look.

1

Terra irredenta

Duelling nationalisms

Πάλι με χρόνια με καιρούς, πάλι δικά μας θα 'ναι. Once more, as years go by, once more it shall be ours.

– Greek folk song

Greek nationalism, like most modern national movements, has its origins in the nineteenth century. As such, it was the natural inspiration for the Greek Revolution, which began in 1821. After Greece became a sovereign nation in 1830, the quest for unredeemed lands became the primary if not 'the *only* ideology' of the Greek state.[1] In the main, this expansionary agenda was successful. To its initial territory in the Peloponnese, *Sterea Ellada* (Central Greece) and a few islands in the South Aegean, Greece added the Ionian Islands, ceded by Britain, in 1864. Following the Russo-Turkish War of 1877–8, the Great Powers compelled the Ottoman Empire to cede Thessaly in 1881. In 1913, Greece acquired Macedonia, Epirus and Crete as the spoils of her successful participation in the Balkan Wars. In 1919, Western Thrace was added, part of the price paid by a defeated Bulgaria at the conclusion of the First World War. In the same manner, Italy was compelled to surrender the Dodecanese Islands in 1947. Through various vicissitudes, however, the island of Cyprus was never incorporated within the Greek state.[2]

In the context of Greek nationalism and its foreign policy manifestation, the *Meghali Idhea*[3] (Great Idea) – which aimed to restore a state akin to the Byzantine Empire in the Balkans and on both sides of the Aegean – *enosis* was a natural aspiration among many Greek-Cypriots. Understanding the foundations of *enosis* – along with the intellectual and historical baggage it brought in tow – are critical to how we analyse the origins of the struggle against British colonial rule, its course, the forces that evolved to fight against *enosis* and the struggle's result. Greek nationalism framed *enosis* as natural, justified and inevitable. It conceived of Cyprus as a 'Greek' island. Its tenets precluded substantive compromise with Turkish-Cypriots or even a recognition of their concerns for their cultural integrity and social status. In practice, it would impose strategic limitations on the movement, leaving the *enosis* cause with almost insurmountable handicaps.

For many Greek-Cypriots, Greek nationalism served as the foundation for Cyprus's inclusion within the framework of the *Meghali Idhea*. As a foreign policy for Greece, this stressed the importance of bringing Greek speakers within the Greek state. In this way, it was a mirror of contemporaneous, and largely successful, Italian and German irredentist campaigns to form nation states based on linguistic and cultural affinities. Although the *Meghali Idhea* was a current in Greek foreign policy from the beginning of the Greek state, it is most commonly identified with the expansionist policies of Eleftherios Venizelos beginning with the outbreak of the Balkan Wars in 1912 and culminating ten years later with the Greek disaster in Asia Minor.[4] Although the Asia Minor Catastrophe[5] dealt a crippling blow to Greece's physical capacity to pursue irredentism, the ideal remained central to the country's education system and political culture. As one modern scholar has described it, even after 1922, Greeks students 'continued to imbibe the highly romantic, irredentist nationalism of their fathers'.[6]

After the Second World War, as opposition to British colonial rule on Cyprus definitively became the project of nationalist Greek-Cypriots working in tandem with the Orthodox Church, the negative impact of the policy of '*enosis* and only *enosis*' on the island's Turkish-Cypriot minority became more acute. Tensions rose between the two communities and Turkey gradually became more wary of developments in Cyprus. Turkish opposition was a major source of international pressure against *enosis*. Difficulties for the cause existed in Greece as well. Greek poverty and the civil war (1946–9)[7] forced Greece to tread cautiously on the issue to avoid losing vital support from Britain, and later, from the United States. At the same time, while *enosis* might have seemed a natural choice among many Greek-Cypriots, its pursuit was not without peril or controversy.

Part of the controversy stems over the perpetual debate, waged across time and disciplines, concerning the 'Greekness' of Cyprus. Most Greek and Greek-Cypriot writers emphasize cultural and historical continuity between Greece and Cyprus.[8] A particular view of history is central to this argument, namely, that 'Cyprus is inhabited by a race, akin to the ancient Arcadians, which has ever belonged to the Hellenic World. . . . Cyprus had an integral Greek character and contributed to the creation of Greek civilization'.[9]

British bureaucrats, on the other hand, were at pains to distinguish between Cypriots and Greeks, pointing out somewhat tautologically, as Turkish and Turkish-Cypriot representatives later would, that the unification of Cyprus with the Greek state was illegitimate because Cyprus had never been part of the Greek state.[10] Overt racial prejudices often characterized the British analysis of Cypriot identity. Sir Charles Belcher, Cyprus's chief justice from 1927–30, conceded the Europeanness of Greek-Cypriots but remained unconvinced of their Greekness. In his view, they spoke 'a dialect of Greek, but you can no more draw racial conclusions from that than you can from American negroes speaking English. They are darker-complexioned than the mainland Greeks, and almost certainly have a large admixture of Asiatic blood.'[11] Belcher's contemporary Sir Ronald Storrs, who served as governor and commander-in-chief of Cyprus from 1926 to 1932, took a different view, writing that '[t]he Greekness of Cypriots is, in my opinion, indisputable'. Perhaps directly refuting Belcher, he wrote that 'Nationalism is more, is other, than pigmentations and cephalic indices. A man is of the race of which he passionately feels himself to be. No sensible person will deny that the Cypriot is Greek-speaking, Greek-thinking, Greek-feeling, Greek.'[12]

Three decades before Storrs, Winston Churchill weighed in on the issue declaring that he thought 'it only natural that the Cypriot people, who are of Greek descent, should regard their incorporation with what may be called their mother country, as an ideal to be earnestly, devoutly and fervently cherished'.[13] Churchill's view was tempered by a characteristically incisive observation, often echoed by Turkish academics and representatives – that those Greek-Cypriots who earnestly sought *enosis* on the basis of their Greek descent should 'not forget that they must show respect for similar feelings of the others'. The 'others' Churchill spoke of were the Turkish-Cypriots. Their 'similar feelings' represented their right to oppose union with Greece, and perhaps to choose to become part of Turkey in the event Britain ceased to govern Cyprus.[14]

Even Storrs, in spite of his apparent sympathy for Greek-Cypriot nationalism, conceded some peculiar limitations of Cypriot Greekness. With a first in classics from Cambridge, Storrs was not immune from the characteristic condescension of the British colonial class. Greek-Cypriots, he observed, might mention Homer and Sophocles as pillars of civilization, but the names of those great authors 'rather than their verses were cited'. Archbishop Kyrillos III (r. 1916–33), who laid some claim to being a scholar of ancient Greek, would, in Storrs's estimation, 'have been defeated by an average Sixth Form boy in a competition in classical Greek prose of iambics'. During a visit to the Central Training College for Boys, Storrs appeared simultaneously appalled and amused that neither a bookcase containing Greek classics nor the books themselves had ever been opened much less read.[15] For Storrs, Greek-Cypriot claims of Greekness were diminished by the absence of a formal scholastic continuity with Hellenism. In his view, a claim of cultural lineage from Homer was less convincing if Homeric verses were not called upon to sustain it. Subsequent British administrators were similarly scathing in their assessment of Greek-Cypriot claims. In 1949, one official attacked what he perceived to be the counterfeit veneer of 'Greekness', which came not from 'accomplishments but by sentiment: by the insistence of the Greek-speaking Cypriot that he is as pure a Greek as any Athenian . . . and the rather shallow nostalgia connected with "Mother Greece"'.[16] These arrogant attitudes coloured relations between Greek-Cypriots and British administrators, thus poisoning whatever potential existed for goodwill, cooperation or compromise.

Genetic links to the people of Athens and a working knowledge of the classics aside, by metrics like culture, religion, language and a shared sense of history, Greek-Cypriots were part of the Greek world. In fits and starts they had been so for more than 2,500 years. Storrs's point, that the Cypriots' own sense of their identity was what mattered, remained profound. Yet as Churchill implied, and others cogently argued, identifying the legitimate Greekness of Greek-Cypriots was distinct from assuring a Greek political future for the island itself. Cyprus's Turkish minority – which could claim to be Turks as much as the Greek-Cypriots could claim to be Greeks – was a major obstacle to *enosis*. Their very existence was an impediment to the concept of a Cyprus that was Greek in political terms. As the anthropologist Peter Loizos noted, 'to attempt to classify Cyprus sociologically as a "region" of Greece is to follow a line of non-thought that concludes that the Turkish minority had no rightful place in the

1960 independent republic'.[17] Loizos, perhaps, overstates the point, but it is important to consider that the conception of Cyprus as a 'Greek' island presented enormous problems for the island's Turkish population. Just as prejudice on the part of British administrators prevented the establishment of a functional relationship with Greek-Cypriots, so did the nationalist attitudes of many Greek-Cypriots preclude compromise and cooperation with the Turks of Cyprus.

For Greek nationalists, Turkish-Cypriots had no political standing in the quest for self-determination leading to unification with Greece. Given the inherent Greekness of Cyprus, Turkish-Cypriots were apart from the island's political society. In its most extreme form, this parochialism denied the existence of Turkish-Cypriots per se. This view acknowledged that a few Turkish soldiers and administrators had come to Cyprus but argued that the rest of the Turkish-Cypriots were simply the descendants of Greek-Cypriots who had been forced to convert to Islam.[18] Following the Ottoman conquest, conversions from Christianity did occur as Christians sought to avoid paying the personal tribute or *gizyia* imposed by Muslims on non-believers. However, research suggests that these numbers were small. The larger contingent of Turks in Cyprus came as colonizers. These were predominantly janissaries and ordinary soldiers who were settled along with deported peasants from Anatolia in the decades following the Ottoman conquest.[19] Supporters of the Greek-Cypriot nationalist line, however, insisted that the majority of Turkish-Cypriots were 'Venetians or Greeks who changed their religion to avoid taxes'.[20] Turkish narratives, on the other hand, focused on the fundamental 'Turkishness' of Turkish-Cypriots claiming that they had come to Cyprus in the late sixteenth century and 'preserved' their 'status as a separate community ... ever since'.[21]

Regardless of their lineage, Turks in Cyprus feared that in the case of *enosis* they would, at best, have to accept the status of second-class citizens, existing as the humble and deferential 'little Turk'.[22] At worst, they could face 'annihilation'.[23] Ignoring such factors, Greek-Cypriot nationalists went to great pains to push the Turkish presence on Cyprus aside in order to justify their view of the island as purely Greek. It was precisely this lack of place within the framework of the cause of *enosis* and its pursuit which made Turks and Turkish-Cypriots the cause's most trenchant opponents. As the movement coalesced around the Greek-Cypriot right and the Orthodox Church, the space devoted to considering Turkey and Turkish-Cypriots shrank further, thus putting greater and greater obstacles in the path of enosis.

The role of the church

In Cyprus, as in other bastions of Hellenism, the *Meghali Idhea* had three intellectual underpinnings: the unifying concepts of the Greek 'nation', Greek history – fusing the classical, Byzantine and modern Greek traditions[24] – 'and the concomitant unity of the core values of Greek national identity as "Hellenic Christian"'.[25] The religious component of Greek nationalism meant that Hellenism and Christianity were often and easily conflated. During the Ottoman period, various *milletler* or nations were categorized based on religious affiliation. In this way, the archbishop of the Orthodox

Church in Cyprus became the *ethnarch* (national leader) of the Greek-Cypriot community during the Ottoman period.[26]

After the Greek Revolution, a tradition emerged that shaped collective identity within the Greek community. This painted the church as the 'principal source of Greek political culture'.[27] The confluence of Orthodox Christianity with the Greek nation did pose some problems in light of the church's history of cooperation with the Ottoman authorities. This cooperation had deep historical roots. In 1453, Lucas Notaras, grand duke to the last Byzantine emperor Constantine XI Palaeologos, was supposed to have said that he preferred to see the sultan's turban to the papal mitre in Constantinople.[28] A few months later, his wish was granted when the city fell to the Ottomans; Notaras was subsequently executed on the orders of Sultan Mehmed II. The church was more fortunate than the grand duke. The Ottomans restored much of the independence and privileges which had been sacrificed in favour of Catholic assistance which proved too little and too late to prevent the end of Byzantium. Orthodox clergy were exempted from the tax levied by the Ottomans on Christian subjects. The patriarch of Constantinople assumed the dual roles of the leader of the Orthodox Church and the head of the Orthodox nation, replacing the Byzantine emperor.[29]

During the centuries of Ottoman rule, with its unique position secured, the church became 'instrumental . . . in securing the allegiance of the sultan's Christian subjects'. To overcome this compromising legacy, the confluence of Orthodoxy and Greek nationalism 'was systematically projected back into the Ottoman past'.[30] Aspects of history were glossed over as more recent actions, favourable to Greek nationalism, were emphasized. In this vein, the critical role of the church in the Greek Revolution took centre stage. Indeed, during the Greek War of Independence, Orthodox clerics played a leading role and were frequently targeted for punishment by the Ottoman authorities. In Constantinople, Patriarch Gregory V was hanged on 15 April 1821, even though he had no connection with the revolutionaries. In Cyprus, on 9 July, Archbishop Kyprianos was also hanged along with the bishops of Paphos, Kition and Kyrenia in an attempt to snuff out the revolution. In spite of this bloody warning, Greek-Cypriots contributed men and supplies to the struggle for independence even though their own island failed to become part of the Greek state.

In this context, while Greece struggled for independence from Ottoman rule, the concept of a 'Greek citizen' and a 'Greek Orthodox Christian' were not distinguished from each other.[31] The same principle applied in Cyprus even during British rule where religious affiliation was a marker or substitute for national identity if not an individual's defining characteristic in its own right.[32] Religious divisions imposed and then codified by the Ottoman conquest had a profound and lasting impact on the problematic relations between the two communities.[33] By fusing 'Orthodox and Greek national identity . . . religious minorities [were excluded] from the dominant political culture and . . . their full integration into society' was 'seriously hampered'.[34] This was true for minorities within Greece and would become a key obstacle for Cypriot *enosis*. This was a legacy of division inherited by the British, exacerbated by them, to be sure, but not their creation.

British rule began in 1878 through the terms of a defensive alliance concluded in Constantinople on 4 June, nine days before the beginning of the Congress of

Berlin. The agreement, formally known as the 'Convention of Defensive Alliance between Great Britain and Turkey, with respect to the Asiatic Provinces of Turkey', offered British support against Russian ambitions concerning 'the territories in Asia of His Imperial Majesty the Sultan', in return for the sultan's agreement that Cyprus 'be occupied and administered by England'.[35] Moving with expedience, Sir Garnet Wolseley arrived on 12 July (a day before the conclusion of the Congress of Berlin) as the empire's first 'Administrator'.[36] Ten days after his arrival, Wolseley met Bishop Kyprianos of Kitium in the port city of Larnaca. *The Times* reported that Kyprianos, in keeping with the unification of the church and Greek nationalism, announced that the Greek people of Cyprus accepted the transfer from Ottoman to British control 'because we believe that Great Britain will eventually help Cyprus, just like with the Ionian Islands, unite Cyprus with mother Greece'.[37] Cyprus was not the first territory in which the precepts of the *Meghali Idhea* ran headlong into the requirements of British imperialism, and the tensions implicit in Kyprianos's message would intensify over time. Still, neither the cause of Cypriot *enosis* nor the British attitude towards it had a clear form at this time.

From the British perspective, there was scepticism about the usefulness of the new acquisition.[38] In many ways, the procurement of Cyprus fit neatly into historian Sir John Seeley's famous contention, made in 1883, that the British acquired half the world in 'a fit of absence of mind'. Only four years after obtaining Cyprus, the opportunistic occupation of Egypt 'put Cyprus in the shade'.[39] Limited in terms of facilities, infrastructure, population and natural resources, the island was considered something of a 'backwater'.[40] As early as November 1912, Cyprus seemed surplus to imperial requirements. Winston Churchill, as first lord of the admiralty, suggested offering the island to Greece as compensation for British basing rights on the Ionian island of Cephalonia.[41] This was ironic in light of the fact that Britain had ceded that very island to Greece half a century before.

Cyprus was offered again in somewhat more perilous (and better known) circumstances in October 1915 but this time as an incentive for Greece to join the war against the Central Powers. Confronting the costly deadlock of 1915, King Constantine I refused.[42] By the time Greece did enter the fray in June 1917, choosing the side of the Triple Entente, the British offer was no longer valid. Greece received modest territorial concessions from Bulgaria at the conclusion of the war, but there was no mention of Cyprus. For Greek-Cypriot nationalists, such painful missteps on the part of the Greek government were compounded at the Paris Peace Conference in 1919–20 when the Greek prime minister, Eleftherios Venizelos, focused on securing continued support for Greek forces campaigning in Asia Minor. Cyprus was never raised in his negotiations with his British counterpart, David Lloyd George.[43] Venizelos clearly subordinated the cause of Cypriot *enosis* to larger issues of Greek policy which prioritized a mandate around Smyrna and aspirations towards Constantinople.

Cyprus and Greece remained, in the words of Virgil, 'lovers bound unequally by love'.[44] Greece never made the acquisition of the island a primary foreign policy goal in spite of Cypriot aspirations and Cypriot pressures. This disconnection of priorities was something the *enosis* movement was slow to recognize. At the same time, the *enosis* movement in Cyprus failed to grasp the limited resources and capacity Greece had for territorial expansion after 1922 – particularly if it meant the renewal of conflict with Turkey.

In contrast, the Greek-Cypriot commitment to *enosis* gathered momentum even when Greece's capacity to support it reached a nadir. In 1922, the very year of the Asia Minor Catastrophe, the archbishop of Cyprus led the formation of a national assembly aimed at applying pressure on the British authorities. In 1929, a Greek-Cypriot delegation formally petitioned for union and was refused. In October 1931, the Cyprus government's attempts to raise new revenues, balance the budget and revamp the education system led to disturbances, a refusal to pay taxes and a boycott of British goods. Rioters burned a police car and the governor's residence. Governor Sir Ronald Storrs called out the British army units based in Cyprus and elements of the largely Greek-Cypriot police force to restore order, probably without quoting from his extensive knowledge of Homer. Eventually, the revolt, such as it was, was suppressed. Seven Cypriots were killed by security forces, 28 were injured, and 400 were arrested. Among the authorities, 39 military and police were also injured.[45] In the aftermath, 3,359 Cypriots were called to appear in court, 2,606 of whom were convicted and given sentences from fines to five years in prison. Most significantly, two bishops, Nicodemos of Kitium and Makarios of Kyrenia, were deported for life along with eight other senior political leaders, including the heads of the communist party.[46] New restrictive laws were promulgated, ending even the appearance of autonomy and self-governance, and which included restrictions on the election of a new archbishop.

In addition to targeting the church, the government's response also fell heavily on the Communist Party of Cyprus (CPC). The party itself was outlawed, its organizations were dissolved, its offices destroyed, and in addition to its exiled leadership, numerous party 'cadres were imprisoned or internally exiled to isolated villages in the countryside'.[47] This internal exile reflected the tendency of colonial administrators to admire (and in this case imitate) the draconian anti-communist policies then in favour in Mussolini's Italy.[48]

In targeting the communist party, the British authorities also laid down the marker that they would ruthlessly suppress any organization which pushed for fundamental reform on the island. The marginalization of the communist party also undermined Greek- and Turkish-Cypriot relations. During the 1920s and 1930s, when it first emerged, the communist party sought to establish cooperation between Greek- and Turkish-Cypriots. Although vigorously opposed to British imperialism, Cypriot communists advocated independence rather than *enosis* in order to reconcile the two communities. At the time, they dismissed *enosis* as little more than Greek imperialism.[49] In the 1920s and 1930s, however, the goal of independence 'had very restricted appeal among the Greek population of Cyprus'.[50]

Although Britain's display of force temporarily restored order, the events of 1931 were a harbinger of the violence to come. Also visible in this disturbance and the response to it was the burgeoning conflict between the British administration and the Cypriot Orthodox Church. A month before the riot, church officials had taken a leading role in opposing the increase in customs taxes which were part of the controversial new revenue plan.[51] Changes to the educational system had also been seen as a blow to the church's authority – the most recent manifestation of a continuing battle fought by the authorities in Cyprus to remove education from the hands of Greeks generally and the church specifically.[52]

Connections between the spiritual and temporal power of the church were deep and powerful. Lacking senior political representatives, the Greek-Cypriot people entrusted their clergy with the dual roles of spiritual and political leadership. An autocephalous[53] branch of the Greek Orthodox faith, the church in Cyprus occupied (and continues to occupy) a unique position of wealth, power and influence on the island. Under Ottoman rule, the church maintained and championed the 'Greek' identity of Cyprus. As *ethnarch*, the archbishop enjoyed political as well as spiritual power as the leading figure of the Greek-Cypriot community. 'In the eyes of the Greeks the church was not only the symbol of their ethnic and religious identities, but also their protector against mistreatment by local officials.'[54] Under British rule, in spite of the administration's desire to firmly separate church and state, leading clerics retained a high degree of involvement in the island's political affairs. Under the framework of the constitution of 1882, they became 'the most active members of the Legislative Council'.[55] As political awareness in Cyprus rose, the political authority of the archbishop over the Greek-Cypriot community became increasingly overt. It also set the stage for conflict with the British authorities. While Ottoman governance had allowed the archbishop of Cyprus free reign as civil and religious leader of the Orthodox community with the privilege to tax members of the church, British governance relied on the 'strict separation of Church and State'.[56] This put the British colonial state and the Cypriot Church in opposition with each other.[57] To a large extent, it was Britain's restrictive policies towards the church 'and the curtailment of the previously broad responsibilities the church had enjoyed under Ottoman rule that eventually strengthened its protest potential and support for political emancipation'.[58]

The church's connection to the cause of *enosis* was even more fundamental than teachers and taxes. As the guardian of Greek identity in Cyprus based on language, culture and religion, the church became the natural incubator for the *enosis* cause. No institution in Cyprus reflected the feelings of Hellenism more deeply than the church with its critical links to Hellenic identity on historical, political and cultural levels.[59] During the first decade of the twentieth century, this political identity took a decidedly nationalistic colour as the church went through a 'crisis of "nationalization"' in which '[t]he more forceful nationalists eventually won. . . . [F]rom then on the Church of Cyprus assumed the uncontested leadership of the nationalist movement in the island, that aspired to union with Greece.'[60]

The church was not alone in advocating for union during this period. In the 1940s, the successor of the outlawed communist party, the Progressive Party of Working People, AKEL,[61] distanced itself from independence as favoured by the CPC. Gradually, AKEL, in spite of the scepticism of many of its members, transformed its platform. In 1942, a year after its founding, the party advocated self-determination. In 1943 and 1944 it spoke of the need for 'national restoration'. By the fourth party congress in July 1945, AKEL openly demanded 'union with mother Greece'.[62] AKEL's stunning recalibration reflected the failed resonance of its inclusive message of independence. Its new advocacy for *enosis*, however, precluded compromise with any members of the Turkish-Cypriot left, who sympathized with broader goals of socio-economic reform. For just as Greek nationalism had manifested itself in the *Meghali Idhea* and the desire for *terra irredenta*, the Turks of Cyprus began to develop their own political goals. Primary among these was the desire to thwart the *enosis* cause.

Duelling nationalisms

For Greek-Cypriots, the *enosis* cause was based on a fundamental sense of connection with the Greek nation. It was the misfortune of the Cypriot *enosis* movement that the same ideology which underpinned Greece's most ambitious plan for expansion, through the Treaty of Sèvres, concretized a rival Turkish nationalism which would eventually prove its most trenchant foe. In the face of the Greek occupation of Smyrna and the advance of Greek forces deep into Anatolia, Turkey's reformist leader, Mustafa Kemal, was able to consolidate his authority and lay the groundwork for a new Turkish nation. This work underpinned the modern Turkish Republic, established in 1923, and became the model for the emerging Turkish nationalism in Cyprus.[63]

Some Greek scholars, exemplifying the nationalist claim that in general Greeks have done it first and done it better, argue that 'Turkish nationalism can hardly be dated prior to the Young Turk revolution of 1908, if then'.[64] In other words, Greek nationalism was at least a century older than Turkish nationalism, and in this way, its claims (particularly in reference to Cyprus) were somehow more legitimate. Turkish nationalism, however, had deeper roots than this view allows, although it contained its share of contradictions. Turkish national had roots as far back as the mid-nineteenth century, when the Jewish-Hungarian orientalist Arminius Vambery published on the subject in 1868. Several Young Turk leaders developed close relations with Vambery, and adopted his ideas.[65] Pan-Turkism, as it was primarily called, received a further fillip through the work of a number of Russian-born Tatars who developed their ideas in opposition to the rising tide of Pan-Slavism in the Balkans and in the wake of the Russo-Turkish War of 1877–8.[66] In Cyprus, the emergence of a Turkish-Cypriot nationalism is also connected to the beginning of British colonial administration in 1878, partially as a result of awakening 'the Muslim Turkish elite to the danger of losing its privileged position, the danger of losing Ottoman domination itself and ultimately the incorporation of Cyprus into Greece'.[67]

Over time, two key tensions surrounding the concept of Turkish nationalism developed. Both were based on specific historical conditions. First, the turbulent final decades of the Ottoman Empire witnessed a competition among unifying ideologies: pan-Turkism, pan-Islamism and an Ottoman national identity. Creating an Ottoman national identity 'was a chimera' as the moribund Ottoman construct was precisely what young nationalists aimed to replace.[68] Pan-Islamism had greater support. During the Turkish War of Independence, Islam remained a powerful force. However, the forcible end of the Caliphate in 1924 and the modernization programme favoured by Mustafa Kemal explicitly sidelined Islamism in favour of the more restrictive and modest Turkish nationalism.[69] Modest goals reflected the second tension – this one a function of the political realities which greeted the newly formed Turkish Republic – the tension between traditionally expansionist irredentism and a nationalism focused on purification and consolidation.

In the context of these two tensions, Turkish nationalism began as a tool for the Young Turk movement to oppose the endless victories of Western powers against the decaying Ottoman Empire while at the same time transfiguring the sclerotic and bankrupt Ottoman identity with a vigorous new sense of 'Turkishness'.[70] Its primary proponents were military officers and intellectuals who attempted to synthesize Turkish identity with Western European reforms. Their goal was to stabilize and modernize the Turkish state. Turkish nationalism was central to the political programme of the Committee of Union and Progress (CUP), which was established in Thessaloniki as a secret society in 1889. This movement challenged, marginalized and eventually subverted the Ottoman Sultanate and Caliphate. In 1908, the 'Young Turk Revolution' re-established constitutional government and multiparty politics. Five years later, a coup d'état led by a group from the CUP established a triumvirate.

Under the rule of 'the three pashas', Enver, Talaat and Djemal during the First World War, Turkish nationalism reaped bloody rewards targeting the Ottoman Empire's minorities, particularly its Christian populations. The Armenian Genocide (1915–18) is the most well known of these campaigns, but considerable numbers of Ionian and Pontian Greeks as well as Assyrians living within the Ottoman state were killed or deported during the war and its aftermath. The victory of the Turkish nationalists in the Greco-Turkish War of 1919–22 culminated with the incineration of the Greek-occupied city of Smyrna and the deaths of tens of thousands of Armenians and Greeks at the hands of the Turkish army.

In the 1920s, other minority groups like the Kurds were subject to 'brutal military repression and a campaign of state terrorism, which aimed immediately and ultimately at destroying the Kurds as a coherent ethnic community that could make demands on the Turkish state'.[71] As Speros Vryonis argues, these campaigns represented 'the modern Turkish state's effort to create – which is to say force – a homogeneity of its disparate constituent elements'.[72] Turkish nationalism of this period 'redefined Ottoman Christian and Jewish subjects as outsiders'. Its proponents sought to settle Muslim immigrants on the property of these 'outsiders' after their relocation.[73] Within the narrative of Turkish nationalism, such actions were a source of 'creation and purification'.[74] Violent '[c]leaning was necessary to establish the Third Republic. There was no other choice. You could not have such a cosmopolitan Republic.'[75]

Ironically, this objective of creating a cleansed homogenous homeland obstructed Turkish nationalism from holding irredentist goals. Rather than the expansionist nationalism of the Greeks, Turkish nationalism turned to consolidation. Official opposition to 'overt pan-Turkish irredentism' was a problem for the Turks of Cyprus and contributed to the subdued Turkish attitude towards the growing support for *enosis* on the island.[76] Kemal himself had gone so far as to criticize Turkish irredentism as dangerous and self-defeating. Instead, he called on the emerging Turkish nation, as early as 1921, to 'return to our natural, legitimate limits [and to] know our limits'.[77] Kemalism, as practiced by Atatürk himself until 1938 and then by his successor İsmet İnönü, president until 1950, acknowledged that ethnic Turks would live outside the borders of the new Turkish state. Kemalist policies also conceded that caution and prudence were called for in dealing with risky external issues, and made elites 'reluctant to get involved in Cyprus' through the late 1940s and early 1950s.[78]

Turkish 'disinterest' in the political future of Cyprus and its lukewarm opposition to *enosis* during the first half of the twentieth century must be understood in this context. It is not accurate to claim, as some scholars do, that Turkey had no interest in Cyprus before the question of Cypriot self-determination was first brought to the United Nations by Greece in the 1950s.[79] Nor is it accurate to argue that Turks or Turkish-Cypriots were not opposed to the idea of *enosis* until stimulated by the British once violence began in 1955. Tensions between the two communities in Cyprus are attested, for example, during the Cretan crisis of 1897. That year, the high commissioner issued a proclamation 'prohibiting provocative meetings, assemblies, processions or written articles' by both Greek and Turkish-Cypriots relating to Crete.[80]

While Cyprus was administered by the British but still formally part of the Ottoman Empire, there was a 'persistent appeal of the Turkish-Cypriots to Ottoman authorities', continued 'efforts to avoid severance of this link, and the continued rise of tensions with strong nationalist overtones with the island's Orthodox Greeks'.[81] Such tensions were not invisible to the colonial administrators. As the high commissioner Sir Charles King-Harman noted in 1905, 'the feelings between the two races in Cyprus must ever be strained, and the cause of collision [pan-Hellenic aspirations] must exist which although dormant, may be easily aroused'.[82] *Enosis* demonstrations in April 1906 resulted in a tense stand-off between Greek- and Turkish-Cypriots. In 1907, a formal appeal was launched to Istanbul for financial aid for the Turks of Cyprus. In October that year, shortly after the arrival of Winston Churchill, who was then undersecretary of state for the colonies, a local official and Turkish-Cypriot notable declared that '[w]e absolutely repudiate the union of the Island with Greece, and request that the delivering of speeches on the subject in places of official and high standing may be categorically prohibited'.[83] The Young Turk Revolution of 1908 only accelerated support for Turkish nationalism in Cyprus, thus further raising opposition to *enosis*.[84]

In the broader historical context, Turkish hesitancy in relation to Cyprus – such as it was – was a transient aberration. The Ottoman Empire controlled Cyprus until 1878 and Britain only formally annexed the island from the defunct Ottoman state following the Treaty of Lausanne. Turkish disengagement, such as it was, occupied a window of two decades between the end of the Greco-Turkish War and the end of the Second World War. During this time, Turkish weakness and a need for domestic development and internal consolidation shaped attitudes. Once the global conflict ended and Greek-Cypriot nationalists moved to push their claims to the fore once more, Turkey's response was swift and unambiguous opposition.

Turkish-Cypriots also voiced their opposition. After the establishment of the new Turkish Republic, nationalist support among the Turkish-Cypriots grew in parallel with the Greek-Cypriots. They

> replaced old-guard Turkish-Cypriots in various colonial institutions in the 1920s, and in the 1930s and early 1940s many more became politically active through professional associations and newly founded newspapers and political organizations. . . . By the mid-1940s the nationalists dominated not only the emerging Turkish-Cypriot bourgeois class but the Turkish-Cypriot political elite as well.[85]

These Turkish-Cypriots looked to Ankara for support like never before. As the Cyprus crisis deepened, their claims 'in favour of the colonial status quo [expanded] ... for partition of the island and union with Turkey and Greece, respectively', in the event of decolonization.[86] Following the *enosis* referendum of January 1950, Turkish-Cypriots launched a series of protests and the leader of the Turkish-Cypriot community, Fazıl Küçük, sent a strongly worded telegram to the secretary of state for foreign affairs.[87] In April 1951, the governor of Cyprus reported to the secretary of state for the colonies that 'certain local Turkish associations ... have requested an interview to bring to my notice anxiety felt by the Turkish community over *enosis* and "to request whether anything could be done to alleviate great uneasiness felt by local Turks on this account" ... Turks and other Cypriots have been genuinely disturbed by recent events relating to Enosis which means more menacing aspect than usual'.[88]

The success or failure of the *enosis* cause came to revolve around the outcome of the duel between competing nationalisms. They had similar origins and were grounded in, if not beholden to, the strategic concerns of 'parent' powers. But while Turks and Turkish-Cypriots were keenly aware of the dangers posed to them by Greek nationalism, Greek-Cypriot nationalists discounted the forces gathering against them. Instead, they convinced themselves that Turkey had little interest in Cyprus and no legitimate claim in any case. Turkish-Cypriots, lacking a coherent identity or distinctive culture, would perforce go along with *enosis* and simply accept the will of the majority. As Holland and Markides argue, the *enosis* movement's 'mistake lay in the assumption that both the chief minority and Turkey, as its "motherland", could be kept on the margins'.[89] In their view, this error was 'understandable'. While the exclusion of Turkey and Turkish-Cypriots does not defy comprehension, it does demonstrate fundamentally flawed strategic thinking on the part of the leaders of the *enosis* movement. It was an extraordinary error. As early as 1951, the British ambassador in Ankara, Noel Charles, had explained the roots of Turkish concerns in Cyprus:

> Turkish public opinion would be bitterly opposed to the cession of Cyprus to Greece for several reasons. First, there is the legitimate anxiety of the Turks about the fate of the Turkish minority under Greek rule. Secondly, the Turks are determined not to see any more islands off the Turkish coast fall under Greek rule. It is significant that the agitation about Cyprus has recently stimulated interest in the Dodecanese, and more than one Turkish journalist has threatened that, if the Greek demand for Cyprus is pressed, Turkey will retaliate by demanding the return of these islands. Thirdly, the Turks are sensitive to the Communist threat in Cyprus and fear that if the island is handed over to Greece, this threat will become more acute and the strategic uses of the port of Iskenderun will be completely nullified. Lastly, there is the Turkish historical claim to Cyprus which, in Turkish eyes, is far more solidly based than that of Greece.[90]

Turkey's concerns in Cyprus were clearly and concisely articulated. As Charles pointed out, they were hardly secret; many had even been voiced through the media. The leaders of the *enosis* cause, however, appeared blind to the scale of the storm their actions were about to unleash. As the commander of Britain's Middle East Land Forces noted in a letter to the vice-chief of the Imperial General Staff, 'there is a strong and virile Turkish minority in the island which would be extremely discontented under Greek rule'.[91] Greek-Cypriot nationalists acted in wilful blindness of this constraining reality.

As the Second World War drew to a close, concerns among the various actors provided the British government with what they considered an opportunity to diffuse tension on the island and move towards a productive new chapter as a stabilizing force in the Eastern Mediterranean. Their plan, however, ran straight into the conflicting attitudes of parties on all fronts. The collapse of their plan demonstrated more clearly than ever the division which existed among multiple sides and pushed Cyprus, slowly but surely, towards attempts to solve those differences through violence.

2

Imperial constitution

Rejection and radicalization

Do not the great mass of people living in Cyprus realize that by belonging to the British Empire they get a square deal?[1]
– Air-Commodore Harvey in the House of Commons, 9 June 1948

Better a poor mother than a rich aunt![2]
– Traditional Cypriot saying

In spite of the 1931 revolt and the subsequent repressive policies imposed by the British colonial administration, the *enosis* movement did not resort to violence during the Second World War. In Palestine, by contrast, Zionist insurgents effectively ceased operations against the British at the outbreak of the European war in September 1939 but restarted them again in February 1944. Greek-Cypriot nationalists held back throughout the world war and its immediate aftermath. During the post-war period, *enosis* forces continued to focus on negotiation, political pressure and appeals to the international community. In spite of its muted epilogue, the 1931 revolt had signalled the latency of greater radicalism. After the Second World War, Greek-Cypriot nationalists moved ever closer to the 'Cretan pattern, with its emphasis on the dynamic, even violent, claim for liberation'. This approach would culminate in the armed revolt of 1955–9.[3] Still, violence, although commonplace against British colonialism after the Second World War, was not a foregone conclusion in Cyprus. It was a mutual inflexibility on the part of Greek-Cypriot nationalists who were committed to *enosis* and British policymakers who remained intransigent on the possible scope for self-government during the critical years at the war's conclusion and in its aftermath, which set Cyprus on the course to violence.

British policymakers knew the direction of the wind before the war's end. In 1944, a senior Colonial Office official observed: '[T]he impetus given to democratic ideas by the war is likely not only to produce a clamorous demand in Cyprus for the participation of the people in their own government . . . but very strong support for [this claim] in this country [Great Britain] and elsewhere.'[4] While recognizing its inevitability, British policymakers nevertheless wanted to avoid this clash for as long as possible. As Hugh Foot, the colonial secretary and acting governor of Cyprus, reported to the Colonial

Office, the administration was 'anxious to avoid a show-down on the Enosis issue in present circumstances'.[5] Foot, of course, would return to Cyprus as its governor and commander-in-chief in 1957.

Enosis pressure was reinvigorated by the end of the war and presented British policymakers with important decisions. London aimed to use diplomacy to soften these tensions. The government's stated goal was to reach some sort of solution that would allow for the continuation of British sovereignty, while at the same time provide for the Cypriot people a degree of self-government. This programme's failure highlighted significant differences between the British government, the Greek- and Turkish-Cypriot communities, and eventually Athens and Ankara. At issue were the security of British interests in Cyprus, the nature and scope of Cypriot self-government, the rights of Turkish-Cypriots and the future of the *enosis* movement itself. Even at this inchoate stage, the fundamental divergences among the various actors came into clear focus and made for insurmountable obstacles.

Cyprus confronted the British government with three distinctive challenges that were to shape London's policy and complicate a possible solution in the years to come. First, rhetoric on the island centred on political union with Greece instead of the traditional colonial goal of independence. This fundamental goal created a particular set of difficulties since it involved a second sovereign nation, Greece, and, ipso facto, considerations of that nation's allies and rivals. Second, during this time, perceptions about Cyprus in London were changing. Once a backwater, Cyprus was now seen as an integral British possession. Moreover, because of its small size, British policymakers were convinced that sovereignty could be maintained on the island even as the empire scaled back its overseas possessions and broader military establishment. Finally, in Cyprus, Britain faced a divided population; each community had established states as their advocates, and, if necessary, protectors. Further complicating the issue were the relationships both Greece and Turkey had with Great Britain and with each other. Both countries were British allies and, after February 1952, members of NATO.

Constitution and controversy

The initial strategy of the British government was to marginalize the *enosis* forces with a new constitution granting increased powers to local actors. Domestic elites would have their focus turned from advocating *enosis* to dealing with a narrow set of internal issues. At once, it was hoped this would marginalize the more strident pro-*enosis* voices, particularly within the clergy, while at the same time 'defuse nationalistic agitation'.[6] Arthur Creech Jones, the new Labour government's secretary of state for the colonies, announced the constitutional plan at the end of October 1946. His written statement sounded a hopeful note that such an initiative would pave the way for social progress, economic development, improvements in infrastructure and increased political freedom for the citizens of the island.[7] The plan also called for a consultative assembly of all Cypriots to cooperate in establishing both a new constitution and a new legislative assembly. This assembly would work in close conjunction with the British administration. It was hoped that, when put into practice, this plan offer would allow Britain to maintain control of Cyprus by undercutting support for *enosis* through material progress and increased local participation in the domestic government. Significantly, the proposals involved the cooperation of the island's Greek majority and Turkish minority.

In spite of aspirations, the announcement of the new constitutional proposals was met with a discouraging reception among Greek-Cypriots. In immediate reply to the parliamentary comments of 23 October 1946, the Ethnarchic Council[8] cabled London, rejecting 'categorically and with indignation any solution of the Cyprus question not granting [the Cypriot people] their national liberty by union with Greece which constitutes our only national claim and aspiration'.[9] Undeterred, the British government responded with a two-track offensive designed to improve Cypriot perceptions of the British administration. The first of these was the 'hearts and minds' campaign emphasizing British plans for the development of Cyprus's economy and social welfare. Reforms and improvements would be initiated as part of a decade-long project designed to address the island's infrastructural needs from transport to agriculture, health, electricity and water supply. A lack of funding from London had always put a brake on Cypriot development but now four million pounds were made available towards the goal of getting the consultative assembly to 'meet in the hopeful atmosphere created by a long-term programme of economic development'.[10] In attempting to siphon off support for *enosis* through economic growth, British policymakers were ignoring the sentiment of the Cypriot expression (had they ever heard it) that it was better to be a 'poor mother than a rich aunt'.[11]

The British also pressed forward with improvements to public health. Malaria was the focal point of the health drive and substantial resources were devoted to eradicating the disease through the widespread spraying of pesticides. Cypriot agriculture was targeted with schemes of reforestation and irrigation, which were designed to improve the yield of farmland and to prevent food shortages in drought years. For a predominantly agricultural society, these were important steps. Plans were set for upgrading the island's unsophisticated road system, creating a modern electricity grid and for expanding the airport facilities. The stated goal was 'to establish a contented Cyprus as a self-governing member of the Commonwealth'.[12] Through its very rigour, however, this development programme put the British authorities on the back foot with those favouring self-determination. The scale of the reforms and the announced ten-year duration of the project made it clear that the British had every intention to stay in Cyprus. This reality was openly acknowledged as something Cypriots would have to accept as the constitutional process began.[13] Under these preconditions, finding common ground would prove difficult from the start.

Concurrent with the programme of material reform, the British openly pursued a policy of reconciliation. The government's response to the events of 1931 had been 'unusually firm, even Draconian repression, including the suspension of constitutional government in the colony'.[14] The legislative council of local notables had been dissolved. As punishment for their role in the riots, the bishops of Kition and Kyrenia were deported. Archbishop Kyrillos III, who was allowed to remain in Cyprus, died in 1933 and the absence of the two deportees, coupled with a series of laws implemented by the British in 1937, prevented the enthroning of a new archbishop. The most restrictive of these, Law No. 34, stated that in all future elections, the archbishop-elect would not be enthroned until approved by the governor.[15] As part of the reconciliation agenda, the restrictive laws were revoked and the deportees of 1931 were permitted to return.

The Labour government entrusted the programme of Cypriot development and political rapprochement to a new governor, the former minister for civil aviation, Reginald Lord Winster. Winster was a personal friend of Creech Jones[16] and his appointment apparently broke with the recent tradition of appointing senior civil servants as colonial governors.[17] Along with his questionable qualifications, the incoming governor's commitment to his responsibilities was also debatable. In his early correspondence with Creech Jones, Winster's primary concern appeared to be the reduction of his time away from Britain and not the establishment of a new and workable regime in Cyprus. Initially, the Colonial Office favoured a standard appointment of five years. In a letter of 22 January 1947, Winster made his contrary intentions clear, writing that he expected to accomplish his mission within a year to eighteen months.[18] Creech Jones was quick to reply that eighteen months would be the barest minimum and that a commitment of two years was probably more likely. Winster, however, was clear about his priorities. Once the new constitutional proposals were adopted, he wished to return at once, 'in order to resume my political activities which, as far as I can see at present, I have no wish or intention to abandon'.[19] On one major point, however, the secretary and the reluctant new governor were in agreement – no change to the sovereignty of Cyprus was being contemplated. At most, the possibility was that after working under a new constitution for a trial period, control of domestic governmental affairs could be turned over to Cypriots while British officials retained the portfolios of foreign affairs and defence.[20] The motivation behind such constraints was simple: to circumscribe the potential for unification with Greece, thus preserving British interests and allaying Turkish fears.

Just as the British had a new political figure in Cyprus, so the Greek-Cypriots, freed from the constraints of Law No. 34, proceeded to elect an archbishop for the first time since 1916. In June 1947, Leontios, bishop of Paphos and the locum, secured his election to the archiepiscopal throne with the support of the Greek-Cypriot left. After being officially enthroned on 20 June, Leontios continued to express his strong support for union and his vehement opposition both to the constitutional concept and to any compromise that would leave Cyprus separate from Greece. In this, Leontios was quite different from his predecessor, Kyrillos III, who had neither spoken out for *enosis* nor participated in the riots of 1931.

In Ankara, the Turkish government was acutely aware of both the security concerns of the Turkish minority, emanating from demographics, and the strategic concerns rooted in geography. Contrary to narratives that Turkish opposition to *enosis* was belated, stage-managed by the British or otherwise counterfeit, Cypriot *enosis* was not an acceptable option for Turkish policymakers. Turkey was adamant on this point for two reasons – one emotional, one practical. Emotionally, Turkish rhetoric claimed that Turks refused to live under Greek rule. Turkish-Cypriots feared that under Greek rule their identity, rights and property would be eroded and subsumed. Practically, the Turks claimed that they had reason to fear the spectre of communism in Cyprus and that a

British withdrawal might precipitate a communist takeover, throwing the strategically placed island into Soviet hands and pressuring Turkey's southern ports. Even if the nationalists were victorious, a Greek-controlled Cyprus was seen as a security threat to Turkey's southern flank given the long-standing hostility between Athens and Ankara. Some Turkish observers were even concerned that the union of Cyprus and Greece was simply the first step for reinvigorating the notion of the *Meghali Idhea*.[21]

When he arrived on 27 March 1947, Winster was given a lukewarm reception. Many Turkish-Cypriots waved British flags and cheered, but the majority of the Greek-Cypriot population remained subdued. At the official reception the next day, leading Greek-Cypriots including the newly elected archbishop, the bishop of Kyrenia and the mayor of Nicosia were absent. Only a few secondary government officials attended. Four Greek-Cypriots from the Advisory Council who absented themselves from the formal welcome dinner were promptly dismissed.[22] The rocky beginning was a harbinger of the difficulties that would follow.

In July, Winster invited senior local officials, various union leaders and the heads of a number of professional associations to assist in forming the consultative assembly tasked with framing the new constitution. Existing political parties were deliberately neglected as was the Cypriot Orthodox Church, which, in Winster's words, 'had better keep out of these matters'.[23] Nationalist pressure against anything short of *enosis* coupled with fears that 'the dominant political force in any of the future elector contests would be the Left of Centre coalition under the leadership of AKEL' kept the political right from participating in Winster's constitutional exercise.[24]

From a British perspective, excluding the church was natural, both on the grounds of the separation of church and state favoured by British policymakers and because of its uncompromising stance on *enosis*. The right was largely absent through its own choice coupled with pressure from the church. The left, even though it would form the bulk of Cypriot representation, protested over the exclusion of AKEL and several of its affiliates.[25] As a result of these tensions, only eighteen of the thirty-two members invited by the governor participated in the constitutional debate. These were a Maronite, eight leftist Greek-Cypriots (five town councillors, two trade unionists and a representative from the cooperative society), seven Turkish-Cypriots and two Greek-Cypriots appointed by the British government, and therefore sympathetic to its positions.[26] Sir Edward Jackson, the chief justice of Cyprus, served as chairman.[27] The formation of the assembly hit a snag almost immediately when, on 26 July, Archbishop Leontios died suddenly of typhus. He was succeeded by the aged bishop of Kyrenia, Makarios II, who was an *enosis* hardliner and veteran exile of 1931. Despite their shared commitment to *enosis*, the two men had a history of animosity. Makarios II has even been described as Archbishop Leontios's most 'implacable enemy' on account of their political differences.[28] Even before the assembly's first meeting on 1 November 1947, the church, led by the new archbishop, began to pressure the Greek-Cypriot assembly members to avoid concessions to the British and not to compromise on the cause of *enosis*.

Even without the representatives from the church and the right, the negotiations were contentious. The central principle at issue was the degree of self-government that would be exercised by the Greek-Cypriot population. As the island's majority, the Greek-Cypriots regarded self-determination and self-government as nothing less than their fundamental rights if they were to consider themselves as free people. The British position was not as cut and dried. British policymakers felt the need to balance strategic and political requirements – bases and supply centres to project power throughout the Middle East and Africa – with the principle of Cypriot self-government. In addition, London had to balance constitutional protections for the rights of the Turkish-Cypriot minority so as to avoid creating tensions with Turkey since such tensions could undermine the security of Cyprus and Britain's broader regional concerns. Greek-Cypriot leadership seemed to ignore the reality that, even at this stage, Turkey and Turkish-Cypriots supported the continuation of British sovereignty in Cyprus and were vehemently opposed to the notion of self-government. This was largely because Turks and Turkish-Cypriots knew (as the Greek-Cypriot side openly proclaimed) that self-government in Cyprus was a stepping stone towards *enosis*.

On 18 November, the eight leftist Greeks submitted a memorandum for the secretary of state for the colonies arguing for the broadening of the terms of reference of the constitutional committee and the possibility of self-government.[29] Although the assembly represented the first time Greek- and Turkish-Cypriots had been brought together 'with a "mandate" to arrive at an agreed outline for a constitution', division rather than unity was the dominant feature of the discussions.[30] As Jackson reported to London, '[T]he seven Turkish members have shown ... the deepest distrust of the intentions of the Greek majority ... towards their community.... They have repeatedly asserted, with obvious conviction, that it is the declared intention of the Greek majority to destroy the Turks as a community in Cyprus.'[31]

Striving to maintain control of Cyprus, the British government tread cautiously in order to avoid a breakdown in the negotiations.[32] Officials within the Colonial Office, who among the various branches of the government were least in favour of concessions, were 'against granting self-government and instead preferred a transitory regime which would not concede Cypriot ministers, but would offer this prospect in five years' time'.[33] Military considerations, given developments in Egypt and Palestine, were also at the forefront of British thinking. 'In January 1948 the British Government finally decided to accept the Colonial Office position, [against granting self-government] but without any mention of a five-year transitory period for giving ministries to the Cypriots. The government also noted that recent Middle Eastern developments made it imperative not to risk losing control over Cyprus.'[34]

At this stage, the constitutional proposals under discussion included suffrage for men aged twenty-one and over. (The voting rights of women remained to be taken up at a future date at the discretion of the assembly.) There would be a unitary legislature of twenty-two members: eighteen elected from the Greek-Cypriot community and four elected from the Turkish-Cypriot. As in the Constitution of 1882, they would be elected from separate electoral rolls. Four additional seats would be reserved for several senior appointed officials of the British government in Cyprus.[35] 'The presence of these officials', it was argued

> would ensure that the Legislature is properly informed on executive subjects and on the policy of the Government, both by speeches and by answers to members

questions, and would also ensure that the members of the Legislature themselves, as the representatives of public opinion in the Island, would be able to make their views known directly and in the free exchange of debate to the most senior officials.[36]

Nevertheless, the Greek-Cypriots would enjoy a clear majority in the assembly, thus satisfying an aspiration dating to the very beginning of British rule. Although this was an important concession to the Greek-Cypriots, significant issues remained unresolved.

Three critical gaps existed between what the British could accept on the one hand and Greek-Cypriot aspirations on the other: the control of ministries (excluding foreign affairs and defence), the ban on debating the position of Cyprus within the Commonwealth in the Cypriot legislature and the strong executive powers of the governor.[37] The Greek-Cypriot representatives wanted the critical portfolios of foreign affairs and defence, not only because of their significance but also because of their particular relation to the *enosis* cause. Britain baulked at this idea precisely for this reason. In addition, handing key ministries to Greek-Cypriots would be seen as marginalizing the island's Turks and threatened to create an unstable political dynamic between the two communities. The British government felt that debate on the position of Cyprus in the Commonwealth would also only serve foster disunity between Greek- and Turkish-Cypriots, essentially nullifying any benefit derived from the new constitution by constantly calling Britain's position in the island into question. It also had the potential to quickly diminish the utility of Cyprus as a base. Finally, the strong executive power of the governor, including the right to veto legislation and to enact legislation unilaterally, was thought necessary to maintain stability and to protect British interests. To Greek-Cypriots, it smacked of pure imperialism.

The British government realized that the constitutional process was on treacherous ground but were not about to give in. Harsh experience during the partition of India, coupled with the empire's painful retrenchments, had hardened attitudes even among the Labour leadership. Prime Minister Atlee was in no mood to compromise with communists in Cyprus or to see half measures and interim constitutions applied which would undermine Britain's control of the island, particularly on the issues of security and foreign policy.[38] Already there was a fundamental gap between what British policymakers were willing to concede and what Greek-Cypriot nationalist were willing to accept. In a memorandum of 26 April 1948, the minister of state for colonial affairs openly acknowledged that 'it is necessary to remember that to offer less than a certain minimum degree of self-government is to court entire rejection'. Then, he speculated that '[i]f the move . . . to grant Cyprus a more liberal form of Government were now to end in total rejection . . . the dissident element in the Island would be greatly strengthened, with adverse consequences within and possibly outside Cyprus'.[39] But to agree to self-government would endanger Britain's ability to use Cyprus as a military base, and threaten an open break with the Turkish-Cypriot population. The Turkish-Cypriots supported the proposals but had made it clear to the British that they would not consent to full-blown self-government 'which would place the minority under the majority's domination'.[40]

Under heavy pressure from the ethnarchy, the Greek-Cypriot members insisted on their demands. The British government conceded that only after five years of functioning under an interim constitution would it be acceptable to consider transferring the ministerial portfolios excluding defence and foreign affairs to the Greek-Cypriots. In time, these might be transferred as well.[41] This offer too fell short of what the Greek-Cypriots were willing to accept. On 7 May, Governor Winster received a message from the Colonial Office, copies of which were to be distributed to the members of the consultative assembly on 11 May. The letter confirmed that the British government

> saw considerable difficulties in the way of accepting the proposals of the eight Greek members, which embodied the principle of fully responsible government in the internal affairs of Cyprus. Further consideration of these proposals since that date has confirmed His Majesty's Government in the view that they are unacceptable.[42]

With the minimum demands of the two sides apparently irreconcilable, and with every negotiating point seemingly exhausted, the eight leftist Greek-Cypriot representatives voted against the new constitution on 20 May and withdrew from the assembly.[43] In spite of this, votes in favour of the proposals from the ten remaining representatives carried the constitution. Given the nature of this 'success', the British government decided that the constitutional process could not move forward. The assembly was dissolved on 12 August, and a 'temporary shelving of the constitution' became the government's stated policy.[44]

Even though it failed, the constitutional exercise provided impetus for Turkish concerns over the future of Cyprus. Pro-*enosis* demonstrations in Greece sparked a 'reaction of the Turkish press, a section of which lashed out against Enosis and criticized the Republican People's Party (RPP) government for neglecting the Turks of Cyprus'. In November 1948, President İnönü received a delegation of Turkish-Cypriots 'and the Turkish Foreign Ministry sought British assurances that there was no intention to hand the island over to Greece'.[45] For the British, especially for Winster, the constitution's failure was a major blow. In his yearly budgetary address to the executive council early in 1949, recounting events of the previous year, Winster spoke bluntly about the disappointment. The constitutional process had 'foundered upon the rock of a demand for the transfer of a vastly greater degree of authority than I could possibly regard as advisable in the interests of the people of Cyprus'. Winster continued, pulling no punches against those he felt responsible for the constitution's failure:

> The action of certain members of the Assembly in refusing what was possible because they were not given what it would have been disastrous to grant, was in itself a reflection upon the sense of responsibility with which I had credited them, and upon their fitness to exercise the powers they were demanding.[46]

With the failure of the constitutional initiative, Winster, who had accepted his appointment only reluctantly, concluded by announcing his resignation since his 'primary purpose in coming to Cyprus' had failed.[47] He had been in Cyprus for twenty-one months.

Naturally, Greek-Cypriot opinion did not agree with Winster about the reasons for the failure of negotiations. In response to Winster's address, the Pan-agrarian Union of Cyprus (PEK), an important network representing village farmers, issued a statement that was published in the newspaper, *Neos Kypriakos Phylax*, on 17 February 1949: 'The Consultative Assembly has failed because it was based on foreign psychology. The Government has never been able to trace the road leading to the Cyprus soul. In the case, however, of the Consultative Assembly it was kept far away from the Cyprus soul in a deplorable manner.'[48] This 'deplorable' separation from the 'Cyprus soul' centred on the failure of the consultative assembly to allow for unification with Greece. That a leftist organization would speak in such terms was symptomatic of both the widespread commitment to *enosis* and the need of even leftist groups to toe the nationalist line.

Although the 'Winster Constitution' was never implemented, it influenced the political landscape in Cyprus for years to come. The disagreements which plagued its drafting remained contentious. In some ways, the Winster proposals represented a more advantageous solution to the Greek-Cypriot side than the agreement reluctantly signed later on in 1960. As with the nearly concurrent UN proposal for the partition of Palestine, it seemed, in retrospect, to offer a more stable situation than that which developed in both territories after years of struggle and human trauma. In both instances, the resort to violence served to harden prejudices, increase mistrust and add to the divides that negotiations would seek to bridge. Nevertheless, the offer on the table in 1948 satisfied important Greek-Cypriot demands: it moved the island towards self-government and had the potential for eventual self-determination. It had no provisions for the interference of Turkey in Cypriot affairs. The failure of the constitutional initiative left all sides disappointed, but while the British hoped for a period of salutary neglect in Cyprus, *enosis* supporters of every political stripe, not satisfied with merely blocking the Winster proposals, soon turned to more activist methods to further their cause. To put those methods into action, they would first need to seize unambiguous control of the nationalist narrative in Cyprus and marginalize Greek-Cypriot opponents who might seek a more moderate message.

3

'This sacred goal'

Communists, churchmen and the struggle for the nationalist narrative

> [W]e seek what it is possible to obtain, self-determination. For the Cypriots, however, self-determination will automatically develop into Enosis. . . . I think that we will succeed.[1]
>
> – Archbishop Makarios III, 30 November 1954

The collapse of the constitutional proposals of 1948 left Cyprus politically deadlocked and deeply divided. British policymakers officially left the moribund constitutional proposal in play, but there was almost no chance the Greek-Cypriot community would choose to re-engage on those terms. Britain's failure to improve the offer of 1948 spurred the *enosis* forces in Cyprus to further action. More concretely, it set the stage for a confrontation *among* Greek-Cypriots – between the church and the left – over who would control the *enosis* cause. In the years between the failure of the constitutional assembly and the outbreak of violence, this struggle would be won by the Orthodox Church in partnership with the Greek-Cypriot right. Their victory meant that their agenda would control and drive the *enosis* movement. This control would manifest itself in both the domestic and international escalation of initiatives directed against British rule and culminate in the launching of a campaign of violence designed to achieve *enosis* once and for all.

During the summer of 1948, as the constitutional process collapsed, church leaders convened and drafted a 'Blueprint for the National Struggle'. This document is a brief but critical source for understanding the attitude of the church to the *enosis* cause and the deep and powerful influence it exerted in the planning of resistance to British rule. The 'Blueprint' made it clear that the church would continue and expand its central role in working for *enosis*. Resistance would proceed in two primary directions: a struggle against the British government in Cyprus and an action against local communist elements.[2] In addition to the practical steps the church took during this period, the 'Blueprint' sheds important light on its attitudes and strategies towards achieving *enosis*. According to this strategic plan, efforts would be made along the twin tracks of creating international tensions for Britain through diplomacy and disorder in

Cyprus through 'political disobedience'. The goal, in the initial phase, was to 'deprive the government of all its collaborators and aspire to the creation of political chaos which England [would] not be able to conceal'.[3] The document highlighted the three core ideological principles of the church. These principles would serve as mainstays of the right during the struggle: anti-colonialism, anti-communism and a commitment to the Greek Orthodox identity.

Frustration in the continued failure of negotiations played a major role in stimulating impatience on the *enosis* issue as did the church's fear of communism. These fears were stoked by AKEL's strong showings in municipal elections.[4] The church's ideology made communism a focus of deep suspicion and distaste. In 1948, the plan was clear that 'an intense anti-communist struggle' would be conducted in conjunction with opposition to British rule.[5] The pillars of Greek nationalism and anti-communism would shape the church's role in the struggle. It was essential not only to fight Britain for *enosis* but also to fight the communists in order to win control of the *enosis* narrative. The marriage of the church with the nationalist right reinforced a basis for conflict within the Greek-Cypriot community. Given the context of the ongoing Greek Civil War, this is not surprising. But these divisions would shape the struggle to come.

Attitudes towards Turkish-Cypriots also fashioned a path for the future. As with many Greek-Cypriot documents, the 'Blueprint' did not detail the place of the island's Turkish-Cypriot minority. Throughout the conflict, the *enosis* movement was slow to appreciate the extent of Turkish and Turkish-Cypriot hostility to their goals; Greek-Cypriot nationalists never fully realized the power of the Turkish government to influence events. Too many Greek-Cypriot nationalists regarded Turkish-Cypriot concerns as irrelevant to the workings of an effective democracy based on the will of the majority. In time it would prove a dangerous oversight.

Financial support was at the heart of the church's role. As the 'Blueprint' detailed, in order to achieve the political goals of *enosis*, 'a powerful fund is needed to finance the entire struggle. The basis of the fund ought to be the funds of different monasteries. It is about time that they be used entirely for this sacred goal. Simultaneously, it is possible to implement an additional system of receiving subscriptions for the national struggle.'[6] As far as church leaders were concerned, the time for pushing the British out had arrived. 'The struggle will begin with system and method and above all with boldness', they concluded. It will not wait 'for events to progress, and act or react accordingly, but will seek to pre-empt and provoke events'.[7] In the immediate term, nothing would prove more provocative than the church's plans for an island-wide petition for *enosis*.

Plebiscite and procrastination

In seeking to organize an island-wide plebiscite on *enosis*, the church aimed to advance its position as the leader of the *enosis* cause at the expense of AKEL. During this critical period, Greek-Cypriot society 'was polarized between the church and the communists, and *enosis* became the key to political supremacy'.[8] Under the new leadership of Ezekias Papaioannou, AKEL increased its vocal support for *enosis* even while continuing to excoriate the Greek government as a 'monarchist-fascist' regime.[9] Papaioannou's turn 'to the intransigent line of non-negotiable and immediate *enosis*' in March 1949 contributed to AKEL's loss of 'the initiative to the ethnarchy'. Instead of leading or shaping opinion and action, the party became 'a mere follower in the logic of the "absolute solution", leaving the people of the "Rally for Self-Government" rudderless, prey to the fancies of a Cypriot Great Idea'.[10]

The explanation of AKEL's attitudes during this stage is problematic. If Cyprus had indeed become part of Greece in 1949, it is unlikely that the Greek government's anti-communist sentiments would have spared AKEL members from persecution and possible imprisonment. One theory, advocated in parts of the British government, argued that Greek-Cypriot communists were gambling that Turkey and Great Britain would simply not agree to *enosis*. AKEL was therefore willing to support it as a way to sow dissent within the Western Alliance and 'to profit from any confusion caused in the Eastern Mediterranean'.[11] While this view cannot be entirely discredited, it did not account for two critical facts: the genuine pro-*enosis* sentiments of even leftist Greek-Cypriots and the general opposition of the left to British colonialism. AKEL's ideology opposed British imperialism and supported any movement which undermined it. Even in Greece, the communist party was forced to bow to nationalist sentiments and advocate territorial 'claims against Turkey in eastern Thrace and against Britain in Cyprus'.[12] AKEL had its own explanation for why it supported *enosis* in spite of the potential for political persecution at the hands of the Greek military regime. Their argument was that Greek-Cypriot communists should place more faith in their cultural identity as Greeks than in their political affiliation. The government of Greece could change, but the bond between Greeks and Greeks in Cyprus would not. AKEL articulated this view openly in 1954:

> Some people abroad find it difficult to understand why the people of Cyprus should fight for union of Cyprus with Greece when Greece itself had a monarcho-fascist regime and is actually under American subjugation and control. The struggle of the people of Cyprus for national rehabilitation must be viewed in relation to the struggle of the Greek people for national independence and not separately. . . . Governments come and go in Greece but the Greek people are always there.[13]

There is also a cynical explanation for AKEL's support of *enosis*. Within the party, it was feared that opposition to *enosis* would erode AKEL's domestic support because of the broad-based Greek-Cypriot backing for *enosis*. The party's immediate concerns were heightened by setbacks in the local elections of 1949. In the hopes of reinforcing its electoral strength, AKEL 'sought to protect its flank by becoming more nationalist than the nationalists' even going so far as to declare a willingness 'to raise the question of *enosis* at the United Nations'.[14]

AKEL's attempt to turn national rhetoric into political advantage prompted a strong response from the right, particularly from the church. With the groundwork for action having been laid during the summer of 1948, the church 'trumped AKEL's call for a "national assembly" by declaring on 1 December 1949 that a plebiscite would be held on the question of *enosis*, and when the Governor responded that the issue of sovereignty was closed, the Archbishop decided to go ahead unilaterally'.[15] The plebiscite's organizers hoped that an overwhelming 'yes' vote would clearly demonstrate the unified desire of the Greek-Cypriot population to the British government. At the same time, it was hoped that the result would draw criticism of British colonialism from all over the world. Most importantly, however, the exercise would outflank AKEL and place the *enosis* cause firmly in the hands of the church.

From the start, the church stamped its authority on the process. 'Greek Orthodox congregations through the island were called upon to sign a resolution after Sunday mass on 15 and 22 January 1950.'[16] Greek-Cypriots who held government positions under the British administration were excluded from voting.[17] Given that the petition was to be signed after Sunday mass, Turkish-Cypriots were also marginalized. However, a few Turkish-Cypriot signatures were later appended.[18] To ensure a robust vote in favour of *enosis*, strongly worded sermons threatened the denial of burial and baptismal rites for those who failed to sign the petition.[19]

Given the growing political tensions on the island and the full support of the church, the results were hardly surprising. A communiqué issued by the Ethnarchy Council on 27 January 1950 proudly announced that 215,108 of the 224,744 Greek-Cypriot voters – almost 96 per cent – had signed in support of union with Greece.[20] It was a significant victory for the *enosis* movement and a clear, if not unimpeachable, expression of the sentiments of the majority of the Greek-Cypriot population. An implicit assumption from the conduct and result of the plebiscite was that the voice of the island's Turkish-Cypriots was largely irrelevant to the Greek-Cypriot dream of union with Greece; the will of this majority, the church and nationalists maintained, was all that mattered.

Makarios, the bishop of Kitium (who would soon rise to international prominence as Archbishop Makarios III), expressed these sentiments clearly at a press conference in February. When asked about attitudes towards the Turkish minority in the event of *enosis*, he replied:

> I can assure you that the anxiety of the Turks in Cyprus about *Enosis* is not well-founded. When the Turks claim union with Turkey in the event of Britain leaving Cyprus they don't really mean it themselves. We must always have in mind that it is the majority's wish that counts and not that of a minority. The Turks in Cyprus will have nothing to lose as a minority under Greek rule in Cyprus. They will have all the usual privileges as is the case with the Turkish element in Thrace.[21]

Makarios's reasoning was flawed on almost every point. The Turks were serious when they spoke about union with Turkey; in fact their politicians still argued that the entire island should revert to Turkey if British sovereignty ended.[22] The wish of the minority, in this case, required consideration because both the British and Turkish governments, each more powerful than the Greek government, would not accept a solution which did not account for those feelings. Finally, whether the rights of Turks in Cyprus would be secure or not under Greek-Cypriot government was immaterial given the fact that Turkish-Cypriots regarded their rights as threatened. Statements like those made by the soon-to-be archbishop would hardly have given them confidence.

For its part, the British government appeared as uninterested in the will of the Greek-Cypriot people expressed in the plebiscite as the Greek-Cypriots seemed in that of the Turkish-Cypriots. This dual misunderstanding was a salient feature of the crisis in Cyprus. 'The British grossly underestimated both the measure of sympathy for enosis ... [and] the Greek-Cypriots showed themselves equally unmindful of the Turkish dimension.'[23] Once it was clear that the plebiscite had failed to shift the attitude of the British in any way, the Greek-Cypriot nationalists broadened their attack, seeking material support for their cause in Greece and moral support from the rest of the world. A delegation from the ethnarchy visited the United States and Greece at the end of 1950, but neither nation was receptive. In America, burgeoning Cold War tensions made disturbing Britain, or the Mediterranean balance, unpalatable. Self-determination for the Greek-Cypriots was peripheral to maintaining peace and stability in the Eastern Mediterranean. Although America was sympathetic to Greek-Cypriot opposition to British colonialism, Britain was too important an ally to offend over such an apparently minor matter. In Greece, other issues took precedence over Cyprus including maintaining cooperation with the United States, avoiding an open rupture with the British government, healing the political, economic and social divides of the civil war, preventing hostility with Turkey and protecting the Greek minority in Turkey, particularly in Istanbul.

The British ambassador in Athens noted in a January 1951 telegram to Ernest Bevin at the Foreign Office: 'No other single factor is likely to have so much influence here [in Greece] as the knowledge that the United States Government are opposed to the raising of the question in present circumstances.'[24] Prophetically, Ambassador Clifford Norton remarked that, although the Cyprus question had been pushed into the background by 'the gravity of the international situation', he feared that 'all those interested ... [would] do their utmost to ensure that it is not allowed to remain there'.[25] In April, the Foreign Office reported that 'the State Department recently instructed the United States Ambassador at Athens to speak to both the Greek Prime Minister and the Archbishop of Cyprus and to impress on both M. Venizelos and Archbishop Makarios the view of the United States Government that this was not the time to press the Enosis issue'.[26]

American pressure further deflated the Greek appetite to support the *enosis* cause. This factor was critical, because the *enosis* movement could hardly move forward politically, or otherwise, without material or even tacit backing from the motherland. For the present, it would be up to the people of Cyprus to change attitudes in Greece and abroad. To that end, Archbishop Makarios III made one of his many visits to Greece, travelling to Athens between 13 March and 13 April 1951. It was a highly publicized trip, during which he devoted himself 'solely to furthering the cause of *Enosis*'.[27]

In Turkey, and among Turkish-Cypriots, attitudes towards *enosis* were already strong and well formed. The early days of April 1951 saw a great deal of official British correspondence devoted to the heightening of Turkish feeling with regard to Cyprus. On 6 April 1951, Governor Sir Andrew Wright,[28] who had replaced Winster in August 1949, wrote to the secretary of state for the colonies that members of Cypriot-Turkish associations had requested an interview to bring to his 'notice anxiety felt by the Turkish community over *Enosis*' and 'to request whether anything could be done to alleviate great uneasiness felt by local Turks on this account'.[29] According to Wright, 'Turks and other Cypriots have been genuinely disturbed by recent events relating to *Enosis* . . . [which had taken on a] more menacing aspect than usual because from press reports the Greek government now appears to be treating Cyprus as a claim to be negotiated rather than as an aspiration to be pursued'.[30]

Opinion was also rising in Ankara. The British ambassador in Ankara wrote to the Foreign Office on 23 April:

> Turkish public opinion would be bitterly opposed to the cession of Cyprus to Greece for several reasons. First, there is the legitimate anxiety of the Turks about the fate of the Turkish minority under Greek rule. Secondly, the Turks are determined not to see any more islands off the Turkish coast fall under Greek rule . . . agitation about Cyprus has recently stimulated interest in the Dodecanese . . . if the Greek demand for Cyprus is pressed, Turkey will retaliate by demanding the return of these islands. Thirdly, the Turks are sensitive to the Communist threat in Cyprus and fear that if the island is handed over to Greece, this threat will become more acute and the strategic uses of the port of Iskenderun will be completely nullified. Lastly, there is the Turkish historical claim to Cyprus which, in Turkish eyes, is far more solidly based than that of Greece.[31]

The radicalization of both sides was proceeding in earnest. When a group of Turkish-Cypriot notables met with Governor Wright in April, they toed the Ankara party line. Wright tried to mollify their concerns by reaffirming Britain's commitment to the status quo in Cyprus. The Turkish-Cypriots, however, were adamant that conditions on the island were taking a new and dangerous turn with pressure for *enosis* generating tensions unique in Britain's seventy-year history on the island. The delegation asked for assurances 'that *Enosis* would never come' and that Britain would not leave Cyprus as they had withdrawn from Palestine or India.[32] Aware of the violence that had followed British withdrawals elsewhere, Turkish-Cypriots feared a similar result in Cyprus. British policymakers too were determined not to repeat those mistakes.

Britain's determination was supported by the increased perceptions concerning the strategic importance of the island. A report from the British Chiefs of Staff on 24 April 1951 was clear on the need for both a strategic presence in Cyprus and a firm stance by the British government on the issue of Cypriot sovereignty. British troops would not be moved around the Middle East haphazardly. A clear commitment to maintaining the island 'as a firmly held British stronghold' was needed. Full control of the island and its garrison was considered a strategic imperative.[33] The chiefs recommended an 'unequivocal statement . . . that His Majesty's Government will not consider any alteration to the status of Cyprus'.[34]

The change from a Labour government to a Conservative government in the election of October 1951 did not alter London's position on Cyprus. Almost as an annual ritual, questions about Cyprus were raised in Parliament. Time and again the issue of bridging the chasm between the Winster Constitution and the result of the plebiscite came to the floor only to receive the same response: no change in the sovereignty of the island was contemplated and the proposals of 1948 remained open for discussion.

These terms were far from what the new archbishop, Makarios III, was willing to accept. Makarios assumed his position as archbishop of Cyprus in October 1950, at the age of only thirty-seven, supported by the Cypriot right. Although Makarios II had headed the church during the plebiscite, Makarios III had been instrumental in its organization.[35] Makarios III shared his predecessor's political affiliation and goals, and fully adopted the nationalist slogan of '*enosis* and only *enosis*'. The new archbishop was born Mihalis Christodoulou Mouskos in rural Paphos, and was educated at the University of Athens and later at Boston University on a World Council of Churches' scholarship. In the years to come, Makarios's energy and relentless travel made him a fixture on the international scene, canvassing support for Cypriot self-determination.

Evangelos Averoff, soon to be the Greek foreign minister, captured the reality that from Makarios's election, '[i]t was clear that there was a new and rapid change of course. The overall organization of the struggle became more efficient and the issue assumed greater urgency in Cyprus, in Greece and in the international arena.... Truly, Archbishop Makarios moved heaven and earth to bring the Cyprus issue to a head.'[36] From the pulpit he preached the gospel of *enosis* and the liberation of Cyprus from British control. Makarios took Cyprus's cause to the world, travelling to Athens in 1951, to Washington, New York (where he visited the UN General Assembly), London and Athens in 1952, to Greece, Egypt, Lebanon and Syria in 1953. In 1954, he was again in Athens and New York, once more attending the UN General Assembly. In 1955, the archbishop attended the Afro-Asian Conference in Indonesia and yet again travelled to Egypt and Athens.[37]

Makarios worked to shape the character of the *enosis* movement within Cyprus as well, formalizing its organization and control through the authority and ideology of the church and the right. The archbishop's international lobbying effort seemed to succeed at the end of 1952 when a small victory was won at the UN. In December, a resolution supporting the universal principle of self-determination as a right for non-self-governing and trust territories, the validity of plebiscites, and a ruling that such questions were within the purview of the UN Committee on Human Rights was passed. Greece supported the measures but was still reluctant to court an open breach with Great Britain (or Turkey) through explicit referral to Cyprus. This cautious policy drew criticism from Makarios, first privately, then publicly. Evangelos Averoff, the then deputy foreign minister, recounts a testy exchange with the archbishop during the latter's visit to Athens in 1952:

> I [Averoff] reminded the Archbishop ... that Greece had still not recovered from the havoc wrought by ten catastrophic years, that neither the prosperity nor the national identity of the Greek-Cypriots was at risk and that there was no danger of any change in the ethnic composition of the island's population. For the time being, therefore, there were for us just two matters of paramount concern: first, to do all we could to feed the hungry, to house the homeless and in general to raise the Greek people's standard of living; second, to do nothing that might rebound on the precious Greek community in Constantinople.... Coolly, and with clinical detachment, the Archbishop replied that he agreed in principle, but with two important differences: first, that the liberty of Greek people takes precedence

over their living standards; second, that the Greek community in Constantinople, though precious indeed, was doomed to annihilation for a variety of reasons. It is hardly being overdramatic to say that his words stabbed me to the heart.[38]

During the same trip, Makarios had had an even more heated exchange with Sophocles Venizelos, the Greek foreign minister and deputy prime minister. According to Venizelos, Makarios had threatened to 'expose' him 'before the Greek people for refusing to bring the issue before the United Nations'. Unmoved by the threat, Venizelos responded: 'You can expose me before anybody you want and with whatever accusations you find appropriate, but I will not allow you to direct the foreign policy of Greece.'[39]

By the summer of 1953, Greece's unwillingness to give sufficiently active support to Makarios's uncompromising position prompted the archbishop to unilateral action. In a sermon at Nicosia's Phaneromeni Church on 28 June, he expressed his disappointment with Greek procrastination. In the most forceful terms yet, Makarios claimed:

> we do not rely entirely on the Greek government, nor do we put our faith exclusively in the United Nations. We rely above all on our own might and we put our greatest faith in *the struggle on our own soil* . . . under the flag of the Ethnarchy, we shall fight with consistency and determination . . . *using every method and every means available*, [Averoff's italics] with our eyes turned always towards one goal: liberty and union with our mother country.[40]

On 10 August, a letter was sent to New York asking specifically for the self-determination of Cyprus to be inscribed on the UN agenda for that summer's council. Since Cyprus was not a sovereign state, a full member of the UN was needed to sponsor the motion. The natural choice was Greece, but the Greek government was still cautious. In September 1953, the Greek representative to the United Nations, Alexis Kyrou, himself of Cypriot origin,[41] delivered a compromise statement before the General Assembly. Kyrou referred to a resolution from December 1952, which had reaffirmed the principle of self-determination, and to the strong feelings of the Greek population in support of the Greek-Cypriot majority's desire for self-determination. In spite of his personal advocacy for *enosis*, Kyrou stopped short of directly asking the UN Assembly to take charge of the issue saying that Greece preferred 'the method of friendly bilateral discussion', due to its 'long-standing cordial relations with the United Kingdom'.[42] The Cyprus problem, in spite of Kyrou's diplomatic language, was beginning to strain the 'cordial relations' between the two nations. On 15 March 1954, Anthony Eden, the then foreign secretary, articulated the government's position in response to questions about negotiations with Athens saying that the government would not 'agree to discuss the status of Cyprus'.[43] The issue seemed closed.

Hopkinson's 'no' and the failure of politics

Greece's cautious performance in New York preceded a series of unsuccessful backchannel overtures to Britain on the Cyprus issue.[44] By an unfortunate coincidence, as opposition to British rule on the island was becoming more active, the perceived importance of Cyprus to British grand strategy was increasing. The withdrawal from India had convinced many high-ranking British officials, both civilian and military, that Britain's future as a great power lay in her continued influence in the Middle East and Africa.[45] The vision was to create a remodelled British Empire, which would project power from the Eastern Mediterranean into Africa and the Middle East. Cyprus was essential to this policy. Developments in Egypt had added to the importance of Cyprus. A policy memo on the strategic importance of the island, issued by the ministry of defence in September 1954, encapsulated the prevailing wisdom. It differed little from the similar document of April 1951, maintaining that Cyprus's value was based on the importance of the Middle East to Britain's strategic position as 'the one major power with special responsibilities for the stability and general strategic interests of the area'. Cyprus was essential to upholding British treaty obligations to Iraq, Jordan and Libya. The Middle East as a whole was 'an important link in our Commonwealth sea and air communications', and, finally, of 'long established economic interests'.[46] Cyprus was

> the only remaining British territory in the Middle East [although Aden was added by hand in the draft] . . . the only place which can provide permanently and free from risk of inadequate internal security and of externally imposed restrictions on our military requirements, a peacetime base for our Middle East land and air headquarters where we can keep troops permanently in peacetime to meet sudden emergencies of any kind.[47]

Britain had reason for concern about future emergencies. The newly created state of Israel was precarious, as were the British supported regimes in Jordan and Iraq. British policymakers were still engaged in counter-insurgency operations in Kenya. During the summer of 1954, the importance of Cyprus was further sharpened. First, London, under pressure from the Egyptian government, took the decision to abandon the military bases in Suez and substitute its functions with expanded facilities in Cyprus. This move had been agreed in principle in December 1952 and planning began in January 1954.[48] Second, the Greek government, rebuked in its bilateral attempts to come to an understanding with Great Britain, announced in June its intention to bring the Cyprus issue to the UN later that summer. The British government had at once to assert its control over the island more firmly while at the same time providing a shield for this policy in the UN.

As part of this process, Henry Hopkinson, the minister of state for colonial affairs, took the floor in the House of Commons and announced another 'fresh initiative in the development of self-government institutions in Cyprus'.[49] Just how fresh this initiative could be – with its accompanying constitution designed to support the continuation of British rule and foster amity between the Greek-Cypriot and Turkish-Cypriot populations – was open to debate. Its main purpose was to build support for Britain in the UN through improvements in Cyprus. The plan's freshness was further circumscribed by Hopkinson's wish to 'make it clear once again that [the government] cannot contemplate a change of sovereignty in Cyprus'.[50] The apparent dichotomy of Hopkinson's statement, promising substantive steps towards self-government while insisting on no change in British sovereignty, sparked immediate challenge from the opposite benches. Labour MP James Griffiths countered sharply: 'Are we now to understand that, so far as Cyprus is concerned, it is not proposed that this constitutional development shall take its normal course which it has in other places, in conformity with the policy of this House?'[51]

Hopkinson returned to the substance of his previous statement, insisting that '[i]t has always been understood and agreed that there are certain territories in the Commonwealth which, owing to their particular circumstances, can never expect to be fully independent'. Boos echoed through the House and Hopkinson muddled on: 'I think the right hon. Gentleman will agree that there are some territories which cannot expect to be that [fully independent]. I am not going as far as that this afternoon, but I have said that the question of the abrogation of British sovereignty cannot arise – that British sovereignty will remain.'[52] British sources conveyed to their American counterparts through unofficial channels that Hopkinson had gone 'completely off his prepared brief', with these remarks.[53] But this was likely a gesture of face-saving placation to the Americans. Hopkinson's remarks were consistent with the firm opposition of the British government to *enosis*. If he had gone off his brief, his comments had not represented an alteration of British policy.

Opposition from the Labour backbenchers was just one indication that, on the political level, maintaining British sovereignty in Cyprus was becoming more difficult. Domestic forces questioned its necessity as the international community prepared to debate its validity and forces in Cyprus gathered to challenge its legitimacy. Arms and funding were dribbling into the island from Greece and the ideology of the *enosis* movement increased in radicalism with every 'no' from the British government. Departing from Cyprus presented its own difficulties. It meant a retreat from empire that was unconscionable to the Eden government. Internationally, it threatened British strategic considerations in the Eastern Mediterranean and, most importantly, raised the spectre of a Turkish response. In the bigger picture, it represented the enduring problem that an uncompromising position over Cyprus could not be maintained indefinitely in the face of Greek pressure internationally and the unwillingness of the United States to support Britain in maintaining the status quo.[54]

Hopkinson's presentation on Cyprus, awkward though it may have been, was meant to respond to each of these challenges: to reassure the British administration on Cyprus, to warn off *enosis* forces on the island, to maintain Britain's strategic position in the Eastern Mediterranean and to assuage Turkish fears. In form, it had provoked much; in substance, it promised to change little. As the 28 July debate closed, the Labour MP Richard Crossman warned prophetically: 'May I say that the tragedy of the Middle East is that there is not a country there whose people have got their rights from the British without murder? In every case we have resisted as long as they made their demands peaceably, and we conceded appeasement when they began violence against us.'[55] Violence in Cyprus was now simmering just below the surface and one final 'no' remained to bring the pot boiling over.

The final 'no' from the United Nations

Despite their prevarication over Cyprus, the Greek government were stung by Hopkinson's statement. 'It was a stupid thing to say', wrote Averoff later, 'first because there is no such word as "never" in human affairs and secondly because in this particular instance it ran counter to the obligations which Britain had accepted by signing the United Nations Charter.'[56] This rigid position of the British government paved the way for Greece to proceed at the United Nations. There was no illusion that the UN would 'liberate' Cyprus from British control or set the island on a path to self-determination and *enosis*. There was no question that the United Nations could provide 'a solution to the Cyprus problem'. British intransigence, combined with pressure from domestic opinion and Cypriot activists (not least Makarios), tipped Greek policymakers to action. They were guarded in their expectations, acknowledging 'that the United Nations, at the most, could only *lead* to a solution'.[57]

While Greece planned its case at the UN, preparations for an armed uprising in Cyprus had progressed a great deal. With the left effectively sidelined from the *enosis* debate and diplomatic overtures collapsing, the *enosis* cause would find expression in violence planned and executed by the right wing. Formal authorization from Makarios was all that was required.

The UN debate during September 1954 demonstrated an awareness that *enosis* sentiment was precariously close to violence. The debate contrasted the Greek delegation's position that the Cyprus problem was one of the self-determination of peoples (and therefore a fundamental right to be defended by the international community) against Britain's position that the UN had no authority to interfere with the sovereignty of a member state. Both Selwyn Lloyd, the British spokesman, then minister of state for foreign affairs, and Alexis Kyrou were in agreement on the principle that the Cyprus dispute posed a much greater threat than simply the agitation of the UN Assembly. Naturally, they differed on predicting the form this agitation would take.

Britain's position, articulated by Lloyd, was that the debate would 'do nothing but exacerbate feelings, set Christians against Moslems and produce internal strife which the Cypriots and hitherto been spared. The resulting tension might extend far beyond the island of Cyprus itself.'[58] For their part, the Greeks contended that the UN needed to take up the cause of Cypriot self-determination in order to avoid unrest in the island directed at British control. The Greek government was bringing the Cypriot case to the UN and putting its faith in the international system in order to avoid a more direct and violent method of achieving *enosis*. Kyrou laid out his case to the assembled delegates in plain language:

> There has already been disquieting signs of the gravity of the situation in Cyprus, and I must assure the Members of this august body that, had it not been for the prospect of resort to the United Nations, the situation in that island would have taken an even more ominous turn. . . . Passive resistance has already begun. Clandestine publications, bearing such titles as 'Freedom or Death'[59] . . . and posters inciting to revolt, are in the hands of almost everyone in Cyprus. The

apparent calm is the quiet that precedes the storm. . . . If the safety valve [of the United Nations] is shut, there will be no other means of lowering the tension.[60]

The response from Selwyn Lloyd touched on several key points in an attempt to discredit Kyrou's argument. First, Lloyd challenged the Greek representative's bleak picture of Cyprus, denying that any violence existed on the island and sniping that 'the only place where people have been sent to prison for differing with the political views of the Government is, in fact, in Athens'.[61] Second, Lloyd insisted that since Cyprus was a crown colony, any disturbance was a matter of 'domestic jurisdiction' which naturally fell outside the purview of the UN. Interference in the domestic affairs of a country was dangerous business. 'If this principle is accepted', Lloyd cautioned 'then no frontier would be permanent. The way would be open to foment discord, to agitate for territorial adjustments, to cause racial and religious discord, and to use this Organization for these purposes.'[62] Third, Cyprus did not represent 'a question of self-determination and independence in the accepted sense of those terms'. This was because, in addition to the Greek majority, Cyprus had a Turkish minority. In the case of Greek-Cypriot self-determination (leading to *enosis*), the Turkish-Cypriot community, Lloyd argued, would under no circumstances 'be given the right to determine its own future' by the Greek-Cypriots.[63] This unequal process of self-determination inherent in *enosis* rendered its application impossible in the view of the British government. The Turkish-Cypriot minority, he continued, remained 'bitterly opposed to *enosis*. . . . This Turkish-speaking community of Moslems is composed of 100,000 people just as devoted to their religious beliefs, just as conscious of their racial and cultural ties with Turkey as the Greek-speaking people are with the Greek Church and with Greece.'[64] Although it may have been spoken in the service of British colonial control, the obstacle concerning the unequal application of self-determination vis-à-vis the Turkish-Cypriot community was an accurate message which neither Greeks nor Greek-Cypriots wanted to hear.

Lloyd's arguments, however, fell on deaf ears and the assembly voted for the inclusion of the item by forty votes to nineteen with eleven abstentions (including the United States). The match, however, was not over. Before the motion came for debate on the floor of the General Assembly, the British used the New Zealand delegation to outflank the Greek proposal. New Zealand sponsored a resolution to shelve the Cyprus debate. Another contentious argument loomed. In order to avoid this, Colombia and El Salvador stepped forward with an amendment to New Zealand's resolution, adding that debate on Cyprus should be shelved only 'for the time being'. In the previous vote, El Salvador had voted with Greece, while Colombia had voted against inclusion. Now, this key addition, spurred, in all likelihood, by the US State Department prevented a deepening of the developing rift between Greece and Britain.[65] On 17 December, the New Zealand resolution, with the key amendment, was passed in a landslide. The last-minute addition, by allowing the debate to be resumed at a future date, passed with fifty votes (including Greece) and eight abstentions.

The Greeks had lacked the necessary broad-based support for a more strongly worded resolution. Anthony Nutting, the undersecretary of state for foreign affairs, took the floor first and triumphantly declared that 'the vote which has just taken place represents a great and important victory for common sense'.[66] The British government had played the UN game well and dodged the bullet of a debate on its colonial control in Cyprus, but the success was hardly permanent. In less than four months, real bullets would threaten British control in Cyprus and explosions of dynamite rather than debate would force a substantial reappraisal of London's position.

4

Taking up arms

The continuation of politics through force

> *I swear in the name of the Holy Trinity that I shall work with all my power for the liberation of Cyprus from the British yoke, sacrificing for this even my life.*[1]
> – EOKA oath

The failure of the UN debate at the end of 1954 left those Greek-Cypriots favouring a political solution with little ground and fewer ideas. For activists, it was the final proof that violence was the only way to achieve union with Greece. After more than a century of working to join the Greek state through diplomacy and negotiation, the decision of Greek-Cypriot nationalists to resort to force was neither impulsive nor bloodthirsty. Over the course of the struggle, however, Giorgos Grivas – EOKA's commander – and Archbishop Makarios III confronted problems for which they had not been prepared and limitations beyond their original considerations. Their prism of Greek nationalism blinded them to the extent (and even existence) of Turkish-Cypriot and Turkish fears and interests. Their committed anti-communism created tensions with leftist Greek-Cypriots. Their desire to remove Britain from the island completely reduced space for a negotiated solution with London. And even though Makarios and Grivas were unified in these goals, their differences over the use and scope of violence created fissures within the nationalist movement itself. These tensions would dog and define the struggle over the next four years.

Leadership and creation EOKA

EOKA was the spearhead of the *enosis* movement. Reflecting the long history of *enosis* agitation in Cyprus, its formation was a gradual process. In the years following the Second World War, disappointment over the lack of progress through negotiation with Britain, coupled with the example of organized violence in other colonies, inspired groups of Greek-Cypriot nationalists to consider the use of arms to further their cause. One of the foremost voices in favour of armed action was a retired colonel, Giorgos Grivas. Grivas was a Cypriot, born in the district of Famagusta in 1898. At eighteen, he left Cyprus and enrolled in the military academy in Athens and became a Greek national.[2] After serving in the First World War and in the Greco-Turkish War (1919-22), Captain Grivas won a scholarship to study in France. He completed his studies at the '*École de Guerre* in Paris and lectured on tactics at the War School in Athens'.[3] During the Second World War, he saw service as a staff officer, eventually ending up serving as the chief of staff for a division on the Albanian front.

After the fall of Greece, Grivas rose to some notoriety as the founder and commander of the resistance organization '*X*'.[4] In this capacity, Grivas had his first experience leading insurgent operations. Composed mostly of royalist Greek officers, *X* was aggressively anti-communist. It was dedicated to Greek irredentism and the return of the monarchy.[5] Its pro-monarchy credentials were reinforced by the claim, probably apocryphal, that its name 'was derived from the signature of the King of Greece (Georgios Gliksbourg), which resembled the Greek letter x'.[6] *X*'s record against the Germans was not distinguished within the context of the Greek resistance. Speculation remains as to whether this was due to 'weakness, excessive caution, and a lack of adequate Allied support' or due to a primary focus on 'a bitter running vendetta with the rival Communist underground'.[7] Once the Axis powers withdrew their forces from Greece, *X* played a small role in the civil war, where its anti-communist role in the street battles of Athens had placed it front and centre. *X*'s rather dull performance during the occupation and its invigorated activity after the liberation have led some to argue that a number of *X*'s 'associates were tainted with the stigma of collaboration; and its weapons, on the Colonel's [Grivas's] own admission, were obtained from the enemy [Germany]'.[8] This intent of some modern authors to shade Grivas through Nazi collaboration is somewhat overdone. It was the goal of the Germans to foment civil war in Greece. To this end, the Wehrmacht left behind a quantity of weapons, many of which they could not carry in any case, in the hopes that various right-wing elements would use them against the left.[9] In all likelihood, this was how German weapons came into Grivas's hands, and not through direct collaboration with Nazi forces.

In 1946, as the Greek Civil War raged, Grivas first met Makarios through Zafeiris Valvis, who was a political adviser to *X*.[10] Grivas recorded in his *Memoirs* that Makarios had published several articles in *X*'s newspaper attacking communism.[11] Later in 1946, when *X* came to be considered something of an embarrassment on the international scene for the Greek government, its offices in Athens were closed.[12] As *X* faded and the Greek communists were defeated, Grivas became progressively marginalized as a political figure. He attempted to convert *X* into a purely political movement but failed miserably at the polls and retired to private life. It was after his failure to achieve political distinction in Greece that he seemed to have begun considering forming a military organization geared towards Cypriot *enosis*.

Grivas's methods in the pursuit of *enosis* had their roots in his beliefs and experiences. Grivas was religiously devout, a committed royalist and nationalist. He regarded Cyprus as an inexorable part of Greece for historical and cultural reasons. He was remarkable for his zeal and energy. A hostile contemporary biographer described him as doing everything, fighting, exercising, praying or stamp collecting, 'with a fanaticism that verges on the insane'.[13] His MI6 profile characterized him as a man of enormous industry with an unremitting attention to detail. His 'great grasp of detail

[and] his lucid mind', gave him an 'exceptional facility for expressing himself clearly'.[14] He was 'personally always clean and regularly shaved . . . neither smoked nor drank and was abstemious in matters of food to the point almost of vegetarianism'.[15] Rumours persisted that he subsisted on little more than two dozen oranges a day.[16]

Grivas believed deeply in the cause of *enosis* and was prepared to pursue it with complete ruthlessness. He was also very much a product of his time, straightjacketed in a mind-set of strict discipline and the belief that violence was an essential, effective and legitimate tool to further political objectives. To historian Robert Holland, 'Grivas had no ideas beyond a hatred of Communism, a love of Greece and a sincere and highly romanticized belief in *Enosis*.'[17] These ideological foundations meant that Grivas and his comrades fused irredentism, religiosity and patriotism characteristic of traditional Greek nationalism with the newer elements of anti-communism and post-war anti-colonialism.[18] These beliefs directly influenced the nature of the struggle he led and contributed to making his relationship with Makarios at once symbiotic and problematic.

In May 1948, Grivas approached Christodoulos Papadopoulos, the brother of his former aide in *X*, with preliminary ideas about beginning an armed struggle in Cyprus.[19] Papadopoulos, a lawyer who served on the Ethnarchic Council, travelled to Cyprus at Grivas's request in August 1950 to gauge whether the situation would be favourable for such operations. The response in Cyprus, according to Papadopoulos, was encouraging.[20] Grivas continued his overtures within nationalist circles in Greece, next approaching his former commanding officer from the war, Giorgos Kosmas, who had risen to the position of Chief of the General Staff. According to Grivas, Kosmas was also 'in the confidence of' Field Marshal Alexandros Papagos. Kosmas promised to work to convince Papagos 'that only force could liberate Cyprus'.[21] The struggle to persuade Greek political and military leaders to make the cause of *enosis* their own would be a familiar theme throughout the struggle. By mid-1951, both the philosophical and the physical foundations for an armed struggle were coming together. At the start of that year, Grivas approached Giorgos Stratos, Greece's former minister of war. This, in turn, led him to a meeting with Socrates and Savvas Loizides. The Loizides brothers were Cypriot-born lawyers living in Athens as political exiles. They were members of the Ethnarchy Council and known *enosis* activists. In 1951, Savvas had published a monograph arguing for union based on international law. On 1 May 1951, the Loizides brothers, Stratos and Grivas met at a cafe in Athens. The outcome of their discussion, according to Grivas's *Memoirs*, was that he should 'undertake the leadership of an armed struggle to throw the British out of Cyprus'.[22]

It was apparent Grivas wished to move quickly. He immediately secured a visa and in July travelled to Cyprus to conduct a personal reconnaissance.[23] He met Makarios soon after his arrival and spoke encouragingly to the archbishop about the prospects for the success of an armed struggle. The two men met again in August, and although Makarios seemed to agree in principle with the colonel's arguments, Grivas understood that 'he had grave doubts' and 'was not really convinced' that guerrilla warfare on Cyprus could be used to achieve *enosis*.[24] It was not the first manifestation of Makarios's nebulous style. His agreement with Grivas was more theoretical than practical; for now, violence would have to wait.

In spite of Makarios's hesitancy to endorse violence, the archbishop took a lead role in putting the *enosis* movement on a more organized footing with the direct support of both the church and the nationalist right. As previously discussed, this was partially due to the church's desire to avoid having the movement co-opted by the left wing. To this end, Makarios secured the election of a protégé, Andreas Azinas, as secretary general of the powerful PEK and extended the church's influence over a breakaway confederation of right-wing trade unions.[25] A centrepiece of Makarios's initial actions within Cyprus was his creation of the Pancyprian National Youth Organisation (PEON)[26] in January 1951. The goal was to 'unite all members of nationalist youth organisations under the leadership of the Ethnarchy and, specifically, Makarios III'. Makarios exercised 'absolute control' over the organization. He appointed all organization officials and had to approve any amendments to the organization's constitution, whose parameters he no doubt set. PEON, a 'youth' organization, required its members to be '18–40 years old, loyal to the Ethnarchy, national ideals and the traditions of the Greek race'.[27] PEON would focus on promoting the cause of *enosis* while inculcating Greek nationalism and counteracting the prevalent communist youth organizations.[28] At the inauguration ceremony for PEON's Nicosia branch in March 1952, Makarios boasted that PEON would 'be the cornerstone of the general organization of the internal front and vanguard of the Cyprus struggle'.[29] In time, it would become a recruiting ground for EOKA.

As Makarios worked hard in Cyprus to create the foundations of resistance organizations, his diplomatic initiatives abroad, as described earlier, were equally dynamic though less fruitful. Their failure forced him back on Grivas and those advocating violence. Back in Athens to pressurize the Greek government, Makarios attended the first meeting of a group the Loizides brothers had named the 'Sacred Liberation Committee'.[30] Makarios officially chaired the committee's meeting on 2 July 1952. Most of the attendees were hard-core nationalists and former *X* members: Professor Dimitrios Vezanis, formerly of *X*; Giorgos Stratos, the Cypriot-born general of the Greek army; Nicolas Papadopoulos; Colonel Elias Alexopoulos, also formerly of *X*; Professor Yerasimos Konidaris; and the lawyer Antonis Avgikos.[31] Grivas urged immediate action through sabotage and guerrilla operations while Makarios cautioned that the moment was not yet right.[32] When the committee met again nearly three weeks later, Makarios was discouraged by the perceived lack of support from the Greek government. The Cypriot contingent decided that it was time to escalate their actions. Makarios openly attacked the Greek leadership in his farewell radio broadcast, and in October, Grivas returned to Cyprus for further reconnaissance. In Cyprus, Makarios arranged for Azinas to meet Grivas at the home of Grivas's brother. They discussed how Grivas planned to proceed with the struggle.[33]

By the start of 1953, Grivas, who returned to Greece in February, prepared a plan detailing his vision for operations in Cyprus.[34] Unlike the general resistance described by the church's 'Blueprint' of 1948, Grivas laid out in detail how violence would be employed to further the cause of *enosis*. Being an experienced soldier, Grivas was not under any illusions about what his small group could accomplish militarily. Instead of military victory, the objective was '[t]o arouse international public opinion, especially among the allies of Greece, by deeds of heroism and self-sacrifice, which will focus attention on Cyprus until our aims are achieved'. Grivas knew that whatever paramilitary organization he could form, it would not be capable of defeating the British in the field. Instead, his goal was to make the British feel 'continuously harried and beset until they are obliged by international diplomacy exercised through the United Nations to examine the Cyprus problem and settle it in accordance with the desire of the Cypriot people and the whole Greek nation'.[35] Like the 'Blueprint' of 1948, Grivas acknowledged the importance of creating international pressure against Britain as well as the danger of opposition within Cyprus. While the church in 1948 focused on communism, Grivas, in 1953, was vague, writing only that he 'would take measures to neutralize all opposition in Cyprus, from whatever quarter, as well as to put out of action and severely punish any Cypriots acting as British agents to the prejudice of our struggle'.[36] In spite of the absence of a direct reference to communism, there is evidence to suggest that Grivas's thinking was nevertheless influenced by the experience of the Greek Civil War and also by the Greek guerrilla war against the German occupation.[37] Critically, although his plan laid out how it would punish Cypriots working against *enosis*, like the 1948 'Blueprint', it made no explicit mention of the fallout an armed struggle might cause with Turkish-Cypriots or, more importantly, with Turkey.

Grivas planned three courses of action: '1) Sabotage against Government installations and military camps. 2) Surprise attacks of small and highly mobile combat units against the British forces. 3) Organizing the passive resistance of the population.'[38] The first two were components of what Grivas considered 'guerrilla warfare', which he believed was 'a suitable weapon in the hands of nations and states for the promotion of their national military policy'.[39] Grivas thought of guerrilla warfare as a means which 'from time immemorial' had been used by the 'weak, subject peoples ... against their masters to recover their freedom'.[40] Grivas's historical awareness and personal experiences shaped this view. He had seen the effectiveness of guerrilla operations first-hand, when fighting against Mustafa Kemal during Greece's war with the new Turkish Republic.[41] From a historical perspective, he described guerrilla operations as fundamental to a number of conflicts, from origins of the Greek Revolution through opposition to Germany within the occupied countries of Europe to the expansion of Soviet communism following the Second World War.[42] In Cyprus, he would try and emulate these examples.

In the plan of 1953, Grivas wrote that '[b]ecause of the difficulty of conducting a systematic, large-scale armed guerrilla campaign, and in view of the fact that the territory is not capable of absorbing large guerrilla forces, the main weight of the campaign will be placed on sabotage'.[43] He did not, however, exclude expanding guerrilla operations provided there were sufficient weapons at hand and a 'favourable turn' of events.[44] In carrying out sabotage operations, Grivas was clear that he alone, as the leader of EOKA, would be responsible for selecting targets.[45] Military operations would be used to support the sabotage groups and, if possible, to carry out 'more important missions against military targets'.[46]

Struggles

Planning for military operations in addition to sabotage highlighted the emerging tensions between Grivas and Makarios. These would become an omnipresent feature of the EOKA struggle, not least because Grivas resented Makarios's attempts to exercise operational control over EOKA. These tensions reflected a fundamental division in how the two men viewed the utility of violence and the *enosis* struggle itself. Makarios and Grivas were individuals of very different background, experience and temperament. Their differences were as apparent to individuals within the struggle as to those who opposed it. The MI6 officer who prepared a report on Grivas in 1959 wrote that 'the relationship between Grivas and Makarios was never easy. They appear as mutually unsympathetic characters.'[47]

While this is perhaps to overstate the point, as identified earlier, the debate over the use of violence was present from the first meetings in 1951. By 1953, Makarios authorized Grivas to begin preparations for a struggle, but the *nature* of this struggle had been left to political developments.[48] This prevarication gave Grivas scope to deliver a plan of operation along the lines he desired. In March, Makarios and a group of followers met to formalize their participation in a resistance organization.[49] The ceremony was 'consciously styled on the model of the *Philiki Etairia*', where they swore an oath 'to translate their designs into action'. In echoing earlier rituals, Makarios and his supporters revealed a 'somewhat outdated nationalist outlook', which was a 'throwback to the romantic nationalism of the nineteenth century'.[50] In spite of the forward progress, Makarios conveyed to Grivas in March 1953 his opposition to violence and his 'sabotage only' policy. He reiterated this position through Azinas in June. He was willing to authorize the use of force within a limited scope along the lines of his stated preference for sabotage.[51] Makarios was also dragging his feet about committing to a start date for operations. A continued failure of diplomatic initiatives and Grivas's control of operational planning, however, created a momentum towards violence.

Grivas – as his debates with Makarios (and his general plan) make clear – aimed at a broader and bloodier struggle. As an experienced soldier, Grivas felt Makarios had no understanding of the nature of military affairs: 'He [Makarios] cannot grasp military developments, nor can he anticipate the reaction of fighters or security forces on the battlefield, what developments will be like and how one control them. A fire cracker, a firework, a shot in the air and no one can tell how the crowd will react.'[52] It was Grivas's opinion, and probably a correct one, that once unleashed, violence would be difficult to control. In addition, Grivas believed that it would take more than throwing a few bombs for Britain and the world to take notice. In Grivas's view, once Makarios gave the green light for the struggle, he would have to accept the consequences.

Greece's defeat at the UN, coupled with more positive murmurings from Prime Minister Papagos (no doubt spurred by the Hopkinson 'no' and his rebuff at the hands of Prime Minister Eden), prevented Makarios from holding Grivas back any longer. Papagos had resigned his military command in April 1951 upon entering politics and securing his position as prime minister following an electoral victory in November 1952. In early 1955, Grivas and Makarios discussed beginning the struggle on 25 March, that is on Greek Independence Day. Grivas thought that was too long a delay and pushed for an earlier start. Then on 25 January 1955 the conspirators suffered a massive setback. The *St. George*, a caique from Athens loaded with explosives purchased by the church, was captured by the destroyer HMS *Comet* along with the boat's crew and Socrates Loizides. Makarios wrote to Grivas with marked defeatism that 'it seems that we have lost before we have started'.[53] Although Grivas records in his *Memoirs* that '[t]his was a staggering blow', he had no intention of giving up. Grivas went into hiding after the capture of the *St. George*, leaving Nicosia and moving to the small village of Kakopetria in the Troodos Mountains. All EOKA training ceased.[54] The British authorities, however, were unable to follow up on their success, and soon, Grivas was confident enough to come out from the shadows.

The first months of 1955 were filled with activity. Grigoris Afxentiou, a Cypriot who had served in the Greek army as a reservist officer, had been introduced to Grivas through Azinas a few days before the capture of the *St. George*. With explosives now in short supply, Afxentiou suggested following the example of fishermen who dove in shallow water off the coast of Famagusta to retrieve landmines and artillery shells dumped by the British after the end of the Second World War.[55] The effort to acquire dynamite from mines was redoubled.[56] Makarios also made cash available for the purchasing of explosives, where necessary, from the black market.[57]

With sufficient supplies and increased concern about discovery, Grivas again pressured Makarios for formal permission to begin. The plan of 25 March was scrapped as being too dangerous in the face of a possible increase in British preparedness due to the significance of the date for the Greek community. Grivas contacted Makarios on 21 March reporting his readiness and highlighting that any delay would place the entire project in danger.[58] On the evening of 29 March, Grivas and Makarios met in secret. At last, the archbishop gave permission to begin the campaign. Grivas prepared for immediate action. He sent word for the area commanders to meet him the next day. Operations would begin at midnight of 31 March–1 April.

At half-past twelve on 1 April, men armed with dynamite and home-made explosives attacked wireless stations, police stations and army barracks inflicting damage on property rather than specifically attempting to kill or injure security personnel. Sixteen separate explosions rocked Cyprus's four major towns: Nicosia, Famagusta, Larnaca and Limassol. Inauspiciously for EOKA, the only casualty was its member Modestos Pantelis, who electrocuted himself as he attempted to cut power lines in the city of Famagusta. Later that morning, EOKA released a proclamation announcing the beginning of 'the struggle to throw off the English yoke'. Grivas, styling himself 'Dighenis' after a legendary Byzantine hero, tied his organization's cause to the greater ideals of Hellenism and freedom. The narrative of Cypriot slavery at the hands of the British was a common trope among supporters of the *enosis* cause.[59] Characterizing the status of Cypriots under British colonial rule was an exaggeration to be sure. While their condition was something less than slavery, it was also something less than freedom. Cypriot citizens remained in a condition where majorities could be frustrated and their will sidelined.

Having begun the struggle, Grivas was not about to relax the pressure on the British. In fact, the onset of violence provided the opportunity to expand operations and further increase his role in the struggle. He wrote in his diary on 2 April that sabotage would continue until the police were 'unable to cope with the situation'. This would force the government 'to use military forces for its security' and allow Grivas the scope 'to organize the rebel struggle which is already being prepared'.[60] Further attacks were carried out over the next seven days on military installations in Nicosia, Limassol, Larnaca and Famagusta. EOKA tried to sabotage the electricity in Nicosia and also attacked a police station in the capital. High-profile targets were hit leading to tens of thousands of pounds in damage.

After the accidental electrocution of Pantelis, no fatalities were recorded on either side. During this stage, the evidence suggests that Grivas respected Makarios's preference for sabotage. The archbishop's dual desires for caution and control were immediately apparent. Just days into the struggle, the EOKA leader received a letter from the archbishop. In his diary for 4 April, Grivas wrote in obvious frustration:

> Gen[ikos][61] sends me a letter and gives his opinion that our activities must stop in the towns so that we may re-organise ourselves!! I must take lessons now from the various faint-hearted fellows who surround Genikos and give advice to him because they are afraid of their skins and are interested in their leisure. Because such are the men who give their opinions to Genikos who, only yesterday wrote me, 'Go ahead, you are doing well.' It is a critical turn of the struggle now.[62]

EOKA, however, did pause to regroup; 9 June saw the final small-scale attacks of the initial phase of operations. The respite was brief. While it is possible that Grivas was sensitive to Makarios's entreaty, it is more likely that he was simply reorganizing his forces. Around 10 May, a group of eight Greek-Cypriots attending college in Athens returned to the island, committed to the *enosis* cause. While in Greece, they had formed their own anti-British organization, and with the help of sympathetic Greek army officers had received arms and explosives training. Some had even travelled to Crete and trained for two weeks in guerrilla tactics, again, under Greek officers.[63] Once in Cyprus, they met with Grivas. After an impassioned speech about freedom and the struggle, the colonel explained that EOKA needed leaders, educated and committed men of intelligence, who could serve the organization as regional commanders.[64] Grivas later wrote in his *Memoirs* that these 'keen and energetic boys' would form 'the nucleus of . . . [the] first mountain guerrilla groups'.[65] The colonel assigned each man a different command, and instructed them to recruit new members and to monitor British and police targets for future attacks.[66] Grivas also planned a new series of larger operations to begin later in June.[67]

With their new leadership in place, Grivas's men resumed operations in earnest on 19 June with several grenade attacks in Nicosia and one in Famagusta. A report by the Cyprus Intelligence Committee (CIC) distinguished this new violence as phase 'B'. A number of bomb attacks were conducted on 20 June, along with armed raids on police stations and arson. The insurgency heated up through the summer as attacks became a nearly daily feature of life on the island. According to his *Memoirs*, Grivas's plan was to continue the heightened level of violence at least through to October, at which time the issue of Cyprus would again be raised by Greece at the UN.[68] This objective was supported by a report sent from Grivas to Makarios on 23 May where he wrote, 'The struggle must be organized in such a way that it may last at least until next October, when the Cyprus question will be discussed in the UNO.'[69] From the beginning, Grivas was aware that the international perception of EOKA and its fight would be an important consideration for British policy in Cyprus. He was keenly aware of the effect military operations could have on the political negotiations.

On 21 June, the first fatality inflicted by the insurgency occurred during a bomb attack on the Nicosia central police station. On 22 June, a police sergeant was killed in Limassol. A British policy brief in August clearly identified the shift in strategy:

> The April campaign was apparently directed primarily against property and in order to intimidate rather than injure persons. The campaign which started on 20 June, however, while deliberately intending to kill and injure persons, particularly amongst the police and army, was sufficiently indiscriminate to endanger the lives of persons in the vicinity of the explosions.[70]

This escalation represented a clear shift in the organization's operations and was the result of a mandate for intensification from Grivas. On 21 June, the colonel recorded in his diary: 'I have communicated an order to Heron and Thalis, saying that I am not satisfied with the results of the Nicosia groups and demanding the intensification of activity, particularly against the police traitors, no matter if they are Greeks or Turks. My design is to terrorize the police so that we may be given more freedom of action.'[71] Grivas was raising the stakes and pushing the struggle beyond the limits envisioned by Makarios. The scale of violence would soon be beyond the archbishop's ability to control.

Grivas's escalation brought mixed results. The British administration had been placed firmly on the back foot. Initial response to EOKA, although it lacked strong organization, training and supplies, were weak. The Cypriot police suffered serious losses, most particularly to their credibility. Internationally, there was a buzz about the subject of *enosis* far greater than anything in the past. But these advances came with costs. As Grivas persevered in escalating the campaign over Makarios's wishes, his relationship with the archbishop was becoming more problematic. At the same time, successes in the field meant increased British resources and scrutiny were likely to fall on the island in the near term. In addition, Grivas's actions had opened two critical fissures within Cypriot society. First, by resorting to violence, he had reopened divisions between right and left in a dramatic way. The central committee of AKEL responded to the first bombings with a public statement of their own on 1 April, arguing that 'such activities can only cause damage to our cause and struggle [for *enosis*].... History has no example where a people have won their freedom except through the heroism of a united mass struggle. The patriotic people of Cyprus are in no way connected to these terrorist activities.'[72] Although AKEL's political leadership maintained sympathy for the principle of *enosis*, it vehemently opposed EOKA and its methods.

Second, the resort to violence realized deep-seated fears within the Turkish-Cypriot community for their physical security and political future. As the governor of Cyprus, Robert Armitage, who had replaced Wright on 19 February 1954, noted to the secretary of state for the colonies: 'Turkish feeling is, as you know, running high, and if a Turk is killed by Greek terrorist action, that will provide just the spark that is needed to set off a conflagration of communal strife.'[73] To mitigate the prospect of communal strife, while also trying to control Greek and Turkish antagonism and restore some degree of peace to Cyprus, Britain launched both military and diplomatic offensives. In Cyprus, this manifested in the appointment of a senior soldier, Field Marshal Sir John Harding, the Chief of the Imperial General Staff, as governor and commander-in-chief. Diplomatically, efforts were directed towards convening a Tripartite Conference where Britain, Greece and Turkey could hopefully talk out their differences.

The resort to violence had shattered the illusion of British authority, but no one could know the number and shape of the shards. Deep divisions and powerful factions were now in play both in Cyprus and internationally. Policymakers in London, Athens and Ankara as well as EOKA gunmen, Cypriot clerics and the colonial administration now scrambled to get what they could from the evolving situation.

5

Deepening divides

Political and ethnic fractures

> *So all the toils and moils of weeks and months are brought to an abrupt end in a manner which we have been repeatedly told could never be contemplated. What a difference if they had done this [the Tripartite Conference] last year. No EOKA, no tension, no loss of friendliness.*[1]
>
> – Sir Robert Armitage, Diary Entry 29 June 1955

After working for years to characterize the conflict over Cypriot *enosis* as a purely domestic problem for the British government, policymakers in London rapidly shifted course following the outbreak of violence in Cyprus. They called for a Tripartite Conference in an attempt to bridge the various divides. Britain, Greece and Turkey would be invited; representatives from the Cypriot communities would not. The failure of this conference to provide a resolution to problems in Cyprus reflected the escalation of Turkish fears towards the *enosis* movement, the deterioration of relations between Britain and Greece, and a rupture in relations between Greece and Turkey. The conference would vividly present the tangible differences which existed between the parties involved. Its failure to mitigate violence on the island led to a new phase of action by the British government characterized by increased repression through military means and negotiations with the Greek-Cypriot community in the person of Archbishop Makarios III.

EOKA's violence raised the stakes in Cyprus considerably. Part of the plan worked out by Grivas and Makarios was to win support of the international public opinion and to use that international support to make some form of self-determination possible.[2] Greece would once more play a key role by bringing the Cyprus question before the UN in the fall of 1955. British policymakers were determined to avoid this, fearing that they were particularly vulnerable on this front.[3] This was partially because Washington had informed London that American support would cease without some 'forward' move on Cyprus.[4] In a cabinet memorandum, the foreign secretary, Harold Macmillan and, the colonial secretary, Alan Lennox-Boyd recommended 'that Her Majesty's Government should take a new initiative in the near future, and that this initiative should take the form of a proposal to the Greek and Turkish Governments that they should join with ourselves in tripartite discussion of the Cyprus question'.[5]

For the government of Prime Minister Anthony Eden, this Tripartite Conference was a necessary political gamble leavened with the cynicism of realpolitik. On the one hand, it made a key concession (from the point of view of the British government) in that it acknowledged the *international* character of the problem in Cyprus. This was something the British had consistently resisted. The volte-face shocked Governor Armitage and represented one of several fissures between him and London. As he recorded in his diary on 29 June: 'So all the toils and moils of weeks and months are brought to an abrupt end in a manner which we have been repeatedly told could never be contemplated.'[6] In essence, the conference was an admission by the Eden government that the concerns of the two 'mainland' countries had to be addressed if a durable solution was to be found.

The Tripartite Conference has been pilloried after the fact. Historian Robert Holland dismisses it as a poor attempt by Harold Macmillan, the foreign secretary, to '"solve" the Cyprus problem through complicated international means, rather than by engaging with the details of internal Cypriot politics – details which he looked upon with disdain'.[7] The 'dangerous' tactic of attempting to bring 'international leverage to bear' on the crisis was representative of Macmillan's 'preferred *modus operandi*' and nothing less than a 'hare-brained Foreign Office' scheme.[8] This line of argument overlooks two critical factors: first, the British had made attempts to bridge the gap with several direct overtures to the people of Cyprus between 1947 and 1954. The offers were not everything Greek-Cypriot nationalists hoped for, but they did give some scope of self-government. By necessity, the offers were modest, cautiously navigating between the Scylla of Greek-Cypriot hopes and the Charybdis of Turkish-Cypriot fears, not to mention the practical considerations of British grand strategy. Second, to argue that the internationalization of the Cyprus problem was the result of a 'hare-brained' scheme on the part of Macmillan or the Foreign Office is to ignore the fact that Greek-Cypriot nationalists had decided to 'internationalise the problem by bringing it to the UN in 1949'.[9]

Archbishop Makarios III, in particular, had been canvassing support for *enosis* across the world since 1950. A call to *enosis*, by its very nature, internationalized the Cyprus problem, as did Turkish-Cypriot recourses to Turkish support. Internationalizing the Cyprus question had been one of Makarios's fundamental objectives since his ascent to power.[10] His busy schedule of international travel lobbying for support for *enosis* between 1951 and 1955 confirmed this and belied the simultaneous claim that the Cyprus problem concerned only Greek-Cypriots and Britain.[11] Holland himself acknowledges that the 'root of an internationalization of the conflict inside the island' was not the policy of the British government but dated back to a declaration by AKEL in October 1949 to join a national assembly and 'raise the question of *enosis* at the United Nations'.[12] We must read this in the restricted sense that the internationalization of the *enosis* conflict, as expressed in appeals to the UN and the campaign of EOKA, had its roots in AKEL's potential UN appeal of 1949. Such a view, while precise, distorts the reality that Cyprus was an international issue from the time that Britain secured administration of the island from the Ottoman Empire in 1878. Subsequent appeals to Greece, Turkey and international opinion broadened this reality. Links between Cyprus and Greece emerged from the Greek Revolution. From 1878 onwards, the

Turkish government maintained an interest in Cyprus whether the British or Greeks wanted them to or not. Turks and Turkish-Cypriots continually spoke against *enosis*; the emergence of EOKA only exacerbated these feelings of concern. These were the practical considerations behind Britain's change of course represented by the gamble of the Tripartite Conference.

At the same time, there was a dose of cynicism in the planned conference. It was hoped that the simple act of the conference itself, regardless of the outcome, would be seen as a positive move by the broader international community and the United States, in particular. Turkey, it was acknowledged within British government circles, would not need much convincing to attend such a conference since it 'would be a recognition of their right to be consulted on an equal footing with Greece'.[13] Greece would perforce attend, or be easily cast as unwilling to come to some resolution of the problem with her NATO allies. The British ambassador in Washington, Roger Makins, approached the American secretary of state, Alan Foster Dulles, about using American influence to encourage the Greek government to attend the conference. In Washington, Dulles understood this tension and, in a seemingly innocuous way, asked Makins 'how the Greeks would feel about the inclusion of Turkey'. If Dulles's fairly harmless phraseology masked a truly serious issue, Makins's reply ignored (perhaps with sarcastic intent) the realities of the situation. He answered Dulles by stating that 'since they [the Greeks] were allies of Turkey both in NATO and in the Balkan Alliance, they ought to welcome the invitation unless they were completely intoxicated by their own propaganda'.[14]

Propaganda was not entirely the province of the Greeks. The Turkish press responded to EOKA's initial acts of violence with a series of articles challenging Britain's willingness to remain in Cyprus in the face of an armed insurrection. Britain, the Turkish press contended, could not be counted on to remain stalwart. While alerting Britain to the very real concerns in Turkish quarters, these articles also had the calculated effect of raising the alarm within the Turkish community. Since Turkish-Cypriots were not invited to the conference, the Turkish voice would loudly oppose *enosis* and seek to protect the Turkish-Cypriots from the perceived dangers of living under Greek rule. The largest lacuna of the conference, however, was that Greek-Cypriots, who were, after all, responsible for the violence, were not invited to attend.

It is easy to criticize the British policymakers for excluding the Greek-Cypriots, but there were at least two good reasons for this: first, to include the Greeks would have raised the question of including representatives from the Turkish-Cypriot community. Negotiations would then have potentially involved British, Greek, Turkish, Greek-Cypriot and Turkish-Cypriot parties in an unwieldy quin-partite arrangement. Second, it is highly unlikely that the Turks would have accepted Greek-Cypriot participation, as it would put the Cypriots on a par with representatives from three sovereign powers. Britain too, for obvious reasons, was also reluctant to treat the Cypriots (whether Greek or Turkish) on the same level as representatives from sovereign states.

Because of the implications of the conference for the future affairs of the island, Turkey, unsurprisingly, was first off the mark in accepting the British offer. Greece remained reluctant, but two days later it accepted and the three sides prepared to meet in London. Although the Turkish government agreed to the conference and expressed a cautious optimism about the talks, it was under no illusions about what the conference could deliver for their interests. The Greek-Cypriots were offended that the future of their island was to be discussed without a single representative from their community. Archbishop Makarios denounced the forthcoming conference in strong words. A meeting among British, Turkish and Greek representatives would solve nothing, primarily because

> [t]he Cyprus question does not constitute a political issue between Britain on the one hand and Greece and Turkey on the other. The Cyprus issue is purely a question of self-determination and concerns the British Government and the Cypriot people only, and it can be extended so as to concern the Greek Government, whenever the latter, in interpreting the feelings of the Greek and especially the Cypriot people, acts as the people's mandatory for the safe-guarding of the island's right of self-determination. . . . Personally we have no doubts about the failure of the conference [because] the Cypriot people will not accept any decision on the part of the Tripartite Conference, not in agreement with its rights and aspirations, even if the Greek Government were to undersign this decision.[15]

Makarios's accusation that Britain had unnecessarily widened the conflict through the inclusion of Turkey reveals a fundamental inconsistency and a fateful omission. Britain's preference, throughout its involvement in Cyprus, had been to treat any disruption as a sovereign issue without recourse to other parties. *Enosis* was a question to be settled between the British government and the Cypriot people. Fatefully, Makarios's statement also implied the absolute denial of Turkish and Turkish-Cypriot interests, which was characteristic among the leaders of the EOKA cause. For Makarios, the 'Cypriot people' were the *Greek*-Cypriot people. Neither Turkish-Cypriots nor Turkey should have any role in determining the future of Cyprus.

Makarios's tone provided a bleak backdrop for the beginning of the conference. The British government was aware that the negotiations would be difficult. In internal communications, they discussed the likelihood that the conference would fail to achieve any firm result. Still, a debate of the issues and Britain's admission of the existence of a serious problem with international ramifications represented an important development. In addition, whether or not the Greeks and Greek-Cypriots accepted that Turkey had a right to participate in the Cyprus issue, Turkey was an involved and extremely important party to the unfolding events. As observed by Harold Macmillan, who as foreign secretary would chair the conference: '[I]t was common sense to recognize the fact that no new arrangements in Cyprus could work successfully unless it was acceptable to both the Greek and Turkish Governments.'[16]

In preparing for the conference, British policymakers mapped out several key points for their position. These were outlined in a memo from the Colonial Office private secretary to the prime minister. It was of primary importance 'not to gang up with the Turks or stimulate their resistance to self-determination'. Such a delicate balance would be partially achieved through reassurances of Britain's enduring intention to remain in Cyprus and to not cede the island to Greece. In conjunction, a central goal of the conference was an open airing of the views of all three sides from which the direction of a solution might be determined.[17] Once these views were articulated, the next task was 'to define in writing the differences between the three Governments and to make sure that the other two agreed with the definition. When this had been done, probably not without some argument on drafting, we should say that we must now address ourselves to the task of reconciling the differences by a process of compromise.'[18]

Britain's main aim during the negotiations 'would be to bring the Greeks up against the Turkish refusal to accept *Enosis* and so condition them to accept a solution which would leave sovereignty in our hands until at least there was tripartite agreement to make a change'.[19] This was another aspect of British cynicism. London policymakers hoped to use the Turks to achieve this goal during the conference, which would 'provide the opportunity for Turkey to demonstrate that if Britain leaves the island, this would create a cause of dissension between Turkey and Greece and that it is therefore better that she should stay'.[20] Any mention by the British government concerning self-determination for the Greek-Cypriots, the central and only significant desire of the Greek negotiators, was to be avoided.[21] The consensus view was that such a move would not be tolerated by Turkey, would be impossible to implement on the island and would not be in the interests of Britain. The conference had the support of the United States, and Britain hoped that American influence could be used to make the Greeks more amenable to compromise.[22] As Makins wrote to the Foreign Office on 20 July: 'The [American] State Department hope that these negotiations will provide for the first time an acceptable rallying point for moderate opinion both in Greece and in Cyprus in opposition to the extreme demands of the ethnarchy.'[23] The British government felt that it needed 'unequivocal support from Washington' for the conference.[24] Further, British representatives in the United States voiced their opinion that America should also 'urge the Greeks ... to resist such demands as they do not themselves consider to be in their national interest. In other words to stand up to Makarios.' If this should fail, the British hoped that the Americans would make it clear that they would oppose the next Greek attempt to raise the Cyprus issue at the UN.[25]

America's strategic goals entailed achieving a modus vivendi between Turkey, Greece and Britain. These countries were all important NATO allies. 'Extreme' demands on the part of the Cypriot ethnarchy for prompt self-determination to be followed by *enosis* were direct obstacles to these goals. These demands were also problematic for the Greeks, who still wished to avoid a fissure with either Britain or Turkey. They were incompatible with British interests, which centred on maintaining Cyprus as a sovereign British base and military headquarters. Finally, they were unacceptable to Turkey, because of the uncertain future of the Turkish-Cypriot minority and the geostrategic implications of a Greek-controlled Cyprus.

In his opening speech, Macmillan emphasized the friendship existing between the three governments present and the need for them to discuss openly their different points of view on the Cyprus crisis so as to come to an understanding.[26] On the second day, Stephanos Stephanopoulos, Macmillan's opposite within the Greek government, put forward his arguments, saying that the Greek government was 'acting as interpreter of the will of the Cypriot people'. Britain's position that Cyprus was essential to the defence of the Middle East and to its diplomatic commitments was subordinate to the political stability of the island. Without self-determination for the Cypriot people, Stephanopoulos argued – adopting Makarios's conflation of Cypriot with Greek-

Cypriot – Cyprus would remain in disorder. Only a stable Cyprus could provide the foundation on which all three nations could effectively organize a 'common defence in Cyprus and in the Eastern Mediterranean'.[27] Stephanopoulos appealed to the British nation as 'the very ideal of freedom and justice' and requested 'that Cyprus be granted her basic rights after a period of "free government"'.[28]

The statement of Turkish deputy prime minister Fatin Zorlu during the next day's meetings provided a contrast both in tone and in substance. Gone were Stephanopoulos's flattery and deference. In their place, Zorlu argued forcefully that the Cyprus issue concerned only Britain and Turkey. The island's future had been codified by the Treaty of Lausanne under whose terms 'the parties concerned in Cyprus were only and exclusively Turkey on the one hand and Great Britain on the other'.[29] Zorlu argued that Cyprus 'by its geographical structure, is a prolongation of the Anatolian Peninsula, of which the soil is Anatolian soil, of which the climate is Anatolian climate, has, ever since the time it came under Turkish sovereignty, been attached to the Motherland as any other province of Turkey, and has constituted an inseparable part thereof'.[30] Zorlu emphasized the continuity of Turkey and Cyprus in population terms as well by adopting the faintly menacing line that 'it is not sufficient to say . . . that 100,000 Turks live there. One should rather say that 100,000 out of 24,000,000 Turks live there and that 300,000 Turkish-Cypriots [individuals of Turkish-Cypriot decent] live in various parts of Turkey'.[31] Turkish-Cypriots were not a minority, per se, but as part of a larger majority that deserved consideration. Zorlu concluded by calling for the Cypriot Church to 'refrain from dabbling in politics' and then launched a thinly veiled threat against Greece. Zorlu reminded the participants that the 'Greek-Turkish friendship, cooperation and alliance is based on a political agreement in principle established by the Treaty of Lausanne'. Any change in the status of Cyprus would nullify that agreement.[32] Zorlu's arguments had clear biases, but the latent threat that they carried was grounded in truth. While the 100,000 Turks of Cyprus were a minority of less than 20 per cent, Zorlu was correct in highlighting the power in the hands of the 24 million Turks less than 50 miles to the north. The local balance of power favoured Greek-Cypriot nationalism, but the broader geopolitical balance was in the hands of Turkey.

An ill-tempered back-and-forth continued throughout the conference. Macmillan attempted to retrieve something positive from the proceedings during his statement on 6 September. His vague generalities and political manoeuvring did not obscure the reality that the conference was at best, futile, and at worst, detrimental, to bringing peace to Cyprus. The foreign secretary emphasized such similarities between the parties as he could, arguing that all three delegations recognized the strategic importance of Cyprus and sought to maintain friendship and cooperation while being cognizant of their respective duties to the people of Cyprus.[33]

The progress of the people of Cyprus would take place in the context of 'real, genuine advance towards internal self-government'.[34] Of course, this self-government would not mean self-determination. Any new constitution would come from the minds of British policymakers and be implemented by a British governor in a colony that would remain British territory. Stephanopoulos, keenly aware of the absence of the Greek-Cypriots from the negotiations wondered how any 'constitution for Cyprus could be described as democratic if Cypriots were not associated with the task of working it out'.³⁵ The strongest and most ominous words came, not surprisingly, from Zorlu. The Turkish representative laid the blame for the Cyprus crisis at the doorstep of the Greeks whose persistent 'demands in spite of the sincere and friendly warnings made by Turkey during the three years prior to this Conference have brought us to this inextricable position today ... the question of Cyprus', he continued 'is of such importance ... that it is extremely difficult to maintain and to safeguard the friendship and the alliance with Turkey while seeking at the same time in one way or another to arrive either at the union of Cyprus with Greece or the giving of self-determination to the Island of Cyprus'.³⁶ But Turkey's 'friendly warnings' had already turned into devastating actions in a pogrom directed against the most vulnerable Greek community within its reach – the Greeks of Istanbul. As Averoff had predicted to Makarios in 1953, it was this precarious population who paid the price for Turkey's discontent over Cyprus.

At the Yassıada Trial in 1960, the prosecutors contended that it was Zorlu himself who originated the idea of an attack against the Greek minority and that Menderes had supported him.³⁷ *Kıbrıs Türktür Cemiyeti* (KTC) – the 'Cyprus is Turkish Association', formed in August 1954 with the support of Menderes – had been happy to turn the concept into reality. As explained by Vryonis:

> [T]he pogrom's intent was twofold: first, it was a planned and successful effort to destroy the forty-five Greek communities spread out over the vast area of greater Istanbul and its environs; second, it served certain domestic and foreign policies of the Menderes regime. Domestically, Menderes's economic policies had, to a certain degree, proved to be a failure, leading to inflation and, consequently, to hardship on a large part of the Turkish population. . . . In foreign affairs, his [Menderes'] open change of policy on the Cyprus issue in 1954-55 transformed the status of the Greeks of Istanbul from that of a hostage to the Turkish minority of Greek Thrace to that of a sacrificial offering to Turkey's policy on Cyprus.³⁸

The careful planning of the 'spontaneous' riots demonstrated Turkey's calculated change of policy in relation to Cyprus.³⁹

The groundwork for the operation had been laid in August 1955, and the closing of the Tripartite Conference struck the Turkish government as the ideal time to demonstrate its concerns over Cyprus. The concept of a protest (or something stronger) in favour of Turkish claims even had support in certain circles of the British government. A Foreign Office note from September 1954 even argued that 'a few riots in Ankara would do us nicely'. The Foreign Office mention of Ankara (which had no Greek community) raises an important difference from the actual pogrom in Istanbul.⁴⁰ The theory of 'a few riots in Ankara', voiced in 1954, *before* EOKA's turn to violence, bore little resemblance to the awful realities of what occurred in Istanbul during 6-7 September 1955.

The immediate provocation was based on a lie. On 6 September, there was a small explosion in the courtyard of the Turkish consulate in Thessaloniki, which was also the house where Atatürk was born. No one was injured. Only the building's window panes suffered any damage, although a crudely doctored photograph circulated in the

Istanbul *Ekspres* later that afternoon which showed major structural damage to the house.[41] In the preceding days, 'large numbers of poorly dressed provincials had been brought into the city [of Istanbul]', and evidence suggests that the fuses for explosives had been shipped from Turkey to the consulate in Thessaloniki on 3 September.[42] In response to this 'provocation', over the night of 6–7 September, the ruling *Demokrat Parti* local administration, student unions, youth associations and members of the KTC launched a savage attack against Greeks and Armenians in Istanbul.[43] The violence brought back memories of the atrocities carried out by Turkish forces during the First World War and the Greco-Turkish War of 1919–22. Using rudimentary weapons, incendiaries and improvised battering rams, angry crowds looted Greek and Armenian shops, burned churches, and assaulted Greek and Armenian citizens. The homes of Greek NATO officers were targeted in Izmir arousing the suspicion of at least one reporter from *The New York Times*, who observed that the 'Turkish mobs . . . were led directly to the inconspicuous and widely separated houses'. His conclusion was that 'at least some aspects of the rioting [were] tolerated by officialdom'.[44] Instructions to the mob focused on the destruction of property and intimidation. Orders to avoid killing were, in the main, observed.[45] This non-lethal intent did not prevent horrendous atrocities. Evidence of rape of both Greek women and boys exists, while some Greek and Armenian men (including priests) were subjected to forced circumcision.[46]

The scale of the destruction was so great that Prime Minister Adnan Menderes called out the Turkish army to contain the violence and placed the two cities under martial law. When the rioting died down, the appalling scale of the damage emerged. *The New York Times* reported on 17 September that '[m]ore than 4,000 shops, mostly Greek or Armenian-owned were totally wrecked by the rioters. . . . Seven hundred homes were damaged . . . eighty out of eighty-five Greek churches in the country were attacked and seriously damaged. Some were ruined by planted fires.' In Istanbul, it was 'as if every third shop on Madison Avenue and half of those on the Avenue of the Americas had been ripped apart and their goods strewn on the streets'.[47] The churches were a particular target. As Vryonis writes, '[T]he all-out attack on Greek religious institutions involved over 90 percent of the Greek churches, but it also included, on a much smaller scale, Armenian and Catholic churches, as well as one synagogue.'[48] Between 15 and 37 citizens of Greek origin were killed and there were hundreds of physical assaults and an estimated 200 rapes.[49] Before, during and after the conference, Turkey continually voiced concerns that its minority in Cyprus would be in peril at the hands of the Greek-Cypriot majority in the event of *enosis*. Events in Istanbul demonstrated just how vulnerable Turkey's own minorities were.

In the short term, the pogrom served to demonstrate the strength of Turkish sentiment on the Cyprus issue. It also demonstrated that real and substantial animosities were present between the Greeks and the Turks. Only minimal provocation was necessary to turn this latent dislike into open hostility. Politically, the purpose of the riots, as described by Robert Holland, was 'to demonstrate unequivocally the seriousness of the Turkish claims over Cyprus. In this vein the actions were directed principally against Greece, but they were a vivid reminder, as well, to the British (and also to the Americans, presently unpopular in Turkey following a cut in aid payments), whose Embassy was afforded scant protection.'[50] Even though the political message of the riots was directed in part towards Britain, the violence in Cyprus and continued Greek action at the UN left some in the British government with very little sympathy for the suffering inflicted on Greeks by the riots in Turkey. As Eden himself quipped to the British ambassador in Athens immediately after the riots: 'The Greeks have sown the wind and are now reaping the whirlwind. It would be as well . . . to let the medicine work.'[51] What effect this bitter medicine had is open to debate, but the failure of the Tripartite Conference left the British in need of a local solution to the ever-increasing scale of EOKA violence.

Modern historians have not been kind to the Tripartite Conference. Richard Lamb, in *The Failure of the Eden Government*, described the conference as little more than 'shadow boxing' on Eden's part. Eden, 'determined not to give an inch to Greek claims', used the conference to place the onus for the failure to reach a compromise on Turkey, in spite of 'liberal' offers on the part of Great Britain.[52] This is somewhat simplistic. Earlier constitutional offers were rejected out of hand by the Greek-Cypriots who, led by the church, maintained a maximalist position. This fundamental unwillingness to accept anything short of *enosis* must be recognized as a significant factor in the failure of negotiations at this stage. The minimum (and only) Greek-Cypriot demand could not be reconciled with maximum British or Turkish concessions. *Enosis* and its precursor steps were not something that the Turkish government would ever accept. Lamb himself comes around to this point, partially contradicting his own argument, acknowledging that '[t]he Tripartite Conference duly revealed the impossibility of Turkish and Greek agreement'.[53] The chasm between the sides was revealed by the conference, not created by it.

The failure of the Tripartite Conference had a significant impact on the Cyprus insurgency. Representatives from Great Britain, Greece and Turkey would not come together again for some time, and then only when the threat of direct armed conflict forced them into compromises that they were not ready to accept in 1955. In the short term, the conference's failure prompted each power to take its own actions. Greece continued to champion the Cyprus issue at the UN and to supply EOKA with arms and money. Although the conference had not furthered Greek aims, many in Athens and in Cyprus felt that the conference itself represented a compromise which had been won through the use of arms. Their view was that continued violence would force the British into greater concessions. As in the case of the defeated UN motion of 1954, a failure in the political arena led to greater violence on the ground. Putting faith in increased action by EOKA, however, ignored the possibility that further violence could gain ground against the British, but at the risk of hardening Turkish attitudes and escalation. Having given international diplomacy a try, the British government now felt justified in attempts to tighten its control of Cyprus and eliminate EOKA on the ground. British policy in Cyprus was about to undergo significant changes.

6

A time to talk

The Harding-Makarios negotiations

> *Either I shall reach some basis of co-operation with the Archbishop, in which case the emphasis will be on constitutional development and improvement in social and economic conditions, or there will be an open conflict involving a full scale emergency campaign.*[1]
>
> – Field Marshal Sir John Harding, 5 October 1955

In many ways, the Tripartite Conference changed the shape of the international arena for the Cyprus crisis. As it concluded, British policy took a new direction, dramatically altering conditions on Cyprus as well. The conference revealed not only the gaps between British, Greek and Turkish interests but also the divisions within the British government. Governor Armitage had been shocked by London's abrupt change of course in calling for the conference. He had been overruled on the inclusion of Makarios or other Greek-Cypriot representatives. He had failed in his efforts to start a new constitutional discussion along a line more conciliatory towards Makarios's demands.[2] These differences and the escalating disorder in Cyprus contributed to pressure within the British government to replace the governor. Armitage's successor would have to fulfil the potentially contradictory roles of suppressing EOKA on the one hand while attempting to negotiate a settlement on the other.

On 9 September, as Armitage prepared to return from London to Cyprus, Lennox-Boyd asked if he was happy remaining in Cyprus in light of the fact that 'a more important governorship' was about to become open. 'Armitage replied that he had taken on the job and would like to finish it.'[3] The message, however, was clear – Sir Robert's days in Cyprus were numbered.

By mid-September, members of the government had approached Field Marshal Sir John Harding, the Chief of the Imperial General Staff. When Harding accepted the post, Lennox-Boyd informed Armitage of his replacement in a letter of 23 September: 'I hope you will realize that this is in no sense a reflection on your administration as Governor. I am making this change not because of any inadequacy on your part, but solely because the present situation calls, as it did in Malaya a few years ago, for a Governor with military standing and experience.'[4] Armitage informed his parents about the decision the very next day, telling them that they would soon read about his replacement by Harding. 'Events here, present and future', he wrote, 'make this the prime job for a military trained man ... now strategic considerations must prevail. It is a bitter blow.'[5] Upon reflection, Armitage claimed that the realities of the situation were such that he hardly regretted leaving: 'When one looks onto the rolls of barbed wire in the garden, the bodyguard and armed vehicles which follow me whenever I go out ... it is not altogether unwelcome that one should move to another atmosphere.'[6]

Lennox-Boyd's mention of Malaya in his note to Armitage had not been accidental. The British government was convinced that a solution which effectively maintained British interests on the island would only be possible if the successes of Templer's tenure in Malaya could be replicated in Cyprus. To this end, Field Marshal Harding would assume a role modelled on Templer's, filling the dual roles of governor and commander-in-chief of Cyprus's security forces.[7]

Harding's first order of business was to open a dialogue with Makarios aimed at ending the violence through a negotiated settlement. The failure to reach an agreement during this time owed much to the incompatible aims of the two sides but foundered on demands by Makarios for concessions beyond what had been agreed to with Harding and because of the inability of the Greek-Cypriot side to recognize the substantial limits Turkish concerns placed on British policy options. When negotiations failed, Harding ordered the deportation of Makarios and several other leading figures in the Greek-Cypriot community. With Makarios removed, the field marshal turned his full attention to trying to crush EOKA as a viable insurgent organization, thus leading to a further escalation of violence.

Field Marshal Sir John Harding came to Cyprus with an impressive military career to his credit. He had commanded major formations during the Second World War both in North Africa and in Europe. After the war, he was the commander of British forces in the Mediterranean. Between 1949 and 1951 he served as commander-in-chief of Far East Land Forces, where he engaged in limited counter-insurgency operations.[8] These positions provided him with a combination of geographical and tactical experience that made him an excellent candidate to take command in Cyprus.

Harding's military career culminated in his appointment as Chief of the Imperial General Staff in 1952. He was made a field marshal in 1953. With the failure of the Tripartite Conference at the beginning of September 1955 and the continuation of EOKA attacks throughout the summer, Eden approached Harding about taking control in Cyprus. On 23 September, Harding met with the foreign secretary, Harold Macmillan, to discuss the situation in the colony.[9] The next day, Harding received a letter from the prime minister: 'I want to tell you how sincerely grateful I have been for the spirit in which you met the offer we have been discussing these last two days', Eden wrote.

> I quite understand how little attraction such a post can have for you at this time. After a brilliant military career there is nothing to be gained, and may be something to be lost, in undertaking such responsibilities, but equally I know how little you allow matters of that kind to weigh in the scale when national interest is concerned.[10]

The prime minister was eager for Harding to assume command at the earliest possible time. As he explained, 'I have been profoundly unhappy about Cyprus for some time past. I do not think we could have avoided this situation.'[11] On the day after Eden's letter, 25 September, Harding was appointed governor of Cyprus. Only a week later, on 3 October, he arrived on the island. The new governor immediately communicated his opinion to Lennox-Boyd that the pending negotiations with Archbishop Makarios would be critical to the course of the insurgency.

Harding was convinced that if the negotiations failed, pro-*enosis* violence would accelerate. In the field marshal's view, new security measures and aggressive operations would be the key to eliminating EOKA. Nevertheless, a negotiated solution remained his priority. For the British, the failure of the Tripartite Conference and continued unrest in Cyprus were a source of strain. The bases meant to solidify Cyprus's position as the new headquarters for British forces in the Middle East were under construction and there were escalating tensions between Israel and its neighbours. These facts made British policymakers eager for a resolution of the Cyprus problem. With their negotiating position apparently strengthened by the demonstration of strong Turkish feeling against *enosis* and the appointment of a field marshal as governor, the British hoped to pressure Makarios into a compromise. Ideally, the compromise would remove some of the pressure for *enosis*, and, most importantly, restore peace to Cyprus under continued British rule.

Makarios drew his own conclusions from Harding's arrival. To the archbishop, the opening of direct negotiations with the British government represented a success. The problem would now be dealt with on a bilateral basis between Britain and the (Greek) Cypriots, as he had advocated in Athens before the Tripartite Conference. Direct negotiations were a further indication that British authorities were finally taking the demands of the *enosis* movement seriously. Leaders within the *enosis* movement, including Makarios, believed that EOKA's violence had paved the way for a discussion on something like equal footing and that this violence had also made the British willing to make genuine concessions to avoid further unrest. What remained was to clinch the deal through negotiation in the space that EOKA had won. This had been the plan all along.[12]

'Let us stand absolutely firm and see the business through'

The Harding-Makarios discussions, which took place between October 1955 and March 1956, clarified the major points of disagreement between Britain and the *enosis* cause that would endure for much of the conflict. The failure of these talks resulted in the deportation of the archbishop with three other leading Greek-Cypriot figures, and the escalation of violence to its peak levels in November 1956. The negotiations were difficult. A mutual obstacle was the fact that both Harding and Makarios were playing conflicting roles. Harding was simultaneously a diplomat and military enforcer.[13] To Greek-Cypriots, the field marshal personified unpopular coercive measures and the oppressive nature of British rule. Harding found it equally challenging to discuss a settlement with Makarios, the man he felt was responsible for the violence that claimed the lives of British soldiers and terrorized Cypriot citizens and law enforcement officials.

On the day of Harding's arrival in Cyprus, Makarios asked the Ethnarchy Bureau for their views on his upcoming meeting with the new governor. Several key points emerged, all along familiar lines. First, the bureau members emphasized that the British had to recognize the principle of self-determination. Second, a predetermined time limit (not exceeding five years), pending the implementation of self-determination, would have to be agreed. Third, the 'nonsense about the Cyprus question being a Greco-Turkish dispute, [must] be cleared up'.[14] Turkey's say in the future of Cyprus had been assured by the Tripartite Conference. The final official British proposals put forward on the last day of the conference (6 September) claimed to offer the prospects of 'a new and liberal constitution leading to the fullest measure of internal self-government'. These concessions, circumscribed as they were with 'the proper safeguards and guarantees required by the international situation and the protection of the interests of the communities concerned' along with the 'strategic requirements of the present international situation' amounted to little more than a rebottling of Winster's 1948 vintage.[15] By design, the carefully worded caveats implied a refusal to accept *enosis* and the need for the acquiescence of the Turkish government to any solution. Nevertheless, they also conveyed a message that the British government was willing to compromise. As the colonial secretary telegrammed to Governor Harding on 17 October 1955, '[I]t is not our position that the principle of self-determination can never be applicable to Cyprus. It is our position that it is not now a practical proposition on account of the present strategic importance of the island and on account of the consequences on relations between NATO powers in the Eastern Mediterranean.'[16] These fraught 'relations between NATO powers', meant the certainty of conflict between Turkey and Greece at the prospect of *enosis*.

Such constrained proposals served as the starting point for the negotiations between Makarios and Harding and demonstrated several critical gaps between the two sides. None was more obvious than the role of Turkey and the position of Turkish-Cypriots. The ethnarchy continued to ignore the reality that an insistence on self-determination, the prospect of placing Turkish-Cypriots under Greek rule and thrusting Turkey out of the picture would be unacceptable to the British, the Turkish-Cypriot minority and the Turkish government. From Harding's first meeting with Makarios, it was clear to the field marshal that Turkey's position in any settlement was the major stumbling block. Turkish interests affected both self-determination and a timetable for its implementation. The new governor was convinced that Makarios's primary aim was to reduce Turkey's influence on decisions in Cyprus and to settle the affair on a bilateral basis between Greek-Cypriots and the British government.[17] Eden perceived this as well and wrote to the new governor on 8 October that

> although the Archbishop's position seems somewhat obscure, I take it that his real purpose is to manoeuvre us into excluding consultation with the Turkish Government or the Greek Government or even both . . . I cannot judge whether the Archbishop's purpose is to probe our thoughts further, or merely to divide us from our allies, particularly the Turks. If the latter, of course we cannot give way to him.[18]

For British policymakers, Turkey and the Turkish-Cypriots needed to be included in the discussion.

The *Times* hit on this important gap in an article on 6 October: '[T]he Turkish view is that there can be no question of even the acknowledgement of the right of self-determination, and how this can possibly be reconciled with the Greek-Cypriots' demand that Britain should at least acknowledge their right to self-determination is a problem which appears to be quite insoluble.'[19] Whatever concessions the British were prepared to make, they could not commit 'themselves to anything that might make *enosis* possible'.[20] As Harding reported to the prime minister, Makarios was seeking a fundamental change in the British attitude towards Cyprus and there was 'no hope' of that.[21] Hubert Faustmann argues that this first round of negotiations failed because of 'the British refusal to exclude a Turkish veto over Greek-Cypriot self-determination and to grant a Greek majority in the parliament'.[22] Turkey was the key factor preventing compromise but not just because of opposition to a Greek majority in Parliament. British policymakers had legitimate fears that Turkish opposition would become violent when confronted with any scenario that hinted at *enosis*. As British diplomats in Ankara cabled London, the Turkish were 'utterly opposed to any form of self-government'. From this, officials deduced that there was 'practically no hope' of securing Turkish acquiescence to even the attempt of introducing a new constitution in Cyprus.[23] Britain was bound to Turkey through both NATO and the Baghdad Pact. Makarios and the pro-*enosis* faction in Cyprus failed to recognize the fundamental limitations this placed on British policy.

On 16 November, Harding announced a new programme of economic and social development to run concurrently with the constitutional overtures. The plan would involve £38 million in expenditures on rural development, irrigation, electricity, inland telecommunications, port development and education, all aimed at bringing new prosperity to the island.[24] Such an investment would improve the standard of living for all Cypriots and was thus aimed at securing popular support for the administration. This initiative took another page from the playbook employed by Winster. As then, if the British government hoped that advertising a massive investment in Cyprus's future would help turn opinion in its favour, it was seriously mistaken. To Greek-Cypriots, the investment represented less the fact that British policy aimed to help the Cypriot population and more the reality that Britain envisaged a long-term presence on the island.[25]

Neither the start of negotiations nor the governor's investment pledge reduced EOKA activity. Attacks became a damaging and regular feature of life. On 19 November 1955, no fewer than forty-one bombs exploded across the island. On 24 November, two British soldiers were killed in a gun-battle. Seventy-four acts of violence were recorded in October, spiking to 217 in November.[26] The rising tide prompted Harding to action. On 26 November, the governor declared a state of emergency, giving him a new series of legal mechanisms to crack down on insurgent activities and public disorder.

Emergency regulations were a common tool used by the British government during this period to wage a counter-insurgency campaign. As explained by historian David French, '[e]mergency powers regulations gave the security forces plenty of latitude but with few of martial law's drawbacks . . . the security forces operation within a clearly defined legal framework' and 'permitted them to employ a very high degree of often lethal force'.[27] In Cyprus, these emergency powers, among other things, translated into large-scale detention of individuals suspected of 'terrorist' activities.[28]

In early December 1955, Harding and Makarios were once more at the negotiating table, but Harding was not optimistic about the prospects for a settlement. As he wrote to the secretary of state for the colonies on 2 December, if discussions break down, 'I shall be forced to take really strong measures over a protracted period, no matter how unpleasant they may be, to keep the situation under control'.[29] Harding's hard-line position was as much a demonstration of his own convictions as an exhortation to Her Majesty's Government to maintain its firm stance with regard to Cyprus, or, in the event of concessions, to make them soon and openly. 'I cannot conceive of anything more damaging for the future of this island', Harding warned, 'or for our world wide strategic position than to make a stand now and later on to surrender to public opinion and coercion. Again with great respect I would urge that if concessions are to be made let them be made now, otherwise let us stand absolutely firm and see the business through.'[30]

On both a professional and personal level, Harding's patience was wearing thin. After their meeting on 21 November it appears that Harding had developed a degree of personal distaste for Makarios.[31] Makarios's 'immediate and unhesitating rejection' of the most recent compromise Harding had brought back from London came as a 'severe shock' and 'put an end to the positive attitude with which he had until then approached the Greek-Cypriot leader'.[32] Harding's antipathy extended to his attitude towards other leading figures in the Cypriot Church. By December, the field marshal was satisfied that the best way to end the violence was the destruction of EOKA, to be achieved, in part, by the removal of Makarios and Bishop Kyprianos of Kyrenia from the political arena. Such a move had been discussed at the highest levels of the British government even before Harding's arrival. In September, the Cabinet had decided against authorizing the deportation of the bishop of Kyrenia due to the possibility of a backlash in public opinion.[33] At the beginning of December, Harding once more laid out his views to the colonial secretary, arguing that removing the 'most extreme element in the Ethnarchy' and restricting the 'movements and freedom of expression of other members' would be necessary if negotiations broke down.[34]

Harding was particularly infuriated by the substance of the bishop of Kyrenia's preaching. On 5 December, he wrote to Lennox-Boyd in exasperation, referencing a particularly incendiary speech and requesting immediate permission to 'proceed with deportation'.[35] In spite of the provocations, the British government, wary of the risks, remained reluctant. W. H. Young of the Foreign Office minuted on Harding's request:

> However justified the Governor's exasperation, the present seems a bad moment tactically to proceed to extremes. We have gone to great lengths to keep the negotiations with the Greek Government alive and the Secretary of State and the Colonial Secretary took great pains in the debate yesterday to leave the way open for the Archbishop and the Greeks. There can be little doubt that the expulsion of a leading Bishop, however justified, would put an end to any hope of a negotiated settlement.[36]

On 9 December, a revised formula for constitutional progress was circulated to the Greek government. In spite of the failure of the Tripartite Conference, British policymakers hoped that a formula devised by London and cleared by the Greek and Turkish governments would serve as a foundation for progress in the discussion with Makarios, providing direction and mutual reassurance. The relevant paragraphs read (points of subsequent contention with Makarios are in bold):

> It is not therefore their [HMG's] position that the principle of self-determination can never be applicable to Cyprus. It is their position that it is not now a practical proposition both on account of the present strategic situation and on account of the consequences on **relations between NATO powers in the Eastern Mediterranean**. If the people of Cyprus will participate in the constitutional development, it is the intention of Her Majesty's Government to work for **a final solution consistent with the treaty obligations [NATO and the Baghdad Pact] and strategic interests of Her Majesty's Government and its allies**, which will satisfy the wishes of the people of Cyprus. Her Majesty's Government will be prepared to discuss the future of the island with representatives of the people of Cyprus when self-government has proved itself a **workable proposition** and capable of safeguarding the interests of all sections of the community.[37]

British policymakers felt that careful wording, particularly the obtuse double negative ('not ... never'), which had been lifted verbatim from Lennox-Boyd's letter to Harding on 17 October 1955, and soft generalities were required to prevent any of the involved parties from reactively negatively. Negative feeling in Turkey had been high for some time. As the ambassador in Turkey, Sir James Bowker noted to the Foreign Office: 'The fact is that the Turks are nervous and suspicious that during the last three months Her Majesty's Government may have shifted their stand on the question of self-determination.'[38] According to Bowker, leading Turkish officials impressed upon him their concern that Britain's position on Cyprus might be modified by continued negotiations with Makarios. They had only 'mistrust of any dealings with the Archbishop'.[39] To prevent a rift with Turkey, Bowker advised that British policymakers should be careful to 'keep the Turks as regularly informed as possible about what is going on over the Cyprus issue and continue to give them all possible assurances calculated to tranquilise them about our position and policy'.[40]

British policy, by necessity, was a balancing act. In a telegram to the foreign secretary, Harding identified 'five major factors to be considered' as part of the Cyprus question. These were, without 'any order of priority a) the position of the Archbishop, b) the attitude of the Greek Government, c) the feelings of the people of Cyprus including the Turkish community, d) the security situation and e) the attitude of the Turkish Government'.[41] The difficulty in reconciling these five points was brought home by a personal letter from Foreign Secretary Macmillan to Lord Home, the secretary of state for Commonwealth relations as they discussed what an agreement might look like. 'All the indications at present', wrote Macmillan, 'are that this [a clause forbidding *enosis*] would be totally unacceptable both to the Greek Government and to the Greek-Cypriots. Conversely, a treaty without such a stipulation would hardly be acceptable to the Turks.'⁴² These were the obstacles facing Makarios and Harding as they prepared for their next round of discussions.

Harding and Makarios began their third, and final, phase of negotiations on 9 January 1956. The situation on Cyprus was precarious and the direction of events on the island hinged on their discussions. EOKA's violence had escalated dramatically in November and December 1955, although rough weather in late December subsequently curtailed operations.⁴³ The sharp decline in EOKA attacks, though not the direct result of moderation by Grivas or Harding's emergency decree, allowed discussions to be renewed in somewhat less strenuous conditions.

Harding cabled Alan Lennox-Boyd in the early hours of 10 January, after his meeting with Makarios. 'I had a meeting with the Archbishop this evening', he wrote, 'which lasted about two and a quarter hours. It was inconclusive but at any rate established that he is prepared to continue discussions on the basis of the revised formula. At the end we agreed to meet again shortly.'⁴⁴ Harding related an apparently minor detail to Lennox-Boyd in order to reveal something of the character of the negotiations. Makarios, according to Harding, began the discussions by questioning some specific use of wording. 'For example, did "public security" embrace control of the policy [sic]? Surely any administration which aspired to be self-governing must control its executive organ?' Such hair-splitting did not suit the field marshal. As he wrote to Lennox-Boyd, 'I headed him [Makarios] off the pursuit of this hare and we got down to discussion of the revised formula.'⁴⁵

A one page memorandum outlining the British formula had been drafted and given to Makarios. The archbishop raised three points of concern which Harding conveyed to Lennox-Boyd:

(1) The third sentence and particularly the reference to 'consequences on relations between NATO powers in the Eastern Mediterranean'. (2) The statement that a final solution should be 'consistent with the treaty obligations' of HMG and its allies. (3) The qualification that discussion of the future of the island would have to wait until self-government had proven itself 'a workable proposition'.⁴⁶

Although the British formula did not mention Turkish interests directly, points 1 and 2 clearly referred to Cyprus's northern neighbour. To Harding, the reason behind Makarios's objections was clear. As he wrote to Lennox-Boyd, '[Makarios] left me in no doubt that what is behind his objections on points (1) and (2) is the assumption that Turkey would exercise a deciding influence over the exercise of self-determination and the reaching of a final solution.'⁴⁷ Point (3) related directly to the ability of Greek-Cypriots and Turkish-Cypriots to work together in governing the island.

Just two days into their discussions, a further complication regarding the place of Turkey and the Turkish-Cypriot community in the crisis was added to the situation. In spite of Grivas's initial prohibition against attacking Turkish-Cypriots, in early January 1956 Grivas changed his mind; the EOKA leader was, in his own words, now convinced that 'it was impossible to avoid all actions against them'.⁴⁸ As Grivas writes, 'certain Turks in the police worked energetically against the Organisation particularly in Paphos, and the area commander there, Yiannakis Droushiotis, decided one must be executed'.[49] Droushiotis, one of EOKA's most aggressive members, presented Grivas with the case against a particularly active Turkish-Cypriot police sergeant, Abdullah Ali Riza.[50] The sergeant had been a chief witness against six villagers imprisoned for smuggling explosives into the island and had arrested another EOKA man in possession of a Sten machine gun. Grivas approved the request and authorized Riza's assassination. On the morning of 11 January, an EOKA gunman caught up with Riza as he was returning to his home in Paphos and shot him in the chest. He died on his way to the local hospital.[51] Grivas's radical change in EOKA's policy at this critical time was an error. It reinforced claims about the insecurity of Turkish-Cypriots, further raised tensions between the two communities and provided Turkey with opportunities to push its agenda more strongly with the British.

Word of Riza's murder spread quickly throughout the island and by afternoon, Turkish-Cypriot shops in every town had closed in protest. Greek flags were pulled down and Greek-Cypriot shops were stoned, breaking their windows.[52] Telegrams and letters of protest from Turkish-Cypriot groups flooded in to Governor Harding. In his telegram, Dr Fazil Kütchük, the chairman of the KTC in Cyprus, bluntly laid out his feelings: '[T]he Turkish community is enraged at the unprovoked attack on the Turkish police sergeant who was killed by Greek terrorists this morning. . . . This act of violence . . . is bound to spread and with catastrophic repercussions for the whole Middle East'. Kütchük closed with a veiled warning about the possibility of a violent reaction: '[W]e are doing our utmost to keep the enraged Turkish community at bay telling them that we have utmost confidence in your government and in the Turkish Government which we know will not stay idle at this cowardly attack on the peaceful Turkish inhabitants of the island. We trust that you will not fail us at this most critical hour.'[53] According to British reports, Turkish-Cypriot rioting on 11 January damaged twenty-eight houses and shops belonging to Greek-Cypriots.[54] It was just the beginning of intercommunal conflict and the British administration would be hard-pressed to bring it under control. While the Turkish-Cypriot factor gained force, the negotiations between Harding and Makarios were reaching a critical stage. Partially due to EOKA's escalation, British policymakers had even less flexibility for concessions to Turkey than they had before.

Decisions

Two days after the riots, Makarios and Harding met for the sixth time. According to the minutes kept by the ethnarchy secretary Nikos Kranidiotis, the meeting 'was carried out in a polite manner compared to that of the previous meeting'.[55] Increased courtesy did not narrow the divide. Makarios asked for the deletion of three phrases from the revised British formula of 9 December. First, the caveat from the British government that self-determination could not be applied immediately in Cyprus because 'it is their position that it is not now a practical proposition both on account of the present strategical situation and on account of the consequences in relations between NATO powers in the Eastern Mediterranean'. Second, Makarios wanted Harding to remove the statement that the government would work towards a final solution of the Cyprus problem 'consistent with the treaty obligations and strategic interests of Her Majesty's Government and its allies'. And third, he wanted discussions on the future of the island to be reserved until (limited) self-government had proved itself 'a workable proposition'.[56]

On the first point, Harding was willing to modify the phrase 'on account of the consequences in relations between NATO powers', to read 'on account of the present strategic and political situation in the Eastern Mediterranean'. He hoped that the removal of the reference to NATO would reduce the spectre of Turkey. Makarios was unsatisfied, however, arguing that the word 'political' had to be deleted as redundant since 'the obligations stemming from it are contained in "strategical"'.[57] Harding countered that the concession was sufficient and, when he refused to concede anything further, Makarios suggested moving on to the second point. The archbishop felt that the reference to 'treaty obligations' in relation to the nature of a final solution was unnecessary and asked that it be removed. Harding was unwilling to concede this point because, in his view, the British government would be open to being accused of bad faith, both in Cyprus and by its allies, if it did not mention the significance of treaty obligations.[58] This was another subject where Turkey's presence loomed large. As Harding and Makarios debated the point concerning 'treaty obligations', the discussion melted into the third point of contention dealing with the political situation during a period of self-government and its effect on a final solution. The back-and-forth on this subject point provides an illuminating microcosm of the talks and is worth quoting at length:

> Gov [Harding]: HMG recognize straight away that no treaty exists which excludes the application of the principle of self determination to Cyprus. In any case, I would not like to prolong the discussion. I would simply like to know whether you regard the retention of treaty obligations and of the condition of the political situation as a cause for the discontinuance of the talks.
>
> H[is] B[eatitude] [Makarios]: I know the views of my people and of my counsellors and I am sure that this reference to the treaties will not make a good impression. On the contrary it will give grounds for England to be accused of bad faith.
>
> Gov On the contrary, Great Britain must put forward these conditions right from the beginning so that she may not be accused by her allies. If you really wish for an agreement, you must accept this point . . . .
>
> HB The application of obligations resulting from a treaty is obvious. Why should therefore special emphasis be attached to them in the particular case of the self-determination of the people of Cyprus?
>
> Gov In order that Great Britain may persuade her allies and make her intentions clear to them . . . I fear that HMG will not accept the amendment and it would indeed be most regrettable if the formula were to be rejected for these reasons.
>
> HB As I have already said I discussed the subject with my advisors and I say that this phrase is completely unacceptable . . .
>
> Gov If we fail to find a solution this will be due to the unwillingness of Y[our] B[eatitude] to understand the obligations of Great Britain in this part of the world.

HB I am sorry to give such an impression . . .
Gov Would HB [sic] accept the formula if these two points were omitted?
HB Yes. I would accept if there were to be omitted from the first sentence 'the' and 'political' and from the second 'the existing treaty obligations'. The same arguments apply to both these points.
Gov I am afraid this will cause misunderstanding between our allies to whom we must be clear.
HB We and myself are also among those to whom Great Britain must be clear.
Gov Yes, but not only you.[59]

The two men remained apart in both style and substance. John Reddaway, the administrative secretary in Cyprus, nicely captured this dynamic in his memoir on Cyprus, describing the Harding-Makarios talks as

a fascinating, but frustrating, game of Knight versus Bishop with neither able to make much impression on the other owing to the nature of the tactical powers they possessed (or perhaps because they were playing the game by different rules), the Knight always pressing bold forward in search of a decision, leap-frogging obstacles from his own side as well as his adversary's, the Bishop sliding elusively this way and that, playing for position rather than attack, but always threatening to seize some commanding diagonal.[60]

On the side of substance, to Harding's mounting frustration, the crux of the dispute remained Makarios's unwillingness to accept Turkish interests or Britain's need to account for Turkey's interests in a solution. Harding could not budge on this point because of the importance of the Turkish Alliance to Britain and the damaging prospect of a conflict between Greece and Turkey. Makarios's final quoted sentence voiced the Greek-Cypriot desire to be the primary, if not the sole, consideration for the British policymakers. Harding's response was equally telling and demonstrated the gap between the two parties. His phrase 'not only you' referred obliquely to the concerns of Turkey and Turkish-Cypriots – concerns Makarios showed no intention of considering. Indeed, during this exchange, there was no direct mention of Turkey or Turkish-Cypriots. It is unclear whether these issues were avoided intentionally to remove further divisiveness, or because Makarios did not wish to legitimize Turkish claims.

Leaders in London realized both the extent of the Turkish factor and how assiduously Makarios was trying to avoid it. A personal note from the deputy undersecretary of state, J. G. Ward, at the Foreign Office encapsulated the situation:

In his two latest talks with the Archbishop the Governor now seems to have established pretty definitely that the Ethnarchy will not agree to a formula containing any reservations covering our 'treaty obligations or any reference which implies that Greco-Turkish relations must be taken into account in considering the possibility and timing of self-determination'. Our view in the Foreign Office is that we cannot possibly drop these reservations – quite apart from the inherent unwisdom of doing so, there is no doubt that the Turks will blow up. We therefore feel that a break in the negotiations for a settlement cannot be long avoided, despite the grim implications.[61]

A Foreign Office minute codified Ward's informal letter and highlighted the difficulties posed by Turkey if the British government were to accept Makarios's modifications:

> Both amendments proposed by the Archbishop are aimed at excluding any Turkish interest in Cyprus. Despite the fact that we have repeatedly told the Archbishop and the Greek Government that there is no question of a Turkish veto and the decisions about Cyprus rest solely with Her Majesty's Government, the Governor has concluded that the Archbishop will refuse the formula if political considerations affecting Turkey could be taken into account in coming to a solution.

As for the Turks, they 'would resent our accepting either of the Archbishop's amendments. To them the amendments would seem to remove all the safeguards in the formula which we have assured them we would maintain. . . . If we propose further amendments to these passages the Turks will be convinced that we are giving in to the Archbishop.'[62]

In the view of the Foreign Office, any formula that omitted all reference to the political situation in the Eastern Mediterranean, as Makarios requested, 'would be unrealistic'.[63] Their quite correct conclusion was that since the problems in Cyprus were mainly political, 'all relevant political considerations' needed to be taken into account. This included the 'genuine and strong' interest of the Turkish government.[64] The minute closed with a statement that mixed frustration and disbelief, positing that 'there can be no possible gain to anyone, including the Archbishop, from neglecting a fundamental factor [Turkey] in the situation'.[65] In January 1956, as during the plebiscite in January 1950, the UN overtures of 1954, and the decision to launch a campaign of violence in 1955, the *enosis* forces in Cyprus, spearheaded by the Orthodox Church, were ignoring Turkey and the Turkish-Cypriot minority. They would not acknowledge the existence of a distinct Turkish-Cypriot community who remained directly opposed to *enosis* nor would they come to grips with Turkey's 'genuine and strong' interest in Cyprus.

Makarios's intransigence caused great frustration in London and prompted attempts to shift him through Greek intervention. A telegram from the Foreign Office to Sir Charles Peake, the British ambassador in Athens, made both points quite clear. 'If you have not already done so you should see the Greek Minister for Foreign Affairs. . . . You should say that the Archbishop's reactions are most disappointing. His only answer to our attempt to meet his criticisms was to raise further difficulties and to be highly evasive about his attitudes towards terrorism.'[66] Second, Peake was encouraged to 'invite the Greek Government to consider urgently what they can now do, in their own interest, to make the Archbishop see reason'.[67]

British policymakers felt that a reasonable compromise was being offered along the lines laid out in the newly revised formula put to Makarios on 18 January.

Slight adjustments of language attempted to address the archbishop's critiques while maintaining good faith with Turkey. The operative paragraphs now read:

> It is not therefore their position that the principle of self-determination can never be applicable to Cyprus. It is their position that it is not now a practical proposition on account of the present strategic and political situation in the Eastern Mediterranean.
>
> Her Majesty's Government have offered a wide measure of self-government now.
>
> If the people of Cyprus will participate in the constitutional development, it is the intention of Her Majesty's Government to work for a final solution consistent with the existing treaty obligations and strategic interests of Her Majesty's Government and their allies which will satisfy the wishes of the people of Cyprus. Her Majesty's Government will be prepared to discuss the future of the island with representatives of the people of Cyprus when self-government has proved itself capable of safeguarding the interests of all sections of the community.[68]

The changes accounted for two of Makarios's original three objections. Gone was the reference to NATO along with the words 'a workable proposition'. 'Strategic and political' remained along with the mentions of 'treaty obligations' and 'allies'. For Makarios, it was not enough; he pressed his previous objections and added new ones. Reference to 'treaty obligations' and 'allies' had to be removed along with the words 'political situation' in reference to the Eastern Mediterranean. Wary of Turkish attitudes, Harding did not budge. On 26 January, he had received a report that in Larnaca, a Turkish-Cypriot organization that called itself *Volkan* (Volcano) had distributed leaflets with the subject: 'Betrayal of Turks by Bargaining with a Priest.'[69]

Slowly but surely, the bargaining priest was extracting concessions from the British policymakers. As Makarios noted in letter to Andreas Azinas on 23 January, '[T]he talks with the Governor have not until today produced a result. I have the impression that the British will finally give in. They are waging a war of nerves on us. Fortunately, our nerves are strong.'[70] When Makarios and Harding met again on 27 January, the governor had just returned from a trip to London where he discussed the archbishop's reservations with Britain's political leadership. Harding reported to Lennox-Boyd that the meeting had lasted for two and a half hours and that Makarios 'was on the defensive throughout practically the whole discussion and clearly did not like it much.'[71] Harding's conclusion was that Makarios had found 'himself in the difficult position of having to accept an agreement on our latest terms or of taking the blame for refusing a good offer'.[72] Both men, it seemed, overestimated the strength of their position and the resolve of the other side.

As discussions resumed, the disagreement centred on the nature of the constitution that would codify Cyprus's development towards self-government. Makarios argued that the formula under discussion 'could not be considered separately from the constitution. For they might agree on the formula and yet disagree on important terms of the constitution which would stop cooperation.' Harding countered that an agreement on the formula needed to precede discussion of a constitution and that the decisions on the framing of the constitution would have to be taken, and here he alluded to Turkish-Cypriots, 'not only with the Archbishop but also with all sections of the community'.[73] Makarios hoped for another meeting, but Harding's patience was running out. The field marshal replied that 'he would only consent to meet the Archbishop again if the latter wished to have an elucidation of some point in the documents which he would be sending him on the following day'.[74]

Makarios seems to have taken Harding's warming temper into consideration. He called a meeting of the Ethnarchy Council for 30 January and on 28 January he met with Grivas. During this period, Grivas recorded that Makarios's tone suggested a belief that the armed struggle may have run its course. Two points were foremost in the mind of the archbishop: first, in his view, 'the people were getting tired'. Second, he was concerned about 'the big financial expenditures incurred because of the struggle'. Both factors inclined him to a solution.[75] Makarios did believe that he could extract British agreement to Cypriot self-determination, ignoring the Turkish factor, once more.[76] Grivas was sceptical, but gave his consent to the potential agreement, provided that, in addition, an amnesty could be arranged for his EOKA fighters.[77] Amnesty had not been discussed with Harding and would prove to be a thorny new issue.

At the meeting of the Ethnarchy Council on 30 January, however, the bishop of Kyrenia led the attack on compromise: 'I consider the Governor's proposal unacceptable and we must turn it down. Had the Governor accepted a predetermined time limit of 3 to 5 years [before self-determination], we would accept. But if we accept this it would be tantamount to an affront. I insist on the historical slogan "*Enosis* and only *Enosis*".'[78] Makarios admitted that the differences between his plan and the governor's plan were great. In theory, the bishop of Kyrenia stated that in spite of his objectives, he would accept three to five years' time limit delaying self-determination. Makarios, backtracking from one of the ethnarchy's earlier conclusions, did not support the idea of set time frame, arguing that they would not be able to predict the political situation in either Cyprus or Greece at the conclusion of such a period. Besides, by avoiding any particular time frame, 'we would be in a position to put forward our demand for self-determination immediately'.[79]

In contradiction to the attitude recorded by Grivas, Makarios claimed to the Ethnarchy Council that he was confident that the high morale among pro-*enosis* advocates in Cyprus would sustain his rigid stance. The lawyer, Socrates Tornaritis, agreed that armed resistance had brought results and supported the continuation of a hard line: 'I also am a follower of the intransigent policy which has given results such as the right to self-determination in Cyprus. I am confident that the morale of the people will remain high.'[80] Harding's new formula would not be accepted. Here again, Makarios seemed to be changing his attitude. Grivas, apparently, had understood from their meeting that a peace deal with close. On 31 January he had informed the guerrilla group operating around Kykkos Monastery that an agreement would soon be concluded and even permitted a photograph to be taken of him with his men.[81]

Meanwhile, Makarios's rejection of the terms was communicated to Harding by letter on 2 February.[82] 'The text in question', Makarios wrote,

> recognises indirectly the principle of self-determination and states that its application, however, is made dependent on conditions so general and vague,

subject to so many interpretations and presenting so many difficulties as to the objective ascertainment of their fulfilment, as to create reasonable doubt about the positive nature of the promise which is given regarding the final solution of the question in accordance with the wish of the people of Cyprus.[83]

Harding had been busy between his meeting on 28 January and the receipt of this note. On 31 January, he had met with Cyprus's Turkish consul general to discuss the British formula (newly reworded in an attempt to address Makarios's concerns). Their exchange confirmed the fears of the Foreign Office that Turkey's interest in Cyprus was diametrically opposed to the concessions sought by Makarios. The consul made two points: first, he emphasized to Harding that, despite their recent silence on the issue, the Turkish people maintained very strong feelings on Cyprus. Second, he argued 'that any system of self-government for Cyprus based on majority rule by the Greek-Cypriots could never be acceptable to the Turkish minority and would inevitably lead to civil war or something approaching it'.[84]

While Harding tried to soothe the concerns of Turkish-Cypriots, the Foreign Office was encouraging Ambassador Bowker to work on reducing the hostility of the Turkish government in Ankara. 'You must try to persuade the Turkish Government that we are not presenting them with a *fait accompli* on the constitution questions. As the rejoinder to the Archbishop makes very clear, the form of the eventual constitution can only be determined after full consultation and discussion with all sections of the population of Cyprus.'[85]

In light of these realities, Harding was reluctant to make any specific promises on the constitution to Makarios. He was not a constitutional expert nor was he qualified to put forward the arguments for the Turkish-Cypriot side. Turkish-Cypriots, like Greek-Cypriots, had long rejected constitutional initiatives. This somewhat muted acknowledgement that some sort of constitutional process might begin, was inchoate and therefore vulnerable. As Harding wrote to Makarios on 14 February: '[Y]ou will understand that Her Majesty's Government could not enter into commitments about the position of separate communities under the constitution before discussions have taken place at which representatives of those communities have expressed their views.'[86] Harding's letter continued: '[I]t must be recognised that persistent violence and disorder have increased the difficulties of introducing constitutional government. Fear of intimidation has stifled free expression of opinion. The minorities are more concerned than before about the possible consequences for them of the advent of self-government.'[87]

To overcome some of these hurdles, British policymakers began discussions of tasking someone with legal qualifications to draft a new Cypriot constitution. This would provide for internal self-government (under British sovereignty), increased powers for the Greek-Cypriot community and minority protections for Turkish-Cypriots. While the British government's move towards a new constitution was cautiously optimistic, the headlines of *The Times of Cyprus* were positively hopeful. The cover of the edition for 15 February 1956 ran the following headline: 'All the Archbishop's main terms find acceptance. Governor Agrees: Peace Is in Sight at Last.' The story promised that 'from the day when agreement on the broad outlines is announced – and that surely is very near – Cyprus can hope for an ending of the violence which it has endured too long and to move into a period of full self-rule.'[88]

On that day, 15 February, Grivas also received a letter from Makarios asking him to 'avoid any actions against the British because in all likelihood an agreement would be reached with Harding'. Grivas was battling his own doubts about peace. On 16 February, the abbot of Kykkos played on these fears, pointing out the gaps existing between the positions of Makarios and Harding.[89] Grivas wanted a mutual ceasefire, but Makarios refused to bring such a proposal to Harding because it would 'reveal his connections' with EOKA.[90] In spite of his misgivings, Grivas recorded in his *Memoirs* that he secretly ordered a suspension of all attacks.[91] The absence of reporting on major actions over the next two weeks supports this claim.[92]

In spite of the hope for peace, getting the constitutional debate started was proving extremely difficult because the formula had still not been agreed to. Makarios would not accept Harding's vagaries and was anxious to prevent concessions to Turkish interests. Makarios and his advisers debated these issues again at a meeting of the Ethnarchy Council on 21 February. One representative insisted that the inclusion of Turks in the Cabinet would have to 'be avoided at all costs'. Makarios was sympathetic in principle. 'Perhaps you are right', he said, 'but in practice this would be unattainable.' Even Bishop Kyprianos was cautious, but cynical, about appearing to be openly anti-Turkish. 'We must not appear to be against the Turks, on the contrary, we must succeed in gaining their confidence so that we may attain *Enosis*.' On the constitution, however, Kyprianos held nothing back: 'I reject the constitution and insist on immediate self-determination.'[93] In this attitude, even among the pro-*enosis* Ethnarchy Council, he was alone. The other members pressured him to reconsider his position, but Kyprianos remained adamant: 'Under no circumstances will I change my opinion. Each of us has his opinion and cannot be deprived of this. If we are fighting for liberty, we must respect the liberty of others.' Makarios urged him to reconsider, pointing out that it was 'not democratic to create a split'. Kyprianos would not be swayed: 'I have my opinion', he replied, 'and you may proscribe me.' Theodoulos Sophocleous, assistant principal of the Pancyprian Gymnasium, posed a final reaction to the exchange muttering, 'A grave danger will arise the moment the people are filled with fanaticism.'[94] Kyprianos, alone among the twenty-six councillors, refused to approve of Makarios's draft reply. *The Times of Cyprus* reported that the 'portly firebrand', finding 'himself in defiant isolation', stormed out of the meeting in Nicosia and drove back to Kyrenia alone.[95] Makarios would not press for immediate self-determination, but his remaining differences with the formula proposed by Harding meant that the two sides were still a long way off.

Grivas's request for an amnesty for EOKA fighters was also now a new factor dividing the two sides. By 21 February, however, *The Times of Cyprus* optimistically reported that the governor was 'ready to amnesty most if not all' of the detained EOKA fighters.[96] Although it would remain an open issue to the end, it does not appear to have been the central cause for the inability of the two sides to reach an agreement. The primary concerns remained the scope of self-government, its transition to self-government and the place of Turkey and Turkish-Cypriots.

On 25 February, Makarios conveyed his concerns to Harding. The archbishop's cooperation 'in the framing and operation of self-government' could be achieved if this phrase was openly acknowledged 'as a transitional stage towards self-determination, which ever remains our sole and final aim'. Moreover, such cooperation was only possible 'in so far as the fundamental democratic principles . . . described in our previous letter were clearly established now as a basis of the constitution which is offered'.[97] These democratic principles involved an assembly elected to reflect the demographic advantage of the Greek-Cypriot community, the control of that body over the cabinet of ministers (which would exclude Turkish-Cypriots) and guarantees that executive responsibility for public security would revert to (Greek) Cypriots once order was restored.[98] Makarios also insisted on an 'early repeal' of the emergency laws and 'the granting of an amnesty for all political offences' as 'indispensable' to any agreement. These terms, wrote Makarios, constituted 'every possible concession beyond which our national conscience and natural dignity do not permit us to go'.[99]

In London, it seemed that Makarios was moving the goal posts, pushing for new and problematic concessions:

> [O]n the main issues . . . the Governor and the Archbishop had come very near to reaching an agreement. At this final stage, however, the Archbishop had put the agreement in jeopardy by asking for an amnesty for all political offenders in Cyprus. . . . The Governor was most reluctant to make any offer of an amnesty until the Archbishop had abjured the use of violence and had given practical proof of his ability to induce his followers to abandon it.[100]

More significantly, by continuing to hammer the line that self-determination (meaning *enosis*) remained the 'sole and final aim' of the Greek-Cypriot people, Makarios continued to ignore the reality that such a claim was impossible because of the Turkish factor.

The archbishop's approach to these negotiations reflected his characteristic brinksmanship. While a novice at Kykkos Monastery, he had refused to grow a beard. The abbot had beaten him, but he still refused. Finally, Makarios was threatened with expulsion from holy orders. He packed his bags and a taxi was called. As Makarios put his foot on the step of the taxi the abbot relented and asked him to stay.[101] Makarios's biographer, Stanley Mayes, thought that 'such brinksmanship was later to become a familiar part of Makarios's technique'.[102] Later, another Makarios interlocutor, Sir Hugh Foot, would acknowledge that Makarios 'was a man of political skill . . . [with] confidence in his own opinion. But I sometimes think he enjoys to gamble, to go right up to the edge, to pit his wits against everyone else.'[103] While the abbot of Kykkos backed down, Harding did not. The gambling style that cost Makarios little as a novice in the monastery carried a high cost for Cyprus in 1956.

On 28 February, Lennox-Boyd arrived in Cyprus with hopes of clinching a deal. The arrival of the colonial secretary was a clear indication of both the seriousness of the discussions and the sincere British expectation that an agreement was close at hand. On 29 February, Lennox-Boyd met with representatives of the Turkish-Cypriot community and with Makarios. Before their meeting, some ten explosions were reported in various parts of Nicosia. *The Times of Cyprus* accused the communists of planting the bombs in order to prevent an agreement.[104] This is highly unlikely since communist violence in Cyprus during this period was almost non-existent and Harding had already arrested more than 130 leading communists. In his *Memoirs*, Grivas claimed to have authorized the bombs as a 'warning demonstration' of EOKA's strength 'before the final round of talks'.[105] Regardless of their origins, the bombs, by themselves, did not prove the decisive factor in scuttling a solution.[106]

Lennox-Boyd had arrived to clinch a deal and was willing to make concessions, even on Makarios's new demands, in order to do so. He informed Makarios that the British government would take a number of actions in return for the archbishop's condemnation of violence and his aid in restoring peace on Cyprus. These undertakings on the part of the British government would consist of an amnesty for all detainees 'except those involving violence against the person or the illegal possession of arms, ammunition or explosives', the repeal of the emergency regulations 'at a pace commensurate with that of the reestablishment of law and order', and the drafting of 'a liberal and democratic constitution in consultation with representatives of all sections of opinion in the Island'.[107] Makarios, however, was not prepared to accept Lennox-Boyd's statement 'as a basis for cooperation', and 'could not accept the exclusion of those carrying arms, ammunition and explosives from the amnesty or the reservation of public security to the Governor "for as long as he thought necessary"'. In addition, Makarios insisted that 'the composition of the elected majority . . . be defined to this satisfaction in advance of the recommendations of the Constitutional Commissioner'.[108] Lennox-Boyd had travelled thousands of miles and made concessions on Makarios's new demands in order to achieve an agreement. But his actions and offer were deemed insufficient by the archbishop.

This rejection was the final straw. Plans were put into motion to remove Makarios from the scene if he did not perform a volte-face and agree to the offer. In Lennox-Boyd's opinion, after five months of talks, '[t]he time for negotiation was now past and the time for decision had arrived'.[109] Harding and other British officials had communicated to Makarios that time was running out for the negotiations. Concessions had been made by both sides. Lennox-Boyd regarded the British offer as positive and felt that the proposals should be made public, 'confident that they [the proposals] would be recognised everywhere as generous and constructive'.[110] He 'emphasised to the Archbishop the generosity of the offer of amnesty in its present form and urged that relatively unimportant doubts and uncertainties about its operation should not be allowed to obstruct an agreement'. He argued that the issue of an elected majority in the future Cypriot assembly was 'for the Constitutional Commissioner'. Lennox-Boyd conveyed that he was eager to 'see the constitutional talks started . . . [and] earnestly asked the Archbishop, therefore, not to make an issue of this point such as to obstruct our getting the talks started and to disappoint our hopes of bringing the Emergency to an end'.[111] In spite of the archbishop's professed desire for a solution, he did not feel that Lennox-Boyd's statement provided a 'basis on which he would like to see an agreement concluded'. Makarios blamed his predicament on the attitude of the people, 'a large section' of whom 'did not wish to follow his lead in reaching an agreement. If he accepted, without having a wide measure of popular support, he would become an object of severe attack and criticism.'[112]

Makarios's attitude was problematic on two counts: first, he portrayed himself as a prisoner of the will of the Cypriot people. This argument diminishes his agency as a leader capable of taking important decisions and shaping public opinion rather than being driven by it. Lennox-Boyd understood the prevarication, noting that 'it was the responsibility of a leader to lead his people and not to follow them'.[113] Second, the archbishop had been at the forefront of shaping and radicalizing that opinion which he now claimed prevented him from agreeing to Harding's terms. Makarios had long preached the gospel of '*enosis* and only *enosis*'. He had organized the plebiscite of 1950 and, upon his elevation to the archiepiscopal throne, had undertaken to canvass support for *enosis* across the globe. It was disingenuous for him now to claim that public opinion prevented him from agreeing to measures of compromise when he had been instrumental in shaping public opinion. Confronted with disagreements on major points, Lennox-Boyd could see no way forward. His trip had been in vain.

As *The Times of Cyprus* reported, '[h]opes of peace were deferred last night'.[114] In Cyprus, events now proceeded rapidly. Harding secured agreement from London for the deportation of Makarios and the bishop of Kyrenia. On 9 March, Makarios was taken into custody as he attempted to board a plane to Athens from Nicosia Airport. Kyprianos was arrested at his home in Kyrenia. Polykarpos Ioannides, Kyprianos's secretary, was arrested on the street in Kyrenia and Stavros Papagathangelou, the priest of Phaneromeni Church and a leading recruiter for EOKA youth groups, was also arrested at his home in Nicosia. The four were sent into exile in the Seychelles. The move was greeted by riots and violence in Cyprus, by attacks from the opposition in Parliament and by international condemnation. It was a calculated risk reflecting Harding's frustration at the failure of the talks.

These sentiments were apparent in a letter written on 4 March by Harding to his son. '[I]t was very disappointing that after such long and tedious negotiations we were unable to get an agreement', wrote the governor. 'At the beginning of the meeting we had on Monday night – the Colonial Secretary and myself with the Archbishop – I thought it might take a different form from all my previous meetings with him, but it was soon apparent that he was determined to shield the terrorists and to [illegible] our bargaining. Looking back I cannot think of anything more we could have done to secure an agreement.' The negotiations, 'of the past five months', he confided,

> have done a good deal to clarify the problem and to put it into perspective. Apart from that it was an essential political exercise to exhaust all possibilities of reaching a basis for cooperation by negotiation before resorting to other methods – rather like the amnesty proposition in Malaya – and it might have come off – it probably would have if it had been tried a year or two earlier.

What remained clear to the field marshal was that 'By his persistent refusal to denounce violence the Archbishop forces us to the conclusion that he believes in violence as a political weapon and would not hesitate to use it again – a curious attitude for a so-called Christian leader'.[115]

With Makarios and Kyprianos removed from the picture, Harding hoped to enjoy greater freedom of action in the fight against EOKA and to undercut some of the organization's strength. Confined in exile, Makarios would neither be able to rally international support for *enosis* nor would he be in an effective position to denounce

British policy in Cyprus and stir up the population against British rule. Makarios's enforced departure also meant the struggle for *enosis* was unequivocally in the hands of Grivas. As the colonel recorded in his *Memoirs*:

> The exile of Archbishop Makarios meant that I had now to take on the political as well as the military leadership of the resistance. I did not shrink from this double burden: indeed, the additional responsibility gave me greater freedom of action and added strength, just as the Archbishop's deportation, far from quenching the fires of revolt, fanned them into flames. I launched a new offensive designed to transform the whole island into a battlefield.[116]

In Grivas, Harding would find an opponent as uncompromising as he was. Moreover, with Makarios outside Cyprus, there was no prospect for a negotiated solution.

The decision to deport Makarios was a heavy one – heavy in responsibility, risk and potential reward. Harding was eager to make the most of the opportunity he saw to crush EOKA militarily without having to work simultaneously along the tortuous path of negotiation with the pedantic and uncompromising cleric. As he wrote to his son,

> Up to date I have had to pursue two divergent policies – appeasement by negotiation and restoration of law and order – which has compelled me to refrain from some security measures while negotiations were still in progress. Now I can give the restoration of law and order, and the elimination of the terrorists overriding priority – so in that result my task will be simplified but it may involve doing some pretty unpleasant things, and the next phase may be a bit grim – we shall see.[117]

A new phase in the struggle was indeed about to begin: one which not only saw the escalation of violence between EOKA and the British but also witnessed a campaign by the British government against Makarios in absentia and against the Cypriot Church. In many ways, the last of these was retaliation for years of violent abuse hurled down on the British from pulpits across Cyprus. Harding now had the chance to destroy EOKA, but an escalation in violence also provided an opening for attacks by the British government's opponents against what they characterized as unacceptably draconian methods. A new battle for security was about to begin.

7

'To destroy EOKA and re-establish law and order'

I have carried out a review of the resources available to me for carrying on the security campaign and have come to the conclusion that certain additional units and personnel are urgently required to destroy EOKA and re-establish law and order with the minimum delay.[1]

– Field Marshal Sir John Harding, 7 January 1956

From his very first day as governor, Field Marshal Sir John Harding had to manage between fighting EOKA and attempting to negotiate peace. His discussions with Makarios ended in March 1956 with the archbishop's deportation, but the battle between EOKA and the security forces continued. As Harding predicted, the failure to reach an agreement with the archbishop would present circumstances for 'a full scale emergency campaign'.[2] During 1956, this is precisely what occurred. As illustrated in the previous chapters, violence and negotiation proceeded in tandem, with one influencing the other. During Harding's time in office, a significant increase in EOKA violence was met with increased troop deployments to Cyprus and reforms to the island's security services. Harding organized a new security apparatus around emergency regulations (instituted at the end of November 1955), which gave the administration significant new powers, a redesigned police force and a massively reinforced army. Harding used these means to implement a comprehensive approach to combating EOKA on the ground. New forces were used to attack EOKA guerrilla groups. Security forces widened their activities, conducting large search and cordon operations, mass arrests, and summary detentions. Harsh interrogation methods – even torture – of detainees became common. Abuses 'were reported and at least two officers were subsequently court-martialled. As a former Intelligence Corps non-commissioned officer put it, "torture was endemic" in Cyprus.'[3] After Makarios was deported, emergency powers were even used to apply the death penalty to several captured EOKA fighters.

During and after the Harding-Makarios negotiations, violence in Cyprus remained a complicated cocktail. EOKA forces targeted the police and British armed forces, but they also continued efforts against 'traitors' who collaborated with the British or those, mainly leftists, who opposed EOKA on ideological grounds. British forces, in turn, focused their efforts on eliminating EOKA. At the same time that British security forces struck back against the Cypriot population, the British leadership attempted to discredit the Cypriot Orthodox Church by linking it to terrorism. Underpinning all these conflicts were the unresolved international political disputes and the local quarrels between Greek- and Turkish-Cypriots. It was a deadly and combustible concoction.

While Harding made a clear effort to adapt the lessons of counter-insurgency experiences from elsewhere in the empire, particularly Malaya, this learning process was fundamentally crippled in Cyprus by a lack of room for compromise at the political and strategic levels. Parallels between Cyprus and Malaya were imperfect for a number of reasons, and while tactical lessons were applied, strategic order effects were not achieved. Through 1956, neither the British nor the Greek-Cypriot nationalists were able to achieve their political objectives through violence in spite of escalating its use dramatically. Their respective failures created a small opening for a negotiated compromise but such a denouement failed to materialize.

Malayan model

The campaign in Cyprus has been characterized as a British success,[4] a failure,[5] an 'acceptable' defeat[6] and, with frustrating prevarication, a military failure but political victory.[7] The approach used in Cyprus reflected earlier British experiences in Malaya. Harding's very appointment echoed the choice of General Templer for command in Malaya, and Harding's approach as governor attempted to put lessons from Malaya into practice.

Harding identified 'five main elements of disorder and subversion which must be brought under control'. These were EOKA, 'the secondary schools, the Church, the Communists and the organs of hostile propaganda'. Countering EOKA was Harding's priority. The organization's activities, he wrote, 'extend into two fields, the planning and execution of acts of terrorism and the organisation of public disorders and lawlessness'. If the population failed to help the security services, or aided EOKA, Harding felt that he should strike back at the people directly through the use of collective punishments such as fines and curfews taken under emergency powers. EOKA would also be targeted specifically through vigorous military offensives. Such operations took time and required both an expansion of the available military forces and the isolation of EOKA from weapons and supplies from abroad.[8] The focus on these coercive measures was consistent with Britain's approach in other colonies confronted with unrest. It did not do much in the way of 'hearts and minds', but criticizing the British effort along these lines misses key aspects of the nature of the problem. 'Hearts and minds' were not spaces the British were capable of contesting in Cyprus where they 'were much less flexible politically' than in other areas where there was unrest.[9] Some attribute this inflexibility to Cyprus's importance as a military base and imperatives of empire.[10] But flexibility and a programme of hearts and minds lacked applicability in Cyprus. Even if British policymakers had been willing to contemplate compromises towards *enosis*, Turkish-Cypriots and Turkey would have prevented it. As argued by Thomas

Mockaitis, 'Britain was not in a strong position to mount a hearts and minds campaign for the simple reasons that it could not grant *enosis* even if it had wished to do so.'[11] A hearts and minds campaign was always contingent on the possibility of a political solution being reached by Britain, Greece and Turkey. For much of the emergency in Cyprus, such a solution remained illusory both domestically and internationally. Opposition from Turkey and Turkish-Cypriots to concessions that the British might consider making to the *enosis* cause were the most intractable obstacle.

'Hearts and minds' is itself a problematic concept. The term is perhaps most closely associated with Templer's experience in Malaya, and is derived from his statement made during a speech that the answer to the uprising in Malaya 'lies not in pouring more troops into the jungle, but in the hearts and minds of the people'.[12] But the concept, indeed the phrase itself, has a much older history, dating back to one of Britain's earliest counter-insurgency experiences – the campaign in North America during 1775–81. It was General Sir Henry Clinton who perhaps coined the term when he wrote to the secretary of state for America, Lord George Germain, that military force would be insufficient to end the American insurgency. Instead, Clinton believed, it was necessary 'to gain the hearts and subdue the minds of America'.[13] As in America, so later on, the concept had limited success. As in America, so later on, its application has been criticized as incomplete at best, and deceptive propaganda at worst.

David French's reassessment in *The British Way in Counter-Insurgency 1945–1967* is highly critical of the idea that British policymakers made much use of 'hearts and minds' in their doctrine. French argues that '[c]oercion, not conciliation, was the mainstay of British policy'.[14] Others have agreed with this assessment. Hew Strachan describes 'hearts and minds' as nothing more than a euphemism for giving the natives a 'firm smack of government'. It 'denoted authority, not appeasement'.[15] Paul Dixon similarly argues that in Malaya, and elsewhere, in spite of the lip service to the theory of 'hearts and minds' the British approach was 'highly coercive'.[16]

The military campaign in Cyprus reflected many of the tensions presented by 'hearts and minds'. British policymakers needed to avoid a level of violence which would result in international condemnation, while demonstrating effective military action against EOKA. There was a need to balance the maintenance of the rule of law within the colony with the harshness which might be used to maintain that rule of law. French argues that during this period, the balancing act usually tilted towards coercion and repression and that doctrines of 'minimum force' and 'hearts and minds' were little more than window dressing. An attack on 'minimum force', however, is incomplete in the case of Cyprus. British policymakers and soldiers knew they would be fighting insurgents if they wished to achieve certain political outcomes. Grivas openly declared that he was waging a war against Britain's 'occupation' of Cyprus. It is naive to believe that any war can be waged without violence, coercion and brutality. British policymakers were also genuinely constrained by both world opinion and domestic British politics. Violence was used, but as even French admits, in Cyprus it did not reach the levels inflicted by other colonial powers. A comparison with the actions of France in Algeria is a sobering view of what might have occurred had it not been for Britain's different thinking on counter-insurgency methods.

Of particular importance to British security practices and reforms was a report produced by Templer himself in late April 1955. Harding read this before his arrival in Cyprus and supported its recommendations.[17] Templer's lessons included an emphasis on intelligence (particularly the need for effective counter-intelligence and a powerful special branch), the importance of political as well as military progress in defeating an insurgency and the vital significance of having a large and capable local police force. Templer's report was released on 23 April 1955, only three weeks after the outbreak of EOKA violence. Its purpose was 'to suggest ways and means for preventing trouble from breaking out in the Colonies during the longish period of cold war . . . and to ensure that, in the event of a hot war, the Colonial armed forces are well adapted to the role they would probably have to play'.[18] In framing his report, Templer applied his experiences in Southeast Asia. He also visited Cyprus and Uganda to gather additional information. During his brief stay in Cyprus between 14 and 16 April 1955, Templer met with Governor Armitage and took stock of the situation. Coming, as they did, from two very different backgrounds, the two men demonstrated little appreciation for each other. As Armitage wrote to his parents, 'Templer was here for 3 days . . . we had to give him several meals and I had many discussions with him over security matters. He is a nervous, highly strung type, not the sort of person one could imagine getting as high in military circles as he has.'[19]

Templer was equally unimpressed by the governor. Templer described Cyprus as undeniably a 'trouble spot' with a 'burning problem of *Enosis* . . . diligently fed by both the national priesthood and by a foreign government [Greece]'. Templer's greatest concern, however, was the fact that Cyprus possessed 'the largest and best organised Communist Party in any Colonial territory outside the Far East'. This was significant not only because of the Cold War but also because Cyprus was 'the key to the Eastern Mediterranean . . . on which the defence policy not only of the United Kingdom but of the West hinges'.[20] As the foundations of the *enosis* cause made clear, and as EOKA's progress demonstrated, these perceived linkages with communism in Cyprus were misplaced and inhibited a more complete understanding of the phenomenon on the part of British policymakers. It also overlooked the genuine divisions that existed among Greek-Cypriots over the methods employed by EOKA and its supporters.

In Templer's view, Armitage did not understand the magnitude of the situation or the methods best suited to handling it. 'It might be thought', Templer concluded,

> that in these circumstances, the internal security of the base would have the first call on the Government's money, man-power, and general interest. But the Governor himself has told me that in his view the top priorities in Cyprus today are the Information Service, agricultural reform, water, intelligence and police, in that order. I can appreciate, as well as anyone, the importance of matters such as agricultural reform in the long term fight against Communism, and the particular needs in respect of the fight against *Enosis*. But, with respect, I cannot understand how law and order can fail in Cyprus to have top priority.[21]

Harding's appointment reorganized the priorities of the government of Cyprus according to Templer's way of thinking and provided a soldier's determination in implementing those priorities. With the exception of integrating political progress with military success, however, the recommendations of the report were more tactical than strategic. Combating the goal of union with Greece was a different animal from Chinese-Malay communism. Foremost, the British had already agreed upon the key condition of Malayan independence. The Malays were willing to help the British fight against a minority Chinese population which hoped to impose a radical political system with limited appeal to the Malay majority. In Cyprus, much of the Greek-Cypriot majority population supported the cause of *enosis*. Britain was adamant that union with Greece was impossible and even that any sort of self-government would be highly circumscribed. The minority community in Cyprus, the Turkish-Cypriots, opposed *enosis* with near unanimity and their cousins in Turkey threatened Britain and Greece with violence and the collapse of NATO if *enosis* was considered. This left very little room for any sort of political solution in Cyprus similar to the one agreed to in Malaya.

Another aspect of the Malayan model involved declaring a state of emergency. Armitage had requested this at the end of September 1955, only to be bluntly denied at the highest level and informed that such matters would be decided by his successor.[22] When Harding took command in October 1955, there were seventy-four attacks across the island. In November, the number jumped to 217.[23] In the face of such a dramatic escalation, Harding declared a state of emergency at the end of November 1955. Emergency powers gave Harding a series of legal mechanisms with which to crack down on EOKA. The most significant of these included the power to arrest without warrant and to stop, detain and search persons and vehicles; to restrict movement through house arrest, and the prohibition of movement in certain areas; the power of security forces to enter, close or search premises; the power to impose curfews; a mandatory death sentence for carrying arms; and restrictions on the press. Collective fines, curfews and the expansion of the death penalty were all carry-overs from the experience in Malaya.[24] They would also be among the most contentious of the new powers employed by Harding's administration. As a result of the new regulations, curfews and cordon searches – with their resultant stresses in relations between the British and the Greek-Cypriot community – became daily features of life on the island.

Such operations frequently resulted in the detention of suspects. Since the prison facilities in Cyprus were limited, most of these individuals were held in specially constructed detention camps. During 1956, the camps swelled. Under the Detained Persons Law, 132 detainees (communists whom Harding had arrested in December 1955) were held in January 1956. By mid-October, this number rose to 508 and continued increasing, reaching 688 by mid-December and 735 by the end of December.[25] Detained persons were held in communal barracks (most commonly Nissen huts), which were locked at night and ringed by barbed wire. Prisoners received visitors and care packages and attempted to refashion some sort of community life. They even maintained observance of major religious holidays with the help of priests who were allowed to visit them to perform services.

Limited measures were also taken for the welfare of their families. From 1 March 1956, payments were made to the dependents of detainees at the maximum rates of '£10 per month for a wife, £4 per month for the first child and £3 per month for every other child'. Payments were determined by a full investigation carried out by the welfare department 'into the circumstances of the detainee's family'. Though most EOKA men were young and unmarried, with few children, the government spent £25,423 on assistance to their families between March and July 1956.[26] In contrast, in June 1956, the government estimated that it was spending £43,000 per *week* on the maintenance of the army.[27] Widespread detention of Greek-Cypriots without warrant betrayed the lack of substantial evidence gathered by security forces. At the same time, it appeared that the mass detentions did little to impede EOKA operations, which continued to grow in number and effectiveness throughout late 1955 and into early 1956.

The legal mechanisms of the emergency regulations were supported by a new structure for the security and administration of the island, also designed on Templer's Malayan model. Authority was centralized in Harding who, as governor/commander-in-chief, had a complete view of operations and governance. In his own words, the field marshal would work 'in double harness' with the civilian deputy governor, George Sinclair, who would, as Harding described in a telegram to the colonial secretary

> deal directly with the five District Commissioners, the Commissioner of Police and the Commander of the troops. The Directors of Intelligence and Information Services [would be] . . . under our general direction and . . . [would] serve the whole Governmental organisation. The Commander Cyprus district and his forces would be [Harding's] . . . commander for security operations, but the commander would continue to be directly responsible to C-in-C MELF [Middle East Land Forces] for the organisation, equipment, training and administration of all troops under his command.[28]

The arrangement, as Harding made clear, 'would be an exact parallel to the system in Malaya when Templer was High Commissioner'.[29] Centralizing authority, responsibility and information with Harding allowed the field marshal to get a comprehensive understanding of the situation and develop coordinated strategies.

The establishment of an effective intelligence service was another high priority. A report prepared by Brigadier George Baker, Harding's chief of staff, in early 1958 identified some of the major shortcomings of the intelligence service at the start of the insurgency. First, conditioned by the experience of the 1931 disturbances, the army failed 'to appreciate the seriousness of the threat'. Security forces suffered from having 'no proper command structure, no close liaison or cooperation with the administration and police, inferior communication and lack of training in internal security duties. Above all', argued Baker, 'the army was handicapped by a lack of direction. Greater demands were made upon it than it had the resources to meet'.[30]

These misperceptions and miscalculations within the military, it was argued, were rooted in intelligence failures. Soon after Harding's arrival, the CIC provided the governor with a report entitled 'The Nature of EOKA, Its Political Background and Sources of Direction'. The paper traced the emergence of PEON and the role of Grivas and Makarios in cultivating *enosis* forces on the island. Nikos Zachariades, the secretary general of the Communist Party of Greece, had revealed Grivas's identity as Dighenis in a radio broadcast on 24 April 1955, only three weeks into the struggle.[31]

The CIC report confirmed Grivas's identity as Dighenis and was also correct in placing the control of EOKA's campaign was 'solely' in his hands. It underlined that EOKA represented a nationalist movement focused on *enosis*, which recruited its strength from middle- and working-class young people, the church and its youth organizations. Indeed, some 60 per cent of those convicted or detained under the emergency regulations were twenty-four years old or below.[32]

EOKA's organizational structure, and the youthfulness of its members, made counter-intelligence and infiltration particularly challenging. The Secret Intelligence Service (SIS)[33] felt that it could not introduce 'agents from outside, as these would be speedily detected in the small island'. Greeks and Greek-Cypriots serving in the Special Operations Executive in Egypt were also deemed unusable. It was suggested that MI5 might 'investigate the possibility of using Cypriot students studying in the United Kingdom'.[34] While EOKA members did give information to British forces through both interrogation and collaboration, no evidence has yet emerged suggesting that either MI5 or the SIS was able to introduce agents into EOKA. Intelligence gathering was further hampered by the lack of Greek speakers within British forces, particularly those with 'military or intelligence knowledge' in all branches of the security services.[35]

One clandestine success came through the establishment of a top-secret 'Q (or Irregular) unit' on the island in early 1956. This unit consisted 'of a British leader, a second leader who [was] an ex-terrorist, and local men who [were] either ex-terrorists, or ... trained in terrorist methods'.[36] The structure was a refinement from the experience in Palestine where 'Q Patrols' had been established within the police force.[37] The Q unit in Cyprus also had similarities to the pseudo-gangs in Kenya.[38] Posing as an EOKA mountain group it would go 'into villages claiming to need shelter from pursuing security forces' in the hopes of 'unmasking local group leaders and supporters'. In over six months of operation during 1956[39] the unit, 'never more than ten strong, killed, captured or obtained information leading directly to the identification and capture of: 35 hard core EOKA members, 47 village groups (average strength 5), 5 policemen, 20 priests who were actively helping EOKA, 68 weapons and quantities of bombs, explosives, etc'.[40] It was eventually disbanded in late 1956 since, as explained by a British intelligence officer assigned to the Cyprus Police Force (CPF) Special Branch, there was

> a limit to the number of times the same tactic could be repeated successfully in a small island with tight-knit communities, quite good communications, and no long distances. Word got around, and local group leaders or supporters simply ceased to surface in response to the group's demands. There was no other tactic it could use without giving its real purpose away, so no point in continuing, whether with same or different members, and it was disbanded.[41]

At the same time, many Greek-Cypriot villagers in the mountains 'were pro-EOKA, and always suspected the intentions of strangers'. This further reduced the effectiveness of the Q units and meant that their operations never led to the capture of the top stratum of EOKA leadership.[42] No subsequent groups were created along similar lines and the gathering of intelligence remained a challenge for much of the insurgency.

Implementing the various aspects of Templer's Malaya model also ran into the challenge of an evolving and active opponent in EOKA. From the time of Harding's arrival in Cyprus, through the negotiations with Makarios, and after the archbishop's deportation, Grivas was determined to use as many of the tools and tactics at his disposal to combat the British in Cyprus. This meant civil disobedience, an escalation in attacks on British military personnel and the ruthless targeting of the CPF.

'Terrorize the police'

Grivas targeted the CPF from the very beginning of the insurgency. It was a mark EOKA hit early, often and hard. Following the initial spate of bombings in April 1955, Grivas ordered a halt to reorganize. After enlisting additional support and refining EOKA's command structure, Grivas relaunched operations in June 1955 with new mandates. 'The aim of our next offensive', he ordered '[w]ill be to terrorize the police and to paralyse the administration, both in the towns and in the countryside.' The result of these actions would be that '[d]isillusionment will spread through the police force so rapidly that most of them, if they do not actually help us, will turn a blind eye to our activities'.[43] Grivas's assessment, though optimistic, came closer to reality than British policymakers would have liked. Policemen loyal to the British administration were singled out for intimidation by EOKA proclamations and assassination by its hit squads.[44] Numbers and effectiveness for the CPF declined precipitously.

Harding arrived to find a police force incapable of mounting a serious defence of law and order. His predecessor had informed London of the dire situation as early as 4 July 1955. 'Morale in the police is extremely low as a result of campaign of smear and intimidation carried out by EOKA', Armitage wrote. 'Police who arrest suspects immediately become liable to assassination. If suspects are released and steps are not pressed on vigorously to eliminate EOKA, police will not be prepared to run these risk in future.'[45] Harding set about to remedy the situation immediately. A week after his arrival he wrote to Lennox-Boyd that 'my most urgent task in restoring and maintaining respect for law and order [is] . . . the strengthening of the Cyprus police force'.[46] This was an important goal in itself, but it would also allow the police 'at the earliest possible moment [to] assume full responsibility for internal security and relieve the army of this commitment which at present absorbs a large number of troops and diverts them from their proper tasks'.[47] For British policymakers, it was a 'cardinal principle of internal security that military forces act in support of the civil power, and are called upon only when the police can no longer contend with a situation – and then with the arms in which they are trained to use'.[48] Maintaining law and order was the province of the police, not the army. '[P]olice patrolling and crowd control', were tasks 'for which [the soldier] was neither intended nor trained' and which forced him 'constantly to "rub shoulders" with the population'.[49]

The recognition that military resources were meant for what modern armies call 'warfighting' rather than local security – the province of the police – was an important counter-insurgency lesson, and one which the British had acquired before operations in Cyprus. It was a 'basic tenet of British doctrine on internal security . . . that the police, and not the military, should play the predominant role in upholding the law and maintaining civil order'.[50] In Cyprus, however, the size and reliability of the police force was such that it simply could not fulfil the primary role in counterterrorist operations. The lesson was learned in theory but impossible to apply in practice.

Harding undertook to remedy the situation launching a complete overhaul of the force. He proposed nearly doubling the permanent force from 1,800 in 1955 to 3,500; there would be reinforcement of the officer cadre, and major reforms to the Special Branch and intelligence services.[51] Replacing soldiers with policemen in Cyprus was slow work. It was not until August 1956, for example, that the police were able to assume responsibility for security in the towns.[52] The wholesale replacement of the military with the police force was a goal that the British never achieved.

As a small, colonial police force, the CPF was in no way prepared to deal with the scale and scope of EOKA's activities. The force itself was keenly aware of this fact. 'The Police Force was neither staffed, organised, equipped nor trained to cope with these conditions [of terrorism]. A high priority had to be given to Police requirements and in April [1955] approval was given for major increases in all ranks, for supply of radio and transport, for arms and equipment'.[53] In addition to combating EOKA's mountain guerrillas and preventing smuggling, security forces were also faced with the challenge of stopping EOKA assassinations of individual police and military personnel in urban areas.[54] Combating this 'very difficult problem' and cause of 'much worry' was something Harding identified as 'rightfully a task for [the] regular police'. In the governor's opinion, however, the forces were 'quite incapable of taking it on at present'.[55]

Arms and equipment, were secondary shortages; what the police force fundamentally lacked was reliable recruits, particularly Greek-Cypriots. To EOKA, Greek-Cypriot policemen were primary targets for assassination and intimidation. Greek-Cypriot officers were threatened by EOKA verbally and in leaflets. They were excoriated as traitors and collaborators and promised a bullet in the back. All too often the promise was kept. As Grivas recorded in his diary, his instructions were that 'town groups would execute police who were too zealous on the British behalf, while my countryside groups would attack police stations, kill isolated policemen [/] and ambush policy patrols'.[56] In the summer of 1955 Grivas circulated a leaflet address '[t]o the Police' claiming,

> I have warned you and I shall carry out my warning to the letter. Darker days await the tyrants of Cyprus, heavier punishments the traitors.... Do not try to block our path or you will stain it with your blood. I have given orders that: anyone who tries to stop the Cypriot patriots will be executed. Anyone who tries to arrest or search Cypriot patriots will be shot. You have nothing to fear so long as you do not get in our way.[57]

Over the course of the insurgency, 15 of the 51 policemen killed by EOKA were Greek-Cypriots as were 43 of the total 185 wounded – approximately a quarter of the police force's casualties.[58]

EOKA pressure on Greek-Cypriot officers reduced their numbers, dramatically hampering the effectiveness of the force. At the end of 1954, Greek-Cypriots had numbered 850 out of a total police force of 1,386 – slightly more than 61 per cent. In comparison there were 508 Turkish-Cypriots – almost 37 per cent.[59] During 1955, the first year of the insurgency, these numbers began to move in opposite directions. Large numbers of Greek-Cypriots resigned from the force – some out of fear of EOKA, others out of sympathy for it. Recruitment drives aimed at increasing the force's strength, netted only Turkish-Cypriots almost entirely. By the end of 1955, 1,003 out of the 1,838 members of the force were Greek-Cypriots compared with 734 Turkish-Cypriots.[60] A special police commission report during the first half of 1956 described a 'virtual cessation of recruitment' among the Greek-Cypriot population due to '1) Fear of EOKA, 2) Antipathy to the Government, heightened by the curriculum in Greek schools, preaching Greek Nationalism, and 3) Poor pay and conditions of service'.[61] By 31 December 1956, the number of Greek-Cypriot policemen had plummeted to 697. The remaining 1,135 members of the regular police force were now Turkish-Cypriots; the relative proportions within the force had been almost reversed in less than two years.[62]

Comparison of the Composition of the CPF by Religion, 1954–6

Religion	1954 All Ranks (Percentage)	1955 All Ranks (Percentage)	1956 All Ranks (Percentage)	Increase/Decrease (1955–6)
Greek-Cypriot	850 (61.3%)	1,003 (54.5%)	697 (37.5%)	–30.5%
Turkish-Cypriot	508 (36.7%)	734 (40.0%)	1,135 (60.0%)	+54.6%
Other	28 (2.0%)	101 (5.5%)	47 (2.5%)	–53.5%
Total	1,386 (100%)	1,838 (100%)	1,879 (100%)	+2.2%

The haemorrhaging of Greek-Cypriot officers meant that a large increase in the regular police force – a key policy objective designed to bring the insurgency under control – was not achieved during 1955–6. The actual increase of 2.2 per cent was negligible. This was not the result of a failure to recruit Turkish-Cypriot officers – who increased by 54.6 per cent – but as a result of the loss of Greek-Cypriots, whose numbers decreased by 30.5 per cent. In addition, some of those Greek-Cypriots who remained were of dubious loyalty, collaborating with EOKA by giving the organization vital information and even helping prisoners escape.[63]

The newly recruited Turkish-Cypriot officers were not well trained and were mistrusted by the Greek-Cypriot civilian population. By the end of 1956, the ethnic composition of the regular police force no longer represented the demographics of the population, further undermining its legitimacy. In addition, the police force as a whole remained significantly below the new authorized establishment. Although 498 new recruits were brought in to the various branches of the force during 1956, only 2,417 were serving on 31 December 1956 against an establishment strength of 3,643.[64] This force, still small and ineffective, confronted a massive increase in violence. Over the course of 1956, cases of 'serious crime' (almost entirely due to EOKA operations) shot up by more than 36 per cent from 6,335 to 8,655.⁶⁵

From the very beginning of the insurgency, British policymakers decided that the presence of officers with experience from other colonial emergencies would be useful in Cyprus. On 23 August 1955, Governor Armitage asked the Colonial Office for 'seven police officers . . . with experience of emergency conditions in Malaya or Kenya'.⁶⁶ Ten days later, the deputy governor of Kenya was in contact with the Colonial Office offering a list of qualified police inspectors 'willing to volunteer for three year contract service in Cyprus'.⁶⁷ Further expert advice was also offered. Anthony Head, the secretary of state for war, suggested to the prime minister that the administration might benefit from having 'a Lieutenant-Colonel who had had experience of the working of joint headquarters in similar circumstances in Kenya or Malaya'.⁶⁸ As a result of these initiatives, the number of British nationals serving the CPF grew dramatically. The increased use and recruitment of expatriate forces represented an effort by the British government to provide effective law enforcement in Cyprus and to avoid deepening the divide between Greek- and Turkish-Cypriots. It was also hoped that such transfers could leverage the expertise acquired by these officers in other trouble spots. Regardless of their expertise, their small numbers limited these expatriate officers from having a significant impact on the course of the insurgency.

The size and composition of the regular police force were only part of the picture. An auxiliary police force was also created in August 1955. This force had lower educational and medical standards for its recruits than for the regular force. 'The original establishment of 400 was increased to 900 by August 12th, and in late October a further increase to the present figure of 1,400 was authorised.' Because of the difficulty in recruiting Greek-Cypriots, the force was almost exclusively Turkish-Cypriot.⁶⁹ In addition, a mobile reserve of approximately 500 men, also formed in 1956, was completely Turkish-Cypriot.⁷⁰ This latter force personified one of the most contentious aspects of the insurgency – the Greek-Cypriot claim that Britain's recruitment of Turkish-Cypriot constables and auxiliaries represented a policy of divide and rule designed to heighten hostility between the two communities and justify the continuance of British rule. It would be a mischaracterization, however, to view the mobile reserve as a punitive force designed to strike at the Greek-Cypriot community or to maintain or establish a minority rule of the Turkish-Cypriots over the Greek-Cypriots. As described by General Darling in a top-secret report on the course of the insurgency, members of the mobile reserve were used in a limited way 'as static guards over magazines and some vulnerable points'.⁷¹ According to Darling, this formation 'did excellent work until the intercommunal disturbances when it was considered impolitic to use them. They were used in mixed Police/Army confidence patrols with success after their last anti-riot operations which were in January 1958.'⁷²

Contrary to a narrative that British policy in Cyprus was governed by a policy of 'divide and rule', the government was cautious about the uses of the Turkish-Cypriot mobile reserve and the largely Turkish auxiliary police force, because it hoped to avoid further exacerbating intercommunal hostility. In fact, in this circumspection, Harding diverged from the Malaya model, as well as from British practices in Kenya. In both Malaya and Kenya home guards had been recruited 'from amongst those ethnic communities ... opposed to the insurgents'. The British refused to take this additional step in Cyprus in order to avoid worsening 'already fragile intercommunal relations'.[73] The mobile reserve and the auxiliary police were used in a circumscribed manner to prevent the escalation of intercommunal tensions. This was because, in general, British policymakers viewed intercommunal hostility as undermining rather than supporting Britain's position on the island. A Cabinet note by Selwyn Lloyd from July 1955 argued that 'communal strife would seriously impair the efficiency of Cyprus as a base'.[74]

Maintaining Cyprus as a base was a key component of Britain's interest in the island. They had little interest in creating conditions of communal strife which they recognized would endanger the functionality of the base they were trying so hard to protect. Such considerations were also at work internationally, where Britain's primary concern was maintaining NATO and an effective position in the Eastern Mediterranean against the Soviet Union. Civil war in Cyprus threatened war between Greece and Turkey – a move which would damage NATO and open the entire Middle East to Russian expansion. In addition, the British government continued to be active in its desire to recruit reliable Greek-Cypriots into the force throughout the insurgency. Records show that authorities made no attempt to limit or reduce the number of Greek-Cypriot applicants and were pleased when Greek-Cypriot applications rose in 1957.[75] By 1957, the British government brought officers from Britain and other colonies in larger numbers in order to make up the shortfall rather than rely totally on the Turkish-Cypriot element, which was progressively kept away from front-line service to reduce ethnic tensions.

In spite of the cautious use of the mobile reserve, the intercommunal fighting that characterized 1958 strained police resources and legitimacy to their limits. The increased scale of violence in 1958, after the lull of 1957, forced a redoubling of efforts to expand the police force. As a result, the number of police jumped from 2,692 at the end of 1957 to 3,014 at the end of 1958, only 185 below establishment, largely due to the influx of expatriate officers and the continued high number of Turkish-Cypriot recruits.[76] In addition, upwards of 1,800 Turkish-Cypriots served either in the auxiliary police force, along with a handful of Greek-Cypriots, or in the completely Turkish-Cypriot mobile reserve. This meant that, in 1958, of the approximately 4,900 men in police uniform, less than a fifth were Greek-Cypriots, although they represented almost four-fifths of the island population. This fundamental demographic shift in the composition of the CPF represented a victory for Grivas and EOKA. Through their use of targeted violence and intimidation, they significantly undermined the ability of the British to recruit and maintain a police force that reflected the ethnic configuration of Cyprus. This undermined both the force's effectiveness, due to a lack of legitimacy, language capability and community awareness. It also put the responsibility for conducting the counter-insurgency campaign largely on the shoulders of the military.

With the police force generally prevented from carrying out effective counter-insurgency operations, the British administration in Cyprus was forced to rely on soldiers for the day-to-day conduct of security tasks. Military formations were responsible for protecting targets from EOKA attack, carrying out crowd control, patrolling both city streets and mountain tracks, guarding detention centres, and also for offensive operations against enemy targets. Harding's desire to go on the offensive, beginning in late 1955 and continuing through the summer of 1956, required more troops. With these additional soldiers, Harding was determined to carry the war to EOKA and end the campaign for *enosis* by military means.

'To Victory'

Less than two weeks after his arrival, Harding's security review convinced him that while 'an effective command system' was being built up, he needed one more infantry battalion and one more infantry brigade headquarters for operations.[77] The field marshal wrote to Prime Minister Eden with a modest request for approximately 700 additional combat soldiers plus logistical and command support. The 1st Royal Norfolks were duly flown out to Cyprus on 17 October, followed by the headquarters of the 50th Infantry Brigade on 19 October with the addition of extra support for the HQ's radar unit.[78] Harding was convinced that the forces now at his disposal – some seven combat battalions compromising 5,000 fighting men supported by approximately 8,000 more in other units (support staff, headquarters personnel and several units of Royal Marine commandos) – would be sufficient to deal with 'any situation short of a complete breakdown in morale and discipline in the police force'.[79] This 'breakdown', however, was essentially what Harding confronted in the ensuing months, with the result that Britain's military presence in Cyprus continued to grow.

Escalating violence by EOKA was the primary driver of Harding's difficulties. In October 1955, a number of factors converged to convince Grivas that both the tempo and scale of operations needed to be increased. First, was the arrival of Harding himself. Second, was the disappointing conclusion of another debate at the UN. Third, the first round of negotiations between Harding and Makarios had not gone well for the *enosis* cause. As a result, on the day these discussions broke down, 9 October 1955, Grivas ordered the commencement of a new stage of operations, which he called 'Operation Forward to Victory'. This phase of the campaign would consist of 'attacks on enemy agents and unfriendly policemen, combined with raids on village police stations'. The intent was not only to shatter the CPF but also to 'dislocate the intelligence service and draw out the army'. EOKA members also raided mines and military warehouses in order to gain explosives and arms.[80] These attacks continued through October in conjunction with widespread demonstrations that frequently escalated to riots. Demonstrations of EOKA's capabilities were also meant to win concessions for Makarios as he renewed his discussions with Harding.

Harding's problems compounded at the end of October. On 28 October, a British court sentenced Mihalis Karaolis – an EOKA gunman who had been convicted of shooting an officer in the CPF – to death. Karaolis was only twenty-two.[81] This was the first death sentence handed out in relation to the insurgency. Harding banned all demonstrations on that day, but the date was a Greek national holiday, *Oxi* day,[82] which commemorated the Greek government's refusal to accept an ultimatum by Mussolini in 1940. Grivas 'ordered the ban to be defied and there were bloody clashes all over Cyprus'.[83] There were also large-scale demonstrations of sympathy in Athens. The rejection of Karaolis's appeal on 14 November provided another occasion for protest, though Harding held off on the actual execution so as not to pour oil on the fire while conducting negotiations with Makarios. Across Cyprus, mass demonstrations in the cities and the harassment of security patrols throughout the countryside were becoming a way of life. Grivas encouraged this form of resistance writing, '[e]very village must organise its own defence against such attacks [intrusions by the security forces] of the barbarians and receive them with any means'.[84] Students were even more active in demonstrating against the British forces than villagers. During the 'first half of the autumn term, 21 secondary schools had taken part in demonstrations and 46 strikes by students were reported'.[85]

On Cyprus, the situation was dire enough to warrant reassurances, accurate or not, directly from Prime Minister Eden to Prime Minister Menderes of Turkey on 10 November. 'Security is now much more firmly in hand, as a result of the strong reinforcements we have sent and of the measures taken by the Governor. To break the terrorist organisation may take a long time. This task is being resolutely undertaken.'[86] Harding's resolution translated into a request for additional powers. In order to 'stick to the principle of minimum force' but still fight effectively to maintain law and order, Harding required 'powers of collective punishments . . . at least as extensive as those used by Templer in Malaya'.[87] This sort of response, he reasoned, would be effective against both EOKA's targeted violence and the broader protests of the people of Cyprus. On 18 November, Grivas launched 'the main phase of "Operation Forward to Victory"' with more than fifty bombs across 'thirty separate attacks all over the island'.[88] It was in the context that Harding finally secured the consent of London for his declaration of a state of emergency on 26 November 1955.

Harding put his new powers to use. In the first instance, this meant conducting search and cordon operations, usually carried in villages surrounding an area where an ambush had occurred.[89] Kenneth Neale, seconded by the Colonial Office to Cyprus, noted to John Martin, the deputy undersecretary of state for the colonies, that these early measures resulted in 'a depressing lack of tangible success against the terrorists'. It was only by late December, that this trend was somewhat reversed by a few, small successes.[90] On the night of 10/11 December, Operation Foxhunter, spearheaded by the seventy men of the 45th Commando Royal Marines, shot one terrorist armed with a revolver and captured another in possession of a rifle. An EOKA team exchanged fire with a patrol but escaped into a thick mist. Five caves filled with food and supplies for approximately twenty fighters were discovered.[91]

In Operation Foxhunter II, the very next day, two more villages were cordoned and searched by the 1st Gordons. The battalion found only 'one RAOC sergeant's battle-dress blouse'. In the neighbouring village of Kyperounda, a priest with detonators and four time pencils was arrested with his two sons. No major EOKA targets were killed or captured, but nineteen people were detained for interrogation.[92] Search and cordon operations continued on a nearly daily basis in the mountain towns, but the results were still disappointing. This mechanism was simple, as described by a member of the 45th Commando Royal Marines:

> Once the troops carrying out the search arrived at a village, a Land Rover with an officer manning a loudhailer would drive through, well before anyone was awake,

giving instructions '*Attention – Attention, women and children remain in your homes, all males make your way to the Cage.*' The 'Cage' was usually constructed of barbed wire and erected on a suitable open space in the village. Once all males were in the cage and under guard, each one was interrogated whilst being watched most of the time by an 'informer', who would be masked and in a vehicle out of sight. The informer then pointed out any suspect terrorist, who was then taken away for further interrogation by the Security Forces and MI5. The remaining troops would be systematically searching through every house and outbuilding for arms and explosives.[93]

Interrogation methods were harsh. Captured EOKA described a number of tortures ranging from being forced to wear heavy metal boots in the hot Cypriot sun to having cigarettes extinguished on their skin and having their genitals beaten.[94] One member of the 45th Commando Royal Marines recalled that, while his unit behaved appropriately, he was 'uncomfortable' with the interrogation methods of an unnamed captain from the Special Branch.[95] One intelligence officer assigned to the Special Branch dismissed the most egregious claims of mistreatment, arguing that British intelligence in Cyprus 'wanted reliable information, not confessions' and that prisoners had to be produced 'in court within about a week of arrest' and 'all new arrivals were examined and notes made of bruises, etc, in case they blamed us [British authorities] for them in court'.[96] Nevertheless, there was strong evidence of gross mistreatment.[97]

Harding hoped that by pressing the fight against EOKA's guerrilla groups during the winter, he could take advantage of the cold weather, which, along with supply difficulties was hampering EOKA's operations. To this end, Harding wrote to Lennox-Boyd in early January requesting another combat battalion.[98] By mid-January 1956, the War Office announced that Harding would get more than he had initially requested. Two battalions of paratroopers and a second independent brigade headquarters arrived in Cyprus later that month.[99] By February, British forces on the island had grown to nearly 20,000 men and included fourteen major combat units. British forces on the island had nearly doubled in size between October 1955 and February 1956. Still, Harding had remarkably little to show for his efforts.

While struggling to gather high-grade intelligence, deter EOKA attacks and capture high-value targets, security forces suffered surprisingly high casualties. At the end of February 1956, Harding informed Lennox-Boyd of the losses. Since 1 April 1955, EOKA killed seventeen members of the British security forces and twenty-one Cypriots, including six policemen and fifteen civilians. Around 100 British military personnel were wounded along with twenty-three policemen and fifty-three civilians. Against this, Harding reported that British security forces had killed only eight EOKA fighters and wounded fifteen. In addition, twenty-eight captured EOKA fighters were under arrest, facing charges that could result in the application of the death penalty. Another twelve captured members of EOKA faced a maximum sentence of life in prison if convicted.[100]

The statistics reflected not only the intensity of violence on the island but also the ability of EOKA to inflict damage without significant loss to itself. This was largely a function of EOKA's tactics which focused on attacks with explosives and the targeted assassination of security personnel. Laying mines along mountain roads to destroy army trucks or throwing grenades and explosives at police stations and army barracks provided opportunities to inflict casualties on British forces while exposing EOKA men to little danger. The second major aspect of EOKA operations – attacks on security personnel engaged in routine patrols – were carried out in largely urban settings. Their targets were conspicuous due to their duties and were usually fired on from behind. After the attack, the civilian-clothed EOKA gunman was frequently able to melt back into the populace, using the disorder that followed the attack as cover. Such operations had more to do with organized crime 'hits' than military operations and were subject to particular vilification both during and after the conflict. Grivas was quick to defend them in his book on guerrilla warfare published in 1964:

> Of course, our use of execution groups came in for criticism on the part of our opponents who called us 'murderers' because we struck from behind. Such a charge is, to say the least, naïve, because to kill your opponent by assailing him at his weakest point, from the side or rear, is a tactic as old as Alexander the Great, Epaminondas and Marathon, and in more modern times was adopted during the wars of Frederick the Great and Napoleon.[101]

A conventionally trained soldier and something of a military historian, Grivas was aware of the traditional use of deception by great commanders. His defence, however, glossed over the fact that a flank attack on a battlefield by one uniformed army against another was palpably different from a civilian-clothed gunman firing into the back of an officer on a routine patrol along city streets and then disappearing into the crowd.

With Makarios removed, EOKA had carried out 246 attacks in March and followed that with 234 in April. In May, they conducted a staggering 395 attacks – the most for any single month of the insurgency to date.[102] In part, this escalation may have been spurred by EOKA's desire to retaliate for the executions of Andreas whose sentences were carried out by hanging on 10 May 1956. EOKA's heightened pace of operations during the spring raised eyebrows among Turkish-Cypriots. In April 1956, *Volkan* issued a communiqué 'To the Turkish people of Cyprus'. It promised that 'communal clashes will soon start'. *Volkan* seemed eager to equal EOKA's rhetoric of violence and terror: '[T]hose who either deliberately or through vain display dare to give the slightest information regarding the Organisation will be penalised by being shot like dogs. The colonial lackeys who are in love with the British will be treated not as Turks but as traitors. . . . policemen who carry their duties to the extent of treachery shall be punished.' *Volkan*'s message finished menacingly, reminding Turks in Cyprus of the threat EOKA posed to them: 'Do not forget that every fired shot is a step towards Enosis, and every dying Englishman drags us a little closer to the abyss of Enosis. . . . [E]very bomb thrown by EOKA is thrown at us.'[103] *Volkan* did not act on its most violent threats and it is doubtful that it was ever supplied with the arms or training necessary to carry them out. However, the organization was able to organize protest marches and riots to make its feelings known.

For all the violence, Harding's new security apparatus started to make headway. Particularly after the exile of Makarios, the security forces, spearheaded by the army, pursued EOKA ferociously. With an ever-improving intelligence service, and plenty of boots on the ground carrying out operations in both towns and rural areas, Harding was able to inflict setbacks on EOKA. At the end of May 1956, British forces commenced a major security operation, code-named 'Pepperpot', which damaged a number of mountain groups. It was followed in June by 'Operation Lucky Alphonse' which achieved even greater successes, capturing a 'complete mountain gang of seven terrorists including two men with a price of £5,000 on their head', along with significant quantities of equipment and weapons.[104] Security forces even came close to capturing Grivas himself. Contact was made with the EOKA commander's 'headquarters' team in the Troodos Mountains, but he escaped. The security forces, however, did succeed in recovering Grivas's diary covering 10 May to 9 June 1956, along with numerous other documents, including correspondence between Grivas and Makarios from a broader period.[105]

Grivas's narrow escape was a disappointment for the security forces, but other successes followed; soon they began to snowball. Intelligence gleaned from Grivas's diaries, from the interrogation of captured EOKA suspects and from increasingly efficient military operations began to shift the tide in the favour of the security forces. When the number of EOKA attacks dropped to 276 in June, Grivas wrote disapprovingly to an area commander at the end of the month: '[T]he results of our continued struggle, when we think of what we intended to do, are very poor.'[106] In spite of Grivas's frustration, EOKA was in no position to turn the tables on the security forces. Their capabilities continued to deteriorate and only sixty-six attacks were launched in July. Hindered in their operations against the security forces, Grivas turned much of EOKA's fury on domestic 'traitors'. In August 1956, EOKA killed only one policeman; the army did not suffer any casualties at all.[107] In contrast, however, EOKA gunmen murdered twelve Greek-Cypriot civilians identified as 'traitors' and one Turkish-Cypriot.[108] These killings often took place 'in cafés to accentuate the public ritual of the horror'.[109]

EOKA's escalation of violence was tearing the Cypriot community apart, setting Turkish-Cypriots against Greek-Cypriots and Greek-Cypriots against each other while making the international situation even more inhospitable to the *enosis* cause.[110] A lack of progress in the field combined with this ugly turn to the murder of Cypriot 'traitors' weakened support for EOKA in Athens. The Greek government was also in the picture regarding Britain's latest constitutional initiative, which was proceeding in spite of both the deportation of Makarios and continued violence on the island. In Athens, Prime Minister Karamanlis had secured his own electoral mandate in February 1956. Karamanlis had succeeded Papagos after the latter's death in 1955 under somewhat controversial circumstances. To some extent, Karamanlis's stance on Cyprus at the start of his premiership had reflected the delicacy of his situation. With his own position now more firmly secured, Karamanlis developed assertiveness in dealings with Grivas. Karamanlis and, the Greek consul general in Nicosia, Angelos Vlachos pressured Grivas during the summer of 1956 to rein in violence.[111] As further evidence for the potential for compromise on the international scene, on 12 July 1956, Eden announced his government's acceptance of the principle of self-determination for Cyprus. This 'concession' was not a fundamental revelation. British proposals to Makarios during the failed Harding-Makarios negotiations of December 1955 and January 1956 had made a similar declaration, but it was evidence that the situation of complete deadlock was beginning to budge.[112]

Hopes for compromise even managed to survive a serious blow on 9 August when three more EOKA fighters, Andreas Zakos (aged twenty-five), Harilaos Michael and Iakovos Patsatsos (both aged twenty-two), were executed after Governor Harding refused to commute their sentences. On 15 August, as Cypriots celebrated the Feast of the Assumption, Harding gave an interview to *The Times of the Cyprus*. Though he 'defended the recent executions vigorously', he also invited EOKA and Grivas to 'make the first move' towards peace and compromise and support the constitutional proposals that were being discussed at the time. There was also a hint that Makarios could be brought 'back into the picture' to renew political discussions.[113] The combination of factors – reverses in the field, conflict among communities in Cyprus, a political opening and pressure from Greece – apparently began to tell on Grivas, who, somewhat surprisingly, announced a unilateral EOKA ceasefire on 16 August.

According to Averoff, Vlachos, a critic of the unbridled pursuit of *enosis*, drafted the ceasefire announcement. In tone, it seemed to reflect the sober political perspective rather than the flamboyant rhetoric of Dighenis.[114]

> I am ready to suspend operations and await the response of Britain to the demands of the Cypriot people as set out for discussion by the Ethnarchy, Archbishop Makarios. As proof of my unshakeable will to press forward to that happy end, the completion of the work undertaken by Ethnarch Makarios, and to provide him with an opportunity to solve our national question, I order from today the suspension of operations by all sectors under me . . . . EOKA, The Leader, Dighenis.[115]

Reading the ceasefire as a sign of weakness, Harding issued surrender terms to Grivas on 22 August. Insulted by the offer, Grivas demanded its revocation and the relaunching of negotiations with Makarios. When these demands were not met, EOKA resumed action.[116] Grivas's revocation of the ceasefire on 23 August had none of Vlachos's pragmatism. It was pure Dighenis:

> The Victors do not surrender. On Two historic occasions for the Greek nation, when the invader asked for the surrender of arms he received the reply 'Come and take then for yourselves' at Thermopylae and then from Pindos 'No'. As military leader of the fighting Cypriot people, in reply to the demand for surrender, I too say 'Come and take them for yourselves'. There can be no let-up in the struggle until a final solution is found. . . in order to show my goodwill once more and avoid further bloodshed I am willing to wait until the 27th of this month. I hereby state that if the impertinent demand for surrender is not withdrawn by midnight on that date and negotiations are not begun on the terms drawn up by Archbishop Makarios, I shall no longer consider myself bound by the ceasefire which I declared on my own initiative and I shall resume freedom of action.[117]

Even with the two-week ceasefire, there were some 71 incidents in August resulting in 14 fatalities and 18 injuries. One policeman was killed and another wounded. Three soldiers were wounded. Continuing the trend begun in June, civilians were now the most vulnerable group to EOKA's violence – fourteen killed and eighteen wounded.[118] EOKA returned to form in September launching 285 attacks inflicting 18 fatalities (10 British and 8 Greek) and followed in October with 129 attacks claiming 20 lives (6 British and 14 Greek).[119] While the British continued their military operations during this period, the most substantial response came in the form of a propaganda document designed to undercut support for the *enosis* cause by linking violence in Cyprus to the Orthodox Church.

War with the church

In the minds of British policymakers, the war against EOKA was irrevocably linked to the Cypriot Orthodox Church. There were a number of reasons for this: the church had been the driving force behind the *enosis* movement since the beginning of British rule. Archbishop Makarios was its loudest spokesman, carrying the rallying cry of '*enosis* and only *enosis*' throughout the world. He had continually refused to condemn violence and with other Cypriot clerics, notably the bishop of Kyrenia, had preached in support of the armed struggle. EOKA drew recruits from church organizations like PEON. Monks and priests had been caught transporting and storing arms.

In December 1955, while London continued to frustrate Harding over his desire to deport leading clerics, he attempted to make full use of the new emergency powers to strike at the church directly and to prove its connections with EOKA. In the early morning of 8 December, twenty-four monasteries were raided throughout the island as troops searched for weapons caches, EOKA propaganda and correspondence. Finds were meagre. At the wealthy Kykkos Monastery, security forces found only a few sticks of dynamite and some EOKA leaflets. Two pistols were found at Agia Varvara and a monk was detained.[120]

This was merely the first phase in what would be a long and ugly war between Harding's administration and the church. While the rhetoric and actions of leading clerics supported Harding's hostility, the failure of security forces to find more than a handful of weapons in their raids on churches and monasteries bring their utility into question. Raids on ancient holy sites in the early morning hours and the forced search of monks and priests were politically damaging and militarily insignificant. They also exposed the British administration to vociferous attacks by EOKA propaganda. During operations, claimed one leaflet, British forces 'do not hesitate to use methods much worse and more abominable, under the circumstances, than those used by Hitler during the war... in due course we shall demand that the criminals of the British S.S. like Hitler's S.S., be judged by the International public opinion'.[121] Another leaflet, from several weeks later, made even more outrageous claims: '[T]he vandalisms of the British soldiers have surpassed medieval barbarities and orders in the Nazi Concentration Camps. Without any word of excuse they murder unarmed citizens and arrest others whom they subject to unbearable ordeals which only criminals by nature and most degraded men of the lowest social rank could devise.'[122]

Tensions regarding the behaviour of security forces extended from EOKA proclamations to direct exchanges between Makarios and Harding. On 15 December 1955, the archbishop's cousin, Charalambos Mouskos, was killed in an action against security forces. He had been part of a team that ambushed a patrol and killed a British soldier. His funeral became a public relations disaster. A crowd assembled, flouting the ban on assemblies, to follow the coffin from the church. Tear gas was used to disperse the funeral procession and relatives had to proceed to the cemetery via a side street.[123]

Harding received a strongly worded protest from the archbishop:

[That] even enemies of the dead should respect them, taking care for their burial has always been custom and universal written law. We regret sincerely and protest strongly against foul act which was committed yesterday against dead man by British military authorities in Cyprus and by uncivilized Turks who have recently been recruited as policemen. Entirely unprovoked they attacked with tear gas and clubs funeral procession which was following in reverence coffin of Charalambos Mouskos. They did not respect the holy cross and religious symbols which accompanied dead. This sacrilege is black stigma in history of British occupation of Cyprus.[124]

Harding's reply matched the churchman's acerbic tone: 'It is repugnant to me that any disturbance should take place at a funeral', he wrote to the archbishop, 'but I cannot accept allegations contained in your telegram. Muskos [sic] was an outlaw who two days before had taken part in ambushing and murdering a British soldier. . . . Responsibility for any disturbance to funeral must rest squarely on shoulders of those who deliberately disregarded instruction issued by authorities.'[125]

Harding demonstrated a similar attitude with regard to Makarios's deportation. Shortly after Makarios and Kyrenia were sent to the Seychelles, British forces raided the archbishop's palace and carried off a substantial quantity of official and private papers. This was done partially to gather intelligence against EOKA and partially to justify the deportations. Included in this stash were the minutes of the Ethnarchy Council and Ethnarchy Bureau meetings during the winter of 1955–6 describing deliberations relating to the Harding-Makarios negotiations. Evidence gathering against the church continued during the summer of 1956 with expanded operations in the Troodos Mountains. This time, searches 'in and around Kykko Monastery confirmed the authorities' view that the monastery has been a centre of terrorist activity'. Weapons, ammunition, EOKA leaflets and explosives were all discovered in the monastery or in nearby 'hideout' caves constructed as terrorist safe-havens. In response to the discoveries, the monastery was closed to the general public.[126] The revelations in Grivas's captured diary from this period added more substance to the official view that EOKA was in close contact with the church.

On 1 September, Harding wrote to Lennox-Boyd that security forces had acquired evidence 'that the Church has not only been exploiting its position for seditious ends but has been actively engaged in a conspiracy to overthrow the Government by force . . . practically the whole leadership of Cyprus has been deeply and directly implicated in launching the campaign of violence on Cyprus'. The evidence was strong enough for Harding to feel that it presented the British with 'a unique opportunity to take such actions with the least offence to religious opinion throughout the world'.[127] It was eventually published in Nicosia in late October 1956 in a report entitled *The Church and Terrorism in Cyprus: A Record of the Complicity of the Greek Orthodox Church of Cyprus in Political Violence*. Designed to put forward the British position to the world and to justify the security measures taken against the church, including the deportations, the pamphlet set out to demonstrate the complicity of churchmen of every position in the violence on the island.

The document is remarkable for its unabashed agenda and its overt hostility – an indication of the government's frustration both with the church's policies and with the continued violence in Cyprus. Plenty of evidence was found in the correspondence between Makarios and Grivas, and in Grivas's own captured diaries, although it was presented with unrestrained bias. 'Above all', the report argued, 'it was he [Makarios] who brought to Cyprus a brutalized and disappointed soldier [Grivas] to organise the campaign of violence and to terrorise his compatriots into acquiescence in the pursuit of Makarios' political ambitions.'[128] The authors of the report argued that 'It is abundantly clear that Archbishop Makarios took the leading part in the formation of Grivas' secret terrorist organisation, later to become known as EOKA, and it was he who controlled its preparations and determined when it should go into action'.[129] The British document went on to defend the deportations in stunningly blunt language:

> Is it not then a question whether the removal from the Cyprus scene of ecclesiastics, who thus prostitute their religion in support of political violence, may be as necessary for the revival of true religion in their Church as it is for the pacification of their country. [. . .] It is clear that the Ethnarchy never considered self-government on its merits at all and regarded it as 'a short truce' which should be exploited 'for the purpose of immediately pushing on to self-determination', and at the same time, as the only way by which 'we can neutralize the Turkish factor'. . . . the real reason for his [Makarios'] deportation was that he had so far forsaken the path of true religion as to procure the use of violence in support of his political ambitions, and, having done so, had become so deeply committed to it that he either could not, or would not, abandon it.[130]

In spite of the harshness of the language, the British report correctly identified the unwillingness among supporters of the *enosis* cause to compromise with 'the Turkish factor'. This continued to obstruct any solution. The propaganda war against the church – indeed the entire struggle with EOKA – was soon put on the back-burner. Larger events, with implications far beyond the insurgency in Cyprus, were about to take centre stage, providing Grivas with an opportunity to strike back at the British in stunning fashion.

Suez and 'Black November'

Even as levels of EOKA violence remained high during the late summer of 1956, the insurgency in Cyprus was becoming a secondary concern in Eastern Mediterranean international affairs. On 26 July, President Nasser of Egypt announced the nationalization of the Suez Canal and of the Suez Canal Company that operated it. Because of the dependence of Britain on oil supplies passing through the canal, this move confronted British policymakers with a grave crisis. Conferences were held in London among the interested powers from 16 to 23 August and again from 19 to 21 September in an attempt to solve the problem and to re-establish a canal users' association that would be acceptable to Egypt, Britain and France. Without satisfactory progress or guarantees from Egypt, Britain and France began secret discussions in mid-October about a possible Anglo-French military intervention. Soon, their planning involved cooperating with the Israeli government in an invasion of Egypt that would allow Britain and France to intervene between the two warring factions, occupy the Canal Zone and topple Nasser's government. On 29 October, Israeli forces – with British and French collusion – invaded Egypt. The next day Nasser rejected an Anglo-French ultimatum to end hostilities. On the night of 5–6 November, in keeping with their prearranged plan, British and French troops occupied Port Said and the Canal Zone. On 7 November, the Soviet Union, the UN and, surprisingly, the United States, condemned the Anglo-French invasion. The threat of sanctions, particularly from the United States, combined with very real economic fears in Britain forced Eden into calling a ceasefire that very day. Eden's premiership was fatally wounded by Suez. The prime minister's health deteriorated rapidly from the stress caused by the operation's failure, and he left Britain for Jamaica in November. The government fell into the hands of his chancellor, and former foreign secretary, Harold Macmillan. When Eden resigned on 9 January 1957, Macmillan formally assumed control of the government.

In Cyprus, the British move into Egypt caused frantic activity on the part of EOKA. Several elite paratrooper battalions had been withdrawn from operations in the run-up to the crisis and were now in Egypt. With insufficient troops, there was no follow-up to the successful summer operations. EOKA got a second wind, and Grivas was determined to use it. As one of EOKA's district commanders noted in her memoirs, 'the day after the British attack on Suez, we received urgent orders from Dighenis to step up action and intensify our ambushes. We wished to harass the British as a diversion from their activities in Suez.'[131] November 1956 witnessed no fewer than 416 attacks, the highest number in any single month of the entire insurgency.[132] With British troops remaining in the Canal Zone while negotiations continued to establish a timetable for withdrawal, EOKA continued its attacks, targeting the security forces. Although casualties in the security forces spiked, civilian losses remained steady. During November, sixteen members of the armed forces and four police were killed, along with nine Greek-Cypriot civilians, four British civilians and one Turkish-Cypriot civilian.[133]

Civilian Casualties (August 1956–20 February 1957)[134]

Month	Greek-Cypriot	Turkish-Cypriot	British
August 1956	12	1	Nil
September 1956	8	2	1
October 1956	14	Nil	Nil
November 1956	9	1	4
December 1956	12	Nil	1
January 1957	7	Nil	4
February 1957 (to the 20th)	2	Nil	Nil

In spite of the high losses in November, casualties among British security forces decreased to almost nothing in December. It seemed as if EOKA had shot its bolt.

Security Forces Casualties (August 1956–20 February 1957)[135]

Month	Service	Police
August 1956	Nil	1
September 1956	7	3
October 1956	6	Nil
November 1956	16	4
December 1956	1	1
January 1957	1	2
February 1957	4	1

In spite of EOKA's best efforts, British security forces were able to hold their own and reassert control. Although the number of attacks increased massively in November, no major successes were achieved against British forces; the fundamental dynamics of the situation remained unchanged. Once the Suez situation settled, the British forces on Cyprus struck back. As troops returned to the island, so did successes. In mid-December, a joint police and military operation in Limassol and Larnaca arrested fifty-two terrorists of importance, including the Larnaca district commander.[136] The security services considered the arrests 'to be undoubtedly the most important single haul since the beginning of their campaign against EOKA'.[137] On 19 January 1957, the security forces killed mountain group leader Markos Drakos in a gun-battle. On 1 February, area commanders Evangelos Evangelakis and Andreas Chartas were captured. In March, Yiannis Droushiotis, the Paphos commander, was taken by security forces.

By mid-February 1957, the Special Branch described EOKA as 'trying to maintain pressure' in spite of their leadership losses. These losses forced the organization 'to employ less experienced personnel', leading 'to a marked rise in the number of casualties inflicted on terrorists in the actual commission of their crimes'. Security was also strengthened through the arrest 'of a number of Greek-Cypriot police officers for complicity in EOKA activity'.[138] The CIC echoed Special Branch, reporting on 21 February 1957 that '[f]or the first time since EOKA terrorism started in April, 1955, there are genuine signs that the movement is on the wane, and for the first time it has been possible to frustrate terrorist plans by reason of precise advance knowledge of what was being planned. This is a most satisfactory state of affairs, and is the result of the cumulative effect of much painstaking intelligence effort.'[139] By this time, twenty of the thirty individuals (including one woman) who had served as district leaders throughout the island had been killed or arrested. Under interrogation, many of those in custody gave information leading to the capture of additional EOKA members.

On 3 March, the security forces scored their greatest victory in the mountains near Macheras monastery. After an intelligence tip-off, a detachment of the Duke of Wellington's Regiment was led to a wooded area containing the hideout of EOKA's most notorious commander, Grigoris Afxentiou. Afxentiou, a former officer in the Greek army, refused demands to surrender. According to many accounts, he repeated the declaration Grivas had used in his bulletin of 23 August, quoting the Spartans at

Thermopylae. When asked to surrender his arms, he had replied with the words of King Leonidas, Μολὼν λαβέ – 'Come and take them.' After a gun-battle that raged for several hours, Afxentiou was killed when his hiding place was saturated with petrol and set alight. His charred body was recovered from the cave several hours later.

EOKA was staggered. As the CIC noted in its biweekly review, 'The terrorists have never before suffered such a succession of severe reverses as they have during the past two months.' While mindful of the organization's resilience, the CIC was optimistic that with continued pressure EOKA would be smashed, particularly since it appeared 'unlikely that external distractions, such as the Suez crisis, will cause a division of the counter-terrorist effort, as happened the last time the terrorists showed signs of cracking'.[140] This view seemed to be confirmed on 14 March when Grivas announced a suspension of operations and offered a truce if the British would release Makarios.

The intelligence services were convinced that EOKA had been defeated. In January 1957, the Colonial Office suggested that Brigadier Baker write a review of

> the more important aspects of the Emergency in Cyprus with a view to assisting Colonial Governors of other Territories in considering what steps they would have to take should they find themselves faced with an Emergency situation, and in considering the measures required to forestall or prevent it.[141]

With Afxentiou's death and the subsequent ceasefire, the drafting of the report moved forward. It seemed EOKA's days as a fighting force were numbered.

The close of 1956 and the beginning of 1957 were significant not only for the military successes of the security forces but also for political developments that suggested that Harding's successes in the field had created an opportunity for a negotiated solution. Proceeding with new constitutional proposals, the British approached both the Greek and Turkish governments in conjunction with the people of Cyprus, in an attempt to end the violence. These proposals opened a new phase of discussion and diplomacy, culminating in renewed attempts to solve the problem at the UN and within NATO. The failure of these attempts would lead not only to the most violent and dangerous phase of the insurgency but also, in time, to its end.

8

False dawn

The failed road to peace

> H.M.G. consider that the situation in Cyprus has considerably improved and is sufficiently under control for them to take a liberal view of the conditional appeal which the Archbishop has now made. I have accordingly instructed the Governor of Seychelles, with the full agreement of Sir John Harding, to cancel the orders for the detention of the Archbishop and his three compatriots, and to arrange passages from Seychelles by the first available vessel.[1]
>
> – Prime Minister Macmillan, 24 March 1957

Britain had long considered the establishment of a workable constitution for Cyprus to be a mollifying influence on the *enosis* cause. This was the principle behind the Winster proposals of 1947 and the declaration at the conclusion of the Tripartite Conference in 1955. In February 1956, as senior policymakers within the British government believed that an agreement was at hand through the Harding-Makarios talks, serious consideration began about the drafting of a new constitution for Cyprus. This constitution was meant to set Cyprus on a path to self-government while blocking *enosis*. By mid-February 1956, London had chosen their man to lead this process. He was Cyril Lord Radcliffe, an Eldon Law Scholar and former Fellow of All Souls College, Oxford, who was already famous for his work in the creation of India and Pakistan in 1947, where he had drawn up the partition line that separated the two countries. Radcliffe's task in Cyprus would prove as difficult as that in India. His constitutional proposals would have to satisfy not only the nationalistic aspirations of Greek-Cypriots but also the security concerns of Turkish-Cypriots, and the strategic needs of Great Britain, Greece and Turkey.

In spite of the failure of the Harding-Makarios negotiations and Makarios's subsequent deportation, Radcliffe's work on drafting a new constitution proceeded. Completed in December 1956, Radcliffe's proposals were the subject of continuing debate for most of 1957. These proposals, and the debate they sparked, reflected changing conditions in Cyprus. More significantly, they were evidence of an evolving international environment. Britain's failure at Suez, and the fall of the Eden government, created an opportunity for new approaches towards the Cyprus problem under the leadership of the new prime minister, Harold Macmillan. 'Britain had lost the capacity for acting ... without a nod of approval from Washington.'[2] Moving forward, the United States would play a larger, though still secondary, role in resolving the problem of Cyprus. At the same time, British policymakers were forced into an even greater reliance on Turkey to support their position in the Eastern Mediterranean. This limited the degree of concessions British policymakers felt that the new constitution could grant to the Greek-Cypriots.

Although Radcliffe's proposals in their final form would not include partition, the prospect of dividing Cyprus along ethnic lines emerged in the middle of 1956 as ethnic tensions continued to build. Attempts by British policymakers to leverage Greek and Greek-Cypriot concessions against the threat of partition remains one of the most cynical devices employed by London to combat the *enosis* cause. Although partition was avoided in the context of the 1950s, the permanent division of their island is sadly a fear Cypriots continue to live with.

By the summer of 1957, violence on Cyprus began to simmer again with no solution having been reached. Reinvigorated by the long truce, EOKA returned to operations; security forces were forced back into a reactive role. The *enosis* movement, along with the governments of both Greece and Turkey, refused to come to an understanding on Radcliffe's proposals. Now that partition had been raised as a potential option, Turkey pressed for it as the only solution to Cyprus's problems. As in previous years, the failure to reach a negotiated settlement led to an increase in hostility; 1957 proved to be a year of false dawn and lost opportunities.

A new constitution and familiar obstacles

Reeling from a series of blows, EOKA declared another truce on 14 March 1957, which was conditional upon the release of Archbishop Makarios.[3] The ensuing moratorium on attacks seemed to confirm the hope that the situation in Cyprus was moving towards a permanent end to violence. On 24 March, the new prime minister, Harold Macmillan authorized the release of Archbishop Makarios from detention as a move towards re-establishing the basis for a negotiated settlement. Makarios made his way to Athens but was not yet allowed to return to Cyprus.

Although British security forces had made some advances on the ground, British policy in the Eastern Mediterranean, more broadly, had suffered dramatic reverses over the same period, largely as a result of the Suez debacle. By the start of 1957, the new Macmillan government hoped to take advantage of the progress in Cyprus to achieve a lasting solution on the island that could recoup some of Britain's damaged prestige in the region. Macmillan's succession brightened the prospects for compromise. He was not considered to be as rigidly imperialist as Eden, and had been an early advocate of the idea of British bases in Cyprus rather than Cyprus as a British base.[4] Such a course of action was discussed with Governor Harding by the new minister of defence, Duncan Sandys, during a visit to Cyprus in April 1957. Sandys looked to end national service and reduce defence costs. In support of these overarching goals, he suggested to Harding 'that sovereignty over the whole island was no longer a *sine qua non* to meet the military requirement'.⁵ This key modification to Britain's position left room for compromise. It was hoped that Britain, Greece, Turkey and the two communities on the island could reach an understanding within that space.

In the spirit of Macmillan's desire for compromise, the Radcliffe constitutional proposals of December 1956 represented an only slightly different approach towards a familiar goal. Instead of encouraging the Cypriot people to discuss a framework for a constitution under British auspices, constitutional proposals were drafted by a British legal expert then circulated for approval to the Greek and Turkish governments. Once approved, they would be applied to Cyprus. Makarios's removal meant that there was 'no one on the Greek-Cypriot side to accept . . . a settlement' and that 'the only other way to a settlement was at the international level, with all the difficulties of direct Greek and Turkish involvement'.⁶ Just as the Radcliffe report proceeded along familiar lines, it foundered along familiar lines. The Greek-Cypriots would not agree to it because it did not provide for self-determination and a clear path to *enosis*. It gave too much power to a non-elected governor and kept Cyprus under British sovereignty.

Radcliffe's odyssey began in February 1956 when he was approached about drafting constitutional proposals for Cyprus. During this time, as previously discussed, an agreement with Makarios seemed likely, and the British government was planning the implementation of a possible solution. The position of the British policymakers was that an understanding between Harding and Makarios – along the lines of the proposed British formula – would be followed by constitutional negotiations involving Britain and the Greek- and Turkish-Cypriot communities.

At the start of February 1956, Harding wrote to the colonial secretary, Alan Lennox-Boyd, in support of appointing a constitutional commissioner. Less than a week later, Lennox-Boyd informed the governor of his choice. While willing to assume the responsibility for leading the constitutional commission, Radcliffe was not entirely comfortable with the scope of his new task. As he confided to the deputy undersecretary of state for the colonies, Sir John Martin:

> I do not regard myself as a constitutional expert in any sense: and I have the strongest belief that no Constitution is likely to have validity or strength unless it is produced from genuine discussion by those who are to be responsible for working it. . . . To produce a Constitution 'in the air' would, I think, put me in a false position, and would prejudice any further contribution one could make to the evolution of one.⁷

Choosing to lay the foundation for his proposals on the ground rather than 'in the air', Radcliffe planned a trip of several weeks to Cyprus. During this time, he hoped to meet representatives from both the Greek- and Turkish-Cypriot communities and take stock of the situation himself. Meetings on the details of his visit and of the broader approach to the drafting were held in early June with Harding and Lennox-Boyd. On 8 June, it was decided that Radcliffe would be appointed the sole constitutional commissioner and that he would fulfil this role with the help of 'a panel of advisers upon whom he could draw for assistance as necessary'.⁸

Radcliffe arrived in Cyprus on 14 July 1956. In a statement shortly after his arrival he admitted that the task facing him was a difficult one. 'I do not want anyone inside or outside this island to think it will be easy. There are a great many interests to be taken into account and reconciled before any recommendations can be made. I am here now to listen.'[9] For the next three weeks Radcliffe worked to get a better understanding of the situation first-hand, meeting with leaders from both the Greek- and Turkish-Cypriot communities. By 3 August, having done his best to get an accurate picture on the ground, he was on his way back to London. In London, Radcliffe discussed the drafting of his proposals with the most senior officials in the British government.

At the end of September, Radcliffe went to Cyprus for another ten days. He returned to London on 5 October. Over the next month and a half he drafted his proposals. Lennox-Boyd presented them to the British Cabinet on 16 November 1956, in the wake of the Suez debacle. Radcliffe's terms of reference made four points clear: Cyprus was to remain under British sovereignty; the island's primary function as a base to fulfil British 'international obligations' and 'defence . . . interests' had to be assured; the governor of Cyprus and/or the Government of Britain would retain control of external affairs, defence and internal security; and the constitution was 'to be based on the principles of liberal democracy and . . . [was] to confer a wide measure of responsible self-government on elected representatives of the people of Cyprus', while protecting the rights of minority communities.[10] The terms of reference made it clear that the constitution would safeguard the primary British interests in Cyprus while attempting to replace the Greek-Cypriot goal of *enosis* with the palliative of self-government. Turkish-Cypriot opposition would be mitigated by providing minority protections. Partition was not mentioned. It would not play into Radcliffe's recommendations, since his mandate was to create a constitutional framework under continued British sovereignty. Radcliffe was explicitly ordered not 'to consider or envisage the possibility of an eventual change of status [for Cyprus]'.[11]

The constitutional commissioner was in no doubt as to the obstacles standing between his proposals and the creation of a functioning new constitution for Cyprus. In his report to the Cabinet, Radcliffe made it clear that the conditions of 'terrorism and intimidation' in Cyprus, along with the British emergency countermeasures, had distorted 'ordinary life' and made the implementation of his proposals impossible.[12] In spite of these realities, Radcliffe remained hopeful that once adopted, his proposals could bring real and positive change to the island. At the same time, Radcliffe hoped that the proposal for constitutional development, in itself, would help bring the emergency to a close.[13]

In the eyes of the government's conservative elements, the constitution would help create a 'climate of compromise' through the ironical means of demonstrating British firmness. As the Tory MP Julian Amery explained, the nature of the constitutional proposals would 'bring the Greeks to understand that there cannot be self-determination for Cyprus in the foreseeable future'. British resolve on the issue would 'convince . . . friends and . . . foes alike in the island and in the Eastern Mediterranean' of Britain's determination 'to stay in Cyprus'. Anyone trying to put Britain out of Cyprus was 'biting granite' and would 'break their teeth'. Greek-Cypriot desires for immediate self-determination and *enosis* would only be stopped once they were 'convinced that they cannot hope to enforce them'.[14]

In substance, the proposals were balanced and flexible. As the author freely admitted, the proposals were 'to be read as instructions for a draftsman, not as a draft itself'.[15] Still, Radcliffe's draft carried weight. The proposals fulfilled the mandate of the terms of reference and outlined a continuation of British sovereignty. The governor would retain significant executive power. In addition to appointing six members of the legislative assembly, he would serve as the chief executive of Cyprus. He would be 'the final judge' in matters pertaining to 'his reserved subjects', such as foreign policy and internal security. He would also determine whether any bill from the assembly stepped into his reserved subjects. Providing for a Supreme Court or other outside referee to fulfil this role, Radcliffe wrote, was 'not possible'.[16]

Finally, '[a]ll legislative acts of the Assembly and all executive administration actions or decision on the self-governing side ... [would] be subject to the condition that they must not conflict with certain guaranteed rights relating to religion, education, charitable, religious and cultural institutions and use of languages'.[17] Radcliffe felt that his purpose was to create 'a fair balance between the different and often conflicting interests which are involved'.[18] The conflicting interests, however, were hardly reconciled by the proposals in front of them. The powers of the governor were particularly contentious for the Greek-Cypriots. Nevertheless, Radcliffe had made three major concessions to the Greek-Cypriot side. First, Greek-Cypriots would have an elected majority in the legislative assembly. Twenty-four of the thirty-six representatives would be elected from the general roll. Another six would be elected by Turkish-Cypriot voters exclusively. Six more would be appointed by the governor. This gave Greek-Cypriots a real majority that could not be blocked by a coalition of Turkish-Cypriot and appointed members. Second, this assembly would be the sole legislative body, unchecked by any 'upper house' where Turkish-Cypriots or officials appointed by the governor would have a disproportionate voice. Third, any mention of partition was excluded. It remained to be seen whether these concessions would be sufficient to secure Greek-Cypriot acquiescence.

For their part, Turkish-Cypriots would have their rights protected by several special features. A two-thirds majority of Turkish-Cypriot members of the legislative assembly would be necessary to implement 'any law which alters the existing laws of Cyprus regulating Turkish-Cypriot domestic affairs'.[19] In addition, an Office of Turkish-Cypriot Affairs would be created and the relevant minister (a Turkish-Cypriot) would be part of the Cabinet. Although Radcliffe was sympathetic to Turkish-Cypriot misgivings regarding life under Greek-Cypriot majority rule, he did not accept that the Turkish-Cypriots 'should be accorded political representation equal to that of the Greek-Cypriot community'. In Radcliffe's opinion, organizing Cyprus as a federation was not logical. There was 'no pattern of territorial separation between the two communities and, apart from other objections, federation of communities which does not involve also federation of territories seems to me a very difficult constitutional form'.[20] The crucial point for Turkey remained the possibility of partition. Although any mention of formally dividing the island was not included in Radcliffe's proposals, it was part of the ongoing diplomatic dialogue between British policymakers and leaders in Athens and Ankara as they discussed Cyprus in late 1956.

At the time when Radcliffe's proposals were brought forward, British policymakers had more to concern themselves with than the situation in Cyprus. Through the autumn of 1956, the crisis over Suez had become an international issue of enormous proportions. After the failure in Egypt, British prestige, particularly in the Middle East, was at an all-time low. The Eden government had neither the time nor the political will to force through Radcliffe's proposals. When they were brought to the Greek and Turkish governments in mid-December, Eden's government was crumbling. The prime minister himself was ill and soon to resign.

In spite of the inauspicious backdrop, Lennox-Boyd met with Prime Minister Karamanlis in Athens on 14 December 1956. The Greeks had received the proposals the day before. Lennox-Boyd explained that, after the establishment of a working constitution along the lines proposed by Lord Radcliffe, Her Majesty's Government 'would review the question of the application of self-determination'. After this vaguely hopeful message, Lennox-Boyd hit Karamanlis with the critical threat of partition. 'Because of the difficulty of the problem of the interests of the Greek and Turkish communities in Cyprus, when the time came for this review, HMG would be guided by the principle that the Turkish-Cypriots as well as the Greek-Cypriots should be allowed to exercise self-determination. Therefore HMG would not rule out the eventual partition of the island.'[21] The threat failed to move the Greek prime minister. Karamanlis attacked Radcliffe's proposals claiming that they were neither liberal nor democratic. The scope for self-government was 'of a very limited nature'. Karamanlis felt that 'on the question of the position of Archbishop Makarios [still intimately linked to terrorism in the British view] and of self-determination the views of HMG were far from those both of the Greek Government and of Archbishop Makarios himself'.[22] The non-elected governor retained too much power and no firm date for self-determination was mentioned. Karamanlis could not endorse Radcliffe's report. Greek-Cypriots were simply not being given enough.

The Greek reaction came as a great disappointment to many within the British government. Within the Foreign Office the reaction was particularly bitter. 'The visit to Athens went badly', wrote D'Arcy Patrick Reilly of the Southern Department:

> The Greeks were ungracious and ungenerous, and very stupid. They hardly bothered about self-determination, and concentrated on the constitution.... They complained that they had had not time to study it [Radcliffe's proposal], and yet within a few hours of Mr. Lennox-Boyd's very clear exposition they made up their minds to reject it, giving reasons that were nearly all trivial. They obviously wanted to pick holes and put the worst interpretation on everything.... My impression is that they were thoroughly frightened by the prospect of a constitution that worked, and were determined to prevent if it they could. They may be afraid that with self-government, enthusiasm for Enosis may wane.[23]

In spite of the anti-Greek rhetoric, the Foreign Office was still worried by the deterioration of relations with Athens. Members of the staff of the American embassy in Athens were fearful that the hostility of the Greek government could shift it away from the Atlantic Alliance altogether, and even tilt towards Moscow. As a result, both American and British policymakers hoped that the United States could use its influence to prevent the Greeks from rejecting the proposals outright so soon after they had been shared.[24] Instructions came in from the State Department to the American ambassador in Athens that he was to communicate to the Greek government 'that it would be unwise of them to react prematurely in an adverse sense to the Radcliffe proposals', and that Greece's attitude towards the proposals would determine America's reaction to Greece in the upcoming UN debate over Cyprus.[25]

The British ambassador in Athens, Sir Charles Peake, similarly tried to prevent an outright rejection. Peake suggested to Foreign Minister Averoff that the Greek government's public statement might admit that 'though the proposals at first sight did not seem to offer as much as had been hoped, the document was long and intricate and the Greek government would need further time for close study before any view could be pronounced'. Averoff responded with despondency, saying that no such course was possible as he was 'a "prisoner" of his government'.[26] On 19 December, the Foreign Office asked the American State Department for a positive statement about the plan and to apply direct pressure on the Greeks not to reject it so soon. Washington was receptive, but disagreed over the optimum timing; the Americans suggested issuing a statement 'in the very near future'.[27] A partial explanation for the slight difference in American and British strategy comes from the relative importance of Greece to both countries. Both American and British policymakers regarded Greece as an important ally, but two camps within the British government favoured Turkey over Greece if a black-and-white decision was required. The first group, from within the Foreign Office, considered Turkey to be Britain's most important asset in the Middle East, largely because of its dual role in NATO and the Baghdad Pact. The second group, within the British administration in Cyprus itself, felt that Turkish-Cypriot support and participation were essential to the day-to-day operations against EOKA, and knew that Turkey could provoke civil unrest on the island at will, which would dramatically complicate the security situation. The Americans took the different view that Greece and Turkey functioned like 'two blades of scissors' in relation to NATO. Each was 'presumed to be as important as [the] other'.[28] This attitude was reinforced by the influence of Greek-Americans on domestic politics and by American fears that Greece might drift away from NATO. As a result of these factors, the Americans were reluctant to back the Greeks into a corner.

In spite of the State Department's hesitation, a showdown was approaching. On 19 December, as the Foreign Office appealed to the State Department, Lennox-Boyd presented Radcliffe's report to the House of Commons. The colonial secretary supported it as a 'statesmanlike document', which represented 'a fair balance between the different and often conflicting interests which are involved'.[29] Crucially, he then clarified the British position on the issue of Cypriot self-determination and its bearing on partition arguing that self-determination needed to be applied equally to both communities in Cyprus. Turkish-Cypriots and Greek-Cypriots would 'be given freedom to decide for themselves their future status. In other words, Her Majesty's Government recognise that the exercise of self-determination in such a mixed population must include partition among the eventual options.'[30]

The premise that partition could not be ruled out – broached with the Greeks in private on 14 December – had now been repeated in Parliament for the whole world to hear. For the Greeks, it was the death knell for Radcliffe's proposals. As Foreign Minister Averoff recorded in his memoirs, 'this statement, made by the Colonial Secretary in Parliament . . . constituted an official declaration of intent, and as such it was binding. Thereafter the Greek government could not possibly agree even to discuss the Radcliffe proposals, although strong pressure was put upon it to do so.'[31] The British intent, however, had not been to bring about partition but to bring about Greek concessions through the *fear* of partition. Later the same evening, an official statement was issued from Athens. In it, the Greek government claimed that the proposals did not 'provide for the exercise of self-determination by the people of Cyprus' and did not 'comply with fundamental principles of the United Nations Charter'. The proposals were 'neither democratic nor liberal' and, while they granted 'the principle of majority in form – and that only in limited measure – they nevertheless suppress it in substance, by vesting the Governor with practically unlimited powers. . . . [T]he [Greek] Cabinet have unanimously decided that the proposals could not be considered as providing a basis for a solution of the Cyprus question.'[32]

Many British policymakers now expressed an open hostility to the Greek attitude. In their view, the Greeks had not examined the proposals in good faith. The precipitate rejection was evidence to them of how little attention had actually been given to Radcliffe's document. As Ambassador Peake wrote to London, the statements confirmed 'that the Greek Government took their negative decision on December 14, scarcely 24 hours after they had received the Radcliffe report and directly following the colonial secretary's conversation with Mr. Karamanlis'. The timing suggested to British officials that the Greeks had not 'given detailed consideration [to Radcliffe's proposals] but simply made it appear that they had been presented with a *fait accompli* . . . as soon as the Greek Government realized that Her Majesty's Government's proposals did not provide for self-determination within a fixed period, they determined from weakness to have nothing to do with them'.[33]

In all likelihood, Peake had misread the situation. The Greek rejection did not come after the closed-door meetings between Lennox-Boyd and Karamanlis; it followed immediately after the announcement of the possibility of partition in the House of Commons, not from the broader content of the constitutional proposals. Frustration on the Greek side was understandable. Although substantial concessions towards self-government were being given, the same obstacle that had doomed all constitutional proposals from Winster onwards remained. Because of strategic considerations and its alliance with Turkey, Britain was unwilling to pave the way for *enosis* except to hint at self-determination after a delay of a decade or more. Critically, a clear route to *enosis* seemed to be the only solution Greek-Cypriots were willing to accept. In Greek eyes, including partition as a possible denouement damaged the proposals beyond repair.

The official tone of the Greek rejection paled in comparison with the visceral condemnations from the Cypriot *enosis* movement. A leaflet from EOKA's political wing on 10 February 1957 denounced the Radcliffe exercise with unrestrained anger:

> The 'sold to the Colonialists' mind of Lord Radcliffe was for seven months pregnant with his legendary constitution for Cyprus. A year later he gave birth to

his spiritual son, but alas! It was a monster with arms of Democracy and the mind of a British dictator.... The worn-out colonialists seek with violence to impose on us this political monster, whilst they keep our Ethnarch imprisoned thousands of miles away from his people.[34]

An EOKA publication on 22 February decried the proposal with similar vehemence: 'No Radcliffe! Your constitution is not even applicable to negroes. It is a shame to try to convince a people with a better civilization than yours, your stubbornness to enforce it as being the proper one shows your audacity and impudence.'[35] It was only a foretaste of the chauvinism that was to define the violence to come.

For its part, the Turkish government hoped to use the Radcliffe proposals as a springboard towards partition. After meeting Prime Minister Menderes, Reilly conveyed to the foreign secretary that it was clear 'that the Turks have decided that, since HMG are committed to self-determination, the only solution is partition, and the sooner the better'.[36] Lennox-Boyd's presentation in the House of Commons had reinforced the view in the Turkish government that continued pressure on the British could make their goal of partitioning Cyprus a reality.

Turkish opinion and the widening gap

By December 1956, a great deal of Turkish diplomatic effort had already gone into making sure that Radcliffe's proposals would be supported by a statement confirming the right of the Turkish-Cypriots to self-determination. Just as Greek-Cypriot self-determination was a veil for *enosis*, advocacy of Turkish-Cypriot self-determination became a thin screen for partition (*taksim*). Many Turks and Turkish-Cypriots were adamantly opposed to the idea of Turks living under Greek rule. They were also concerned to maintain elements of Turkish culture on Cyprus. Their rhetoric, that Cyprus was geographically and historically part of Turkey, had not dimmed. The strongest argument on the Turkish side, however, was the premise that, if the principle of self-determination was to be applied on Cyprus, it would have to be applied to Greek- and Turkish-Cypriots equally.[37] British policymakers were sympathetic to this view.[38] Sympathy and implementation, however, were entirely different.

During late 1956, Prime Minister Menderes hammered away that partition was the only solution Turkey could accept and the ultimate sacrifice that it was willing to make.[39] Partition was the bogeyman of the *enosis* movement. Like the British use of Turkish-Cypriots in the island's police force, the concept of partition is seen by many Greek-Cypriots as another manifestation of the empire's policy of divide and rule. Britain had partitioned India in 1947 (with Radcliffe himself drawing the line). In 1948–9, a bloody series of wars created a de facto partition of Palestine into the Jewish state of Israel and remaining Palestinian territories that were soon swallowed up by Egypt and Jordan. According to this reasoning, the instability inherent in dividing the Greeks and Turks of Cyprus into two autonomous (or quasi-autonomous) units would necessitate a British presence and allow them to maintain control of the island. The issue, however, was more complex than this line of argument suggests.

Different parties within the British government professed different opinions on the subject. The damaging experiences in India and Palestine made many British policymakers wary of proceeding with a similar course in Cyprus. It would be difficult to implement as there was no geographical separation of the two communities. On a practical level, a divided Cyprus was not viewed as easier to control. Most British policymakers were convinced that partition would lead to a civil war within the island and possibly a regional war between Greece and Turkey. Such events would threaten rather than strengthen Britain's position in the region. British policymakers had been clear as early as 1955 that intercommunal strife in Cyprus 'would seriously impair the efficiency of Cyprus as a base'.[40] On the cynical side, some within the British government hoped that partition could be manipulated and used as a threat directed against the Greeks, in order to sustain British control of the island and delay concessions to the *enosis* movement. As the Radcliffe mission picked up steam, the British began to consider the issue of partition in depth and how it could be turned to their advantage.

On 7 June 1956, Sir John Martin from the Colonial Office, sent a secret report to Governor Harding on partition. It laid out some of the key points and also explained the divisions within the government on the issue. Martin told Harding that most senior officials in the Foreign Office, including the permanent secretary, Ivone Kirkpatrick, favoured the idea of partition largely due to their inclinations towards Turkey.[41] Martin and the Colonial Office were opposed to the idea, wishing instead 'to maintain undisputed British control'.[42] As a negotiating point, however, the concept had its uses. Martin believed that

> nothing can be better calculated than the threat of partition to cause the Greek-Cypriots to think twice before exercising their right of self-determination in order to secede from British sovereignty . . . . It also seems to me that possibly the threat of partition provides a more manageable stick to beat the Greeks over the head with than the 'ostensible alternative' of a tripartite administration which was proposed in Your Excellency's Appreciation.[43]

By mid-June 1956, the Turks were also aware that partition was being considered. They seized on the concept eagerly and compounded it with a threat. On 18 June, Suat Ürgüplü, the Turkish ambassador in London, visited the Foreign Office where he voiced his preference for partition. The threat came in his argument that 'a British withdrawal from Cyprus would modify the Lausanne Treaty of 1923 and endanger the Greeks of Istanbul'.[44] Abrogation of the Treaty of Lausanne was a threat for nothing less than the renewal of war between Greece and Turkey. It threw into the fire not only the status of Cyprus but also all the lands conceded by Turkey in 1923, as well as threatening the already vulnerable population of Greeks remaining in Istanbul. A Turkish threat of war over Cyprus was made even more clearly by Settar Iksel, the Turkish ambassador in Athens. In September 1956, in a series of meetings with the Greek foreign minister, Iksel 'had repeatedly mentioned war as a means for solving the Cyprus problem'.[45]

In Nicosia, Harding understood partition as a forcing mechanism to be used against the Greeks in order to leverage concessions. The governor communicated his support for the tactical discussion of partition, not its implementation, to the colonial secretary in a telegram from October 1956: 'By all means let us use the threat of partition as a bargaining counter in the exchanges that take place between the parties concerned in the search for a solution', he wrote, 'but I earnestly hope that we ourselves shall never come to regard it as anything other than a counsel of despair'.[46] This was a highly risky negotiating strategy. Britain's choice to invite Turkey to the Tripartite Conference in 1955 had fuelled Greek and Greek-Cypriot fears that Britain was actively seeking to involve Turkey in an issue that concerned only Greece, Great Britain and the people of Cyprus. The latest strategy of bluffing the Greeks with the threat of partition reinforced this view of Turkish-British collaboration. In Greek eyes, it also undermined Britain as an honest negotiator genuinely seeking a compromise settlement with Greek/Greek-Cypriot ambitions.

One of the strongest arguments against implementing partition was what carrying it out would mean in practice. Lloyd wrote to Lennox-Boyd on this issue on 8 August 1956, arguing that

> partition can only be regarded as the last expedient when everything else has failed. We only resorted to it in Ireland, in India and in Trieste when it became clear that there was no means of reconciling the divergent views of the interested parties; and I do not think we should put it forward for Cyprus until the same situation arises.... We have never fully worked out a partition plan [for Cyprus].[47]

He suggested to Lennox-Boyd that Radcliffe should see the ethnic map of Cyprus (which would demonstrate the near insurmountable obstacles to a partition in Cyprus due to the geographical mixing of the two communities) 'and give him an account of the various ideas which have occurred to us'.[48] Greek- and Turkish-Cypriot villages were spread throughout the island. Only the mountainous region around Troodos at the island's centre was composed entirely of Greek-Cypriot villages. Everywhere else the two communities were interlaced. All the major cities had considerable Turkish minorities. Ironically, the largest urban concentration of Turkish-Cypriots was in Paphos in the west; the smallest was in Kyrenia, closest to Turkey on the island's north coast.

Governor Harding agreed with Lloyd in seeing partition as nothing less than 'a confession of failure and only to be contemplated as a lesser evil than Enosis'.[49] Prime Minister Macmillan concurred.

> If we give it [Cyprus] to Greece, there will be a war between Greece and Turkey. If we 'partition', it is a confession of failure – means (perhaps) civil war in the island followed by full war between Greece and Turkey. We really want only air-bases for ourselves, for Baghdad pact and general ME and Persian Gulf Defence.[50]

With so much pressure from senior policymakers against partition, it is understandable that it was never implemented. Past experiences, combined with the particular difficulties on the ground, made it appear a poor choice. The Chiefs of Staff supported this view, although they did not rule out partition permanently. The military's position was as clear as it was cynical. Partition was 'preferable to either: (a) unconditional Enosis, or (b) a continuing deterioration of relations between Greece, Turkey and the United Kingdom, and a continuing decline in our international prestige as an enlightened and liberal power'. In practice, any partition scheme would have to ensure 'the retention of certain areas as British territory in perpetuity in order to meet our continuing military requirements here after partition had taken effect'. Finally, the Chiefs of Staff 'agreed that after a period of probably some ten or fifteen years our military requirements here are likely to be much reduced, and it is then and then only that we could contemplate putting partition into effect'.[51]

The different sides of the partition debate also reflected the different priorities of the actors within Britain. While the Colonial Office and government of Cyprus wished to maintain British control and avoid another Palestine, the Foreign Office seemed more willing to bow to partition as a means of ending the dispute and putting relations with Turkey back on the right foot. However, it is important to remember that, even among its advocates, partition was not seen as a positive solution, but merely as the least bad option. It would be costly, and 'would undoubtedly entail great hardship and suffering'. At the same time, the problems in Cyprus were based 'on the traditional and very longstanding conflict between Greeks and Turks' and could only be solved by 'an agreement between the United Kingdom, Greece and Turkey'. In these circumstances, partition was not a solution but 'a means of bringing both parties to their senses'.[52] Forces within the Colonial Office remained convinced that, instead of helping to soothe the intercommunal tensions, partition would exacerbate the divide. Separate education and separate control of communal affairs would assure that 'the rift between the two communities will grow still wider and deeper'.[53] A deepened rift would multiply the difficulties of maintaining British control and diminish the utility of the island for Britain's strategic needs.

The partition debate highlighted the significant degree of disagreement between the Greek and Turkish governments on an acceptable final solution. It also demonstrated that successes in the field against EOKA were subordinate to larger geopolitical factors. Harding made this fact clear in a telegram to Lennox-Boyd:

> I must repeat what I have said so many times in recent months: that no matter how successful we may be against EOKA; no matter what happens to Radcliffe's proposals; there can be no real or lasting solution to the Cyprus problem without agreement between the United Kingdom, Greece and Turkey on the question of self-determination and the future international status of the island. . . . The gap between them [the governments of Greece and Turkey] is clearly very wide and it is perhaps the recognition of that fact that has recently led both governments and some of our own people to toy with the idea of partition as a possible solution.[54]

As Harding hinted, both the Greek and Turkish governments took the idea of partition seriously – the Greeks fearfully and the Turks eagerly. In early November 1956, the Foreign Office informed the British ambassador in Ankara that the Turks were lobbying heavily for partition as the only chance for a solution. Menderes even claimed that he was convinced the Greeks would possibly accept the idea as well.[55] Here, Menderes was either exaggerating or bluffing. In public, and in negotiations with both British and American diplomats, partition remained a non-starter for the Greeks.

By the end of November 1956, it looked as if the internal government battle within Britain had been won by the parties that unequivocally opposed such a drastic step. A committee of the Chiefs of Staff presented a memorandum on the 'Military Implications of the Partition of Cyprus', which hammered the point home. The report continued to emphasize the importance of British military bases on the island for NATO, the Baghdad Pact and Middle East policy. It concluded that '[i]f Cyprus is to be of any significant value to HMG, NATO or the Baghdad Pact there is an overwhelming military argument against partition'.[56] This report provides further evidence that in the cynical diplomacy over Cyprus, Britain hoped to maintain a unified island (at least during this period). It was thought that any physical separation would undermine, not support, Britain's strategic needs and desires in the region.

In spite of the recommendations against partition, its threat was implicit in the presentation of the Radcliffe proposals to the Greeks and explicit in subsequent parliamentary debates. This was the compromise chosen by British policymakers. They hoped that, given time and careful study of Radcliffe's plan, the Turks would 'understand the many and great safeguards for Turkey which it contains' and therefore move away from partition as a solution.[57] This hope was slim. As the British ambassador in Ankara admitted, 'I fear, however, that the Turks are pathological on the subject of self-determination and will adamantly refuse to see merits in any plan which fixes a date for it however hedged around by conditions and safeguards.'[58]

British policymakers were now in an impossible position. The Turks would not tolerate the essential condition for satisfying Greek demands. The inclusion of partition in Lennox-Boyd's presentation of Radcliffe's proposals had doomed them to failure from a Greek point of view. In Turkish eyes, the British had not gone far enough. In spite of moving away from partition, Britain could not back away from its broader commitments to Turkey. The Greek-Cypriots were leading the campaign of violence on the island, and Turkey was viewed, in many quarters, as Britain's more important ally. The foreign secretary captured this reality in a letter to the American secretary of state on 19 June 1956: 'Turkey is by far our most solid asset in the Middle East; and I am most anxious that in pursuing the shadow of Greek compliances we should not lose the substance of Turkish friendship.'[59] Subsequent events in the region, such as the Suez crisis, the collapse of the Anglo-Jordanian pact and the coup in Iraq, all added to the importance of Turkey to British policymakers.[60] In March 1957, concurrent with successes in Cyprus, the ceasefire and the Jordanian troubles, Macmillan wrote to Selwyn Lloyd: '[I]t is absolutely vital not to prejudice our relations with the Turks especially now that the Baghdad Pact is looming large in the world.'[61]

As Turkey's stock increased in London, the propaganda war in favour of partition continued in Cyprus. Turkish-Cypriots had begun publishing an English version of the weekly newspaper, *Halkın Sesi*, in April 1956. Article after article attacked the idea of Turks living under Greek rule. 'We have lived in Cyprus with Greeks for centuries. We know what to expect from them', began one article ominously. 'We know what they feel about us and how they think of us. The *megalo-idea* [sic] in them is too much inculcated to be easily forgotten; their Church has preached to them to push the Turk down and root him out of Cyprus eventually.'⁶² In December, just two days before Radcliffe's report was to be published, the paper ran a story about Greek atrocities (entirely unsubstantiated) committed against Turks living in Thrace. The timing of these fabrications was not coincidental.

On 19 December, as the Greek rejection of Radcliffe's proposals was being prepared, the British ambassador in Ankara telegrammed the Foreign Office that 'the Turkish Government were prepared to acquiesce generally in Her Majesty's Government's proposals owing to their inclusion of partition as putting an end to the possibility of self-determination leading to Enosis'.⁶³ Lennox-Boyd's presentation in the House of Commons pleased Ankara while it infuriated Athens. The Turkish prime minister had also approached the American government about pressuring the Greeks to accept partition 'as being the only means of reaching a settlement'.⁶⁴ Menderes continued to play this angle two weeks later in a speech before the Turkish Grand National Assembly. Fixating on the promise of partition, Menderes 'said that the Turkish government consider this statement of Mr. Lennox-Boyd's [promising the application of self-determination equally to Greek- and Turkish-Cypriots] a definite undertaking by the British Government, which Turkey accepted as a safeguard for the rights of the Turkish minority and the vital strategic interests of Turkey'.⁶⁵

The British gambit on partition had gone spectacularly wrong. Instead of mollifying Turkish fears and leveraging the Greeks into supporting Radcliffe's compromise, the mention of partition had galvanized Turkish hopes. In Ankara, Radcliffe's proposals had been seized on not as a substitute for partition but as a stepping stone towards it. As Ambassador Bowker wrote to Selwyn Lloyd, '[B]y thus barring the road to Enosis, Her Majesty's Government have removed Turkey's main objection to a Constitution as being likely to be exploited by the Greek-Cypriots and the Greek Government as a means of achieving union of the Island with Greece.' Turkish interest in a constitution had been 'scant' in early December; now a constitution pointing the way towards partition was the only solution. Radcliffe's proposals were seen as 'a bargain whereby they have accepted the idea of a Constitution in return for Her Majesty's Government's acceptance of the principle of partition'.⁶⁶ It was not the compromise Britain was looking for.

Self-delusion and self-determination

Partition's spectre had killed the Radcliffe proposals and, by illustrating the major gap between Greek and Turkish interests in Cyprus, had dead-ended this new path of negotiations for a solution. The hopeful atmosphere surrounding the hiatus of violence in Cyprus began to evaporate. The Turkish government must have slowly come to the realization that London was reluctant to implement partition, so they set about trying to change the circumstances. Through leaflets, radio addresses and newspaper editorials, Turkish nationalists led the charge in favour of partition.

On 20 January 1957, a Turkish mob set fire to Greek-owned homes and businesses in Nicosia's old town. Two days later *The Times* reported that 'no fewer than 70 fires were started in Nicosia . . . and five of them developed into major outbreaks'.[67] The next day the body of a Greek-Cypriot was found beaten to death after clashes between Greek- and Turkish-Cypriot youths. The violence was reminiscent of the riots in Istanbul and Izmir in the final days of the Tripartite Conference in 1955. Turkish extremists, speaking with fire and fists, were making their own push for partition. As the CIC reported on 22 January, 'Turkish-Cypriots continue to regard the partition of Cyprus as a possibility and support for such a solution of the Cyprus problem is gaining ground.'[68]

EOKA seemed unable to respond to the Turkish-Cypriot provocation. Their leadership had suffered significant losses. Markos Drakos, a senior EOKA member, was killed in a gun-battle in Troodos on the night of 18–19 January. On 21 January, a Greek national, referred to as Karademas, was captured along with the mountain gang leader Kyriacos Matsis. Elsewhere on the island, security forces recaptured a Grivas intimate, Polykarpos Georghiades.[69] Altogether, sixteen 'known hardcore terrorists', comprising 'just under half the known leading personalities in EOKA', were killed or captured during operation 'Black Mak' in the Troodos Mountains.[70]

EOKA struck back as best it could. On 25 January 1957, a Greek-Cypriot general strike shut down Nicosia in protest against the Turkish violence. In Famagusta, a British civilian working for the war department was shot and killed. A few days later a Greek-Cypriot policeman was also killed in a gun attack. Retaliation, however, was sporadic and ineffective. The correspondent for *The Times* in Nicosia speculated that Grivas had lost control of the organization.[71] The Turkish push for partition also opened a new front for EOKA; now it had to combat Turkish-Cypriots as well. In the minds of the advocates of the *enosis* cause, there was a clear link between Britain and Turkey. An EOKA bulletin on 2 February 1957 encouraged the Greeks of Cyprus to 'not be afraid of the four-legged unrestrained beasts of Britain and Turkey who torture you and destroy your properties. Strike them with everything you can. Honour and glory to those who sacrifice themselves for the freedom of your Cyprus.'[72]

Successes by British security forces offset the failure of the Radcliffe proposals, but no new movement towards a political solution in Cyprus came out of these British victories. British attempts to organize a new Tripartite Conference were shot down.[73] Greece also rejected the idea of NATO mediation. Averoff explained this in a conversation with John Foster Dulles on 13 February: 'I told him that most if not all the NATO allies would support Britain, which would mean, in effect, that they were voting against us. If the United States took the same line, the people of Greece would see no reason for remaining in NATO.'[74]

At the end of February 1957, the Cyprus issue reappeared at the UN. This time, Greece was looking for a resolution condemning British atrocities in Cyprus. Such a resolution was not possible, but a modified Indian resolution was adopted in the General Assembly by a vote of seventy-six to two.[75] It was brief but potentially significant:

> The General Assembly, having considered the question of Cyprus, believing that the solution of this problem requires an atmosphere of peace and freedom of expression, expresses the earnest desire that a peaceful, democratic and just

solution will be found in accord with the purposes and principles of the Charter of the United Nations, and the hope that negotiations will be resumed and continued to this end.[76]

The wording of the resolution gave each party some degree of hope. On the Greek side, the phrase concerning the resumption of negotiations was thought to mean that talks would soon begin again 'between Harding and Makarios or more generally between the Cypriots and the British Government'.[77] Reeling from the blows of the security forces and the emergence of violence with Turkish-Cypriots, EOKA took advantage of the resolution to put forward its conditional ceasefire. After conferring with Athens, EOKA published a declaration on 14 March:

> Our Organisation in compliance with the spirit of the United Nations resolution expressing the wish for a peaceful and just settlement of the Cyprus question in accordance with the principles of the United Nations Charter, and in order to facilitate the resumption of negotiations between the British government and the real spokesman for the Cypriot people, Archbishop Makarios, declares that it is willing to order the suspension of operations as soon as Ethnarch Makarios is released.[78]

A week later, at the Bermuda Conference, Cyprus was front and centre for Anglo-American relations. British policymakers clung to the position that, if terrorism stopped, 'discussions could take place with Greek and Turkish-Cypriots on Lord Radcliffe's proposals'.[79] Shifting discussions back to engagement with Cypriots, however, would require the release of Makarios. President Eisenhower, aware that international opinion was strongly in favour of this concession, encouraged the British to allow Makarios to leave the Seychelles.[80] On 24 March, Macmillan conveyed to the Foreign Office his willingness to release the archbishop. The wheels were set in motion and on 17 April the ethnarch arrived in Athens where he was greeted by cheering crowds. New proposals from London, however, were not forthcoming.

In Cyprus, the ceasefire held through the summer of 1957, even as the nationalist rhetoric heated up. The directionless and eerie calm on the island did little to improve Governor Harding's opinion of the situation. The field marshal, who had soldiered through months of pedantic negotiations with Makarios, doggedly combated EOKA, endured abuse from Greek- and Turkish-Cypriots alike and faithfully attempted to fit the round peg of London's policies into the square-holed realities of the island, had finally reached the end of his will. On 19 September 1957, to the apparent surprise of the government in London, Harding sent a letter to Lennox-Boyd asking to be replaced. The field marshal pleaded a number of reasons: his wife's ill health, the maintenance of their home and several properties back in England, along with an 'accumulation of private business and personal matters'.[81] The major reason, however, was that events in Cyprus were deadlocked with no prospect of a resolution; Harding had no desire to continue.

As Harding explained to Lennox-Boyd, '[I]t seems more than likely that discussions in Cyprus will drag on inconclusively for some months and possibly into the New Year.'

The field marshal, who had also suffered from a serious bout of influenza, had had enough of Cyprus. In his letter he proposed to leave the island no later than the end of October 'with no idea of returning'. He suggested that his appointment could officially end sometime around the end of the year.[82] Harding's frustration became more obvious as the note continued. There had been talk in July about ending the job 'in a blaze of glory', but he was convinced otherwise: '[F]rankly, I don't think there is ever going to be much glory to be got out of this business. . . . I am afraid I cannot see my way to wait for it indefinitely.' He closed in much the same vein: '[F]orgive me for bothering you with this so soon after your return, but I cannot go on much longer in the present state of complete uncertainty about the future.'[83]

Lennox-Boyd, although surprised by the turn of events, accepted. 'I have now been able to discuss your letter of the 19th September with the Prime Minister,' he replied on 3 October. 'Needless to say, it will be a very great blow to us all to feel that you are no longer to be at the helm in Cyprus, but both the Prime Minister and I are convinced that it would be very wrong to ask you to reconsider your decision and we agree that you should come home.'[84] The Cabinet turned its attention to finding a suitable successor. By the time of Lennox-Boyd's response, this question was already being 'actively' pursued.[85] Lennox-Boyd persuaded Harding to keep on until the end of October and concluded his brief reply: 'This is not the time to tell you of the intense gratitude we all feel for your superlative work – but I hope you really know it in your heart.'[86] The colonial secretary's note was followed two weeks later by a letter of gratitude from the prime minister. 'I cannot allow the announcement of your impending departure from Cyprus to pass without letting you know personally my feelings. Your tenure of office as Governor of Cyprus has been an extraordinary example of public service and devotion', wrote Macmillan. 'I cannot think of a tougher assignment being given to any man nor can I think of any man who could have discharged it with greater distinction.'[87]

Harding was to be replaced by Sir Hugh Mackintosh Foot, a career civil servant and colonial administrator. British policymakers hoped that the challenges of post-insurgency Cyprus would be better addressed by a man of words than a man of war. In a telegram to Lennox-Boyd on 3 October, Foot expressed his interest in replacing Harding. 'I confirm that I should very much like to be considered for Cyprus appointment and believe I could do a good job if there were a sporting chance of working representative institutions.'[88] Foot proceeded to a bit of lobbying, assuring the colonial secretary that he would 'loyally carry out all decisions of HMG [and] would certainly work wholeheartedly for a settlement that would not be unacceptable to HMG, the Turks and the Greeks'.[89] On the key issue of partition, Foot made his stance clear: 'I believe partition would be a disaster and am bound to say that if all efforts to reach agreed solution failed I should wish to feel free to ask to be replaced rather than have to put into effect a policy which I felt to be wrong.'[90] The new governor would bring a new approach to familiar problems, but, like his predecessor, he would not accept the compromise of partition.

Partitioning Cyprus, however, remained the preoccupation of Turkish policymakers. Through 1957, Turkish newspapers and politicians continued their propaganda blitz for partition. They tacked in various directions to catch the prevailing wind: Turks living under Greek rule would be discriminated against or annihilated; Greece was an unreliable ally for NATO and the West; Cyprus could not be handed over to the Greeks because 60 per cent of the island's Greek speakers were 'Communist sympathizers' who would work to hand the island, and Greece, over to the Soviets. Little of these hysterical accusations stuck in either London or Washington.

Britain's release of Makarios in March 1957 prompted a particularly violent reaction. In an April editorial for *Halkın Sesi*, Dr Kütchük wrote that partition was 'the only lasting solution' in Cyprus. 'Constitutional offers', like that of Radcliffe, 'can never be a remedy for the Cyprus ills. EOKA did not take up arms for the sake of a Constitution – its warcry has been enosis and coincided with the Greek policy in Greece.'[91] In May, another Kütchük article called into question Turkey's relationship with Britain. 'The release of Makarios', he wrote, 'and the regrettable events which ensued in Greece have set the Turkish intellectuals thinking on the value of Turkey's friendship and alliance to Britain and conversely on the value of British Friendship and alliance to Turkey.'[92]

The deterioration in Greco-Turkish relations in Cyprus during the summer of 1957 was apparent to Harding. A paper was prepared by the Nicosia secretariat for Ambassador Bowker in Ankara. While it recognized that relations between Greeks in Turks had been positive in the past, the communal tensions from the two years since the start of the EOKA insurgency could not be denied. The decision of the *enosis* movement to adopt violence in 1955 was identified as the key turning point in the relationship between the two communities.[93] The report also emphasized that the actions of Dr Kütchük had 'done nothing to improve relations between the communities'. In fact, the British reported, Kütchük had 'been particularly careful to exaggerate every instance of communal ill-feeling which may have become apparent.'[94]

The ethnic tensions meant that, in spite of the lack of EOKA activity, all was not well in Cyprus. The cauldron was boiling again. Worse still for security forces, EOKA was ready to return to the field. George Sinclair, acting governor between Harding's departure on 4 November and Foot's arrival on 3 December, wrote to Alan Lennox-Boyd 'that having saved their nucleus of leadership last spring, EOKA are now as powerful and well organised as they ever were. Their grip on the Greek-Cypriot population, which had shown signs of weakening during the summer, has been entirely restored by their recent activities.'[95] If nothing else, Sinclair's report demonstrated that Harding's intelligence services were effective enough to identify accurately EOKA's capabilities even if they were not in a position to destroy them. In a flat admission of failure, Sinclair confided, 'EOKA has seized the initiative from us. This has been made the easier for them by our own reluctance to take full scale and effective counter measures, and thus to bring about a clash which might reduce the prospects of success for the international initiatives now being launched.'[96]

Sinclair's message also hinted at even darker times ahead. While EOKA's power renewed itself, 'a *Volkan* leaflet has appeared which promises that Makarios will be assassinated if he is allowed to return; and the leading Turkish newspaper has proclaimed that the Cyprus government is "losing its authority" and that the Turkish community is being driven to take up arms in its own defence'.[97] This last development was particularly serious. If Turkish-Cypriots chose to take security into their own hands, British control of the island would degenerate into chaos similar to that of Palestine a decade earlier. For the British, it was a nightmare scenario.

The deputy governor's words would prove prophetic. On 27 November 1957, EOKA launched its first attack on security forces since March, shooting a British soldier in the face.[98] On 29 November, leaflets distributed around Cyprus's main towns announced the formation of the TMT.

In theory, its mandate was to protect Turks from Greek aggression and to work towards partition. It was no accident that it announced itself after both the renewal of EOKA attacks and the departure of Harding. TMT's leaflets surpassed EOKA and even *Volkan* in brutality and jingoism. 'How much longer will you wait to throw off your chains of slavery?' it demanded of the island's Turkish minority. 'You are born Turks. You are heroes and cannot become slaves.' Through the campaign for *enosis* Greek-Cypriots were attempting 'to destroy the very roots of Turkdom as they have done in Crete'. The example of Crete stood out as a central rallying cry in the minds of TMT and its supporters. The forced exchange of populations, the end of a Turkish presence on the island and its unification with Greece were precisely what Ankara sought to prevent in Cyprus. Greece had 'annihilated the Turks in Crete, Dodecanese and Western Thrace, and has been nourishing the same desire for Cypriot Turks'.[99] Instead, the Turks looked to other recent history for inspiration, harshly reminding those fighting for *enosis*: '[T]hese disgusting creatures [the Greeks] got a good licking on 30th August (1922). Their "*Megali Idea*" was drowned in the waters of Smyrna. These creatures memory is poor, for they have forgotten the past all too soon. Only a Turkish "smack-in-the-face" can bring them to their senses.'[100]

Cyprus was indeed on the threshold of a new phase, but it was not the constitutional compromise and extension of the *status quo ante* that the British had hoped for. Instead Britain was now caught in a tide of nationalism and intolerance as the two communities attempted to claim the future of Cyprus for their own. This change doomed British sovereignty once and for all. Instead of progress towards peace, 1958 would be characterized by an EOKA resurgence and by ethnic violence on a scale that approached civil war.

9

On all fronts

EOKA, TMT and the threat of civil war

> *The road to Enosis is not through Athens, but through the cemetery.*[1]
> – Leaflet from the Turkish-Cypriot organisation 'Volkan', December 1956.

In spite of the recrudescence of EOKA violence, Sir Hugh Foot's arrival as governor in December 1957 represented another new hope for peace. By replacing a soldier with a career civil servant, London conveyed the message that its goal was a peaceful solution and a possible relaxation of the emergency measures in force on Cyprus. Foot also had links to the island, having served as the colonial secretary of Cyprus between 1943 and 1945. While some Greek-Cypriots reacted positively, the change in leadership reinforced the fears of many Turks and Turkish-Cypriots that London was no longer willing to stand firm against terrorism. Foot's aversion to partition further inflamed Turkish attitudes. Foot brought not only new qualifications but also a concrete peace proposal, informed by an approach of Prime Minister Harold Macmillan, to solve the problem.

In spite of Foot's commitment to finding a negotiated solution, his new peace proposals – like so many previous incarnations – faced old obstacles both in Cyprus and abroad. These proposals would also confront new challenges, undermining any move towards peace for most of 1958. During this critical time, EOKA renewed violence not only against the British but also against the Greek-Cypriot left. Turkish-Cypriots also took up arms for the first time and conflict between the Greek- and Turkish-Cypriot communities exploded in a brief but bloody cycle of intercommunal violence in the summer of 1958. There was, however, a light at the end of this tortured tunnel. The escalating threat of war between Turkey and Greece, the near fracturing of NATO and critical international developments beyond Cyprus finally brought the various sides to the peace table. By the start of 1959, the framework of an agreement had been reached. Although the agreement would not prove a lasting solution of the island's problems, it provided an end to the violence and opened a new chapter of Cypriot history. For much of 1958, however, pessimism reigned and a wider conflict seemed menacingly imminent.

While Greek-Cypriots, led by EOKA, were responsible for bringing an armed struggle to Cyprus, the new and pernicious phase of intercommunal violence was directly provoked by Turkish-Cypriots. Turkish-Cypriots acted to further their goal of partition by proving that the two communities could not coexist. Intercommunal conflict was preceded by conflict *within* each of the two communities along political lines. Within both groups, the forces of the nationalist right carried out a campaign of violence and intimidation designed to secure their supremacy and undermine any left-wing opposition to their respective nationalist goals of *enosis* and partition. British policymakers had few effective answers to the degree of violence confronting them and became more convinced that their sovereignty over the entire island was both unsustainable and undesirable.

'The . . . behaviour of Greeks and Turks seems temporarily reversed'

When he arrived in Cyprus, Hugh Foot already enjoyed the reputation of serving as a senior official in a number of former colonies as they made their transition to independence. Some years later, Michael Foot, Sir Hugh's brother, described his sibling's career in less than flattering terms for the *Evening Standard*:

> He became . . . Assistant British Resident in Trans-Jordan, Chief Secretary in Nigeria, Captain-General of Jamaica, and Governor and Commander-in-Chief in Cyprus. One common feature may be discerned in the modern history of all these territories. All of them, after a suitable period of unrest, riot and rebellion, have been removed from the aegis, direct or otherwise, of the British Parliament. Working himself out of one job after another and hauling down the flag a ceremonial occasions, Sir Hugh has moved on elsewhere to apply the same infallible touch.[2]

Independence for Cyprus, however, was not Foot's mandate. The most pressing issue for his administration was achieving Greco-Turkish cooperation over Cyprus and bringing together a solution that restored peace, while maintaining some degree of British control on the island. Foot's ideas for a solution reflected the current thinking in Downing Street, codified several months before his appointment. On 9 July 1957, Prime Minister Macmillan informed the Cabinet that the government once again needed to 'take a fresh initiative to break the present deadlock'.[3] Macmillan's memorandum hit a few key points that were evidence of both consistency and evolution within British policy. Cyprus was now recognized as 'not a Colonial problem but an international one'. As a result, '[n]o solution will be acceptable which does not satisfy the interests of the United Kingdom, Greece and Turkey'. As from the very beginning of the conflict, the interest of the British government was 'to secure . . . essential military needs', although it was now acknowledged that the government needed 'to reduce . . . [Britain's] Colonial commitment'. As in the past, there was an acknowledgement that Turkey was 'mainly concerned to ensure that the island . . . never pass wholly under the control of Greece'. Greece continued to demand *enosis*, but had to 'be convinced that it cannot be attained'.[4]

Macmillan's proposed solution was a tridominium plan. Britain would retain certain sovereign base areas but surrender the rest of the island 'to a condominium of the United Kingdom, Greece and Turkey, who would jointly share the sovereignty between them'.[5] The rest of the island would be ruled by a governor chosen by the three powers, or, if they could not agree, by the other members of NATO. The administration of the island would basically be along the lines proposed by Lord Radcliffe in his rejected constitution from December 1956.[6] This proposal would not be easy to implement but would avoid further commitments of 'a disproportionate amount' of Britain's military strength. It would also avoid the unacceptable alternative of partition, which would not only 'be a confession of failure' but also 'involve a grave risk of open conflict between Greece and Turkey'.[7] In the end, by trying to placate both Greece and Turkey, tridominium pleased neither.

British policymakers debated tridominium as 1957 wore on, but without a conclusion. By the time of Foot's arrival in Cyprus in late 1957, he had worked out a modified version of this idea. Foot's plan, as proposed in January 1958, centred on four points designed to give something to all parties involved. For the British, a seven-year period would pass 'before any final decision' about the island's status. This would allow British policymakers to reshape their strategic posture in the Eastern Mediterranean without having to deal with a radical change in Cyprus.[8] Britain would retain base areas on Cyprus in full sovereignty.[9] To please the Greek-Cypriots, Archbishop Makarios would be returned to the island, and the state of emergency would be ended. On Christmas Eve 1957, the new governor announced three further goodwill gestures directed towards the Greek-Cypriot community: the reopening of a Greek school in Larnaca 'which had been closed as a punitive measure'; the release of 100 detainees, including all eleven women in custody; and 'the removal of restriction on 600 people who had been required under the Emergency Regulations to stay in their villages and report once a week to the police'.[10]

Establishing 'negotiations in the island with leaders of the two communities to evolve a system of self-government' was a sop to Turkish-Cypriot aspirations to equal treatment as a special minority. Finally, to please both the Greek and Turkish governments, there would be 'an assurance that no final decision would be taken at the end of the five- or seven-year period which was not acceptable to Greeks *and* Turks alike'.[11] As with so many aspects of the problem, positive gestures towards one side were met with hostility and mistrust by another. The release of the detainees, in particular, confirmed the worst fears in Turkish quarters that Foot's appointment represented a weakening of British resolve against EOKA. In spite of Turkish fears, the peace plan retained several features that the Turks should have found appealing. Self-determination would take place seven years after the end of the emergency and 'the Turkish-Cypriots no less than the Greek-Cypriots should be given the right of self-determination as a community'. Moreover, the British government, in another concession, acknowledged that it would accept any solution 'approved by the Greek and Turkish Governments and by both communities in Cyprus' provided that it allowed for the retention of the sovereign bases.[12]

In internal discussions, Foot proposed that a Turkish base could be established on the island to further allay Turkish fears. The new governor did not see a problem with this course and thought that both Greece and Britain would have no reason to object.[13] In this assessment, however, he was mistaken and it was his own military rather than the government in Athens which protested. Major General Douglas Kendrew, the chief of operations in Cyprus, launched a particularly scathing attack. Kendrew wrote to the vice-chief of the Imperial General Staff, Lieutenant General Sir William Stratton: 'On my return here I was absolutely horrified to discover how far the idea of granting a Turkish base in Cyprus had gone.'[14] Kendrew had come to Cyprus in early 1956 as part of Harding's security reforms. During the Second World War, he had commanded a brigade in North Africa and Italy. He later served as the commander of the British brigade of the Commonwealth Division in the Korean War. A four-time recipient of the Distinguished Service Order, and a former England rugby international, the tough career soldier had concerns with the military understanding of his new superior, Foot.

Kendrew listed four major arguments against the proposed Turkish base. First, any such announcement would 'almost certainly lead to an explosion from EOKA'. Second, 'a Turkish base in the island ... [would] provide complete and uncontrollable cover for the introduction of arms for the Turkish-Cypriots', in a manner that the government of Cyprus would be unable to control. Third, the Turks would regard it as 'a minor form of partition [and] a springboard for seizure of a part (or indeed of the whole) of the island'. Finally, 'a rallying point of this nature for the Turkish-Cypriots ... [would] ensure continual clashes with the Greek-Cypriot population and that no form of Government in the island will be able to function unless it acquiesce supinely in Turkish demands'. In other words, a Turkish base on Cyprus would represent a major threat to the internal security of the island and to the British position there. The whole idea, concluded Kendrew, was an 'absolutely scandalous piece of political opportunism ... entered upon with criminal frivolity'. Urgent action by the Chiefs of Staff was necessary to eliminate it as a possibility.[15]

Kendrew's attitude was symptomatic of the attitude many in the military and security forces had towards their new commander-in-chief. Lacking Harding's military background, Foot was exposed to the accusations that he failed to understand the severity of the security situation and the intricacies of intelligence and tactical operations, and that he lacked the resolve to implement effective countermeasures against terrorism. Even before raising the issue of the base, Kendrew had already been highly sceptical of the structure of Foot's peace initiative in his assessment of its security implications from December 1957. Kendrew admitted to Foot that the assessment was 'inevitably a depressing document since, as you are well aware, the risks are indeed very great and I should be failing in my duty if I left you in any doubt as to their magnitude'.[16] Kendrew enumerated a number of concerns, each of which betrayed his belief that Foot was incapable of fully understanding the situation. If EOKA wished to resume the offensive after the implementation of a peace plan, either immediately or at a later date, the organization would 'be far more effective than now and will have the complete initiative'.[17] By suspending operations against EOKA during ceasefires, British intelligence would be chasing the game if violence were renewed. Deferring violence would be extremely dangerous and, in Kendrew's opinion, the longer the deferment, the greater the danger. Foot's peace plan threatened to alienate Turks, 'both locally and in Turkey'. This had to 'be avoided at all costs' because of the security implications on the island. With regard to the Turks there was 'no use assessing what is done in terms of real damage . . . it must be assessed in terms of how they choose to see it'. Kendrew saw two key areas that had to be secured before the military, security and intelligence forces in Cyprus would 'take the gamble' of supporting Foot's proposals. First, obtaining support from the opposition Labour Party would help convince the Turks that a new government in London 'would not let them down on self-determination'. Second, Grivas had to be removed from the island. Kendrew saw this as 'a sticking point in relation to the "peace" plan' and urged Foot to accept it.[18]

Kendrew's preoccupation with Turkish attitudes was shared by others in the Cyprus government. The deputy governor, George Sinclair, noted on the memorandum that '[t]he complete and permanent alienation of the Turks, both locally and in Turkey, *must* be avoided'. In order to do this, Turkey and the Turkish-Cypriots had to be convinced that self-determination would be applied equally in Cyprus after the seven years stipulated in the plan. 'If we fail to persuade the Turks of this', he concluded, 'and if we also fail to come to terms with the Greek-Cypriots, our position then in the island without the support of either community may well become untenable.'[19] The Foreign Office, worried about its policy goals in the Eastern Mediterranean and the Middle East, focused on the relationship with Turkey as its priority. As negotiations for a solution to the Cyprus problem proceeded, the British routinely brought their proposals to Turkey first during this period, largely because the Turks were seen as the largest potential obstacle to peace.[20] Concerns regarding Turkish-Cypriot opinion were shared by the government of Cyprus. Foot and his colleagues knew that the maintenance of security on the island would be a nightmare in the face of Turkish-Cypriot opposition or in the event of conflict between Greek- and Turkish-Cypriots. In a letter to Foot – written when the governor was in London for consultations – Sinclair reiterated that the government's main worry was 'the reaction of the Turks which overshadows everything else'.[21]

Foot recognized the concerns of Kendrew and Sinclair, and understood the potential for a strong and hostile Turkish reaction. After receiving Kendrew's assessment, he admitted to Sinclair that 'we must be prepared for an explosion from the Turks and everything will depend on how big the explosion is and how frightened people here are by it'.[22] The situation was delicate. In the past, Greek refusals had disrupted compromise attempts. Now, by providing apparent concessions to the Greek side, Foot risked the alienation of the Turks. The impasse represented, in microcosm, the obstacles facing the British in Cyprus from the very beginning. Foot returned to Cyprus from London on 18 January with the agreement of the Cabinet for his plan. He was aware of the difficulties, saying on his return that 'he thought a start could be made towards a Cyprus solution – if peace were maintained'.[23] At the same time, Selwyn Lloyd, the foreign secretary, was in Ankara lobbying the Turkish government for its support for the latest proposals.

The Turks, both on the mainland and in Cyprus, would have none of it. To emphasize their opposition, hundreds of Turkish-Cypriot youths and students took to the streets of Nicosia and Famagusta in protest on 21 January 1958. They carried banners calling for partition, denouncing the new governor and his peace plan and accusing him of having a pro-Greek bias. Foot understood that the 'demonstrations were planned' and were 'part of the campaign recently organized to increase feeling amongst the Turkish [Cypriot] community. Though the processions were not hostile and were easily dispersed', he confided to the colonial secretary that 'they represent a new and serious development'.[24] As *The Times* noted, '[T]he traditional role and behaviour of Greeks and Turks seems temporarily reversed. It is the Turks who are doing the demonstrating while the Greeks are hesitant, watchful, and suspicious.'[25]

While Cyprus simmered, negotiations in Turkey were not going well. As Lloyd wrote to Foot on 26 January, '[T]alks with Zorlu yesterday were very uphill. Atmosphere improved at dinner with Menderes.' There were four key issues from the Turkish side:

> (1) The 'Federal nature' of political developments in Cyprus i.e. they hate idea of Greeks ruling Turks. (2) The possibility of a Turkish base. They said they would like one at once. I gave no indication that that would be feasible but said that we would consider possibility at some stage. (3) The incorporating of partition pledge in some formal agreement. (4) (But nothing like so important as other three.) The possibility (weaving) into the new statement idea of a tripartite conference.[26]

With Menderes's agreement, Foot left for Istanbul on 26 January to try and help the discussions between Lloyd and Zorlu. The points transmitted by Lloyd to Foot were an indication of the serious obstacles to a solution. British military leaders were adamantly opposed to a Turkish base on Cyprus. Almost all senior members of the British government were against the idea of partition. Only the first point, concerning a federal Cyprus, appeared to leave any room for compromise.

The day after Foot's departure, Nicosia exploded in violence. As Foot had predicted, the rioting increased in an attempt to influence the discussions in Turkey.[27] Large groups of Turkish-Cypriot youths attacked police with stones and bottles. Tear gas was deployed as police and soldiers battled the crowd. *The Times* grimly reported, 'Grave Riots in Cyprus. Pitched Battle with Turks, Troops Besieged by Nicosia Mob, City Simmering Still'.[28] The next day the rioting spread to Famagusta. Again there was open violence between Turkish-Cypriots and British security forces. Casualties began to mount. In the first day alone, Turkish-Cypriot rioters injured twenty-eight policemen, fourteen members of the fire service and twelve soldiers. Dozens of Turkish-Cypriots were injured and ten were killed, including a woman who was knocked over by an army car.[29]

Although the security situation was brought back under control, the Turks had made their point. They would not accept Foot's proposals and were violently opposed to any solution other than partition. Their rioting was directed against both Greek-Cypriots and the British authorities, contradicting contemporary and subsequent Greek-Cypriot claims that the Turks acted in conjunction with British wishes. TMT propaganda made the gap between the British and the Turks abundantly clear. Leaflets published in the days after the rioting accused the British of 'cruel and blood-thirsty conduct', declaring that because of the actions of security forces against demonstrators 'there remains no possibility not only for the Turks and Greek of Cyprus to live together, but also for the Turks to live under British rule'.[30] The actions of their security forces demonstrated that 'the English have moved farther from their previous partisan actions against the Turks, and have shown whom they are serving and whose friends they are'.[31] An American National Security Council Briefing of 28 January stated:

> Repeated outbreaks of violence (10 [Turkish-Cypriot] deaths) during late January may be forerunners of more trouble in near future. Clashes involving Turkish-Cypriots could also lead to further deterioration in Greek-Turkish relations and even British-Turkish relations . . . Turkish-Cypriots' recent large scale rioting against authorities for first time apparently due: A. Fear that new Governor has been 'too soft' to Greek-Cypriots. B. Hope of emphasizing that Greeks and Turks can no longer live together – thus forcing partition.[32]

According to the Americans, the British were facing an 'almost impossible task in finding [a] new plan for Cyprus acceptable to all parties'.[33] It was a position with which the British were all too familiar. When Foot returned to Cyprus at the end of January, he 'almost immediately went into conference with his senior advisers on the situation in the island'.[34]

In spite of their hostile attitudes towards the British administration, the Turkish-Cypriot organizations remained focused first and foremost on the perceived Greek-Cypriot threat to their liberty and safety. In a leaflet of 31 January 1958, TMT urged Turks that 'we must never forget our principal enemy [the Greeks]'.[35] Although the British treated Makarios as practically the sole legitimate interlocutor for Cypriot demands, Turkish-Cypriot propaganda denounced the archbishop as 'black-gowned and dark-souled'.[36] With the situation deteriorating rapidly, the British would have to rethink their policy.

Political manoeuvres and political murders

The failure of the Foot initiative and the violent Turkish reaction in Cyprus at the start of 1958 created new operating conditions on the island not only for the British but also for Grivas and EOKA. Among other things, it seemed to deliver the coup de grâce to plans for a Turkish base on the island before a final solution had been reached. Writing to the colonial secretary, Foot confided his desire 'to make it finally clear to the Turkish Government that we cannot consider ceding them a military base in Cyprus except as a part of a plan for a lasting political settlement'.[37] The riots had demonstrated just how precarious the ethnic balance on the island was.

Makarios was also keenly aware of this reality. Since his release from detention in the Seychelles, the archbishop had continued to try and regain control of the struggle and avoid further violence. Evidence suggests that he felt EOKA's bomb and bullet methods had served their purpose as early as the truce of March 1957.[38] The continuation of violence (not least because of his exclusion from Cyprus) threatened not only Makarios's position as the leader of the Greek-Cypriot nationalist movement but also the stability of the Greek government, relations between Greek- and Turkish-Cypriots, and the control of the right over the *enosis* cause. The archbishop also continued to be uneasy about the human toll of the struggle. He had been particularly shaken by the death of Grigoris Afxentiou in March 1957, which he felt could have been avoided by agreeing to a ceasefire earlier.[39] Makarios believed that continuing along Grivas's path was dangerous. The British agreed.

In Athens, Foot explained the perils of a renewal of violence to the archbishop during a meeting on 13 February. The governor emphasized that a particular danger now existed because of the 'changed attitude of the Turkish minority', which had manifested itself during the January riots.[40] Makarios made the point to Grivas, and EOKA violence did decline on the island. By the start of March, American intelligence was able to report that Grivas had 'apparently decided to emphasize a campaign of passive resistance following a request from Archbishop Makarios that violence not be renewed'. Such a campaign, the CIA concluded, was 'in accord with the recommendations of many influential Greeks and Greek-Cypriots who believe that only the Turks would benefit from renewed terrorist attacks by EOKA at this time'.[41] On Cyprus, the British had come to a similar conclusion: '[T]he political leaders of EOKA had accepted that renewed violence would play into the hands of the Turks.'[42] Grivas, in fact, had issued orders on 31 March allowing area commanders to act on their own initiative in organizing attacks, 'always bearing the strict order in mind that there be no human casualties'.[43] The prohibition against attacking Turks was also restored. As one area commander ordered during this period, 'I wish the Turkish provocations to be treated with calmness and contempt. Both the youths and the combatant groups must show self-restraint towards any Turkish vandalism or armed attacks by the Turks.'[44]

While EOKA remained measured in its actions against the British and the Turkish-Cypriots, no such prohibitions were in force to protect the Greek-Cypriot left wing. This struggle within the struggle remains controversial. Former EOKA members and their supporters admit to the killing of only seven of the twenty-three left-wing Greek-Cypriots who died during this period. AKEL claims that all were murdered by EOKA and used the killings to argue that right-wing extremists were responsible for the island's ills both during this period and later. One reason for the open hostility between left and right during this time was that the left, largely separate from EOKA but nevertheless persecuted by the British during its struggle, seemed more receptive to Foot and a new approach to peace.

At a meeting of Cypriot communists on 3 December 1957, the general secretary of the Pancyprian Labour Federation, Andreas Ziartides, read a warning from EOKA 'that if he co-operated with the new Governor in any way, or entered into any independence negotiations with him, he would have to accept the consequences'. Ziartides was reminded 'that there was one leader, both in the political and military field, and that was Archbishop Makarios'.[45] The truce had encouraged AKEL to pursue its own policy-line on the Cyprus issue. Grivas, with EOKA inactive for months, was worried about becoming isolated by any productive action on the part of the Greek-Cypriot left. Makarios had become worried that left-wing Greek-Cypriots might 'withhold their support when EOKA resumes terrorism'.[46] EOKA's pamphlets stepped up the rhetoric against the left, accusing it of selling out to Governor Foot in order to prevent any such fissure.[47]

Grivas would not allow *enosis* to be sacrificed by either Makarios or the left. The EOKA commander attacked Foot as 'The Wooden Horse of Troy', denouncing the new governor's peace overtures as nothing more than a cunning new policy 'prepared with a view to deceiving us'. Foot's conciliatory gestures were rebuffed: '[T]he Cyprus people do not demand material benefits (roads, loans, release of political detainees etc) but only one thing – its freedom.'[48] Grivas also encouraged the Greek-Cypriot people to continue the struggle, although he fell short of calling for more violence against the British. Instead, he outlined a path to victory based on a new 'total war', which relied on galvanizing public opinion rather than on assassination and ambush. He called for 'continuous systematic and persistent *preparation* [author's italics] both for armed struggle, and for the passive resistance of the population ... continuous and good propaganda amongst the people ... raising high the morale and fighting spirit of the people'.[49]

While Grivas attacked compromise and the new governor with words, EOKA attacked the left with guns. In order to bring the Greek-Cypriot population in line with opposition to Foot's peace initiative, Grivas felt it necessary to assert his dominance over Cyprus's internal political landscape and push the left away from peace through intimidation and murder. In late January 1958, masked gunmen murdered two members of the Pancyprian Labour Federation, a left-wing trade union, in villages near Famagusta. A forty-eight-hour strike was declared by the union as violence erupted in the streets.[50] Ziartides appealed to the people and the ethnarchy 'to condemn these acts against our organisation'.[51]

Grivas's new campaign had a clear message. He claimed that the left were traitors to Cypriot Hellenism because they were willing to talk with Foot. If they continued to act against EOKA, they had to be neutralized. 'We shall strike the traitors no matter to which party they belong', thundered Grivas. 'The left wing party has officially taken all traitors under its guardianship because this party is also betraying the struggle.... The ideas of AKEL and Foot are in complete accord.'[52] Punishments were brutal and violence escalated. In May, the communist party did well in Greek elections, nearly doubling its strength from 1952 and becoming the main opposition party to the Karamanlis government. This added fuel to the fire. Grivas was determined to prevent a similar turn of events in Cyprus. Famagusta seemed to be the hotbed of violence against the left. There, two women had their heads shaved by EOKA men 'as part of the intimidation campaign'. Such attacks were becoming commonplace. As one official reported,

> [t]hree young men, aged about 24, together with a woman ... called on Mrs. ***** and asked where her husband was. ... Mrs. ***** was tied to a chair, her mouth gagged, and the shaving operation began. They told her that they were doing this because she was against EOKA and against the Archbishop. They alleged that she had called him a Rasputin.[53]

On 23 May, two Greek-Cypriot leftists were killed in the Famagusta district. One, a 22-year-old bus driver, who had previously been beaten by EOKA, was shot to death outside his home. The second was the gruesome murder of fifty-year-old Savvas Menacas. A married man with six children, Menacas was 'seized by a gang of about 50 youths and tied to a tree in a courtyard. The churchbells were rung and he was beaten to death. Police who arrived after the crowd dispersed found a poster nearby saying that Menacas' punishment was inflicted on EOKA's orders because of his anti-EOKA activities.[54] Menacas's 'anti-EOKA activities' were unspecified. Photis Papaphotis, the area commander, claimed that Menacas exhibited 'anti-national behaviour'.[55] In spite of firm evidence of substantive 'betrayals' of the *enosis* cause, the killings continued. On 26 May, a third Greek-Cypriot left-winger was found beaten to death on a street in Famagusta.[56] On 29 May another left-wing sympathizer was beaten by masked men outside the town. He died the next day in the city hospital.[57] The labour unions called strikes and marches in protest.

This was a new kind of violence for Cyprus, but it brought with it the recrudescence of attacks against the British forces which stood in the way of EOKA's new campaign against the left. On 4 May, two British soldiers were shot dead in Famagusta and Foot felt forced to re-impose mandatory death sentences for persons found carrying firearms and throwing bombs. The *Cyprus Mail* commented sadly that many people felt 'that the clock had been turned back – almost two and a half years'.[58]

As the renewal of EOKA operations prompted action by the British, it inspired emulation among Turkish-Cypriot nationalists. In late May, TMT, growing in numbers and capabilities, mounted a charge against the tiny Turkish-Cypriot left. On 11 May, TMT had distributed a leaflet threatening that 'Drastic measures will be mercilessly taken against anyone whoever he may be, who acts or speaks against the organization or mentions names or persons at random, or behaves in a treacherous or thoughtless manner prejudicial to the national interests'.[59] In the second half of May, the organization made good on its threats. In Nicosia, on 23 May, two young TMT gunmen fired shots at a 'prominent Turkish Communist, Ahmed Saadi Erkurt, and his wife'. Erkurt was slightly wounded and his wife more seriously injured.[60] On 25 May, Fail Onder, the former editor and owner of a left-wing newspaper *Reformist*, was murdered in Nicosia.[61] On 30 May, a young left-winger was also shot to death.[62] Both EOKA and TMT were asserting control within their own communities while demonstrating their operational capabilities to the British. They would not be denied a voice in the solutions that were being discussed. To some extent, '[b]y intimidating the leftist element in their respective communities the two paramilitary organizations [EOKA and TMT] were steeling themselves and closing ranks in anticipation of a major intercommunal face-off'.[63] Essentially, they were eliminating forces supporting compromise in order to further their maximalist positions.

The power Turkish-Cypriot nationalists demonstrated through TMT dramatically affected the Cypriot political landscape. TMT represented the Turkish-Cypriot equivalent of EOKA, a right-wing, nationalist force as vehemently committed to partition as Grivas's organization was to *enosis*. Its bulletins proclaimed that Cyprus was Turkish and emphasized the greatness of the Turkish race. TMT claimed that it refused to accept becoming 'slaves' at the hands of the Greeks.[64] 'Partition and only partition' was the organization's rallying cry, mirroring the time-worn EOKA motto of '*enosis* and only *enosis*'. Like EOKA, TMT was willing to use political assassination, terrorism and a campaign of intimidation to further its goals. Like Grivas's organization, it was also willing to eliminate fellow Turkish-Cypriots, generally from the left, whom it regarded as traitors.[65]

Confronted now with these two opponents, British forces found themselves with the dual role of combating the insurgency while attempting to keep the peace between the two communities as intercommunal violence simmered. In spite of its ability to attack leftist Turkish-Cypriots, TMT was not well equipped or organized enough to carry out operations on a scale comparable to EOKA. In mid-1958, TMT remained without military trainers or equipment from Turkey and could undertake only small-scale operations.[66] Unlike EOKA, it had no desire to strike British military or police targets. It was, however, more than up to the task of murdering left-wing Turks and putting pressure on EOKA. In this capacity it was still a threat to security and to British rule.

In managing the new problems posed by an armed organization of Turkish nationalists, Britain was constrained to strike a delicate balance between attempting to incorporate Turkish demands into peace negotiations while resisting those demands it felt to be out of line with its own requirements for peace in Cyprus. Turkish propaganda still pushed for the idea that the island should be partitioned, using the burgeoning violence between Greek-Cypriots and Turkish-Cypriots as evidence that the two sides could not live in peaceful coexistence.[67] Open battle between the two communities on the island was rapidly approaching. By June 1958, British policymakers in Cyprus felt that this internecine violence, coming from within both communities, had made conditions in Cyprus 'undeniably worse than at any previous period of the Emergency'. Only the latest proposals for a solution represented hope for a swift end to the violence. 'If these prove unacceptable to either or both sides', concluded a report by the CIC, 'a serious and rapid deterioration in the situation is inevitable.' The words were sadly prophetic.[68]

Divided and unruled

Despite the failure of the Foot plan, the British government continued to push for a diplomatic solution. By mid-May, proposals sketched out with the help of the prime minister for a modified tridominium were making the rounds between London, Athens and Ankara.[69] In a statement of the obvious, the Cabinet had already concluded that reconciling the diverse views of *enosis* and partition were 'the core of the Cyprus problem'. Achieving a solution acceptable to all three concerned governments would require 'each party to make some sacrifice of its present position'. A departure from the obvious came with the declaration of a previous proposal embedded in the concept of a tridominium that to achieve agreement, 'Her Majesty's Government [were] ready to set an example by renouncing their sole sovereignty over Cyprus, if the other parties will match this by renouncing their demands for unitary self-determination and for the partition of the island'.[70]

The air of compromise generated a mix of optimism and pessimism among British policymakers. Foot's deputy governor, George Sinclair, read the reports coming to him in Cyprus with a great deal of hope. 'I cannot tell you how delighted we are to think that these proposals now hold the field and that they are being heavily backed by

Ministers', he wrote to his boss, still in London for Cabinet-level discussions. 'We are full of admiration for the way in which you have been able to present this case and get it accepted.' Sinclair must have been pleased. Uncharacteristically, the deputy governor, who usually signed his messages 'Geo. Sinclair' or simply 'Sinclair', closed '[w]ith my warmest good wishes, yours, very sincerely, George'.[71]

Foot was less optimistic than his deputy. 'The declaration of the new policy', he wrote to Lennox-Boyd, 'is likely to lead to an outbreak of violence in the island from one side or the other or from both. . . . My main fear is that the developments of the past will bring about something like another Palestine in Cyprus. Civil war is an immediate possibility, and this might well lead to a war between Greece and Turkey.'[72] Foot's caution proved closer to the mark than Sinclair's optimism. Tensions continued to rise through the month of May.

On the night of 7 June, the situation took a dramatic turn for the worse. At 10.30 p.m. a small bomb went off at the Turkish Ministry of Information, a part of the Turkish Consulate in Nicosia. No one was injured and the damage to the building was minimal. Nevertheless, mobs of angry young Turkish-Cypriots flooded the streets. During four hours of rioting and burning, two Greek-Cypriots were killed and tens of thousands of pounds of property damaged and destroyed.[73] The next day, the rioting spread to Larnaca. Two more Greek-Cypriots were killed and a number of Greek-Cypriot owned properties were set on fire.[74] In Istanbul, 200,000 demonstrators took to the streets and burned an effigy of Archbishop Makarios.[75] Turkish tanks, police in riot gear and soldiers with fixed bayonets prevented attacks against what remained of Istanbul's Greek community along with the Greek and British consulates. There were fears that the horrific events of 6–7 September 1955 would be repeated. Dr Kütchük called out to the Istanbul mob that events in Cyprus were proof 'that there was no possibility now for the Turkish and Greek communities to live together'. The Istanbul crowd denounced Britain and Greece as deceitful; *The Times* reported that one voice called for mobilization.[76]

Turkish outrage, however, had one small problem – the entire affair had been carefully contrived. British intelligence noted that the furniture in the office had been moved away from the street to prevent damage from the bomb. A day or two before the explosion, the British ambassador in Ankara had also had word from Cyprus that something was about to happen, but was told by senior Turkish officials that there was 'no reason to suppose that the reports were true'.[77] Subsequent reports from both British and American intelligence were clear that the Turks in Cyprus had faked the bomb attack themselves.[78] This deadly deception was reminiscent of the 'attack' in Thessaloniki at the Turkish consulate on 6 September 1955, the excuse for the Istanbul pogrom, which had been a similarly stage-managed sham. Although the precise identity of the perpetrators in the Cyprus bombing is not known, two TMT men had carried out the attack with the express purpose of igniting intercommunal violence.[79]

Turkish-Cypriots were out to prove that they could not live with Greek-Cypriots and that any compromise short of partition was unworkable. This had been the substance of Turkish rhetoric since 1956. The rioting at the end of January had killed the Foot plan, and now the intercommunal strife doomed the latest tridominium proposals from the prime minister. The Turks had struck while the British government was in recess, before an official policy announcement, in order to undermine progress towards a settlement.[80] As the Cabinet conclusions noted on 18 June,

> the internal security situation in Cyprus had deteriorated in the last few days and the Turkish-Cypriots appeared to be deliberately attempting to create the impression that it was impossible for the two communities in Cyprus to live together harmoniously. Urgent representations had been made to the Turkish Government about the importance of avoiding any fresh outbreaks of violence at this stage.[81]

As the Turks had hoped, intercommunal violence began a physical separation of the two communities as Greek- and Turkish-Cypriots moved to areas where their people were in the majority. The political leadership in Turkey was quick to use this as evidence 'that partition [was] already taking place'.[82] Turkish propaganda exaggerated and claimed that by 16 June, over 1,000 Turkish-Cypriots were refugees, fleeing their homes after being attacked or surrounded by Greek-Cypriots bent on massacre and destruction.[83]

A resolution from the Turkish Grand National Assembly on 16 June fuelled the propaganda of partition with distortions and blatant untruths. The British ambassador, James Bowker, sent the resolution along to the Foreign Office, explaining that the incidents which it referred to were 'either untrue or grossly distorted'.[84] The Turkish resolution read:

> [T]he Turkish community which . . . had serious anxieties over the questions of their existence and future, became even more anxious following the report of an intended massacre by the Greek community on June 1. While the Turkish community in the island was in this state of mind, attacks were carried out on Turkish schools. Photographs of Ataturk, the greatest symbol of union and faith, were destroyed; bombs were thrown at Turkish institution [*sic*]; mosques and houses were attacked; defenceless women were assassinated; fields were burnt; and people were forced to leave their ancestral homes. All these incidents confirm and justify the conviction and resolution expressed many times by the Cypriot Turks of their being unable to live together and under the same administration with those elements which were committing such acts, and above all of their being unable to accept Greek domination in any form. In order to re-establish peace and order in Cyprus the two communities must be separated de jure and de facto one from the other. Above all, an assurance must be given to the Turkish community, which is in a state of great anxiety as regards its future and its destiny, that it will never be left in any way under the domination of the Greek community which intends to suppress its right to life and its freedom.[85]

Bowker bluntly exposed the proclamation's lack of truth and encouraged Lennox-Boyd and Foot to avail themselves of 'the true facts of these incidents insofar as they have been established in order to refute the Turkish allegations'.[86]

A report from Foot to Lennox-Boyd countered each of the false claims with the genuine facts:

> The Turkish communiqué stated that, on 1st June, EOKA threatened to massacre Turkish-Cypriots. There is no evidence or information whatsoever in the possession of the Cyprus Government to substantiate this suggestion. . . . The communiqué says that four days later there was an attack on a Turkish school. The facts are that, on the 3rd June, two Greek-Cypriot boys, aged 11 and 12, broke a pane of glass in one of the windows of a Turkish elementary school in Kyrenia and wrote EOKA in chalk on the door. The total damage was six shillings. The boys were taken before a court, bound over for one year and ordered to pay for the broken pane. The school was not entered, and no photo of Ataturk was damaged. There is, as you know, strong circumstantial evidence to show that the disturbances which broke out on the night of the 7th June had been pre-arranged by Turks. . . . It is true that some Turkish-Cypriots have left their homes for fear of attack by Greek-Cypriots, but it must not be overlooked that the reverse is also the case and that the total number of both communities involved is very small in proportion to the total population. It is estimated that total number of households affected does not exceed 650.[87]

If Greek-Cypriot provocations on the island were imagined, their losses were real enough. The bloodiest single incident occurred outside the Turkish-Cypriot village of Geunyeli on 12 June. British security forces encountered a party of Greek-Cypriots on a bus from the nearby village of Kontemenos. Thinking that they were preparing for an attack on neighbouring Turkish-Cypriots, British forces stopped and disarmed the Greek-Cypriots, then drove them some miles away from Kontemenos before releasing them. This snatch and drop policy was a standard British counter-insurgency tactic during this period. It had been used in Palestine and Kenya to disorient and disorganize potential violent threats. For the people of Kontemenos, the experience would prove deadly. Noticed by the Turkish-Cypriot villagers of Geunyeli, the disarmed Greek-Cypriots were attacked with iron bars, axes, knives and possibly firearms as they marched back to Kontemenos.[88] Seven were killed outright (another would die of his wounds) and more than a dozen were injured. No Turkish-Cypriots were killed. Greek-Cypriots cited the attack as evidence of collaboration between the Turkish-Cypriots and the British authorities, but a subsequent inquiry exonerated the British commander of any complicity in the attack.[89]

Even before the massacre, Makarios began to reverse his stance on avoiding further violence and encouraged Grivas to strike back against the Turkish-Cypriots with all means in his power. Speaking in Athens on 10 June, he called on Greek-Cypriots to organize in self-defence to combat 'Turkish barbarism'.[90] Grivas obliged. In his *Memoirs*, he described the shift in EOKA's operations:

> I turned our attention on the Turks and for the first time they felt the full weight of our blows. I had already ordered raids on police stations, with Turkish policemen as chief targets, and waived all restrictions in killing Turks: we found that Turkish enthusiasm for blood-shed soon showed a sharp decline – they had not expected

such ruthlessness on our part, knowing that we had always held our hand in the past.[91]

In spite of Grivas's bravado, the intercommunal struggle presented EOKA with difficulties. Grivas admitted as much, recording, with unconscious irony that

> [EOKA] could not, of course, stop murders and isolated raids in the no-man's land between the two quarters, where night after night the marauders sought their prey, slaughtering unarmed men and women, pillaging their homes, setting fires to their churches. Nor was it easy to save our people in the countryside.[92]

In spite of his experience as a guerrilla leader, Grivas found it difficult to counter the classic guerrilla tactics of his adversaries. It is one of the Cyprus Emergency's intricacies and greatest ironies that during the summer of 1958, EOKA faced a guerrilla war of its own against a parallel Turkish organization. TMT demonstrated how successful guerrilla-style tactics could be against the guerrillas themselves.

Turkish-Cypriot tactics were not the only obstacle to EOKA achieving full freedom of action. Kendrew's situation assessment on 16 July painted an ugly picture. Any sort of political impetus towards peace had been lost, 'tempers on both sides [were] inflamed' and EOKA probably had orders to attack 'both the Turks and ourselves [the British] (but not necessarily everywhere)'.[93] The police force, still dependent on large numbers of Turkish-Cypriots, was completely ineffectual. In such a state, Kendrew saw only three courses:

> (a) to deal with the extremists on both sides, ie crush EOKA and arrest the Turk rabble raisers [sic]. This is clearly desirable, but in order to crush EOKA, within a reasonable time the active assistance of the Turks is necessary, ie the latter must not be finally antagonised. There will be violent reactions from EOKA if these have not already occurred. We would find it difficult to fight on two fronts. (b) To deal with one set of extremists only. As the Turks (whatever their long term intentions) may be disposed to cooperate, and as EOKA has intimidated the Greek population and are set on an anti-British course, EOKA are the primary target. As in course (a) we can expect a violent reaction, but we might expect Turkish help. (c) To continue a holding (and defensive) operation. We have the ability to retain the main towns and communication routes, ie to keep the base functioning.[94]

Although Kendrew admitted that striking against both Greek- and Turkish-Cypriot extremists was 'desirable', it was not seen as a feasible course of action. On a purely military level, Kendrew saw option (b) as the correct course. Anything else would postpone the inevitable. And tackling EOKA at some point in the future would be more difficult. In spite of suggesting an offensive against EOKA as the soundest military course, Kendrew acknowledged that '[t]he only way an ultimate solution can be achieved is by political action. Political action will be impractical if, as seems likely, the situation deteriorates to the point of open and continued civil war, although in this latter case we should be able to retain control sufficiently to keep the island running as a base.'[95]

Through the middle of July, British forces had been relatively even-handed in their security operations. Since the violence began, 524 Greek-Cypriots and 164 Turkish-Cypriots had been detained. The numbers skewed the actual proportions of the population but were not wildly out of line considering the superior nature of British intelligence relating to EOKA. Moreover, by 15 July, forty-three Greek-Cypriots and forty-eight Turkish-Cypriots remained in custody indicating that British forces were somewhat more even-handed in their assessment of individuals representing the greatest threat.[96]

Foot was reluctant to accept Kendrew's recommendation, but eventually bowed to the pressure from the military and launched a large-scale operation against EOKA. Security forces, however, did not strike EOKA alone. Two days after Kendrew's report, Foot took action. 'Operation Matchbox' kicked off at 1.00 a.m. on 22 July and ran for forty-eight hours over the entire island. Robert Holland writes that 'by the end of the third day, 1,992 Greeks were in custody, plus 58 Turks. To assuage what [Charles] Foley's newspaper [*Times of Cyprus*] lambasted as this "laughable contrast", TMT was proscribed by the Government, but none of its known leaders was touched.'[97] Such assessments do not tell the whole picture. Operation Matchbox had indeed been directed solely against EOKA, but it was only one of two operations planned by the British security forces to run sequentially. On 23 July, after the proscription of TMT, Operation 'Table Lighter' was launched to round up TMT members. In that context, the fifty-eight Turkish-Cypriots were arrested – inflicting a not insignificant blow against that organization.[98]

The respective arrest figures demonstrated the limitations of the security forces. There was little intelligence on TMT, compared to significant knowledge of EOKA. More significantly, security forces had come to rely on Turkish-Cypriot cooperation. As a result, the vulnerability of the British situation dramatically increased with the rise in Turkish-initiated violence. Foot made that fact clear to the Colonial Office in March, informing them that in the event of 'some form of civil war . . . our Security Forces which are so dependent on Turkish[-Cypriot] support and participation would put us at a grave disadvantage to say the least.'[99]

Internationally, Turkish support and strength were also clear. As Governor Foot communicated to the British ambassador in Athens, Roger Allen, in January 1958,

> The Turks hold all the cards, it seems, and they are quite determined to press their advantage to the utmost . . . they have started a campaign of violence amongst the Turkish community here in Cyprus which they can and no doubt will turn on again whenever it suits them to do so. This can in effect give them the complete veto (on everything) for which they seek.[100]

Events outside Cyprus were also working in Turkey's favour once again. On 14 July 1958, a group of Iraqi officers staged a coup against King Faisal II who was overthrown and killed. The British government had supported Faisal, whose country was central to the Baghdad Pact. With the new military regime recognized by Nasser's Egypt, Britain found its crumbling Middle East position more reliant on Turkey than ever. The end of the Baghdad

Pact was perhaps the last direct aftershock of Suez and left Turkey as the only viable ally for Britain in the Middle East. It was not the time to confront Ankara over Cyprus.

For their part, the Turks were not in a mood for compromises. With the manufactured violence raging, the June plan was rejected as 'impracticable'. As before, the position of the Turkish government was 'that the situation calls for a radical and not provisional solution'. In the Turkish government's view, 'the only radical solution [was] partition'.[101] Menderes hammered the point home in a letter of 14 June to Macmillan. '[T]he only point of agreement between the United Kingdom and Turkey is based on this concession [partition] by Turkey . . . despite all our good will we have not been able to accept your proposals.' The June proposal was fatally flawed because 'it brings no final solution to the Cyprus question, that is, it contains no reference to the idea of partition which has been put forth as a compromise formula and accepted by Turkey as a concession and at great sacrifice'. With the situation on the ground 'becoming increasingly grave', Menderes was 'convinced that it is now time to find a solution to this problem by generally adopting the idea of partition which is the most equitable, just, moderate and practical solution'.[102]

In spite of the factors in their favour, pushing for partition and provoking intercommunal violence in Cyprus overplayed the Turkish hand. Menderes's rhetoric did not reflect reality. British policymakers remained opposed to partition as did the British public.[103] The 'Turks had made no proper attempt to think out implications of partition', wrote the British delegation to NATO in Paris. 'The time was surely past in the West when populations could be uprooted and economy of a country upset as they certainly would be if partition was imposed. In this connection Turks had apparently not progressed beyond a Balkan war mentality.'[104] In London, it was understood that partition, in all likelihood, would mean war between Greece and Turkey.[105] It was thus to be avoided at all costs. If British policymakers had been guilty of flirting with partition in the past, they now worked to prevent it.

In Cyprus, the deputy governor was adamant that partition meant 'widespread strife' and would 'gravely prejudice the working of our base'. If the British government started using the partition 'card' again, it would 'divert the attention of our own people in Ankara, Athens and London from our positive plan'. The Turks would understand that it was merely a negotiating ploy and would 'resume their flat-out attempt to get partition'.[106] Foot himself was decidedly against partition and even before taking the appointment in Cyprus had informed Lennox-Boyd that he would resign rather than implement such a policy.[107] Blocking partition, however, did not bring peace to Cyprus. While British policymakers remained reluctant to take the field against the Turkish-Cypriots, EOKA was not. Turkish-Cypriot nationalists had sown a conflict with the Greek-Cypriots, and now they would reap a bitter harvest.

'Tolerance had its limits'

During the initial phase of the intercommunal violence, EOKA found itself unprepared for a struggle against the Turkish-Cypriots and TMT. Their attention had been focused on eliminating left-wing elements in their own community and on the new, largely non-violent methods of resistance to British rule. As a result, the Turkish-Cypriots were able to inflict far more casualties in June than the Greek-Cypriots. On 3 July, the *Cyprus Mail* reported that twenty had been killed in the intercommunal fighting, seventeen Greeks and three Turks.[108] The massacre at Geunyeli was only one factor. There was also the attitude of the British security forces which still focused on Greek-Cypriots rather than Turkish-Cypriots as a source of instability and violence. After years of fighting against EOKA and the Greek-Cypriot community, the British had difficulty shifting their focus onto the Turkish-Cypriot community. While the British, hamstrung by the unreliability of the Turkish-Cypriot police contingent, struggled to keep the peace between Greek- and Turkish-Cypriots, EOKA struggled with shifting its focus from the British and Greek-Cypriot communists to Turkish-Cypriots.

In the middle of June, Grivas sent an order to the execution squads 'to kill a Turk in revenge for every death of a Greek'.[109] According to the Larnaca area commander,

> a few days later one of the groups killed a Turk. Immediately a new curfew was imposed. The Greeks took fresh courage, and the Turks now knew that when they murdered a Greek they could expect retaliatory action at once. EOKA would not allow them to kill Greek citizens. Tolerance had its limits.[110]

If tolerance had limits, appearance suggested that the rhetoric of the two sides did not. Another EOKA order went out to the village defence groups. The order denounced 'the uncivilized wolflike,[111] vandal Turk', who had only recently 'left their wild and nomadic life in the wild [*sic*] and remote tracts of Mongolia. . . . If they attack you, you must strike them pitilessly'.[112]

TMT's propaganda welcomed this fight. A leaflet on 28 May 1958 threatened the Greek 'criminals' and the 'mentally unbalanced people' of EOKA, saying that they could 'only be brought to their senses when they are treated as they were treated in Smyrna where they hit the dust, were thrown out into the sea and were buried in the waters of the Mediterranean'.[113] On 11 June, the organization promised that the 'life-and-death bloody war for our *INDEPENDENCE*', would be waged 'in Cyprus very soon', and would end with 'the perfidious English and deceitful Greek bastards being thrown out by us and buried in the deep waters of the Mediterranean sea. The cries of *ALLAH, ALLAH* of the Cyprus Turks, will be heard under the umbrella of the steel wings which will be coming to Cyprus from the Taurus mountains in the near future'. Cyprus would be converted 'into a cemetery and the Mediterranean into a coffin for you [Greeks] and for your shameless cringing English masters'.[114]

TMT's bark remained worse than its bite. By late June, EOKA, better armed, organized, and trained, began to exact a heavy toll on the Turkish-Cypriots. As the fighting turned against them, Turkish-Cypriot leaders, Kütchük and Denktaş, went to Ankara to ask for direct military assistance from the Turkish government. They met with Zorlu, who remained cautious about deepening Ankara's commitment in such an overt way. According to Denktaş, Zorlu asked if they could assure him that arms shipments would be safe from British capture. Kütchük demurred, but Denktaş vouched that they would be.[115] The arms began coming in to Cyprus by mid-July along with a Turkish army officer, Colonel Ali Vurushkan, who according to Denktaş, became the commander of TMT and was responsible for providing its members with military-style training.[116] The recruitment and professionalism of TMT increased. Cyprus, it appeared, was heading for a full-blown civil war.

During June and July 1958, the fighting was bitter and personal. Isolated individuals from both communities were picked off and killed: shot, stabbed or beaten to death by EOKA or TMT execution squads. No one was safe. As Special Branch reported in its bimonthly intelligence report midway through July, the island was experiencing 'a series of brutal intercommunal murders, which included an eleven year old Turkish-Cypriot shepherd boy and a middle aged Greek-Cypriot nun'.[117]

The scale and brutality of the violence, coupled with the delicate international situation finally sent policymakers in Ankara, Athens and London scrambling for a solution. In spite of their strong feelings over Cyprus, none of the governments in question was prepared to engage in a war in the Eastern Mediterranean. With Britain's position weakened by Suez and the collapse of the Baghdad Pact, Greece under pressure from a communist resurgence, and Turkey confronted with hostile and progressively unstable Arab neighbours, each government had good reason to try and bring the situation in Cyprus under control. Makarios was first off the mark, making a 'carefully qualified appeal for an end of bloodshed' on 24 July, which threw blame at Turkey and seemed to have little effect. On 30 July, Prime Minister Karamanlis made his own appeal for peace, called for a return to the 'peace and concord', which the Greeks and Turks of Cyprus had enjoyed 'for many centuries'. This was followed by a second appeal from Makarios and one from Prime Minister Macmillan calling for an end to the bloodshed.[118] Prime Minister Menderes added his voice to those calling for an end to the killings.

These high-level developments built a positive momentum. In early August, Macmillan reached out to Karamanlis: 'I was extremely grateful to read the appeal which you made for the ending of violence and bloodshed in Cyprus', he wrote in a note delivered through the Foreign Office to Athens. 'As this appeal, coupled with appeals made by the Turkish PM and myself, has produced a certain effect in the island itself, I feel that the moment is ripe for the personal meeting between us which I suggested earlier in our correspondence on this matter.'[119] As Macmillan noted, on the island, the response to the calls for peace was swift. An EOKA leaflet from 4 August by 'Dighenis' stated,

> I have informed Mr. Macmillan that the Cyprus people accepts his appeal. . . .
> I have ordered to cease [sic] any action against the Englishmen and Turks but I declare that if by any means the provocations on behalf of Englishmen and Turks continue then as from the 10th of this month I shall be free to order action on both.[120]

TMT followed suit the next day: 'All armed groups must stop their activities until further orders. . . . Greek owned property will not be damaged unless the [sic] Turkish owned property is damaged. No pressure will be done [sic] to the Greek minority in villages unless the Turkish minority is pressed down.'[121]

In approximately two months of fighting, sixty Greek-Cypriots had been killed and another ninety-eight wounded. The Turkish-Cypriots had got off only marginally lighter, with fifty-five killed and eighty-four wounded.[122] Turkish-Cypriot losses were far higher in terms of percentages of the population, but TMT had demonstrated its lethality. It had been a bitter experience. Achieving a compromise would now require overcoming daunting odds and hitherto insoluble contradictions. Cyprus had been shaken to its foundations. Greek- and Turkish-Cypriot relations were at their nadir. At long last, however, with the support of governments in both Greece and Turkey, there was a dim light of hope flickering on the horizon.

10

End game

Killing a dream

> As I recall the many innocent, peaceful people who were killed, the goodwill and tolerance that were destroyed, the friends and friendships lost and the many brave young men – Greek, Turkish and British – who laid down their lives in what was after all, an unnecessary conflict, my mind is filled with a sadness which is tinged with outrage at the folly of it all. There was not even a 'famous victory'. Nobody won. Everybody lost by reason of this futile conflict.[1]
> – John Reddaway, Administrative Secretary of Cyprus

The intercommunal violence which defined 1958 gave way to compromise in 1959. This compromise rested on three key developments: the defeat of another Greek overture at the UN, the announcement by Archbishop Makarios that he was willing to accept independence rather than *enosis* and the fear of further escalation. The factors spurred political leaders in Greece, Turkey and Britain towards common ground. While the entente among Greece, Turkey and Britain was essential to bringing violence to a close, neither the cause of *enosis* nor the tensions between the two communities were completely reconciled. Sadly for all parties concerned, the compromise provided temporary relief rather than a durable solution.

With the ink on EOKA's latest ceasefire still damp, Prime Minister Macmillan flew to Athens in the hope of making further progress towards re-establishing peace and stability in Cyprus. While the ceasefire – and the appeals for peace from three prime ministers that had preceded it – ended the most damaging phase of intercommunal violence on the ground, the international political situation seemed as resistant to a resolution as ever. However, changing landscapes at the UN, in the broader Middle East and even within Greece and Cyprus were beginning to provide traction for a solution. The Macmillan administration was determined not to miss the opportunity of finally ending the mess in Cyprus.

Turkey, concerned with the course of events in the Middle East, appeared ready to negotiate. Greece, however, remained intransigent, wary of the threat of partition and an enduring Turkish presence on Cyprus. In Cyprus, the rhetoric of EOKA still fixated on *enosis*. Moreover, the fragile truce was almost immediately under threat. EOKA's ceasefire was applied only to British security forces. The organization continued the targeted killing of Greek-Cypriot 'traitors' and Turkish-Cypriots. These activities demonstrated that EOKA remained operational and that the British were still not yet in complete control of the security situation. At the same time, it showed that conflict among different groups in Cyprus remained intractable.

By late summer, both the Greek government and Archbishop Makarios had denounced attempts at a compromise based on the August revisions of Macmillan's June plan. In their view, the plan gave too many concessions to the Turks and involved them too directly in the affairs of Cyprus. In response, Greece once again prepared to attack Britain and its Cyprus policy at the UN during the autumn session. In spite of the apparent obstacles, the British government decided to proceed with their plan and invited Greece and Turkey to send representatives to the island to participate in its implementation. To complicate matters further, violence in Cyprus resumed between EOKA and British forces.

Just when the situation seemed headed towards chaos, two important changes took place. First, confronted with the reality that Britain was moving forward with its plan and that Turkey would soon have a formal representative on the island, Archbishop Makarios publicly acknowledged that he was willing to abandon the cause of *enosis* and accept independence for Cyprus in its place.[2] Second, a Greek appeal for Cypriot self-determination was once again defeated at the UN. With the shift in Makarios's position explicitly stated, the Greek government was approached by the Turkish government on a bilateral basis to solve the problem. British policymakers, as previous policy statements had made clear, had no objection to signing off on a solution agreed to in both Athens and Ankara, as long as British interests in Cyprus were respected. At last diplomacy was gaining traction. Greek and Turkish representatives met in New York, Paris and finally in Zurich to hammer out the details of the compromise. By February 1959, they had reached an agreement. The dogged Greek-Cypriot insistence on *enosis* had been removed and progress towards a solution followed.

The British government kept its word and the agreement reached between the Greeks and the Turks served as a foundation for a general solution to the Cyprus problem. A new, independent state was created. Its independence was guaranteed by Britain, Turkey and Greece. *Enosis* and partition were renounced. Britain was provided with two areas to maintain as sovereign bases. Greek-Cypriots would choose the country's president, but the vice-president, with full veto power, would be a Turkish-Cypriot. A Cabinet and single parliament of Cypriots, Greek and Turkish, would direct the new nation's affairs. In both the Cabinet and the parliament, a certain number of seats were reserved for the minority. One of the world's smallest countries was given the world's largest constitution. The final agreements represented compromises all round, but also a new hope for the future of the island. By 1960, that future was firmly, if reluctantly, in Cypriot hands. Britain's tangle in Cyprus was all but over; sadly, the island's troubles were a long way from finished.

Shuttle diplomacy

In an effort to end the intercommunal violence raging through the summer of 1958, Macmillan visited both Athens and Ankara. In both capitals, the prime minister's mission was to build on the calls for peace that had been made by him and his colleagues at the end of July. It was hoped that intercommunal violence might provide the necessary impetus for compromise. If there was a chance to reach a solution about Cyprus, Macmillan was determined to grab it with both hands. The trip to Athens almost strangled Macmillan's hopes in their infancy. Meeting with Prime Minister Karamanlis and Foreign Minister Averoff on 8 August, Macmillan was confronted with familiar protests. The Greeks had four central objections to the British prime minister's June plan. First, the proposal that separate Houses of Representatives for each of the two communities would have 'final legislative authority in communal affairs' was denounced as 'divisive'. As always, the Greeks preferred a single legislative assembly, which could be controlled by the Greek-Cypriot majority.[3] Second, the Greeks disliked the idea of dual nationality for Cypriots and third the proposal to have representatives on the island from both Greece and Turkey.[4] All three points hit the familiar problem of Greek and Greek-Cypriot opposition to Turkey having equal standing with Greece in any agreement over Cyprus. The proposal for a Turkish representative on the island was particularly jarring. To many Greeks, it smacked of a return to the days of the Ottoman Empire when the administration of the island lay in the hands of a representative from Istanbul. Finally, the Greeks protested that the 'number of elected ministers was unfairly weighted in favour of the Turkish minority'.[5] All these objections were firmly rooted in traditional Greek views about how any final agreement should be structured.

Macmillan was disappointed with the Greek position. In his diary, he noted that, by rejecting the Radcliffe proposals from 1956, the Greeks had actually put themselves in a more difficult position in 1958. The Turks had not baulked at Radcliffe's proposal for a single legislative assembly in 1956. Now they were opposing it. If the Greeks rejected the new plan, concluded Macmillan, 'or made it unworkable by violence and terrorism, the end would certainly be partition in its worst form – territorial partition, with Turkish bases, etc'.[6] While British policymakers still resisted this solution strongly, each Greek rejection made it seem more plausible.

Part of the Greek position, Macmillan noted in his diary, was based on sentiment. According to Macmillan, Karamanlis had become 'very emotional' in the discussions. In his diary, Macmillan recorded that the Greeks 'hated the Turks; they had fought them for 500 years, they would fight them for Greek liberty wherever and whenever they could. They could not be humiliated by the Turks. A Turkish veto on Greek aspirations was humiliating.'[7] Macmillan's prose may have inflated the problem, but his central point, that achieving Greco-Turkish cooperation over Cyprus was challenging for practical and historical reasons, remained valid. Moreover, the intransigence of the Greek government had its roots in weakness. The Greek government was 'frightened of Makarios, frightened of Parliament, and frightened of the rise in the Communist vote at the last (May) elections'. Because of these issues, 'the Government clearly cannot "accept" the plan'.[8]

A day after the meeting with Macmillan, Karamanlis, Averoff and the Greek Foreign Office's head of its Cyprus desk, Dimitris Bitsios met with American deputy undersecretary Robert Murphy and Ambassador James Riddleberger. The Greeks presented the Americans with an explanation of their position over Cyprus. In no uncertain terms, they raised concerns that the Cyprus issue was a threat to the stability of their government and therefore a threat to the future of Greece's participation in NATO. The Greeks argued, in terms that echoed numerous previous statements from Ankara, that they 'had made the ultimate concession', by agreeing 'to shelve self-determination, and now wanted only a greater measure of self-government, within or outside the Commonwealth'. There was pressure against the government, with the possibility of the defection of deputies over the Cyprus issue and hostility towards NATO.[9] The Karamanlis government was committed to NATO and enjoyed the benefits of British and American aid because of that relationship. NATO's secretary general, Paul Henri Spaak, however, recognized that in spite of these links, Greece's membership in NATO could not be taken for granted. He told the American ambassador to NATO, Warren Burgess, that, if Macmillan's plan was implemented over Greek objections, Greece would 'probably take it out on NATO, at least by discontinuing cooperation in the military field and adopting a neutralist line of policy'.[10]

Macmillan followed his trip to Athens with one to Ankara. He sounded out the Turkish government about a solution for Cyprus. He explained to Selwyn Lloyd that the meetings were not an unqualified success. 'I am just leaving Ankara,' he wrote to the foreign secretary on 12 August. 'We finished our business with the Turks last night after three meetings, all of them short and only one of them pleasant, the last.' The prime minister reported that on 10 August 'we ran into rough weather. The Turks were at their most suspicious. Zorlu was rude and truculent. Before I could enumerate the Greek points he interrupted to say that he wanted the same number of Turks on the Governor's Council as Greeks; and partition to be added to partnership as the final solution.'[11] Macmillan was not encouraged by the Turkish attitude. 'It was depressing,' he continued,

> to find that Zorlu, and even Menderes, were unwilling to discuss the Greek points objectively and without commitment, let alone respond to a friendly suggestion that in the world situation now facing us it would be in Turkey's interest if, by means of a slight adjustment of the plan which we said all along was no more than an outline, we could obtain, if the not the whole hearted cooperation, at least a tolerable degree of practical cooperation from the Greeks.[12]

Like the Greeks, the Turks remained immovable in their demands – equal treatment and recourse to partition. Worse still, the Americans and British remained fearful that Turkish hostility to a solution could manifest itself not only in a simple withdrawal from NATO but also through a recrudescence of open violence towards Greeks both in Turkey and on Cyprus.[13] Turkish policymakers had already chosen this course in 1955 during the Tripartite Conference (through the Istanbul riots) and earlier in 1958 (with the auto-bombing of the Turkish Consulate in Nicosia) before the announcement of the Macmillan Plan. The British and Americans had every reason to believe that such things could happen again.

In spite of the hostile atmosphere, a Cabinet meeting on 12 August set the new course of British policy over Cyprus. Macmillan had several impressions from his trips. First, he was convinced 'that the Greek government lacked the political strength to give active support to any plan which would solve the Cyprus problem'. The Turks 'were strongly opposed to any modifications designed to meet the Greek point of view'. The Cabinet concluded that only three courses of action remained: to abandon the June plan, to implement the June plan without making changes to it or to proceed with implementing the June policy 'while modifying it in certain particulars'.[14] The first course was seen, in familiar language, as 'a confession of failure'. It was feared that the second course 'would arouse bitter opposition from Greece', and 'would also involve disregarding the views expressed in the North Atlantic Council and in the United Nations'.[15] Faced with the apparently unpalatable alternatives, the Cabinet chose the third option, boldly announcing that the plan, with modifications, would be implemented with or without the agreement of the various parties.[16]

In the policy announcement that followed on 15 August, Macmillan attempted to reconcile Greek concerns while still keeping the Turks onside. British policymakers had decided on three modifications to Macmillan's original plan, each designed to improve its chance of success with the Greeks. First, the proposal promising Cypriots the option for dual nationality would be 'deferred'. As a policy memo noted, 'This proposal which was originally made to please the Greeks, has not in fact appealed to them.'[17] The plan for separate representative houses was scrapped in favour of a proposal for a single representative institution. Finally, the status of the Greek and Turkish representatives was 'to be changed so that, while their functions are not affected, they will not sit as members of the Governor's Council'.[18] Prime Minister Karamanlis, on holiday in Rhodes, returned to Athens immediately on the news of the modifications, but reaction from the Greek government was reported as 'absolutely negative'.[19]

Makarios's reaction was also immediate and even more negative. The new plan struck the archbishop as being nothing more than 'a restatement of the plan announced on June 19th 1958 which has already been rejected'. The choice to proceed regardless drew special criticism: 'I am also painfully astonished,' wrote Makarios,

> to notice that it is proposed to proceed with the imposition of a plan unacceptable to the Cypriot people in their large majority. It should be made abundantly clear that the Greek people of Cyprus can never accept a plan which disregards their basic democratic rights and denies to them both freedom and peace.[20]

How the archbishop hoped to reconcile the continued pursuit of *enosis* with the pursuit of peace was not addressed.

EOKA violence and the polar opposite demands of the island's Greek and Turkish populations remained fundamental obstacles to peace. Makarios was stretching truth when he expressed his

> profound disappointment that the moderation we have shown in a spirit of good will and compromise in order to reach agreement upon a transitory period of self government has met with no understanding and no response whatsoever from the British government whose policy has proved to be devoid of all sincerity of purpose.[21]

British policy, in spite of its cynicism, was sincere in the desire to avoid an open conflict between Greece and Turkey. By undermining NATO and the security of the Eastern Mediterranean, such conflict harmed rather than served British interests in the region. For their part, Makarios and the *enosis* movement's offer of compromise through 'a transitory period of self government' was hollow. The goal remained *enosis* and the only transition desired was one that would make Cyprus part of the Greek state. From the beginning, Greeks and Greek-Cypriots alike should have understood the huge odds stacked against this cause. Insisting on it now was to invite partition and the war that would surely accompany it. As at the beginning of the struggle, those pursuing the cause of *enosis* chose to ignore these critical factors.

After making the decision to proceed along the lines of the modified June plan, British policymakers looked for other options that might soften the blow for the Greeks and Greek-Cypriots. At the end of August, the Cabinet acknowledged that the 'less favourable' reaction of the Greek government meant that 'there was a serious risk of an early revival of terrorism on the island'.[22] The reaction in both London and Cyprus to such a result would be more balanced than in the past. The Cabinet argued that, 'we should adopt as unprovocative a policy as possible towards Greece by giving effect to the plan unobtrusively and laying the maximum emphasis on measures to restore order in Cyprus and to bring violence to an end'. Beyond this, Governor Foot suggested 'that, for this purpose, we should announce forthwith that, subject to the maintenance of peace in the Island, Archbishop Makarios would be permitted to return within the next six weeks and that, if violence completely ceased thereafter, the state of emergency would be terminated by the end of the year'.[23]

To terminate the state of emergency, however, the British would have to demonstrate gains against EOKA and prevent the organization from undermining the security situation. The August truce had reduced the scope of action enjoyed by the security forces and meant that previously gathered intelligence was becoming less relevant with each passing day. A renewal of violence threatened both the British peace initiative and the hope that Greece and Turkey – along with Greek- and Turkish-Cypriots – could possibly get along.

Violence returns

Any optimism about ending the emergency by the end of 1958 was challenged immediately. After the August announcement that the peace plan would move forward, violence in Cyprus reignited. This occurred in spite of British attempts to apply in Cyprus the same mollifying stance it was adopting towards Greece. To foster support on the island for the plan, Foot's administration scaled down security measures and cut back on large-scale operations. As he explained to the colonial secretary on 23 August, 'activity is limited to successful operations acting on information to seize arms and make individual arrests of terrorists'.[24] Limited operations, as might have been expected, brought in limited results. A security report from late August outlined the situation:

> As a result of Op[eration] Matchbox and the follow-up operation [against TMT], which showed Government's determination to check violence: (a) we

have acquired a great deal of low grade information which has led to recovery of some arms and further arrests of wanted persons. (b) A climate of opinion has developed in which information is slowly building up – more so than at any time since March 1957. (c) We hold a limited advantage. As against this: (a) We have not yet penetrated EOKA high grade elements, or arms traffic. (b) We have not yet been able to establish a large scale network of agents. (c) Makarios and Grivas still retain their strongarm squads so as to exercise a hold over the population and embark on full scale action.[25]

In spite of occasional successes, the security forces had not succeeded on the three important points enumerated in the report. These three problems were as true in August 1958 as they had been in April 1955. As difficult as the situation was, the British did succeed in getting some information. On 23 August, security forces, acting on an intelligence tip-off, killed three 'hard-core' targets in a gun-battle in the village of Lyssi. These were the first casualties since EOKA declared a ceasefire on 4 August; Grivas immediately called off the ceasefire. Two days previously, on 21 August, the EOKA chief had released his first leaflet since the truce. It announced that EOKA would

> not succumb to the Anglo-Turkish conspiracy. Our island is Greek. We accept no compromise. We demand clear self-determination. . . . No power is capable of subjugating us and imposing the abortive British plan for our enslavement to the British and the Turks.. . . No one should cooperate in any effort for the imposition of the plan, and all must carry out the orders of leadership.[26]

The subsequent fire-fight with British forces seemed to confirm this stance.

The security situation in Cyprus continued to deteriorate along with the hope of a peaceful run-up to the implementation of the new plan. Earnest violence was also renewed against leftist elements and other 'traitors' to the nationalist cause. On 27 August, a report from *The Times* described 'a pitched battle . . . between [Greek-Cypriot] right-wing and left-wing factions . . . about 15 miles from Famagusta'. The intra-Greek fighting killed two: a girl of thirteen and a woman of thirty-two. Another twenty were injured.[27] Later that day, another EOKA gunman was killed by security forces.

In July, EOKA murdered two Britons, eleven Greeks and four Turks. The Greek-Cypriot victims included women. Iphigenia Fanti, her husband, Michael Fantis and her daughter, Cristallou Pettimeridou, were all killed by EOKA on 28 July in a village in the Troodos Mountains. An EOKA leaflet from 8 August claimed that the three had been executed 'due to their dishonest and treacherous attitude against our national struggle'.[28] During most of August, the ceasefire had been in effect, but another two Britons, ten Greeks and three Turks were still killed by the organization. September started off even worse. A member of the security forces was killed on the first, and on the second, a member of the RAF was murdered. EOKA tried to blow up a Meteor aircraft at Akrotiri airfield and ambushed a military truck outside Nicosia. The British struck back too, surrounding four EOKA fighters at a barn in the village of Liopetri, near Famagusta. After a hard-fought gun-battle, in which one British soldier was killed and five wounded, all four EOKA men were killed.

On 7 September, Grivas retaliated, announcing that a Briton would be murdered for every Greek-Cypriot killed by security forces. EOKA also continued to strike hard against its Greek-Cypriot compatriots. A Greek-Cypriot was shot to death by masked gunmen on 10 September. On 15 September, two more Greek-Cypriots were murdered in the western village of Mesoyi. Notes were pinned on the corpses saying that they had been killed by EOKA.[29] Murders of Greek-Cypriots, ambushes and attacks against British forces (including a new tactic using electronically detonated landmines) were once more a daily feature of life on the island.

Even the escalation against British forces during the second half of September could not disguise the fact that EOKA's focus remained Greek-Cypriots who could betray the cause. This is reflected in the casualty figures. In each of these three months – even while engaged in intercommunal fighting – more Greek-Cypriots had been killed than Britons. In fact, over those three months, EOKA killed only nine Britons, compared with thirty-five Greek-Cypriots – a ratio of almost four to one.

Violence during the late summer and autumn of 1958 reflected the deep connection between political action and the military operations conducted by both EOKA and the British. Macmillan's August announcement was appreciated by the security forces on the ground because it gave them the clear direction that they had been lacking. The uncertainty about British policy in Cyprus, which, among other things, had contributed to Harding's resignation in 1957 was dealt with. The importance of political direction in fighting an insurgency was explicitly stated by Major General Kenneth Darling, who succeeded Kendrew as director of operations in Cyprus in October 1958. In his 'Report on the Cyprus Emergency', from July 1959, Darling wrote,

> Unless and until there is an agreed and firm long term political policy, the activities of the Security Forces are obviously hampered and it becomes more difficult for them to take the initiative. In Cyprus, once the Macmillan Plan was made known in the latter half of 1958, and once it was made plain that the Government was determined not to be deflected by violence from carrying out that policy, the task of the Security Forces was made easier. The maintenance of the political initiative made it far easier to win and keep the military initiative.[30]

Darling continued: 'The fight against terrorism in Cyprus was not purely a military campaign. The services were acting at all times in support of the civil power and their actions naturally had to be subordinated to political needs.'[31] In late 1958, the two paramount political needs were to avoid upsetting the Turks, who had been brought so close to an agreement, and to hold off EOKA so that the majority of Greek-Cypriots would agree to a compromise short of *enosis*. It was, in part, to prevent this shift in public opinion that EOKA continued to target 'traitors', hoping to undercut support for a compromise solution.

Turkish cooperation was important not only for securing an agreement but also for preventing the rioting and violence that Ankara seemed able to turn on and off at will. The first goal was achieved largely by soft-pedalling security operations against Turkish-Cypriots as much as possible. To achieve the second goal, holding off EOKA, British action continued against the organization throughout 1958. Targets of opportunity were attacked in spite of EOKA's ceasefire announcement. This was not only due to the security services' receipt of actionable intelligence but also due to the fact that EOKA operations continued during the ceasefire, not against British targets, at first, but against leftists, Greek-Cypriot 'traitors' and Turkish-Cypriots. The government of Cyprus felt unable to allow such disorder to proceed unchecked. To support this policy, troop levels remained high. An additional 5,000 troops and support staff had come to the island by the end of June 1958 to deal with the intercommunal clashes. British forces continued to operate at their peak strength of 30,000 men through the rest of 1958.

Political concerns were also clearly present in EOKA's thinking. Already sidelined from the political process by the August ceasefire and not consulted during the negotiations in London, Athens and Ankara, Grivas was looking for a way to remain relevant. Continued attacks on the left and against Turkish-Cypriots demonstrated EOKA's strength and its commitment to achieving the *enosis* for which so many Greek-Cypriots longed. Still, to remain in the game, Grivas needed to continue the battle with British forces. The colonel's unwillingness to be marginalized in a new move towards peace was clearly demonstrated by the course of violence following Makarios's statement at the end of September. EOKA continued its operations unabated, murdering a total of five Britons and fourteen Greeks by the end of the month.[32] It was the single highest monthly total of casualties inflicted by EOKA since 'Black November' 1956. October proved even more deadly. With Britain now the firm focus, EOKA bullets and bombs claimed the lives of sixteen Britons, twelve Greek-Cypriots and three Turkish-Cypriots. It was the first time since November 1956 that EOKA killed more Britons than Greek-Cypriots during any single month.

Although EOKA was suffering losses, its ability to inflict casualties on the British remained intact. At the same time, EOKA had not demonstrated the capacity to push the British security forces to anything close to their limits. As the prime minister noted in Cabinet on 12 August 1958, 'horrible as the atrocities committed by EOKA were, they should be seen in their correct perspective: the British forces in Cyprus had incurred only 90 fatal casualties over the previous five years'.[33] More important than even the casualty figures was the fact that British forces had never lost control of the security situation. By late 1958, with a reworked intelligence system and more boots on the ground than at any previous time, they were killing 'hard-core' targets and closing in on Grivas himself.

During this time, the rhetoric of the *enosis* movement displayed a similar resolve to that demonstrated by its gunmen. The 'Valiant Youth of EOKA' – ANE[34] – declared on 15 October that '[o]ur Ethnarchy has duly warned the British Government not to proceed with the implementation of the Monstrous "Plan". He [Makarios] has also warned Foot and company of the consequences of the introduction of such a monster by force. But no one has heeded this warning.' ANE issued a clear warning:

> There will no longer be any mercy. There will be no hesitation or sentimentalism. Our blows will be terrible wherever they may fall. No one will have the right to accuse us of any act of cruelty to which the powerful forces of Justice and morality, which encompasses our struggle, may push us. The great moment has come.

Nothing can hold us back. This is the supreme struggle. We shall all become free or die.[35]

Freedom or death would have to wait. As EOKA's war pushed on, the political goal on which it based its struggle was disintegrating under its feet. Their own spiritual leader, Archbishop Makarios, had supplied some of the fire's fuel; Greece would supply the rest. Surprisingly, it was Turkey that would provide the spark.

A war of words

The announcement that the revised Macmillan Plan would go forward shifted the landscape of the Cyprus problem dramatically. Seneca wrote that '[f]or those who do not know which port they are headed to, no wind is favourable'.[36] Macmillan's plan gave political direction to the Cyprus problem and allowed the various parties to see where they were headed. Most significantly in the short term, the plan called for the representatives from Greece and Turkey to take up their duties on the island by 1 October 1958. For Greeks and Greek-Cypriots it was a sobering prospect. They were not about to accept the plan without a fight nor were they willing to continue with Grivas's killing only to have it lead to a forced partition. The battle was renewed both on the ground in Cyprus and at the UN. Failure to achieve success in both areas would finally bring Greece to the negotiating table.

Even more significant than the decision to proceed with the Macmillan Plan was Archbishop Makarios's public statement on independence, made in an interview with Barbara Castle, the Labour MP from Blackburn. In a meeting on 22 September, Makarios told Castle that he would accept independence in place of *enosis*, as part of a solution for Cyprus. Tensions were running high. Selwyn Lloyd had informed Foot that Averoff had come to see him on the subject of the Turkish representative in Cyprus. Averoff

> said that if we went ahead with the appointment of a Turkish representative on Oct 1 revolution in Cyprus was inevitable. It was also inevitable that the Greek Government would have to react in some spectacular manner or they would be overthrown. He did not exactly say what form their reaction would take but indicated that it might be Greek withdrawal from NATO and the severance of diplomatic relations with us.[37]

Such a threat seemed less serious to the foreign secretary than failing to follow through on the stated policy:

> I do not think we could at this stage postpone or go back on the plan as the Greeks were asking us to do. The only result would be to encourage an outbreak of violence on the part of the Turkish-Cypriots which could lead to civil war in the island and a reaction in Turkey which would further embitter Greco-Turkish relations with all possible consequences for the community in Turkey.[38]

Makarios made similar statements to Castle on the subject. When she asked what the objection of Greek-Cypriots was to this appointment, Makarios replied, '[W]e know that the British Government are [sic] planning to give the Turkish government sovereign rights in Cyprus either through partition or by some other means. This will make a solution of the Cyprus question impossible.'[39] Castle, a journalist with the *Daily Mirror* before her election to Parliament, probed the archbishop about whether he thought 'the right way to solve this problem . . . [was] to take both the Greek and Turkish Governments out of the dispute'? The archbishop replied in the affirmative. When pressed for details, he added, 'I am anxious to find a way in which peace can be restored in Cyprus and bloodshed on all sides be stopped. I therefore suggest that after a fixed period of self-government Cyprus should become an independent state which is linked neither to Turkey nor to Greece.' Makarios went further, saying that he would 'accept the status of independence for Cyprus on the condition that this status shall not be changed, either by union with Greece, by partition, or by any other way, unless the United Nations approves such a change'.[40]

The man who had preached the gospel of '*enosis* and only *enosis*' for more than a decade was now proposing independence free from both Greece and Turkey. There was some confusion over the significance of the archbishop's statement. For the moment, no dramatic changes took place on the island. EOKA's violence continued as did British attempts to suppress it. The archbishop's proposal was met with scepticism in Turkey, which still did not trust him. The idea of independence, however, was not new. Greek- and Turkish-Cypriot communists had proposed it in the 1920s and 1930s. Krishna Menon, the Indian minister of defence and representative to the UN, became an advocate for Cypriot independence on the basis of it being a legitimate solution to the existence of a Cypriot nationality in 1954 and again in 1955.[41] Lord Home had proposed it in 1955.[42] In April 1957, Greek opposition leader Sophocles Venizelos had confided to Roger Allen that self-determination would have to be abandoned in favour of independence.[43] President Eisenhower was reported as favouring it in 1957.[44] Greece and Turkey had discussed independence as a possible solution through the Greek ambassador in Turkey, Giorgios Pezmazoglou, in the summer of 1957.[45] While the Greek government had not shot down these suggestions of independence, through 1957 their view was that independence would be applied only for a prescribed time period and then followed with a plebiscite to determine the island's permanent status.[46] As late as July 1958, Foreign Minister Averoff suggested to the American ambassador in Paris that independence 'within or without the British Commonwealth' was 'the best all around solution for Cyprus'. But the Greeks were still not willing to consider it a permanent solution. Averoff offered only 'a guaranty that for 25 years the Cypriots would stay within the Commonwealth'. After that, the situation would need to be reappraised, possibly through a plebiscite.[47] It was still widely understood that the desired denouement of such a referendum was *enosis*. Makarios's statement, on the other hand, presented independence as a permanent solution. By its nature, it would thus exclude both partition and *enosis*. While the timing of the statement can be understood, there is no direct evidence from Makarios as to why he chose to make this statement to Castle at this precise moment. Nevertheless, the idea of independence as a final resolution to the crisis had started to gain momentum.

In Cyprus, Hugh Foot began giving serious attention to how independence could 'be made to stick'.⁴⁸ Foot's conclusion, conveyed to John Martin at the Colonial Office in a note on 11 November, was that there should be a tripartite partnership among Great Britain, Greece and Turkey in which the three powers signed a treaty guaranteeing the independence of the island and codifying formal protections for the Turkish-Cypriot minority. Foot was convinced that the right settlement was one 'whereby the island is undivided, self-governing and independent'.⁴⁹ Such an agreement would be naturally complex and would require a degree of Greco-Turkish cooperation that seemed unlikely under the prevailing conditions. It seemed only logical that Greece's appeal at the UN later that month would hardly improve the situation.

The debate on Cyprus opened again on 24 November with a speech by Greece's foreign minister, who described the British plan as 'a knife which had been prepared for the purpose of partition in Cyprus'. The future of Cyprus, he argued, 'should be decided by Cypriots alone, without regard to "the interests of London or the ambitions of Ankara"'.⁵⁰ The British case was made by Commander Allan Noble, minister of state for foreign affairs. He described the complicated and unusual nature of the problem in Cyprus and lamented the trouble it was causing to relations among Britain, Greece and Turkey. The policy of proceeding with the Macmillan proposals was 'based on two principles: that violence must cease and peace be restored in Cyprus; and that agreement on the ultimate status of the Island cannot be reached at the present time'.⁵¹ Noble explained the framework of Macmillan's plan and the August modifications. He gave credit to Turkey for participating in the plan by appointing a representative and especially appreciated that 'To avoid provocation to Greece . . . [they] had arranged for the first holder of this office to be their then Consul-General in Nicosia'.⁵² Noble continued the line that his government did not favour partition and said that 'The Turkish-Cypriot community's preoccupation with partition is caused by distrust and enmity, which exists between the two communities. That distrust and enmity has been produced by the terrorist gangsters of EOKA'.⁵³ The minister concluded by condemning EOKA violence and withholding support for independence. While 'a noble principle', he argued that the 'Endorsement of any one final solution now would upset the delicate balance which our efforts have sought to achieve'.⁵⁴ Presenting for the Turkish side, Foreign Minister Zorlu unsurprisingly dwelt on Cyprus's historical and geographical connections with Turkey and emphasized that the principle of self-determination 'must apply equally to Turks and Greeks'.⁵⁵

A resolution on the Cyprus issue was proposed by the representative of Iran on 1 December. It was reintroduced on 4 December after two revisions. The Iranian draft urged that a conference be convened so 'that all concerned should cooperate to ensure a successful outcome'.⁵⁶ Both Britain and the United States signalled their support of the Iranian draft. Proposed amendments by Averoff were rejected or neutralized by sub-amendments from Zorlu and the Iranian draft was adopted by the committee with thirty-one in favour, twenty-two opposed and twenty-eight abstentions.⁵⁷ It would not, however, be subject to a vote in the plenary session. Greek overtures at the UN had failed to deliver once again. Greece's defeat did not spark a new debate on Cyprus; instead, it resulted in a new diplomatic initiative which would finally bring the conflict to a close.

'A resolution acceptable to both sides'

Greece's defeat at the UN seemed par for the course. Previously, failure at the UN had served as a spark for pro-*enosis* violence in Cyprus. This time, however, the diplomatic manoeuvring at the UN produced a meeting of minds between the foreign ministers of Greece and Turkey, putting Cyprus firmly and finally on a path towards an agreement. In a surprise move, Zorlu approached Averoff in New York during the debate over the Iranian resolution. According to Turkish-Cypriot leader Rauf Denktaş, who had come to New York as an observer, Zorlu went over to Averoff and told him that the UN was not the place to settle the dispute over Cyprus and that the issue should be decided directly between representatives of Greece and Turkey.[58] Turkey was looking for a solution to the problem in Cyprus. The Turks hoped that Greece's failure in New York would create the proper conditions for an agreement. While Denktaş remained concerned about what such an agreement would mean for Turkish-Cypriots, Zorlu reassured him that guarantees would protect their interests.[59]

Dimitris Bitsios also provides a brief account of the encounter between the two foreign ministers in his book, *Cyprus: The Vulnerable Republic*. After the approval of the Iranian draft, Bitsios writes, 'Zorlu approached Averoff in the lobby. He said that he regretted what had happened. He would rather have a resolution acceptable to both sides. They exchanged a few words and then Zorlu asked: "Would you like us to meet?"'[60] This got the ball rolling. In their book, *The Cyprus Conspiracy*, Brendan O'Malley and Ian Craig paint a similar picture. Relying on Averoff's recollections of the events, they record that

> the moment of Greece's humiliation [in the UN debate] became the opportunity for securing a workable compromise. Averoff recalled that at the end of the debate Greek morale was at its lowest ebb when Turkish Foreign Minister Zorlu suddenly approached him, accompanied by Ambassadors Sarper and Keural. . . . He [Zorlu] then offered to hold private talks to iron out their differences. Averoff, startled, would only agree if the Iranian motion was dropped without being put to the full General Assembly.[61]

Passed by the First Committee, the Iranian resolution 'was dropped at the Plenary session that afternoon', after what the official British report on the UN session described as 'private consultations'.[62] The basis for these discussions, in Hatzivassiliou's neat phrase, would be 'that a solution on the basis of independence could be found, as long as the Greek realized that the Turkish-Cypriots were a community (not a mere minority), and as long as the Turks realized that eighty is more than twenty'.[63]

This gambit was followed by meetings between Averoff and Zorlu in Paris during a conference of the foreign ministers of NATO countries between 16 and 18 December. Both London and Washington were well aware of the talks and eager for them to move forward. At dinner with Lennox-Boyd on 16 December, Zorlu informed the colonial secretary that talks with the Greeks were proceeding well. At their first meeting, Zorlu had told Averoff 'that EOKA violence and the conduct of the Greek Govt were forcing the Turks towards partition. If these things were changed it would be possible for the Turks and Greeks to cooperate. The Turks did not want to defeat the Greeks but wanted a success for all three Govts. Averoff responded by agreeing to have a further talk.'[64]

Zorlu was clear to both Averoff and Lennox-Boyd 'that the status for Cyprus he had been discussing with Averoff was not really independence'. Its international status, as defined by its constitution, would be based on 'alliances and the right of veto on either side in regard to the minorities. The island', argued Zorlu, 'must be Turkish-Greek not Greek or Cypriot. Outside the sovereign Brit bases sovereignty would be shared between Turkey and Greece.'[65] Assuring the British on the issue of the bases, both the Greeks and Turks were in agreement that the bases 'must remain under Brit sovereignty'.[66] This, the key concession desired by British policymakers, all but assured their consent to whatever details the Greeks and Turks would arrange between them. Neither Greece nor Turkey opposed the idea of continued British bases on Cyprus. Both governments, in fact, had supported a continued British presence. Makarios and the Greek-Cypriot nationalists remained the only obstacle. Makarios had admitted that he would accept independence, and Zorlu claimed that Averoff had confided to him 'that the Greek Govt would not be deterred by Makarios'.[67] After all, without Greek support, it would be nearly impossible for advocates of the *enosis* cause to carry on alone.

The Americans were getting a similar story from the Greeks. Washington's ambassador in Paris wrote to the State Department on 19 December: 'Averoff said that in discussions with Turks . . . attempt being made to arrive at mutually acceptable formula for an independent Cyprus.'[68] Ambassador Houghton reported that Averoff believed Turkey's motivation to be '(1) the widespread sentiment expressed in the UNGA for independence as best solution, (2) genuine concern over ME developments, and (3) desire to reach relatively favourable settlement before possible advent Labor government in UK'. Turkish diplomats sounded a similarly positive, if still cautious, note to the Americans as well, 'commenting on improved atmosphere between two countries'.[69]

The Greeks also had their reasons for wanting a solution. Developments in the Middle East affected them as well as the Turks. More importantly, the strong showing by the communists in the May 1958 elections weakened the position of the Greek government. A solution on Cyprus and the renewal of the partnership with Turkey leading to a strengthening of Greece's NATO ties would remove the Greek government's largest outstanding foreign policy crisis. The Greek general staff made it a point to highlight the interdependence between Greece and Turkey. As Bitsios wrote years later, solving the Cyprus problem had become a priority for the Greek government. From the Greek perspective, there were real questions

> about how much longer the country could go through a crisis of such magnitude; a crisis which upset its normal progress, and jeopardized our security by putting us at loggerheads with some of our closest allies. In Cyprus, the situation was steadily deteriorating. We had information that the British forces were on the tracks of Dighenis. Many Cypriots were in prison or behind the barbed wires of the concentration camps.[70]

International crises and the deepening of the Cold War, combined with the explosive conditions prevailing in Cyprus, brought the governments in Athens and Ankara to the realization that it was time to make a deal.[71]

Diplomatic progress had a real effect in Cyprus itself. On Christmas Eve 1958, an EOKA leaflet announced another ceasefire. Signed by Dighenis, the paper declared that EOKA would

> stop all ... activities as long as the other side will do the same. And we will wait to see how the British Government intends to implement United Nations decisions. We are ready for either a long armed struggle if Britain continues her intransigence or for a cessation of the struggle if a solution which will satisfy the claims of the Cypriot people is given to them.[72]

While Grivas seemed to hedge about the newly conciliatory attitude from Athens, the bishop of Kyrenia led the most radical *enosis* hardliners in denouncing the Greek government for abandoning their cause. An official response from Foreign Minister Averoff was published in the Greek press on Christmas day. Averoff denounced the bishop of Kyrenia's attack and wrote that by his statement he had 'put himself in opposition first to the will of the great majority of the Cypriots'.[73] The unity of purpose between the Greek government and the Greek-Cypriot nationalists was unravelling.

Averoff had a busy Christmas. Not only did he respond to criticism from the bishop of Kyrenia, but on Christmas morning he was also immediately on the telephone to the British ambassador in Athens. Averoff argued to Allen that the ceasefire was of great significance. 'In his view it was the first step on the road to our getting Grivas out of the island. He [Grivas] could of course never offer to go, but this seemed to have been inspired by the improved atmosphere generally and particularly in Cyprus, and might lead to a real end of violence.'[74] The position of Grivas was critical. Ambassador Allen wrote to the Foreign Office that 'the crux of the matter was the attitude of Grivas ... if Grivas could be won round then of course, there was nothing to be feared from Kyrenia.'[75] Just as the impending Greek agreement with Turkey limited Makarios's scope for action so did it reduce Grivas's options. Peace was within reach; it remained only for the Greeks and Turks to grab it together.

A Greco-Turkish summit meeting was arranged for the start of February and would take place in Zurich at the Dolder Hotel. As Bitsios describes, the meeting between Karamanlis and Menderes was highly significant. 'A summit Greco-Turkish conference on Cyprus [involving prime ministers] implied something more than an exchange of views. It meant that substantial negotiations had already taken place, and that they had sufficiently progressed to justify the expectation that an agreement was imminent.'[76] For the British too, the conference was significant as described in a brief note from Macmillan to Foot. 'You and I are naturally watching Zurich with crossed fingers', wrote the prime minister: 'Much will depend on these talks.'[77] The discussions began on 6 February. With many of the details already agreed on during the previous negotiations among the foreign ministers, progress was swift. By 11 February it was all settled. As Bitsios wrote, '[A] champagne toast ... sealed the agreement between the two Prime Ministers. The foreign correspondents cabled that night the unbelievable news that Greece and Turkey had settled their conflict.[78] The agreement was as swift as it had been unexpected.

As communicated to the British the next day, the settlement had eleven points. Greece, Turkey and the newly created Republic of Cyprus would be allies, cooperating in matters of defence. Greece and Turkey would protect the independence 'and territorial integrity of the Republic of Cyprus'. There would be a tripartite military headquarters with a rotating command on Cyprus, along with 950 Greek and 650 Turkish soldiers who would undertake to train the Cypriot army.[79] The presence of Turkish troops in Cyprus had been the sticking point for Turkish-Cypriots. Kütchük and Denktaş had insisted that guarantees needed to be upheld by Turkish troops. According to Denktaş, they forced Zorlu to include this point.[80] The remaining five points were listed separately as a 'Gentleman's Agreement' between Menderes and Karamanlis. Two minor points dealt with the command of the headquarters and the framing of a constitution by committee. The other three points touched on more substantive issues. First, Greece and Turkey would support the entry of Cyprus into NATO. Second, the two prime ministers would encourage the new president and vice-president of Cyprus to continue the prohibition of the communist party. And last, 'immediately after the signature of the treaties all the emergency measures now imposed in Cyprus will be lifted and a general amnesty shall be proclaimed'. Both Zorlu and Averoff insisted that the provisions of the 'Gentleman's Agreement' had to 'be given top security classification [by the British government] since they do not intend it ever to become public'.[81]

To put the final agreement into place, both prime ministers flew to London to add Britain to the settlement. Karamanlis arrived, but Menderes's plane crashed outside London on the afternoon of 17 February due to bad weather. Menderes suffered only minor injuries, but nine of the sixteen passengers died along with five of the eight crew members. The London Conference, however, would proceed without him. That night, Macmillan invited the Greek delegation to dinner. Karamanlis, Averoff and Bitsios all attended. Perhaps taking the opportunity of having the Greeks alone, Macmillan suddenly, and nonchalantly, asked Averoff what he thought would happen if Grivas's hideout was discovered and the colonel was arrested that very night. Bitsios records what happened next:

> Averoff, after expressing strong doubts on the possibilities of such a measure, added that he did not personally know Dighenis, but from what he had heard of him, he believed that he could not be captured alive. Macmillan beckoned Sir Hugh Foot, the Governor of Cyprus, to approach and after telling him of Averoff's reaction, he said that the Foreign Minister doubted that the British had discovered Grivas' hideout. Foot, in a way of confirming, asked Averoff: 'What would you say about a farm outside Limassol, with a hideout under a trap-door?' Averoff addressing himself to the British Prime Minister said: 'If you arrest Grivas, we shall interrupt the negotiations and return immediately to Athens.' After dinner, he went straight to our Embassy and cabled Nicosia that Dighenis should be alerted at once.[82]

Averoff's swift cable to Cyprus suggests that Macmillan was not making idle threats. Darling's Chief of Intelligence, John Prendergast, had finally succeeded in tracking Grivas down. As Darling records,

> John Prendergast came to my house one evening and told me that we had run Grivas and some of his closest associates to ground. . . . The house was under very tight surveillance; he asked for instructions as to what action should be taken. . . . As I was quite clear in my mind that I was not prepared to risk a single British life in the process, it was unlikely that Grivas would be taken alive. May be this would be rough justice, but Grivas had a very heavy debt of murder, torture and sabotage to discharge. However this may be, to have acted in this way at this critical time would have been irresponsible to a degree. At a meeting held by Mr. George Sinclair, the Deputy Governor . . . it was agreed that the only practical course of action was to instruct John Prendergast to fly home that very night to London, to give the information we had to Hugh Foot and to seek instructions as to whether Grivas's head was required on a charger or whether he should be allowed to stew in his own juice. John Prendergast returned after a very short absence to say that we were to adopt the latter course.[83]

Once again, political factors played a major role in influencing military action. With Grivas apparently at their mercy, the British security forces did not seize EOKA's commander for fear that such an act would undermine the precarious peace agreement that was to be clinched in London. The delicate nature of the situation was reinforced once the conference began, as it soon became apparent that Makarios had ambitions to adjust the terms that had been reached between Greece and Turkey. The archbishop, however, was disabused of his idea by the firmness of the Greek government. The agreements from Zurich represented a commitment on the part of Athens and they would not break it to suit the archbishop. In his account, Bitsios adds that other members of the Greek-Cypriot delegation pressured Makarios. '[P]ressure came from his own people. The Metropolitan of Kition and the Abbot of the Kykkou monastery were again present in our conversation. When Makarios said that, if need be, he would resign, the Abbot of Kykkou retorted: "Do resign, and let somebody else pull us out of this deadlock and give us our independence".'[84] Makarios, apparently having learned little from the course of his failed discussions with Harding, was still demonstrating 'his tendency to push things to the extreme before agreeing'.[85] Nevertheless, this was, according to the recollection of at least one person who spoke with Makarios about the subject, the 'hardest decision' of the archbishop's life. Perhaps it should not have been so fraught. Karamanlis made the situation clear with brutal frankness: 'I give you Cyprus on a plate and you refuse to take it', he supposedly shouted at the procrastinating prelate. 'It's monstrous.'[86]

After a short night's sleep, Makarios made his decision. As Foot wrote to Sinclair back in Cyprus,

> Things have been moving very fast. Last night [the 18th] at another meeting of the conference the Archbishop was pressed to make a definite statement that he

accepted the agreements and the British declaration as the agreed foundation for the final settlement of the Cyprus problem. He waived and said that, if he had to give an answer at once, it would be no. After a short adjournment he agreed he would give a definite answer yes or no by 9.45 this morning [the 19th]. We have just heard that the answer is yes and consequently the full conference with Prime Ministers is to be reconvened this afternoon at 3 pm.[87]

Makarios then handed a statement to Foot. It read:

The agreement reached at Zurich by the Greek and Turkish Governments with the declaration of the British Government constitute a good basis for the solution of the problem of Cyprus. We are prepared in full consultation and cooperation with all the people of Cyprus to work for *the preparation of a detailed constitution and* [hand addition] the establishment of a free and independent Cyprus.[88]

Preparing the constitution would take more months of tortuous negotiations; it was not ratified until 16 August 1960 when the Republic of Cyprus officially came into existence. Archbishop Makarios became the island's first president. Dr Kütchük was installed as his vice-president with full veto power. *Enosis* and partition were formally renounced, even if the hearts of people on both sides had not changed. The politicians celebrated the compromise. In his closing statement, Macmillan admitted that, to reach an agreement, 'each of us, all of us in this room, have had to make concessions, and I am sure that it was right to make these mutual concessions'.[89] The final agreement recognized 'the right of the people of Cyprus to an independent status in the world', and recognized 'the Hellenic character of the majority of the Cypriot people. But it . . . also . . . [protected] the character and culture of the Cypriot Turkish community.' Britain's 'defence facilities . . . essential not only for . . . narrow national purposes but for . . . greater alliances', were preserved.[90] Karamanlis and Zorlu evoked the image of Greco-Turkish cooperation fostered by Venizelos and Ataturk. All sides expressed hope for the future and the importance of goodwill and trust in making the settlement a success.[91]

There were reasons for hope. For all the years of anguish, political manoeuvring and human loss, Greece and Turkey had avoided war. Britain had ended the insurgency and kept two sovereign bases while retreating from the rest of the island. NATO, and the interests of the west in the Middle East, had been secured. The denouement represented a compromise. Much had been given up by all sides, but not everyone was pleased with the final result.

Conclusion

The Cypriot people . . . deserved a better fate than the shackles which were forged for them in Zurich.[1]

– Grivas, *Memoirs*

'We have won'

Among the *enosis* hardliners, the independence compromise was met with a combination of anger and frustration. Grivas described

> Bitterness . . . at leaving the Cypriots before they could be given the full freedom of union with Mother Greece. . . . I did my duty, as I saw it, to the end. But the Cypriot people, who fought so bravely and for so long, deserved a better fate than the shackles which were forged for them in Zurich; and those who bound the people's hands behind their backs in London carry the full responsibility for what they did.[2]

It is an irony with deep roots in the problems of Cyprus, that Greece, the object of so much affection among Greek-Cypriots and the motherland in whose name the sacrifices of the struggle had been made, helped forge the 'shackles' described by Grivas. *Enosis* supporters had longed to put their island under the political control of Athens. For a few key moments during the Zurich negotiations, it essentially was. From the start, Greek leaders had been wary of the cause of Cypriot *enosis*. Support, while real, had always been tempered by the constraints of the possible: by fear of Turkish violence – both against Greece itself and against the Greeks living in Istanbul – by international pressure and by Greece's own lack of resources. In Zurich, finding a way out of the Cyprus tangle, Greek policymakers took the road that opened for them.

Uneasiness in the relationship between Grivas and Makarios, which had been present to varying degrees throughout the struggle, also escalated. Now, it took on a more public character. Even as the agreements were signed, Grivas debated the merits of openly opposing the archbishop and continuing the insurgency. The colonel knew that Makarios, having signed the agreements

> would turn against us if we renewed the struggle, taking with him part of the population, large or small. . . . The prospect of civil war among the Greek-Cypriots was a night-mare; yet if Cyprus had offered more space for manoeuvre and easier communication with the outside world for arms supplies I would have seriously considered turning Greeks against Greeks in confidence that I should quickly

master the situation. Unhappily I had to decide that as things were the odds against carrying on the war in Cyprus was overwhelming. There would be endlessly prolonged bloodshed, but no final victory for either side. In the end I decided with a heavy heart that I must call a cease-fire, leaving the Archbishop and his friends to implement the agreement as best they could in the absence of my approval.[3]

In an order issued to EOKA leaders, Grivas explained that he had 'reached the conclusion that to continue to fight would . . . divide Cyprus and perhaps the whole of the Greek people with disastrous results'. Grivas's personal experiences had a strong influence on his thinking as the subsequent example in his order proved:

I shudder to think of the results of national division, such as the conflict between King Constantine and Eleftherios Venizelos, through which I lived and which not only destroyed the dreams of a greater Greece but was a burden on the whole nation for decades after 1916 with tragic consequences culminating in the Asia Minor Catastrophe. Greece today has still not entirely recovered from this. It is preferable to accept a solution, even one that is not entirely good, than to have civil discord since with the latter nothing remains standing. Because of the likelihood of such terrible consequences and the doubtful results which a continuation of the struggle without the people's full support would bring about, I have been obliged to accept the agreement which has been drawn up.[4]

For the time being, Grivas was putting the greater good of Cyprus ahead of his political ambitions and the sacred cause of *enosis*. The power and influence of Makarios coupled with the deteriorating political situation and the changing attitude of Greek policymakers made continuing the guerrilla campaign increasingly untenable. These were good arguments against continuing the fight, but neither can we discard Grivas's reasoning nor can we ignore the painful experience of the recent Greek Civil War. Grivas remained deeply conflicted over his decision. As subsequent events proved, the EOKA leader never abandoned the cause of *enosis* and was willing to oppose Makarios and eventually divide the Greeks of Cyprus in order to achieve it. But that was for the future.

Immediately after the compromise, a feeling of sorrow and failure settled over the hard-core supporters of *enosis*. Eleni Seraphim, the Larnaca area commander, recorded her reaction upon hearing Makarios pretentiously pronounce the victory of their struggle.[5] The archbishop's 'words ["We have won!"] echoed like a bitter irony in the ears of many of us there', she wrote. 'It was true that we had all accepted the decisions of our political leadership which, with unexplained haste, had now closed the Cyprus question.'[6] For many EOKA hardliners, Makarios's change of heart was nothing less than a betrayal of their life's cause. The archbishop's volte-face split the Greek-Cypriot right in a break that remains to this day. While Grivas obeyed, and agreed to lay down arms in 1959, the hopes of many EOKA men that Cyprus would one day achieve union with Greece did not die.

The defeat of the *enosis* cause had come at a high price in human life, diplomatic relations, political capital and, within Cyprus, social cohesion. Opposition had come not only from the British but also from Turkey and Turkish-Cypriots. Greek-Cypriots in the service of the state had also suffered a great deal and were targeted by EOKA as 'traitors'. Left-wing Greek-Cypriots had also become the targets of lethal violence by EOKA. Often such victims were 'traitors' and leftists only in the imagination of EOKA operatives. EOKA's leaders were characterized by their opposition to communism. Eventually, their anti-communism sentiments translated into open violence against Greek-Cypriot leftists. Both Grivas and Makarios hoped that an armed struggle for *enosis* could alter the political landscape on the island and compel Britain to a compromise leading to unification with Greece. This hope ignored both political and military realities. Turkey had a genuine interest in Cyprus and would not agree to it being handed over to Greece. This political miscalculation and the *enosis* movement's disregard for Turkish and Turkish-Cypriot interests throughout the struggle reaped a bitter harvest.

When considering the forces arrayed against it, it is, perhaps, not surprising that the *enosis* movement failed. Two of the movement's greatest shortcomings were its unwillingness to acknowledge the seriousness of Turkish-Cypriot opposition and its inability to comprehend the broad international situation, particularly the influence of Turkey. *Enosis* activists beginning with Makarios and Grivas considered Turkish-Cypriots a negligible part of the equation from the time they began planning the struggle. They failed to consider the extent of the hostility that would emerge in Turkey and from within the Turkish-Cypriot community as a result of their turn to violence. They underestimated the resolve of British policymakers to retain a presence in Cyprus. In spite of the numerous challenges, EOKA was able to survive in the field for almost four years due to the deep commitment of its members and the reality that a few armed and ideologically committed individuals with some basic organization and external assistance were extremely difficult to eradicate.

Although British forces killed and captured many EOKA leaders, enough fighters and senior members, especially Grivas, remained to perpetuate violence. In the end, EOKA's failure to achieve *enosis* was the result of a combination of political and military factors. By 1959, EOKA could not continue its struggle because the political support for that struggle, both from Makarios and from the Greek government, was evaporating. The Greek government feared a confrontation with Turkey and did not wish to lose British and American aid in the continuing battle against communism. As was often the case, the fate of Cyprus was determined by larger historical forces than those playing out on the island itself. Makarios felt that violence had accomplished as much as it could and that to continue would inflict pointless suffering on the Cypriot people. EOKA's shortcomings in the field prompted its political supporters (at home and abroad) to rethink the situation and to come to a negotiated solution. Britain's response, both militarily and diplomatically had been robust, more robust, perhaps, than the *enosis* cause had anticipated. If EOKA had been able to combat the Turkish-Cypriots more effectively, or to compel the British to withdraw, or if Greece had been stronger relative to Turkey, the political imperatives might have shifted.

The *enosis* movement was no stranger to politics. The battle for union with Greece had been fought out through plebiscites and petitions, UN appeals and diplomatic backchannels long before the recourse to arms. Makarios authorized the beginning of the struggle in the aftermath of Greece's failed appeal at the UN in late 1954. The struggle ended after secret agreements between Greece and Turkey to settle the future of Cyprus set in motion after the UN session in late 1958.

Before that settlement took place, EOKA violence permeated every facet of Cypriot life between April 1955 and February 1959. No one was immune from the organization's threats or attacks. Given the limited scope of EOKA operations, the struggle had been surprisingly costly. In the course of the fighting, 105 British servicemen lost their lives, the great majority of which, 81, came from the army. Another 603 were wounded. EOKA killed fifty-one members of the CPF: twelve British, twenty-two Turkish-Cypriots, fifteen Greek-Cypriots and two Cypriots of other heritage. In addition, 185 policemen were wounded. Sadly, civilians suffered most. Some 238 Cypriot civilians lost their lives to EOKA during the course of struggle, and another 288 were wounded.[7] Ironically, 203 of the dead were Greek-Cypriots killed by EOKA for being leftists or 'traitors'. Altogether, EOKA murdered twice as many Greek-Cypriots as Englishmen – a disturbing statistic when one considers the premise of EOKA's struggle. Turkish-Cypriots also suffered greatly. Approximately 55 per cent of police casualties and 58 per cent of police fatalities were Turkish-Cypriots, clear evidence both of their prevalence in the force and EOKA's deliberate targeting of them. In Darling's final report on the Cyprus Emergency, security forces claimed that they had killed ninety EOKA men in operations.[8] At least another four EOKA men blew themselves up making explosives while nine were hanged by the authorities. One of the hanged, Evagoras Pallikarides, was only nineteen years old. Cyprus, like Palestine, was a rare case where insurgents suffered fewer casualties than security forces.

In spite of the casualty differential, British forces were able to 'hold the ring' effectively against EOKA. In doing so, they employed lessons (and indeed personnel) from emergencies in Palestine, Malaya and Kenya. In spite of Cyprus's particular problems, the insurgency there had echoes in other examples. British policymakers invariably chose to draw lessons from either Malaya or Kenya – where emergency operations had met with some degree of success – although the closest parallel to Cyprus, in many ways, was Palestine. In both areas Britain confronted a determined nationalist insurgency. Both EOKA and the Zionists drew strength from a fiercely nationalist ideology. Their tactics of targeted assassinations, bombings and ambushes were quite similar. Both insurgencies took place in bi-ethnic societies where the 'other' group – the Arabs in Palestine and the Turks in Cyprus – were (over)employed as members of the police force to contain violence. Both the Palestinian Arabs and the Turks of Cyprus demanded equal access to the right of self-determination but failed, during that period, to attain it. Both insurgencies took place in sensitive political regions and had ramifications beyond their borders, regionally and internationally. And, tragically, both conflicts continue into the present and have left scars which remain unhealed.

Through the emergencies of the 1940s and 1950s, the British learned the importance of a strong police force in combating an insurgency, the need for a centralized command structure and the critical role of intelligence. Drawing on experiences from Palestine and Kenya, the British were also able to use covert operations – like the Q unit – to beat the insurgents at their own game. Still, except for brief periods when the politicians stopped talking, as in March 1956 with the exile of Makarios or in the months between Suez and March 1957, operations were always dependent on the political situation. Even the arrest of Grivas himself was called off due to political considerations. Tactical 'lessons' accounted for marginal improvements, but the substance of success or failure was dictated by developments in the political situation.

In the final analysis, the settlement in Cyprus was an incomplete victory for all sides involved. Britain had blocked *enosis*, but British sovereignty was reduced to 99 square miles to serve as base areas. Greek-Cypriot nationalists gained independence but renounced *enosis*; Turkish-Cypriots abandoned partition but accepted membership as a protected minority within the newly created Republic of Cyprus under a Greek-Cypriot president and a Greek-Cypriot majority. Each party was forced into sacrifices and compromises, but each also received critical concessions. Given that the solution was reached through negotiation, this should not come as a surprise. Compromise was the essential ingredient, allowing for the isolation of the most radical elements through concessions aimed at more moderate elements.

For Greek- and Turkish-Cypriots, peace short of victory had its pitfalls. Among Greek-Cypriots, aspirations for *enosis* did not simply disappear with the Zurich-London agreements. Turkish-Cypriots were not entirely convinced that the complex new constitution would prove a workable solution to the island's divisions. Old allegiances, ambitions and fears remained. Within a few years of the agreements, Cyprus was once again on the brink of disaster. This time, conflict would not be with the British occupier, but, as in the summer of 1958, among the Cypriot people. Once again Greek-Cypriots in favour of *enosis* engaged in violence not only against Turkish-Cypriots but also against other Greek-Cypriots, this time the supporters of Makarios and an independent Cyprus. The archbishop played a dangerous double-game, at times opposing, at times encouraging, these groups.

In September 1961, Dr Kütchük, now vice-president of the Republic of Cyprus, sent Makarios a letter asking for the archbishop's 'assistance in order to avoid the recurrence' of incidents of 'humiliation and insubordination' suffered by Turkish-Cypriot lawmakers.[9] Kütchük complained about a number of persons within the government 'openly condemning the Zurich and London Agreements', of statements made in support of the EOKA struggle and of using the current situation as a stepping stone towards *enosis* and of 'discrimination against Turks and anything that is Turkish' displayed by the Greek-Cypriot minister of foreign affairs.[10]

By 1963, the island's complex and fragile constitution had broken down. On his arrival on the island on 7 April 1964, the second British High Commissioner discovered a divided island torn by civil strife:

> The state of tension prevailing in the vicinity of the 'Green Line' [dividing the two communities] in Nicosia extended to a greater or lesser degree through the island. ... Roadblocks, fortified posts and emplacements were much in evidence, manned by well-armed men. ... The situation was worsened by the fact that some of these armed guerrillas, both Greek and Turkish, were at this time operating as 'private armies' outside the control of the Greek and Turkish Governmental authorities, who were unable to call them to account for the abductions, murders and other

crimes which they committed. . . . The Turkish-Cypriot community was, in the view of the Greek-Cypriot administration, in a state of active rebellion, which they claimed justified the most rigorous measures against them, including the arbitrary arrest and cutting off of supplies of food, fuel, water, petrol, medicines, building materials; anything which it was held the community might use to defend themselves.[11]

Hostility between the two communities continued throughout the 1960s and early 1970s, increasing tensions with Turkey. Internationally, conditions contributed to instability. In May 1960, a military coup deposed and hanged Prime Minister Adnan Menderes and Foreign Minister Zorlu – the leaders responsible for Turkey's role in the compromise. Relations between Cyprus and Greece soured, particularly after the Greek military coup in 1967. Relations took a further dive when General Ioannides removed Colonel Papadopoulos from power in a second coup in November 1973. This signalled a change in Cypriot-Greek relations. Ioannides was hostile to Makarios and collaborated with former EOKA men to remove him from power. In 1971, a group opposing Makarios and still committed to the *enosis* cause created an organization they called EOKA-B. In 1974, after the death of Grivas, this group would spearhead a coup against Archbishop Makarios with Ioannides's blessing.

Seizing on the opportunity presented by the coup, Turkish troops moved on Cyprus and occupied the northern city of Kyrenia. Cyprus was once more plunged into war and destruction. Three weeks later, Turkish forces pushed out from their bridgehead and overran more than a third of the island. Approximately 2,000 Greek-Cypriots were killed in the fighting; another 1,600 were declared missing and essentially feared dead. Over 200,000 Cypriots became refugees in the wake of the invasion. Northern Cyprus remains occupied and Nicosia is the world's last divided capital. Unfortunately for Cyprus, while the memories of EOKA's campaign may be bitter, the wounds of the coup and Turkish invasion are raw. And, while monuments, memorials and museums commemorate the struggle of the 1950s, barbed wire and concrete machine-gun nests separate the two halves of Cyprus in a divide that endures to this day.

In the end, the failure of the *enosis* cause had many authors: Makarios's ambition, the inflexibility of Grivas and other *enosis* hardliners (both within Cyprus and within Greece), the slothfulness and cynicism of British policymakers, and Turkey's covetousness of the island. In spite of these factors, a workable solution had almost been achieved. Its failure was a cruel end to the dream of *enosis*.

Notes

Introduction

1 Ένωσις.
2 Εθνική Οργάνωσις Κυπρίων Αγωνιστών.
3 Türk Mukavemet Teşkilatı.
4 Steven G. Galpern, *Money, Oil, and Empire in the Middle East* (Cambridge: Cambridge University Press, 2009), p. 10.
5 TNA, CAB 21/2925, 'Report on Colonial Security by Sir Gerald Templer', 23 April 1955, p. 52.
6 For Malaya see John Coates, *Suppressing Insurgency: An Analysis of the Malayan Emergency, 1948–1954* (Boulder: Westview Press, 1992). For Kenya see David Anderson, *Histories of the Hanged: The Dirty War in Kenya and the End of Empire* (New York: W.W. Norton, 2005), and Huw Bennett, *Fighting the Mau Mau: The British Army and Counter-Insurgency in the Kenya Emergency* (Cambridge: Cambridge University Press, 2012).
7 David French, *Fighting EOKA: The British Counter-Insurgency Campaign on Cyprus, 1955–1959* (Oxford: Oxford University Press, 2012).
8 From the title of his book *Cyprus: Reluctant Republic* (The Hague and Paris: Mouton, 1973).
9 David French, *The British Way in Counter-Insurgency, 1945–1967* (Oxford: Oxford University Press, 2012).
10 John Newsinger, *British Counterinsurgency: From Palestine to Northern Ireland* (Houndmills: Palgrave, 2002).
11 David Anderson, 'Policing and Communal Conflict: The Cyprus Emergency', in *Policing and Decolonisation: Politics, Nationalism, and the Police, 1917–65*, ed. David M. Anderson and David Killingray (New York: St. Martin's Press, 1992), p. 210.
12 Thomas R. Mockaitis, *British Counterinsurgency, 1919–1960* (New York: St Martin's Press, 1990).
13 Robert Holland and Diana Markides, *The British and the Hellenes: Struggles for Mastery in the Eastern Mediterranean 1850–1960* (Oxford: Oxford University Press, 2006), p. 213.

Chapter 1

1 Richard Clogg, 'The Byzantine Legacy in the Modern Greek World: The *Megali Idea*', in *The Byzantine Legacy in Eastern Europe*, ed. Lowell Clucas (Boulder: East European Monographs, 1988), p. 254.
2 There were, of course, other reverses, most significantly the 'Asia Minor Catastrophe' in which Greece's attempt to gain the city of Smyrna and much of the Western coast of Anatolia was defeated by Turkish Nationalists under Mustafa Kemal in 1922.

3 Μεγάλη Ιδέα.
4 Ioannis Stefanidis, *Stirring the Greek Nation: Political Culture, Irredentism and Anti-Americanism in Post-War Greece, 1945–1967* (Hampshire: Ashgate Publishing, 2007), p. 18.
5 Μικρασιατική Καταστροφή.
6 Stefanidis, *Stirring the Greek Nation*, p. 20.
7 The conventional dating of the Greek Civil War is 1946–9 even though there were clashes between communist and anti-communist forces before, notably during the *Dekemvrianá*, December 1944–January 1945.
8 For example, J. G. Peristiany, 'Anthropological, Sociological, and Geographical Fieldwork in Cyprus', *Annals of the New York Academy of Sciences*, Vol. 268 (1976), p. 344. Alexis Kyrou, one of Greece's foremost diplomats involved in the Cyprus issue and permanent representative to the United Nations, was a particularly articulate exponent of this view. He spearheaded the first Greek attempt to get the support of the United Nations for Cypriot self-determination in 1954.
9 USNA, DA/CIA, *Truth about Greece: Cyprus*, Pamphlet XII, Athens, August 1950.
10 For example, G. H. Hall, secretary of state for the colonies TNA CAB 129/11/CP46(260), 'Proposed New Policy for Cyprus', 5 July 1946. Anthony Eden, *Full Circle* (London: Cassell, 1960), p. 395. Harold Macmillan, *Tides of Fortune: 1945–1955* (New York: Harper and Row, 1969), p. 660. This assertion was based on the unique history of the island. At the eastern rim of the Byzantine influence, it had been ruled through a Byzantine–Arab condominium from the seventh through the tenth century. At the end of the twelfth century, it was in open rebellion from Byzantium and became a possession of Richard the Lionheart, the knights Templar and finally the Crusader house of Lusignan in short succession. The Lusignan family retained control until the island passed to Venetian rule in 1489. It was conquered by the Ottomans in 1571.
11 Diary of Sir Charles Belcher quoted in Alexis Rappas, *Cyprus in the 1930s: British Colonial Rule and the Roots of the Cyprus Conflict* (London: I.B. Tauris, 2014), p. 16.
12 Sir Ronald Storrs, *The Memoirs of Sir Ronald Storrs* (New York: G.P. Putnam's Sons, 1937), p. 495.
13 Churchill quoted in Storrs, *Memoirs*, pp. 490–1.
14 Füsün Türkmen, 'Cyprus 1964 Revisited: Was It Humanitarian Intervention?' *Perceptions*, Winter 2005, p. 70.
15 Storrs, *The Memoirs of Sir Ronald Storrs*, pp. 494–5.
16 TNA FO 141/4281. Report on the Cyprus National Party, 22 June 1949.
17 Peter Loizou, 'Notes on Future Anthropological Research in Cyprus', in *Regional Variation in Modern Greece and Cyprus: Towards a Perspective on the Ethnography of Greece*, ed. Muriel Dimen and Ernestine Friedl (New York: New York Academy of Sciences, 1976), p. 361.
18 Mete Hatay, 'Three Ways of Sharing the Sacred: Choreographies of Coexistence in Cyprus', in *Religion, Politics, and Conflict Resolution*, ed. Elazar Barkan and Karen Barkey (New York: Columbia University Press, 2015), p. 91.
19 Elena Brambilla, 'Convivencia under Muslim Rule: The Island of Cyprus after the Ottoman Conquest (1571–1640)'. Working paper. ND c. 2010, pp. 124–6; Joseph L. Scherer, *Blocking the Sun: The Cyprus Conflict* (Minneapolis: Minnesota Mediterranean and East European Monographs, No. 5, 1997), p. 48.
20 Scherer, *Blocking the Sun*, p. 6.
21 Frank Tachau, 'The Face of Turkish Nationalism: As Reflected in the Cyprus Dispute', *Middle East Journal*, Vol. 13, No. 3 (Summer 1959), p. 262.

22 Author's interview with Rauf Denktaş, Nicosia, 10 April 2009.
23 *Halkın Sesi*, Vol. 1, No. 1, 9 July 1956.
24 Yiannis Papadakis, 'Greek-Cypriot Narratives of History and Collective Identity: Nationalism as a Contested Process', *American Ethnologist*, Vol. 25, No. 2 (May 1998), pp. 154–5.
25 Konstantinos Dimaras, *Ellinikós Romantismós* (Greek Romanticism) (Athens: Ermis, 1985), pp. 325–419.
26 Holland and Markides, *The British and the Hellenes*, p. 167.
27 Stefanidis, *Stirring the Greek Nation*, p. 15.
28 Steven Runciman, *The Fall of Constantinople 1453* (Cambridge: Cambridge University Press, 1965), p. 71.
29 Charles A. Frazee, *The Orthodox Church and Independent Greece 1821–1852* (Cambridge: Cambridge University Press, 1969), p. 2.
30 Stefanidis, *Stirring the Greek Nation*, p. 16.
31 Antonis Paparizos, 'Enlightenment, Religion, and Tradition in Modern Greek Society', in *Greek Political Culture Today*, ed. Nikos Demertzis (Athens: Odysseas, 2000), pp. 74–115, p. 89.
32 For example, through 1957, British administrators in Cyprus categorized members of the police according to their religious affiliation rather than their national identity. Only in the annual report for 1958 did 'Greek-Cypriot' and 'Turkish-Cypriot' replace 'Christian Orthodox' and 'Moslem' respectively.
33 Yiorghos Leventis, *Cyprus: The Struggle for Self-Determination in the 1940s, Prelude to Deeper Crisis* (Frankfurt: Peter Lang, 2002), pp. 29–31.
34 Stefanidis, *Stirring the Greek Nation*, p. 16.
35 'Convention of Defensive Alliance between Great Britain and Turkey, with respect to the Asiatic Provinces of Turkey', in *The Map of Europe by Treaty: Showing the Various Political and Territorial Changes Which Have Taken Place since the General Peace of 1814*, Vol. IV, 1875–91, ed. Edward Hertslet (London: Harrison and Sons, 1891), pp. 2722–3.
36 The first four British statesmen to govern Cyprus served as 'Administrators'. Beginning in April 1898 with Sir William F. Haynes-Smith, the title was high commissioner. Sir Malcolm Stevenson was the first to hold the title of governor and commander-in-chief from 1 May 1925 when Cyprus became a crown colony.
37 *The Times* (London), 7 August 1878.
38 Robert Holland, *Britain and the Revolt in Cyprus 1954–1959* (Oxford: Clarendon Press, 1998), p. 20.
39 Holland and Markides, *The British and the Hellenes*, p. 164.
40 Holland, *Britain and the Revolt in Cyprus*, p. 21.
41 Michael Llewellyn Smith, *Ionian Vision: Greece in Asia Minor, 1919–1922* (Ann Arbor: The University of Michigan Press, 1998), p. 14.
42 Venezelist propaganda painted Constantine I as a German sympathizer. He did receive part of his education in Germany and he was married to Sophia of Prussia, the sister of Kaiser Wilhelm II.
43 Holland and Markides, *The British and the Hellenes*, p. 180.
44 Virgil, *Aeneid*, trans. Robert Fitzgerald (New York: Vintage Books, 1990), IV, p. 722.
45 Rappas, *Cyprus in the 1930s*, p. 3.
46 Ibid.
47 Yiannos Katsourides, *The History of the Communist Party in Cyprus: Colonialism, Class, and the Cypriot Left* (London: I.B. Tauris, 2014), p. 175.

48 Rappas, *Cyprus in the 1930s*, pp. 33–4. Under Italian fascism, *confino* – internal isolation and exile – was a common punishment for political dissent.
49 Katsourides, *The History of the Communist Party in Cyprus*, pp. 96–105.
50 Ibid., p. 107.
51 Holland and Markides, *The British and the Hellenes*, p. 186.
52 Holland, *Britain and the Revolt in Cyprus*, p. 10.
53 A privilege from the time of the Roman Empire meaning that the Orthodox Church in Cyprus, while fully in communion with the Greek-Orthodox Church, is independent of the authority of its hierarchy. The archbishop of Cyprus is thus the sole authority for the Orthodox Church in Cyprus.
54 Kyriacos Markides, *The Rise and Fall of the Cyprus Republic* (New Haven: Yale University Press, 1977), p. 5.
55 TNA, CO 926/489, *The Church and Terrorism in Cyprus: A Record of the Complicity of the Greek Orthodox Church of Cyprus in Political Violence* (Nicosia: Secretariat, 24 October 1956), p. 1.
56 Holland and Markides, *The British and the Hellenes*, p. 167.
57 Holland, *Britain and the Revolt in Cyprus*, p. 7.
58 Irene Dietzel and Vasilios N. Makrides, 'Ethno-Religious Coexistence and Plurality in Cyprus under British Rule (1878–1960)', *Social Compass*, Vol. 56, No. 1 (2009), p. 80.
59 Maria Hadjipavlou, 'The Cyprus Conflict: Root Causes and Implications for Peacebuilding', *Journal of Peace Research*, Vol. 44 (May 2007), pp. 349–65, p. 354 and Nikos Chrysoloras, 'Why Orthodoxy? Religion and Nationalism in Greek Political Culture', *LSE Symposium on Modern Greece*, 2003, http://www2.lse.ac.uk/european Institute/research/hellenicObservatory/pdf/1st_Symposium/NicosChrysoloras1s tLSESymposiumPaper.pdf.
60 Paschalis Kitromilides, 'Greek Irredentism in Asia Minor and Cyprus', *Middle Eastern Studies*, Vol. 26 (January 1990), pp. 3–17, p. 12.
61 Ανορθωτικό Κόμμα Εργαζόμενου Λαού. Progressive Party of Working People.
62 Katsourides, *The History of the Communist Party in Cyprus*, pp. 192–3.
63 Rappas, *Cyprus in the 1930s*, p. 8.
64 Adamantia Pollis, 'Intergroup Conflict and British Colonial Policy: The Case of Cyprus', *Comparative Politics*, Vol. 5, No. 4 (July 1973), p. 588.
65 Jacob Landau, *Pan-Turkish in Turkey: A Study of Irredentism* (Bloomington: Indiana University Press, 1995), p. 2.
66 Ibid., p. 8.
67 Chrysosotomos Pericleous, *Cyprus Referendum: A Divided Island and the Challenge of the Annan Plan* (London: I.B. Tauris, 2009), pp. 132–3.
68 Bernard Lewis, 'The Ottoman Empire and Its Aftermath', *Journal of Contemporary History*, Vol. 15, No. 1, Imperial Hangovers (January 1980), p. 28.
69 Ibid., p. 29.
70 Leyla Neyzi, 'Remembering Smyrna/Izmir: Shared History, Shared Trauma', *History & Memory*, Vol. 20, No. 2 (Fall/Winter 2008), p. 107.
71 Speros Vryonis, *The Mechanism of Catastrophe: The Turkish Pogrom of September 6–7, 1955, and the Destruction of the Greek Community of Istanbul* (New York: Greekworks .com, 2005), p. 31.
72 Ibid., p. 30.
73 Neyzi, 'Remembering Smyrna/Izmir', p. 107.
74 Stefan Goebel and Derek Keene, 'Towards a Metropolitan History of Total War: An Introduction', from *Cities into Battlefields: Metropolitan Scenarios, Experiences*

and Commemorations of Total War, ed. Stefan Goebel and Derek Keene (Farnham: Ashgate Publishing Limited, 2011), p. 42.
75 The phrase used is *pisliği temizlemek* (cleaning or cleansing the dirt). From the oral history narrative of Gülfem Iren (born in Izmir, 1915). In Neyzi, 'Remembering Smyrna/Izmir', pp. 121-2.
76 Tachau, 'The Face of Turkish Nationalism', p. 262.
77 Mustata Kemal quoted in Lewis, 'The Ottoman Empire and Its Aftermath', p. 31.
78 Umut Uzer, *Identity and Turkish Foreign Policy: The Kemalist Influence in Cyprus and the Caucasus* (London: I.B. Tauris, 2011), pp. 3-7.
79 Vryonis, *The Mechanism of Catastrophe*, p. 29.
80 Altay Nevzat, *Nationalism amongst the Turks of Cyprus: The First Wave* (Oulu: Oulu University Press, 2005), p. 146.
81 Ibid., p. 152.
82 TNA, WO 32/7533, Charles King-Harman to the Secretary of State, 1 April 1905.
83 Quoted in Nevzat, *Nationalism amongst the Turks of Cyprus*, p. 160.
84 Nevzat, *Nationalism amongst the Turks of Cyprus*, p. 168.
85 Charles Demetriou, 'Political Radicalization and Political Violence in Palestine (1920-1948), Ireland (1850-1921), and Cyprus (1914-1959)', *Social Science History*, Vol. 36, No. 4 (Fall 2012), p. 406.
86 Ibid.
87 CO 537/6235 'Turks of Cyprus Protest against the Desire for Union with Greece'; CO 67/352/2 Küçük Telegram to Secretary of State for Foreign Affairs, 13 December 1949.
88 TNA, FO 371/95133, 3 April 1951, Telegram from Sir A. Wright to the Secretary of State for the Colonies.
89 Holland and Markides, *The British and the Hellenes*, p. 227.
90 TNA, FO 371/95133, 23 April 1951, Telegram from Noel Charles to Herbert Morrison.
91 TNA, FO 371/95133, 24 April 1951, Letter from VCIGS to the Chiefs of Staff Committee.

Chapter 2

1 *Parliamentary Debates (Hansard) Fifth Series* – Volume 451, House of Commons: Official Report, Session 1947-8 (London: Her Majesty's Stationery Office, 1948), p. 2160.
2 'Cyprus: Background to Enosis', *Information Department Memorandum* (London: The Royal Institute of International Affairs, 1957), Appendix I, p.viii.
3 Evanthis Hatzivassiliou, *The Cyprus Question, 1878-1960: The Constitutional Aspect* (Minneapolis: University of Minnesota Press, 2002), p. 14.
4 Rappas, *Cyprus in the 1930s*, p. 182.
5 TNA, CO 141/285, Foot Memorandum 12 October 1944.
6 Leventis, *Cyprus*, p. 192.
7 Speech by Arthur Creech Jones, secretary of state for the colonies, 18 December 1946, *Hansard, House of Commons: Official Report*, Session 1946-47, Volume 431 (London: Her Majesty's Stationery Office, 1947), p. 1943.
8 The assembly of leading clerics, the archbishop and the bishops, as well as other Greek-Cypriot notables: local politicians, lawyers and so on.

9   Cable from the Ethnarchic Council of Cyprus to the British Government, quoted in *The Times*, 24 October 1946.
10 *The Times*, 25 October 1946; Issue 50591; col B.
11 'Cyprus: Background to Enosis', Appendix I, p. viii.
12 TNA, T 220/366 Crombie CA (47) 19 'Constitutional Reform in Cyprus', 19 December 1947.
13 TNA, CO 67/358/1 No. 90752, Winster Letter to Creech-Jones, 9 January 1947.
14 Holland, *Britain and the Revolt in Cyprus*, p. 5.
15 L. Lloyd-Blood, 'Mediterranean', *Journal of Comparative Legislation and International Law* (Oxford: Oxford University Press, 1939), p. 2.
16 George Horton Kelling, *Countdown to Rebellion: British Policy in Cyprus 1939–1955* (New York: Greenwood Press, 1990), p. 74.
17 TNA, CO 67/358/1 No. 90752, Letter from Winster to Creech-Jones, 9 January 1947.
18 TNA, CO 850/206/12 No. 20402/88, Letter from Winster to Creech-Jones, 22 January 1947.
19 TNA, CO 67/358/1 No. 90752, Letter from Winster to Creech-Jones, 9 January 1947.
20 TNA, T 220/366, Memorandum by Mr. Crombie, CA (47) 19 'Constitutional Reform in Cyprus', 19 December 1947.
21 Mustafa Aydin, 'Determinants of Turkish Foreign Policy: Changing Patterns and Conjunctures during the Cold War', *Middle Eastern Studies*, Vol. 36, No. 1 (January 2000), p. 120.
22 Holland and Markides, *The British and the Hellenes*, p. 219.
23 TNA, CO 537/2477, No. 37 Winster to Creech Jones, 14 July 1947.
24 Leventis, *Cyprus*, p. 180.
25 Ibid., p. 193.
26 Doros Alastos, *Cyprus in History* (London: Zeno Booksellers & Publishers, 1955), p. 375.
27 'Cyprus: Background to Enosis', p. 7.
28 Leventis, *Cyprus*, p. 156. Makarios apparently lost his temper completely at Leontios's enthronement ceremony, crying out 'I will not enthrone you and I will not recognize you' as quoted in Leventis, *Cyprus*, p. 156ff.
29 Leventis, *Cyprus*, pp. 206–10.
30 Ibid., p. 201.
31 TNA, CO 537/2478, No. 89a, Interim Report by Chairman Jackson, 27 November 1947, p. 2.
32 Leventis, *Cyprus*, p. 209.
33 Hatzivassiliou, *The Cyprus Question*, pp. 44–5.
34 Ibid., p. 45.
35 Cyprus Constitution: Despatch dated 7 May 1948, from the Secretary of State for the Colonies to the Governor of Cyprus (London: His Majesty's Stationery Office, 1948), Colonial Office Dispatch No. 227.
36 Ibid.
37 Hatzivassiliou, *The Cyprus Question*, p. 46.
38 TNA, FO 371/68074, Note from the Prime Minister to the Foreign Office, 22 December 1947.
39 TNA, T 220/366, Memorandum by the Minister of State for Colonial Affairs, 26 April 1948.
40 Hatzivassiliou, *The Cyprus Question*, p. 46.
41 TNA, CO 67/358/1, Memorandum by Mr. Crombie, 19 December 1947.

42 TNA, CO 67/358/1, Report from Colonial Office, Listowell to Winster, 7 May 1948, p. 1.
43 Hatzivassiliou, *The Cyprus Question*, p. 46.
44 TNA, T 220/366, Memorandum from W. Russell Edmunds to Mr. Pitbaldo, Commonwealth Affairs Committee, 22 July 1948.
45 Ioannis D. Stefanidis, *Isle of Discord: Nationalism, Imperialism and the Making of the Cyprus Problem* (New York: New York University Press, 1999), p. 8.
46 CSA 470/1948/1, Governor's Address to the Executive Council, January 1949.
47 Ibid.
48 CSA, SA1 470/1948/2, Statement of PEK published in *Neos Kypriakos Phylax*, 17 February 1949.

Chapter 3

1 TNA, CO 926/450, Letter from Archbishop Makarios to the Bishop of Kyrenia, 30 November 1954.
2 Archives of the Archbishopric of Cyprus (AAC), Makarios II Δ79 'Blueprint of the National Struggle' (Summer 1948), p. 1. (Author's Translation).
3 AAC, 'Blueprint of the National Struggle', p. 1.
4 Katsourides, *The History of the Communist Party in Cyprus*, p. 195.
5 AAC, 'Blueprint of the National Struggle', p. 2.
6 Ibid., p. 3.
7 Ibid.
8 Markides, *The Rise and Fall of the Cyprus Republic*, p. 13.
9 Evangelos Averoff-Tossizza, *Lost Opportunities: The Cyprus Question, 1950–1963*, Trans. Timothy Cullen and Susan Kyriakidis (New York: Aristide D. Caratzas, 1986), p. 7.
10 Pericleous, *Cyprus Referendum*, p. 84.
11 TNA, FO 371/112862, G1081/587, 'United King Policy in Cyprus and the Enosis Demand', 17 September 1954.
12 David Close, *The Origins of the Greek Civil War* (London: Longman, 1992), p. 161.
13 TNA, CO 926/1056, AKEL Leaflet Quoted in Note on the Communist attitude and strength in Cyprus, September 1957.
14 Holland and Markides, *The British and the Hellenes*, p. 222.
15 Ibid., p. 223.
16 Ibid.
17 Andreas Varnavas, *A History of the Liberation Struggle of EOKA (1955–1959)* (Nicosia: EOKA Liberation Struggle Foundation, 2004), p. 8.
18 Holland and Markides, *The British and the Hellenes*, ff. p. 223.
19 *The Church and Terrorism in Cyprus*, p. 3.
20 TNA, FO 371/87716, Ethnarchy Communique on the results of the plebiscite, 27 January 1950.
21 TNA, FO 371/87717, Answers of the Bishop of Kitium to the Press following statement of the Ethnarchy Council on Plebiscite, 17 February 1950.
22 For example, see the contemporaneous statement of the Turkish National Party of Cyprus, reproduced in *The Times*, 26 April 1950; p. 5; Issue 51675; col C.
23 C. J. Bartlett, *A History of Postwar Britain: 1945–1974* (London: Longman, 1977), p. 116.

24 TNA, FO 371/95132, Report from Clifford Norton (Athens) to Mr. Ernest Bevin (Foreign Office), 2 January 1951.
25 Ibid.
26 TNA, FO 371/95133, Report from George Jellicoe (Washington) to Milo Talbot de Malahide (Foreign Office), 3 April 1951.
27 TNA, FO 371/95122, G1081/47, Memo from Sir Clifford J. Norton (Athens) to Mr. Herbert Morrison (Foreign Office), 20 April 1951.
28 Wright had a great deal of experience in Cyprus having served there in the colonial service from 1922 until 1943. He had become colonial secretary of Cyprus in 1937. Between 1947 and 1949 he had served as governor of Gambia.
29 TNA, FO 371/95133, G1081/42, Telegram from Sir A. Wright to the Secretary of State for the Colonies, 3 April 1951.
30 Ibid.
31 TNA, FO 371/95133, G1081/55, Telegram No. 98 from British Embassy, Ankara (Noel Charles) to Herbert Morrison (Foreign Office), 23 April 1951.
32 TNA, FO 371/95133, Communication issued to the Press, April 6 of Interview at Government House accorded to representatives of Turkish Associations on 5 April 1951.
33 TNA, FO 371/95133, G1081/61, Chief of Staff Committee Report, 24 April 1951.
34 Ibid.
35 P. N. Vanezis, *Makarios: Faith and Power* (London: Abelard-Schumann Ltd., 1971), p. 84.
36 Averoff-Tossizza, *Lost Opportunities*, pp. 15–17.
37 Ibid., p. 18.
38 Ibid., p. 19.
39 Pantazis Terlexis, Διπλωματία και πολιτική του κυπριακού. Ανατομία ενός λάθους (Diplomacy and Policy of the Cyprus Problem: Anatomy of an Error) (Αθήνα: Κέδρος, 1971), p. 92.
40 Makarios's sermon of 28 June 1953, quoted by Averoff-Tossizza, *Lost Opportunities*, p. 23.
41 Evanthis Hadzivassiliou, *Greece and the Cold War: Front Line State, 1952–1967* (London: Routledge, 2006), p. 21.
42 United Nations, *Official Records of the General Assembly, Eighth Session*. Plenary Meetings, 15 September–9 December 1953 (New York: United Nations, 1953), pp. 66–7.
43 *Hansard*, Vol. 525, p. 8.
44 These included an approach of Prime Minister Papagos to the convalescing foreign secretary, Anthony Eden, in the Mediterranean in September 1953, which was sharply rebuked.
45 Ashley Jackson, 'Empire and Beyond: The Pursuit of Overseas National Interests in the Late Twentieth Century', *The English Historical Review*, Vol. CXXII, No. 409 (2007), pp. 1350–66, p. 1355.
46 TNA, FO 371/112862, G1081/592, Draft Memo on the Strategic Importance of Cyprus.
47 Ibid.
48 TNA, CAB 129/65, C (54) 26, 'Memorandum by the Minister of Defence', 23 January 1954.
49 *Hansard*, Vol. 531, p. 504.
50 Ibid.

51 Ibid., pp. 507–8.
52 Ibid., p. 508.
53 USNA, Box 3602 RG 59, 'British Difficulties over Cyprus', Embassy (London) to State Department, 25 August 1954.
54 Diana Markides, 'Britain's "New Look" Policy for Cyprus and the Makarios-Harding Talks, January 1955–March 1956', *Journal of Imperial and Commonwealth History*, Vol. 23, Issue 3 (September 1995), pp. 479–502.
55 Ibid., p. 546.
56 Averoff-Tossizza, *Lost Opportunities*, p. 28.
57 Stephen G. Xydis, *Cyprus: Conflict and Conciliation, 1954–1958* (Columbus: The Ohio State University Press, 1967), p. 22.
58 *United Nations, Official Records of the General Assembly, Ninth Session.* General Committee, 21 September–17 December 1954 (New York: United Nations, 1954), p. 9.
59 This phrase, of course, had been the motto of the Greek Revolution of 1821.
60 Ibid., p. 52.
61 Ibid.
62 Ibid., p. 53.
63 Ibid.
64 Ibid., p. 54.
65 Averoff-Tossizza, *Lost Opportunities*, p. 31.
66 *United Nations, Official Records of the General Assembly, Ninth Session.* Plenary Meeting, 21 September–17 December 1954 (New York: United Nations, 1954), p. 539.

Chapter 4

1 Giorgos Grivas, *The Memoirs of General Grivas*, Trans. and ed. Charles Foley (London: Longmans, Green and Co. Ltd., 1964), p. 25.
2 Sam Coates, Francis Elliott and Roland Watson, 'Gen George Grivas (Obituaries)', *The Times Digital Archive* (London), 29 January 1974; pp. 14; col E.
3 Grivas, *Memoirs*, p. 4.
4 The legacy of X remains contentious. Opponents, particularly on the Greek (and Cypriot) left have characterized it as a brutal fascist organization. Sympathetic voices consider it a legitimate resistance organization opposing the Germans and later the communists under the banner of loyalty to the Greek king and the cause of nationalism. For a sympathetic account, see Omiros Papadopoulos, *Οργάνωσις Χ: Τρία χρόνια τρεις αιώνες* (Athens: Νέα Θέσις, 2000). See Neni Panourgiá, *Dangerous Citizens: The Greek Left and The Terror of the State* (New York: Fordham University Press, 2009) and Edgar O'Ballance, *The Greek Civil War 1944–1949* (London: Faber and Faber, 1966) for more critical accounts.
5 Holland, *Britain and the Revolt in Cyprus*, p. 29; Nancy Crawshaw, *The Cyprus Revolt: An Account of the Struggle for Union with Greece* (London: George Allen and Unwin, 1978), p. 91.
6 Yiannos Katsourides, *The Greek-Cypriot Nationalist Right in the Era of British Colonialism: Emergence, Mobilisation and Transformations of Right-Wing Party Politics* (Cham: Springer, 2017), p. 188. In his *Memoirs*, Grivas contradicts this by writing that the organization was called 'Xhi, after the Greek letter X which symbolises the unknown', p. 5.

7   IMW, GB62, Papers of General Sir Kenneth Darling, Report on General Grivas, WMT Magan (MI6), 11–16 March 1959, pp. 3–4.
8   Crawshaw, *The Cyprus Revolt*, p. 91.
9   David Close, *The Origins of the Greek Civil War* (London: Longmans, 1995), p. 90.
10 Makarios Drousiotis, *EOKA: The Dark Side* (*ΕΟΚΑ: η σκοτεινή όψη*) (Λευυκωσία: Έκδοσης Αλφάδι, 2002), p. 51.
11 Grivas, *Memoirs*, p. 17.
12 Close, *The Origins of the Greek Civil War*, p. 157.
13 Dudley Barker, *Grivas: Portrait of a Terrorist* (London: The Cresset Press, 1959), p. 14.
14 Magan, p. 49.
15 Ibid., p.44.
16 Xydis, *Cyprus: Conflict and Conciliation*, p. 71.
17 Holland, *Britain and the Revolt in Cyprus*, p. 30.
18 Xydis, *Cyprus: Conflict and Conciliation*, p. 69.
19 Grivas, *Memoirs*, p. 13.
20 Ibid.
21 Ibid.
22 Ibid.
23 As a naturalized Greek citizen, Grivas required approval from the Cyprus government to visit the island of his birth. In 1951, he was granted a visa by the authorities. By 1954, he was under sufficient suspicion that he was denied a visa and had to enter the island in secret.
24 Grivas, *Memoirs*, p. 17.
25 Stanley Mayes, *Makarios: A Biography* (London: The Macmillan Press, 1981), pp. 42–3.
26 Παγκύπρια Εθνική Οργάνωση Νεολαίας.
27 Katsourides, *The Greek-Cypriot Nationalist Right in the Era of British Colonialism*, p. 205.
28 TNA, CO 926/455 86400, 18 October 1955, Cyprus Intelligence Committee, 'The Nature of EOKA, Its Political Background and Sources of Direction', p. 1.
29 TNA, CO 926/489, *The Church and Terrorism in Cyprus*, p. 19.
30 Charles Foley and W. I. Scobie, *The Struggle for Cyprus* (Stanford: Hoover Institution Press, 1975), p. 15.
31 Ibid.
32 Ibid.
33 Andreas Azinas, *50 Years of Silence: Cyprus Struggle for Freedom, My EOKA Secret File*, Vol. A (Nicosia: Arlo Limited, 2002), pp. 183–5.
34 Grivas, *Memoirs*, p. 19.
35 Ibid., p. 204.
36 Giorgos Grivas, *General Grivas on Guerrilla Warfare*, Trans. A. A. Pallis (New York: Praeger, 1965), p. 91.
37 Azinas, *50 Years of Silence* (A), pp. 182–3.
38 Grivas, *On Guerrilla Warfare*, p. 91.
39 Ibid., p. 1.
40 Ibid.
41 Grivas, *Memoirs*, p. 4.
42 Grivas, *On Guerrilla Warfare*, p. 1.

43 Ibid., p. 91.
44 Ibid., p. 92.
45 Ibid.
46 Ibid., p. 93.
47 Magan, p. 29.
48 Savvas Loizides, Άτυχη Κύπρος, Πως έζησα τους πόθους και τους καημούς της, *1910-1980* (Unfortunate Cyprus, How I Lived Its Passions and Sorrows, 1910-1980) (Athens: Bergadi, 1980), pp. 99-100.
49 The participants were Makarios, Nikolaos Papadopoulos, Georgios Stratos, Yerasimos Konnidaris, Antonios Augikos, Savvas Loizides, Socrates Loizides, Elias Tsatsomiros, Demetrios Stauropoulos, Demetrios Vezanis and Elias Alexopoulos. Grivas was not present and signed the oath later.
50 Demetris Assos, *Makarios: A Study of Anti-Colonial Nationalist Leadership, 1950-1959* (PhD diss., University of London, 2009), p. 94.
51 Azinas, *50 Years of Silence* (A), p. 209.
52 Grivas quoted in Azinas, *50 Years of Silence* (A), pp. 209-10.
53 Foley and Scobie, *The Struggle for Cyprus*, p. 34.
54 Grivas, *Memoirs*, p. 30.
55 Ibid.
56 Ibid.
57 Grivas Diary, *Terrorism in Cyprus: The Captured Documents* (London: Her Majesty's Stationery Officer, 1956), p. 12.
58 Ibid., p. 19.
59 See, for example, the statement of Archbishop Leontios in 1947 deriding Winster's constitutional proposals as inflicting on Cypriots a 'continuation of their own slavery' quoted in Leventis, *Cyprus*, p. 161; Archbishop Makarios's letter to the Australian foreign minister, complaining that Cypriots were 'still enslaved' and struggling to 'rid themselves of the bonds of slavery', quoted in FO 371/95133, 8 February 1951. Also, author's interviews with Renos Kyriakides (20 November 2008) and Thassos Sophocleous (6 March 2009).
60 Diary, *Terrorism in Cyprus*, p. 22.
61 Makarios is referred to in Grivas's diary as 'Genikos' or 'Gen'.
62 Grivas *Diary*, 4 April 1955, from *Terrorism in Cyprus*, p.24.
63 Author's interviews with Renos Kyriakides (20 November 2008) and Thassos Sophocleous (6 March 2009).
64 Author's interview with Thassos Sophocleous, 6 March 2009.
65 Grivas, *Memoirs*, p. 36.
66 Author's Interview with Thassos Sophocleous, 6 March 2009.
67 Grivas, *Memoirs*, p. 36.
68 Ibid., p. 34.
69 Report from Grivas to Makarios, 23 May 1955, from *Terrorism in Cyprus*, p. 51.
70 TNA, CO 926/270, Brief No. 3 'Terrorism' for Tripartite Talks for the Secretary of State for Foreign Affairs, August 1955.
71 Grivas *Diary*, 4 April 1955, from *Terrorism in Cyprus*, p. 35.
72 ΑΚΕΛ: Κόμμα Εργαζόμενου Λαού, 'Αναφορα στην Αποφαση του ΠΓ της ΚΕ ΑΚΕΛ Σχετικα με τα γεγονοτα της 1ης Απριλιο', p. 145.
73 TNA, CO 926/395, Telegram No. 419, from Governor Cyprus to Secretary of State, 4 July 1955.

Chapter 5

1. RHL, Armitage Diary, 29 June 1955.
2. Grivas, *Memoirs*, p. 34.
3. TNA, CAB 129/29, CC (55) 18, 28 June 1955.
4. TNA, CAB 129/75, CP (55) 33, 11 June 1955, p. 1.
5. Ibid., p. 2.
6. RHL, Armitage Diary, 29 June 1955.
7. Holland, *Britain and the Revolt in Cyprus*, p. 58.
8. Ibid., p. 59.
9. Hubert Faustmann, 'The UN and the Internationalization of the Cyprus Conflict, 1949–58', in *The Work of the UN in Cyprus: Promoting Peace and Development*, ed. Oliver P Richmond and James Ker-Lindsay (New York: Palgrave Macmillan, 2001).
10. Mayes, *Makarios*, p. 41.
11. Averoff-Tossizza, *Lost Opportunities*, p. 18.
12. Holland and Markides, *The British and the Hellenes*, p. 222.
13. TNA, CAB 129/75, CP (55) 33, 11 June 1955, p. 2.
14. TNA, CO 926/268, Sir Roger Makins to Foreign Office, No. 1508, 29 June 1955.
15. TNA, CO 926/268, Translation of Archbishop Makarios's press conference in Athens, 16 July, reported in Telegram No. 348 from Athens (Sir C. Peake) to Foreign Office, 18 July 1955.
16. Macmillan, *Tides of Fortune: 1945–1955*, p. 665.
17. TNA, CO 926/268, 'Cyprus Negotiations: Tactics and Timetable', Memo from the Private Secretary (Colonial Office) to the Prime Minister, 13 July 1955, p. 2.
18. Ibid., pp. 2–3.
19. Ibid., pp. 3–4.
20. TNA, CO 926/268, Telegram No. 488 from Ankara (Bowker) to Governor Cyprus (Armitage), 19 July 1955.
21. Holland, *Britain and the Revolt in Cyprus*, p. 66.
22. America's position throughout the Cyprus conflict was fairly ecumenical. The American government hoped for a quick and fair solution that would avoid further tension in a sensitive, but peripheral, theatre.
23. TNA, CO 926/268, Note from Washington (Makins) to Foreign Office, 20 July 1955.
24. TNA, CO 926/268, Telegram from Foreign Office to Washington (Makins), 25 July 1955.
25. TNA, CO 926/269, Telegram from Athens (Sir C. Peake) to Foreign Office, 27 July 1955.
26. TNA, CO 926/269, Draft of the speech of the Secretary of State to open the Tripartite Conference.
27. Statement of Mr. Stephanopoulos, 31 August 1955, *The Tripartite Conference on the Eastern Mediterranean and Cyprus* (London: Her Majesty's Stationery Office, 1955), p. 15.
28. Ibid., p. 18.
29. Statement of Mr. Zorlu, 1 September 1955, *The Tripartite Conference on the Eastern Mediterranean and Cyprus* (London: Her Majesty's Stationery Office, 1955), p. 21.
30. Ibid., p. 22.
31. Ibid.
32. Ibid., p. 25.

33 Statement of Mr. Macmillan, 6 September 1955, *The Tripartite Conference on the Eastern Mediterranean and Cyprus* (London: Her Majesty's Stationery Office, 1955), p. 30.
34 Ibid., p. 31.
35 Ibid., p. 35.
36 Statement of Mr. Zorlu, 7 September 1955, *The Tripartite Conference on the Eastern Mediterranean and Cyprus* (London: Her Majesty's Stationery Office, 1955), p. 38.
37 Vryonis, *The Mechanism of Catastrophe*, pp. 96–7.
38 Ibid., p. 189.
39 Ibid., p. 77.
40 Holland, *Britain and the Revolt in Cyprus*, p. 69.
41 Vryonis, *The Mechanism of Catastrophe*, p. 95.
42 Ibid., pp. 95–9.
43 Dilek Güven, 'Riots against the Non-Muslims of Turkey: 6–7 September 1955 in the context of demographic engineering', *European Journal of Turkish Studies*, Vol. 12 (2011), p. 6.
44 *New York Times*, 'Disastrous Effects of the Turkish Riots', C. L. Sulzberger, 17 September 1955, p. 14.
45 Vryonis, *The Mechanism of Catastrophe*, pp. 211–20.
46 Ibid., pp. 220–7.
47 *The New York Times*, 'Rioting in Turkey Called Danger Sign', Michael L. Hoffman, 17 September 1955, p. 1.
48 Vryonis, *The Mechanism of Catastrophe*, p. 390.
49 Ibid., p. 549.
50 Holland, *Britain and the Revolt in Cyprus*, p. 76.
51 TNA, CO 926/270, Telegram No. 576, 9 September 1955, from Foreign Office to Athens.
52 Richard Lamb, *The Failure of the Eden Government* (London: Sidgwick and Jackson, 1987), p. 133.
53 Ibid.

Chapter 6

1 TNA, WO 32/16260, Telegram No. 779 from Harding to the Secretary of State for the Colonies, 5 October 1955.
2 Colin Baker, *Retreat from Empire: Sir Robert Armitage in Africa and Cyprus* (London: I.B. Tauris Publishers, 1998), p. 110.
3 Ibid., p. 198.
4 RHL, Letter from Lennox-Boyd to Sir Robert Armitage, 23 September 1955.
5 RHL, Mss Afr. S. 2204, Sir Robert P. Armitage Papers, Box 1, Letter to his parents, 24 September 1955.
6 Ibid.
7 TNA, WO 32/16260 Telegram No. 779 from Harding to Lennox-Boyd, 5 October 1955.
8 IWM, AFH 3, Letter from Malcolm MacDonald, Commissioner-General South East Asia to Harding, 12 December 1949.

9 TNA, FO 371/117662, Minute by Macmillan, 23 September 1955 on Telegram No. 683 from Armitage to Secretary of State for the Colonies, 22 September 1955.
10 IWM, AFH 3, Letter from Eden to Harding, 24 September 1955.
11 Ibid.
12 Evanthis Hatzivassiliou, Στρατηγικές του Κυπριακού, Η δεκαετία του 1950 (*Strategies of the Cyprus Problem*) (Athens: Patakis, 2005), pp. 267–71.
13 Holland, *Britain and the Revolt in Cyprus*, p. 83.
14 TNA, CO 926/450, *Minutes of the Ethnarchy Council and Ethnarchy Bureau and Related Documents, October 1955 to February 1956* (Nicosia: Printed by Direction of His Excellency the Governor), Meeting of 3 October 1955, p. 12.
15 *The Tripartite Conference on the Eastern Mediterranean and Cyprus* (London: Her Majesty's Stationery Office, 1955), pp. 41–2.
16 TNA, PREM 1955, Telegram from Secretary of State for the Colonies to Harding, 17 October 1955.
17 TNA, WO 32/16260, Telegram No. 807 from Governor Harding to the Prime Minister, 9 October 1955.
18 TNA, WO 32/16260, Telegram No. 792 from the Prime Minister to Governor Harding, 8 October 1955.
19 Editorial, *The Times*, 6 October 1955, p. 6.
20 Mayes, *Makarios*, p. 83.
21 TNA, WO 32/16260, Telegram No. 817 from Governor Harding to the Prime Minister, 11 October 1955.
22 Hubert Faustmann, 'The UN and the Internationalization of the Cyprus Conflict, 1949–58', p. 20.
23 TNA, CO 925/277, Telegram from Ankara [Mr. Stewart] to Foreign Office, 13 October 1956.
24 *The Times*, Thursday, 17 November 1955; p. 10; Issue 53380; col E.
25 See Chapter 2 above.
26 Written Answers, 22 February 1957, *Hansard*, Vol. 564, p. 104.
27 French, *The British Way in Counter-Insurgency*, p. 103.
28 In Cyprus, there was a maximum of 2,109 detainees form a population of 369,854 Greek-Cypriots. This represented 570 detainees per 100,000 people, the third most in British counter-insurgency operations during this period after Kenya and Brunei (French, *The British Way in Counter-Insurgency*, p. 111.)
29 IWM, Harding Papers, AFH 10, Telegram No. 1153 from Harding to Secretary of State for the Colonies, 2 December 1955.
30 Ibid.
31 Holland, *Britain and the Revolt in Cyprus*, p. 95.
32 Markides, 'Britain's "New Look" Policy for Cyprus', p. 490.
33 TNA, FO 371/117661, Memo by RW Selby, 17 September 1955.
34 IWM, Harding Papers, AFH 10, Telegram No. 1165 from Harding to Secretary of State for the Colonies, 3 December 1955.
35 TNA, FO 371/117675, Telegram No. 1185 from Harding to the Secretary of State for the Colonies, 5 December 1955.
36 Minute by WH Young (Foreign Office), 6 December 1955, on Telegram No. 1185 from Harding to the Secretary of State for the Colonies, 5 December 1955.
37 TNA, FO 371/123863, Cyprus – Revised Formula Given to Greek Government on 9 December 1955.

38 TNA, FO 371/123863, Note from Ambassador James Bowker to JG Ward, 20 December 1955.
39 Ibid.
40 Ibid.
41 TNA, FO 371/123863, Telegram No. 5 from Harding to the Foreign Secretary, 2 January 1956.
42 TNA, FO 371/123863, Personal Letter from Macmillan to Lord Home, 4 January 1956.
43 TNA, CO 926/547, Telegram No. 39 from Harding to The Secretary of State for the Colonies, 7 January 1956.
44 TNA, FO 371/123864, Telegram No. 50 from Harding to the Secretary of State for the Colonies, 10 January 1956.
45 Ibid.
46 Ibid.
47 Ibid.
48 Grivas, *Memoirs*, p. 73.
49 Ibid.
50 Born in 1932, Droushiotis was, in his own words 'thinking terrible things' against the British. In 1954, he discussed attacking Nicosia Airport with mortars and firebombing all government offices in Cyprus. From the author's interview with Yiannakis Droushiotis, 17 July 2009.
51 *The Times*, Thursday, 12 January 1956; p. 8; Issue 53426; col D.
52 TNA, FO 371/123864, Telegram No. 65, Situation report from Cyprus to Secretary of State for the Colonies, 12 January 1956.
53 CSA, SA1/1087/1956, Telegram 2747 from Cyprus is Turkish Party Chairman Kütchük to Governor Harding, 11 January 1956.
54 TNA, CO 926/416, Telegram No. 110 from MIDEAST Main to War Office, 14 January 1956.
55 TNA, FO 371/123865, Telegram No. 31 from Peake to Harding, Minutes of the Sixth Meeting of HB Archbishop Makarios and the Governor of Cyprus, Sir John Harding, on 13 January 1956, 16 January 1956.
56 Ibid.
57 Ibid.
58 Ibid.
59 Ibid.
60 RHL, Mss. Medit. S. 32, John Reddaway, 'Odi et Amo: Vignettes of an Affair with Cyprus' (c. 1985), pp. 61–2.
61 TNA, FO 371/123865, Personal Letter from J. G. Ward to Sir Gladwyn Jebb (British Ambassador, Paris), 18 January 1956.
62 TNA, FO 371/123865, Foreign Office Minute, 18 January 1956.
63 Ibid.
64 Ibid.
65 Ibid.
66 TNA, FO 371/123864, Telegram No. 59 from Foreign Office to Athens, 15 January 1956.
67 Ibid.
68 TNA, FO 371/123865, Revised Cyprus Formula, Foreign Office Minute, 18 January 1956.

69 TNA, CO 925/416, Telegram from Cyprus (Sinclair) to Secretary of State for the Colonies, 26 January 1956.
70 Azinas, *50 Years of Silence* (B), p. 428.
71 TNA, FO 371/123867, Telegram No. 191 from Cyprus (Harding) to Secretary of State for the Colonies, 28 January 1956.
72 Ibid.
73 TNA, FO 371/123867, Telegram No. 192 from Cyprus (Harding) to the Secretary of State for the Colonies, 28 January 1956.
74 Ibid.
75 SIMAE P405/7/11, Description by Grivas of Discussion with Makarios about Harding Negotiations, February 1956.
76 Drousiotis, *EOKA*, p. 163.
77 Andreas Karyos, 'EOKA, 1955–1959: A Study of the Military Aspects of the Cyprus Revolt' (doctoral thesis, University of London, 2011), p. 82.
78 TNA, CO 926/450, (12) Translation of Minutes of Ethnarchy Council Meeting, 30 January 1956, p. 28. *Minutes of the Ethnarchy Council and Ethnarchy Bureau and Related Documents, October 1955 to February 1956* (Nicosia: Printed by Direction of His Excellency the Governor).
79 Ibid.
80 Ibid.
81 Karyos, 'EOKA, 1955–1959', p. 82.
82 Although the governor and the archbishop would not meet in person for a month, they continued their negotiations through a series of letters.
83 Letter of Archbishop Makarios to Sir John Harding, 2 February 1956, p. 6. Correspondence exchanged between the Governor (Harding) and Archbishop Makarios (London: Her Majesty's Stationery Office, 1956).
84 TNA, FO 371/123867, Telegram No. 235 from Cyrus (Harding) to the Secretary of State for the Colonies, 31 January 1956.
85 TNA, FO/123869, Telegram No. 267 from Foreign Office to Ankara, 13 February 1956, emphasis in original.
86 Letter of Sir John Harding to Archbishop Makarios, 14 February 1956, p. 8. Correspondence exchanged between the Governor (Harding) and Archbishop Makarios (London: Her Majesty's Stationery Office, 1956).
87 Letter of Sir John Harding to Archbishop Makarios, 14 February 1956, p. 9. Correspondence exchanged between the Governor (Harding) and Archbishop Makarios (London: Her Majesty's Stationery Office, 1956).
88 *The Times of Cyprus*, Vol. 1, No. 253, Wednesday, 15 February 1956, 'All the Archbishop's Main Terms Find Acceptance'.
89 SIMAE P405/7/11, Description by Grivas of Discussion with Makarios about Harding Negotiations, February 1956.
90 Ibid.
91 Grivas, *Memoirs*, 64.
92 *Times of Cyprus*, Vol. 1, No. 268, 1 March 1956.
93 TNA, CO 926/450, (13) Translation of Minutes of Ethnarchy Council Meeting, 21 February 1956, p. 32. *Minutes of the Ethnarchy Council and Ethnarchy Bureau and Related Documents, October 1955 to February 1956* (Nicosia: Printed by Direction of His Excellency the Governor).
94 Ibid., p. 33.
95 Editorial, *The Times of Cyprus*, 2 February 1956.

96 Editorial, *The Times of Cyprus*, 21 February 1956.
 97 Correspondence exchanged between the Governor (Harding) and Archbishop Makarios (London: Her Majesty's Stationery Office, 1956), p. 11.
 98 Ibid.
 99 Ibid., p. 12.
100 TNA, CAB 128/30, CM (56) 16th Conclusions, 22 February 1956.
101 Sir Hugh Foot, *A Start in Freedom* (London: Hodder and Stoughton, 1964), p. 184.
102 Mayes, *Makarios*, p. 31.
103 Foot, *A Start in Freedom*, p. 185.
104 Editorial, *The Times of Cyprus*, 1 March 1956.
105 Grivas, *Memoirs*, p. 64.
106 Assos, *Makarios*, p. 138.
107 *Hansard*, Vol. 549, pp. 1717–18.
108 Ibid., p. 1718.
109 TNA, FO 371/123873, Telegram No. 470, 1 March 1956.
110 Ibid.
111 Ibid.
112 Ibid.
113 Ibid.
114 Editorial, *The Times of Cyprus*, 1 March 1956.
115 IWM, Harding Papers, AFH 2, Letter from Sir John Harding to John Charles Harding, 4 March 1956.
116 Grivas, *Memoirs*, p. 66.
117 IWM, Harding Papers, AFH 2, Letter from Sir John Harding to John Charles Harding, 4 March 1956.

Chapter 7

 1 TNA, CO 926/547, Telegram No. 39 from Harding to Lennox-Boyd, 7 January 1956.
 2 TNA, WO 32/16260, Telegram No. 779 from Harding to the Secretary of State for the Colonies, 5 October 1955.
 3 Panagiotis Dimitrakis, 'British Intelligence and the Cyprus Insurgency, 1955–1959', *International Journal of Intelligence and CounterIntelligence*, Vol. 21, No. 2 (2008), p. 381.
 4 Mockaitis, *British Counterinsurgency*, p. 12.
 5 James Corum, *Training Indigenous Forces in Counterinsurgency: A Tale of Two Insurgencies* (Carlisle: Strategic Studies Institute of the US Army War College, 2006), p. 3.
 6 Noami Rosenbaum, 'Success in Foreign Policy: The British in Cyprus, 1878–1960', *Canadian Journal of Political Science*, Vol. 3, No. 4 (December 1970), p. 608.
 7 Newsinger, *British Counterinsurgency*, p. 107.
 8 IWM, Harding Papers, AFH 10, Telegram No. 1165 from Harding to Secretary of State for the Colonies, 3 December 1955.
 9 Simon Robbins, 'The British counter-insurgency in Cyprus', *Small Wars & Insurgencies*, Vol. 23, Nos. 4–5 (October–December 2012), p. 720.
10 Ibid., p. 721.
11 Mockaitis, *British Counterinsurgency*, p. 134.

12 Sir Gerald Templer quoted by Paul Dixon, '"Hearts and Minds"? British Counter-Insurgency from Malaya to Iraq', *Journal of Strategic Studies*, Vol. 32, No. 3 (2009), p. 354.
13 Andrew Jackson O'Shaughnessy, '"To Gain the Hearts and Subdue the Minds of America": General Sir Henry Clinton and the Conduct of the British War for America', *Proceedings of the American Philological Society*, Vol. 158, No. 3 (September 2013), p. 202.
14 French, *The British Way in Counter-Insurgency*, p. 173.
15 Hew Strachan, 'British Counter-Insurgency from Malaya to Iraq', *RUSI*, Vol. 152, No. 6 (December 2007), p. 8.
16 Dixon, 'Hearts and Minds?', p. 355.
17 TNA, WO 32/16260, Telegram No. 810 from Harding to the Secretary of State for the Colonies, 10 October 1955.
18 TNA, CAB 21/2925, 'Report on Colonial Security by Sir Gerald Templer', 23 April 1955, p. 9.
19 RHL, Mss. Afr. S. 2204, Papers of Sir Robert P. Armitage, Box 1. Letter to his parents, 16 April 1955.
20 TNA, CAB 21/2925, 'Report on Colonial Security by Sir Gerald Templer', 23 April 1955, p. 52.
21 Ibid.
22 TNA, FO 371/117662, Personal Minute from the Prime Minister to the Secretary of State for the Colonies, 24 September 1955 on Telegram No. 683 from Armitage to Secretary of State for the Colonies, 22 September 1955.
23 *Hansard*, Vol. 565, Written Answers, p. 104.
24 Holland, *Britain and the Revolt in Cyprus*, p. 92.
25 TNA, CO 926/397, Report on the Number of Detained Persons, 29 December 1956.
26 TNA, CO 926/397, Telegram No. 1579 from Governor Harding to the Secretary of State for the Colonies, 5 September 1956.
27 TNA, CO 926/277, Brief for the Secretary of State, Foreign Office Paper CA (56) 23.
28 TNA, WO 32/16260, Telegram No. 779 from Harding to Lennox-Boyd, 5 October 1955.
29 Ibid.
30 IWM, Papers of Sir John Harding (AFH 6), Brigadier G. H. Baker, *The Cyprus Emergency*, 1958, p. 11.
31 Varnavas, *A History of the Liberation Struggle of EOKA*, pp. 74–5.
32 TNA, CO 926/455, CIC (55), Cyprus Intelligence Committee Report, 18 October 1955, pp. 1–5.
33 Commonly known as MI6.
34 TNA, CO 926/520, Security and Intelligence in Cyprus, 2 September 1955.
35 Author's interview with Geoffrey Jukes, 18 December 2009.
36 Baker, *The Cyprus Emergency*, p. 117.
37 Bruce Hoffman, 'The Palestine Police Force and the Challenges of Gathering Counter-Terrorism Intelligence', (2008) [unpublished], p. 26.
38 Newsinger, *British Counterinsurgency*, p. 101.
39 The exact operational dates and further information on the 'Q unit' remain classified. It began operations in early 1956 and ceased operations before Baker's report was due to be distributed in early 1957.
40 Baker, *The Cyprus Emergency*, p. 117.
41 Author's interview with Geoffrey Jukes, 18 December 2009.

42 Dimitrakis, 'British Intelligence and the Cyprus Insurgency', p. 388.
43 Grivas, *Memoirs*, p. 38.
44 IWM, *Harding Papers*, AFH 6, 'Report on the Cyprus Emergency', Major General K. T. Darling, 31 July 1959, p. 3.
45 TNA, CO 926/395, Telegram No. 419 from Governor Armitage to Secretary of State for the Colonies, 4 July 1955.
46 TNA, WO 32/16260, Telegram No. 810 from Harding to Secretary of State for the Colonies, 10 October 1955.
47 Ibid.
48 IWM, AFH 6, General Sir Kenneth Darling, 'Report on the Cyprus Emergency', Nicosia, 31 July 1959, p. 3.
49 Darling, 'Report on the Cyprus Emergency', pp. 3–4.
50 Hoffman, 'The Palestine Police Force and the Challenges of Gathering Counter-Terrorism Intelligence', p. 1.
51 TNA, WO 32/16260, Telegram No. 810 from Harding to Secretary of State for the Colonies, 10 October 1955.
52 Baker, *The Cyprus Emergency*, p. 20.
53 CSA, V40/503, Annual Report on the Cyprus Police Force for the Year 1955, GH Robins, Commissioner of Police, Cyprus (Nicosia: Chr. Nicolaou and Sons Ltd., 1956), p. 3.
54 TNA, CO 926/547, Telegram No. 39 from Harding to the Secretary of State for the Colonies, 7 January 1956.
55 Ibid.
56 Grivas, *Memoirs*, pp. 39–40.
57 EOKA Leaflet, quoted in Grivas, *Memoirs*, p. 40.
58 Darling, 'Report on the Cyprus Emergency', p. 68.
59 CSA, V40/502, Annual Report on the Cyprus Police Force for the Year 1954, GH Robins Commissioner of Police, Cyprus (Nicosia: The Cyprus Government Printing Office, 1955), p. 4.
60 CSA, V40/503, Annual Report on the Cyprus Police Force for the Year 1955, p. 8.
61 CSA, V12/32, Report of the Cyprus Police Commission of 1956 (Nicosia: The Cyprus Government Printing Office, 1956), pp. 25–6.
62 CSA, V40/504, Annual Report on the Cyprus Police Force for the Year 1956, Lt. Col. G.C. White (Chief Constable of Cyprus), p. 3.
63 For example the officer, 'Fat Costas', mentioned by Elenitsa Seraphim, *The Cyprus Liberation Struggle 1955–1959*, Trans. John Vickers (Nicosia: Epiphaniou Publications, 2000), p. 156.
64 CSA, V40/504, Annual Report on the Cyprus Police Force for the Year 1956, p. 2.
65 Ibid., p. 13.
66 TNA, WO 32/16260, Report from GHQ Middle East Land Forces British Defence Coordinating Committee to Chiefs of Staff, 25 August 1955.
67 TNA, FO 371/117690, Telegram from Deputy Governor Baring (Kenya) to the Colonial Office, 2 September 1955.
68 TNA, WO 32/16260, Note from Anthony Head to Prime Minister Eden, 22 September 1955.
69 CSA, V40/503, Annual Report on the Cyprus Police Force for the Year 1955, p. 32.
70 TNA, WO 106/6020, General Kenneth Darling, 'Report on the Cyprus Emergency', 1959, p. 20.
71 Ibid.

72 Ibid.
73 French, *Fighting EOKA*, p. 255.
74 TNA, CAB 129/76, CP (55) 82, 'Strategic Review of the Cyprus Problem', Note by Selwyn Lloyd, 18 July 1955.
75 CSA, V40/505, Annual Report on the Cyprus Police Force for the Year 1957, Lt. Col. G.C. White (Chief Constable of Cyprus), p. 3.
76 CSA, V40/506, John E. S. Browne Esq., Chief Constable of Cyprus, Annual Report on the Cyprus Police Force for the Year 1958 (Nicosia: Police Headquarters, February, 1959), pp. 2–5.
77 TNA, WO 32/16260, Telegram No. 836 from Harding to Eden, 14 October 1955.
78 TNA, WO 32/16260, Minute from CIGS, 17 October 1955.
79 TNA, WO 32/16260, Telegram No. 836 from Harding to Eden, 14 October 1955.
80 Grivas, *Memoirs*, p. 49.
81 By the time of his execution on 10 May 1956, Karaolis had turned twenty-three.
82 Επέτειος του Όχι. Literally, 'the day of "no!"'.
83 Grivas, *Memoirs*, p. 50.
84 TNA, FO 141/3709, Proclamation of Dighenis, 21 November 1955.
85 Karyos, 'EOKA, 1955-1959', p. 118.
86 TNA, PREM 1955, Telegram from Eden to Menderes, 10 November 1955.
87 TNA, PREM 1955, Telegram No. 1061, Harding to the Secretary of State for the Colonies, 19 November 1955.
88 Grivas, *Memoirs*, p. 50.
89 Charles Hart, *Cyprus Crisis – 1955-56: 'B' Troop 45 Commando Royal Marines v. Dighenis* (Portsmouth: Holbrook Printers, 2003), p. 25.
90 TNA, CO 926/416, Minute from K. J. Neale to John Martin, 2 January 1956.
91 TNA, CO 926/416, Telegram No. 1233 from Harding to S. of S. Colonies, 11 December 1955.
92 TNA, CO 924/416, Telegram No. 1242 from Harding to the S. of S. Colonies, 13 December 1955.
93 Hart, *Cyprus Crisis – 1955-56*, p. 33, emphasis in original.
94 Author's interviews with Thassos Sophocleous, Renos Kyriakides, Andreas Chartas and Constantinos Loizou.
95 Hart, *Cyprus Crisis – 1955-56*, p. 47.
96 Author's interview with Geoffrey Jukes, 18 December 2009.
97 In January 2019, the British government reached a settlement to pay £1 to 33 EOKA fighters over claims of abuse.
98 TNA, CO 926/547, Telegram No. 39 from Harding to S. of S. Colonies, 7 January 1956.
99 *The Times*, Wednesday, 11 January 1956; p. 8; Issue 53425; col A.
100 TNA, CO 926/417, Telegram No. 405 from Cyprus (Harding) to the Secretary of State for the Colonies, 24 February 1956.
101 Grivas, *Guerrilla Warfare*, p. 68.
102 *Hansard*, Vol. 565, Written Answers, p. 104.
103 USNA, CIA, Information from Foreign Documents or Radio Broadcasts, D455107, 15 April 1956.
104 TNA, FO 371/123897, Telegram No. 1177 from Sinclair to Lennox-Boyd, 17 June 1956.
105 TNA, FO 371/123897, Telegram No. 1144 from Sinclair to Lennox-Boyd, 12 June 1956.

106 *Terrorism in Cyprus: The Captured Documents*, p. 53.
107 *Hansard*, Vol. 565, Written Answers, p. 102.
108 Ibid., pp. 101–2.
109 Holland, *Britain and the Revolt in Cyprus*, p. 148.
110 EOKA's targeting of Greek-Cypriot 'traitors', often without substantial evidence of collaboration with the British authorities, remains a subject of controversy within Cyprus. See Drousiotis, *EOKA*, pp. 218–25.
111 Holland, *Britain and the Revolt in Cyprus*, p. 148.
112 See Chapter 6.
113 Holland, *Britain and the Revolt in Cyprus*, p. 148.
114 Averoff-Tossizza, *Lost Opportunities*, p. 91.
115 Grivas, *Memoirs*, p. 87.
116 TNA, CO 926/521, Telegram No. 1702 from Harding to Lennox-Boyd, 23 August 1956.
117 Grivas quoted in Seraphim-Loizou, *The Cyprus Liberation Struggle 1955–1959*, p. 113.
118 TNA, CO 926/671, Report of the Cyprus Intelligence Committee (56), Appendix B.
119 *Hansard*, Vol. 565, Written Answers, p. 104.
120 TNA, CO 926/416, Telegram No. 1212 from Harding to the Secretary of State for the Colonies, 9 December 1955.
121 TNA, FO 371/136401, Translated EOKA Leaflet from 26 January 1956.
122 TNA, FO 371/136401, Translated EOKA Leaflet from 15 February 1956.
123 TNA, CO 926/416, Telegram No. 1281 from Harding to Lennox-Boyd, 18 December 1955.
124 TNA, CO 926/416, Telegram No. 1283 from Harding to Lennox-Boyd, 18 December 1955.
125 TNA, CO 926/416, Telegram No. 1284 from Harding to Lennox-Boyd, 18 December 1955.
126 TNA, FO 371/123897, Telegram No. 1177 from Sinclair to Lennox-Boyd, 17 June 1956.
127 TNA, CO 926/490, Telegram No. 1777 from Harding to Lennox-Boyd, 1 September 1956.
128 TNA, CO 926/489, *The Church and Terrorism in Cyprus*, p. 6.
129 Ibid., p. 7.
130 Ibid., pp. 39–41.
131 Seraphim, *The Cyprus Liberation Struggle 1955–1959*, p. 144.
132 *Hansard*, Vol. 565, Written Answers, p. 104.
133 Ibid., pp. 101–2.
134 Ibid.
135 Ibid., p. 102.
136 TNA, CO 926/454, Telegram No. 2493 from Sinclair to the Secretary of State for the Colonies, 13 December 1956.
137 Ibid.
138 TNA, CO 926/670, Special Branch Fortnightly Intelligence Report Vol. V, No. 3/57 (Chief Superintendent of Police, G. Meikle), 19 February 1957.
139 TNA, CO 926/670, 'Intelligence Review for the First Half of February 1957', Cyprus Intelligence Committee (CIC) 57, 21 February 1957.
140 TNA, CO 926/671, Cyprus Intelligence Committee (57) Eight, 'Intelligence Review for the Second Half of February 1957', 7 March 1957.
141 Baker, *The Cyprus Emergency*, p. 3.

Chapter 8

1. TNA, CO 926/949, Telegram No. 89 from Macmillan to the Foreign Office, 24 March 1957.
2. John Darwin, *Unfinished Empire: The Global Expansion of Britain* (New York: Bloomsbury Press, 2012), p. 362.
3. Grivas, *Memoirs*, p. 115.
4. Harold Macmillan, *Riding the Storm: 1956–1959* (London: Macmillan, 1971), p. 226.
5. Michael Carver, *Harding of Petherton: Field Marshal* (London: Weidenfeld and Nicolson, 1978), p. 224.
6. Evanthis Hatzivassiliou, *Britain and the International Status of Cyprus, 1955–59* (Minneapolis: University of Minnesota, 1997), p. 64.
7. TNA, FO 371/123888, Letter from Radcliffe to Martin, 29 April 1956.
8. TNA, FO 371/123899, Note of Meeting in the Secretary of State for the Colonies' room – Cyprus Constitutional Development, 8 June 1956.
9. *The Times*, Monday, 16 July 1956, p. 8.
10. TNA, CAB 129/84, CP (56) 264, The Radcliffe Constitutional Proposals, 16 November 1956, p. 6.
11. *Hansard*, Vol. 562, p. 1267.
12. Radcliffe Proposals, p. 5.
13. Ibid.
14. *Hansard*, Vol. 556, Speech by Julian Amery in the House of Commons, 18 July, p. 1450.
15. CSA, V11/151. Constitutional Proposals for Cyprus, Report Submitted to the Secretary of State for the Colonies by the Right. Hon. Lord Radcliffe, GBE (London: Her Majesty's Stationery Office, December 1956), p. 6.
16. Ibid., p. 10.
17. Ibid., p. 14.
18. House of Commons Debate, 19 December 1956, *Hansard*, Vol. 562, p. 1267.
19. CSA, V11/151. Radcliffe Proposals, p. 14.
20. Ibid., p. 13.
21. TNA, FO 371/123942, Record of Conversation between Karamanlis and Lennox-Boyd in Athens, 14 December 1956.
22. Ibid.
23. TNA, FO 371/123941, Report from DP Reilly to Selwyn Lloyd, 17 December 1956.
24. Ibid.
25. TNA, FO 371/123941, Telegram No. 2499 from Washington to Foreign Office, 18 December 1956.
26. TNA, FO 371/123941, Telegram No. 877 from Peake to Foreign Office, 18 December 1956.
27. TNA, FO 371/123941, Telegram No. 2511 from Washington to Foreign Office, 19 December 1956.
28. USNA, Embassy Records, RG 84 Box 3, Telegram No. 124 from Ambassador Warren (Ankara) to the American Embassy, Athens, 19 October 1956.
29. *Hansard*, Vol. 562, p. 1267.
30. Ibid., p. 1268.
31. Averoff-Tossizza, *Lost Opportunities*, p. 103.
32. TNA, FO 371/123941, Telegram No. 882 from Peake to Foreign Office, 20 December 1956, Text of Official Statement of Greek Government, 19 December 1956.

33 TNA, FO 371/123941, Telegram No. 884 from Peake to Foreign Office, 20 December 1956.
34 TNA, CO 926/932, PEKA Leaflet 68/57, 10 February 1957.
35 TNA, CO 926/932, EOKA Leaflet, 'The Pseudo-Constitution', 22 February 1957.
36 TNA, FO 371/123941, Report from DP Reilly to Selwyn Lloyd, 17 December 1956.
37 *Halkın Sesi*, Vol. 1, No. 37, 18 March 1957, 'Partition, Is it Harmful?'
38 *Hansard*, Vol. 562, p. 1273.
39 TNA, CO 926/277, Telegram No. 1041 from the Foreign Office to Ankara, 2 November 1956.
40 TNA, CAB 129/76, CP (55) 82, 'Strategic Review of the Cyprus Problem: Note by the Minister of Defence' (Selwyn Lloyd), 18 July 1955.
41 TNA, CO 926/277, Report by Martin for Harding, 7 June 1956.
42 Ibid.
43 Ibid.
44 Hatzivassiliou, *Britain and the International Status of Cyprus*, p. 72.
45 Xydis, *Cyprus: Conflict and Conciliation*, p. 81.
46 TNA, CO 926/277, Telegram No. 2094 from Harding to Lennox-Boyd, 16 October 1956.
47 TNA, FO 371/123897, Letter from Lloyd to Lennox-Boyd, 8 August 1956.
48 Ibid.
49 TNA, CO 926/277, Telegram No. 2094 from Harding to Lennox-Boyd, 16 October 1956.
50 Harold Macmillan, *Riding the Storm: 1956–1959*, p. 660, quoting diary entry for 7 July 1957.
51 TNA, CO 926/277, Note on Mr. Melville's letter to Harding, 16 July 1956.
52 TNA, CO 926/277, Letter from Harding to Melville, 10 October 1956.
53 TNA, CO 926/277, Note on Mr. Melville's letter to Harding, 16 July 1956.
54 TNA, CO 926/277, Telegram No. 2094 from Harding to Lennox-Boyd, 16 October 1956.
55 TNA, CO 926/277, Telegram No. 1041 from Foreign Office to Bowker, 2 November 1956.
56 TNA, CO 926/277, Memorandum by the British Defence Co-ordination Committee Middle East, COS (56) 426, 'Military Implications of the Partition of Cyprus,' 30 November 1956.
57 TNA, FO 371/123899, Telegram No. 480 from Ambassador Bowker (Ankara) to the Foreign Office, 18 June 1956.
58 Ibid.
59 TNA, FO 371/123899, Telegram No. 2959 from Selwyn Lloyd to John Foster Dulles, 19 June 1956.
60 Markides, 'Britain's "New Look" Policy for Cyprus', p.493.
61 TNA, CO 926/949, Telegram No. 88 from Macmillan to Lloyd, 24 March 1957.
62 CTNA, Kyrenia, *Halkın Sesi*, Vol. 1, No. 11, 17 September 1956.
63 TNA, FO 371/123941, Telegram No. 1134 from Ambassador Bowker (Ankara) to the Foreign Office, 19 December 1956.
64 Ibid.
65 *The Times*, Friday, 4 January 1957, p. 7.
66 TNA, FO 371/123942, Telegram No. 234 from Ambassador Bowker (Ankara) to Selwyn Lloyd, 28 December 1956.
67 *The Times*, Tuesday, 22 January 1957, p. 6.

68 TNA, CO 926/670, Cyprus Intelligence Committee 'Intelligence Review for the First Half of January, 1957', 22 January 1957.
69 Georghiades was an EOKA commander. His position in the organization was subject to much scrutiny and controversy. Some modern scholars continue to refer to him as Grivas's 'head of intelligence' (French, *Fighting EOKA*, p. 58), but this is incomplete. In 1996, Onisiphoros Konteatis (who joined EOKA at 18) accused Georghiades of being the leading British spy within EOKA (Drousiotis, *EOKA*, p. 107). During the emergency, Georghiades was captured and escaped multiple times, fuelling this suspicion. After participating in an unsuccessful attempt to assassinate Makarios, Georghiades's colorful career came to an end when he was assassinated in 1970.
70 TNA, PREM 11/1757, Telegram from Harding to Lennox-Boyd, 22 January 1957.
71 *The Times*, Wednesday, 23 January 1957, p. 8.
72 TNA, CO 926/932, EOKA Leaflet Distributed in Kyrenia, 2 February 1957.
73 RHL, Mss. Medit. S. 25, AF John Reddaway, 'Reflections on an unnecessary conflict: Cyprus, 1955–1958 [sic] c. 1981', p. 32.
74 Averoff-Tossizza, *Lost Opportunities*, p. 106.
75 Ibid., p. 115.
76 United Nations Resolution, 1013 (XI), 660th Plenary Meeting, 26 February 1957.
77 Averoff-Tossizza, *Lost Opportunities*, p. 116.
78 EOKA declaration quoted in Averoff-Tossizza, *Lost Opportunities*, p. 126.
79 TNA, PREM 11/1838, Bermuda Conference 2nd Meeting, 21 March 1957, p. 10.
80 Ibid.
81 TNA, CO 967/320, Letter from Harding to Lennox-Boyd, 19 September 1957.
82 Ibid.
83 Ibid.
84 TNA, CO 967/320, Letter from Lennox-Boyd to Harding, 3 October 1957.
85 Ibid.
86 Ibid.
87 IWM, AFH 3, Letter from Macmillan to Harding, 17 October 1957.
88 RHL, Mss. Medit. S. 35, Foot Box 3 Folder 3 181/8, Telegram from Foot to Lennox-Boyd, 3 October 1957.
89 Ibid.
90 Ibid.
91 CTNA, *Halkın Sesi*, Vol. 1, No. 40, 15 April 1957, 'Partition: The Only Lasting Solution'.
92 CTNA, *Halkın Sesi*, Vol. 1, No. 45, 13 May 1957, 'Britain's Friendship'.
93 TNA, FO 286/1441, Paper on Greek/Turkish Relations in Cyprus, Nicosia Secretariat, 26 August 1957.
94 Ibid.
95 IWM Archives, AFH 10, Telegram No. 1782 from Deputy Governor (George Sinclair) to Secretary of State for the Colonies Alan Lennox-Boyd, 25 November 1957.
96 Ibid.
97 Ibid.
98 *The Times*, Thursday, 28 November 1957; p. 9; Issue 54010; col E.
99 RHL, Foot Papers, Mss. Medit. S. 35.Box 2 Folder 2 181/5. Proclamation of the Turkish Resistance Organisation, translated in Telegram No. 181 from Governor Cyprus to Colonial Office, 2 February 1958.

100 TNA, CO 926/938, Turkish Resistance Organisation Leaflet, 25 December 1957. The leaflet references the final day of the battle of *Dumlupınar* (26–30 August 1922) when the Turkish Nationalist army commanded by Mustafa Kemal Atatürk defeated the Greek army in Asia Minor and the burning of Smyrna by Kemalist forces on 13–22 September 1922.

Chapter 9

1. TNA, CO 926/670, Volkan Leaflet, 22 December 1956.
2. Michael Foot in the *Evening Standard*, quoted in Foot, *A Start in Freedom*, pp. 22–3.
3. TNA, CAB 129/99, C (57) 161, 9 July 1957.
4. Ibid.
5. TNA, CAB 128/31, C (57) 51, 11 July 1957.
6. Ibid.
7. TNA, CAB 129/99, C (57) 161, 9 July 1957.
8. Foot, *A Start in Freedom*, p. 161.
9. TNA, CAB 129/91, C (58) 4, Memorandum by Lennox-Boyd, 4 January 1958.
10. Foot, *A Start in Freedom*, p. 161.
11. Ibid., p. 159.
12. TNA, CAB 129/91, C (58) 4, Memorandum by Lennox-Boyd, 4 January 1958.
13. RHL, Foot Papers, Box 3 Folder 3 181/8, Note from Foot to Earl of Perth, 22 October 1957.
14. TNA, WO 216/915, Letter from Kendrew to Stratton, 7 February 1958.
15. Ibid.
16. RHL, Foot Papers, Box 2, Folder 1, 181/4, Memorandum by Director of Operations, General Joe Kendrew to Foot, 31 December 1957.
17. Ibid.
18. Ibid.
19. RHL, Foot Papers, Box 2, Folder 1, 181/4, Memorandum by Director of Operations, Minute by Sinclair, 1 January 1958.
20. RHL, Foot Papers, Box 2, Folder 1, 181/4, Telegram No. 38, Ankara to Foreign Office, 10 January 1958.
21. RHL, Foot Papers, Box 2, Folder 1, 181/4, Telegram No. 32, Sinclair to Foot, 8 January 1958.
22. RHL, Foot Papers, Box 2 Folder 1 181/4, Note from Foot to Sinclair, 7 January 1958.
23. *The Times*, Monday, 20 January 1958, p. 8.
24. RHL, Foot Papers, Box 2 Folder 2 181/5, Telegram No. 89, Foot to Lennox-Boyd, 21 January 1958.
25. *The Times*, Wednesday, 22 January 1958, p. 8.
26. RHL, Foot Papers, Box 2 Folder 2 181/5, Telegram No. 28, Note from Lloyd to Foot, 26 January 1958.
27. RHL, Foot Papers, Box 2 Folder 2 181/5, Telegram No. 89, Foot to Lennox-Boyd, 21 January 1958.
28. *The Times*, 28 January 1958, p. 8.
29. Ibid.
30. RHL, Foot Papers, Box 2 Folder 2 181/5. Proclamation of the Turkish Resistance Organisation, translated in Telegram No. 181 from Governor Cyprus to Colonial Office, 2 February 1958.

31 Ibid.
32 USNA, CIA Records, NSC Briefing, 28 January 1958.
33 Ibid.
34 *The Times*, 31 January 1958, p. 8.
35 TNA, CO 926/938, Turkish Resistance Organisation Leaflet, 31 January 1958.
36 TNA, CO 926/938, Turkish Resistance Organisation Leaflet, 23 January 1958.
37 RHL, Foot Papers, Box 4, Folder 2 181/11, Telegram No. 443, Foot to Lennox-Boyd, 27 March 1958.
38 Assos, *Makarios*, p. 172.
39 Ibid., p. 159.
40 TNA, FO 371/130132, Record of Conversation between Foot and Makarios, 13 February 1958.
41 USNA, CIA Records, Current Intelligence Weekly Summary, 6 March 1958.
42 RHL, Foot Papers, Box 4 Folder 2 181/11, Note from Reddaway to Sinclair, 17 April 1958.
43 Seraphim-Loizou, *The Cyprus Liberation Struggle 1955–1959*, p. 247.
44 TNA, CO 926/935, VA/3, Order from EOKA area commander, 1957.
45 TNA, CO 187/1/07, Telegram No. 2407, Foot to Lennox-Boyd, 11 December 1957.
46 TNA, CO 926/938, Telegram No. 191, Foot to Lennox-Boyd, 3 February 1958.
47 Ibid.
48 TNA, CO 926/938, EOKA Order from Grivas, 3 February 1958.
49 Ibid.
50 *The Times*, 23 January 1958, p. 10.
51 *The Times*, 24 January 1958, p. 6.
52 TNA, CO 926/940, EOKA Leaflet, 29 May 1958.
53 TNA, FO 371/136404, Note from Neale to Aldridge, 29 May 1958.
54 *Cyprus Mail*, Vol. 42, No. 4273, 24 May 1958.
55 Drousiotis, quoting interview with Giorgos Lagoudontis, p. 223.
56 *The Times*, 26 May 1958, p. 10.
57 *The Times*, 31 May 1958, p. 4.
58 *Cyprus Mail*, Vol. 42, No. 4254, 5 May 1958.
59 TNA, CO 926/952, TMT Leaflet, 11 May 1958.
60 *The Times*, 23 May 1958, p. 8.
61 *The Times*, 26 May 1958, p. 10.
62 *The Times*, 31 May 1958, p. 4.
63 Assos, *Makarios*, p. 196.
64 TNA, CO 926/938, 86394, Bulletin of the Turkish Resistance Organization, 25 December 1957.
65 RHL, Foot Papers, Box 5, Folder 3 181/14, Colonial Office Brief for the Prime Minister for his visit to America, 4 June 1958.
66 The arrival of Turkish trainers and equipment would begin in earnest in July. See below.
67 TNA, CO 926/938, Turkish Defence Organisation Leaflet, 31 January 1958.
68 TNA, CO 926/675, Cyprus Intelligence Committee, (58) Fourteen, 'Intelligence Review for the Second Half of May 1958', 7 June 1958.
69 RHL, Foot Papers, Box 5, Folder 2 181/13, Minutes of Meeting of Foot and Lloyd, 15 May 1958.
70 TNA, CAB 129/93, C (58) 102, 9 May 1958.
71 RHL, Foot Papers, Box 5, Folder 1 181/12, Letter from Sinclair to Foot, 16 May 1958.

72 RHL, Foot Papers, Box 5, Folder 1 181/12, Foot to Lennox-Boyd, 16 May 1958.
73 *The Times*, Monday, 9 June 1958, p. 10.
74 Ibid.
75 Ibid.
76 Ibid.
77 TNA, FO 371/136337, Telegram No. 833 from Bowker to Foreign Office, 6 June 1958.
78 TNA, WO 216/915, Memorandum by General DA Kendrew, 'Assessment of the Situation 16 July 1958', 19 July 1958.
79 Author's Interview with Rauf Denktaş, Nicosia, 10 April 2009.
80 TNA, WO 216/915, Memorandum by General DA Kendrew, 'Assessment of the Situation 16 July 1958', 19 July 1958.
81 TNA, CAB 128/32 CC (58) 47th Conclusions, 10 June 1958.
82 RHL, Foot Papers, Box 6, Folder 1 181/16, Telegram No. 942, Ankara to Foreign Office, 18 June 1958.
83 TNA, FO 371/136337, Telegram No. 925, Bowker to Foreign Office, 17 June 1958.eve n.
84 TNA, FO 371/136337, Telegram No. 923, Bowker to Lennox-Boyd, 17 June 1958.
85 Ibid.
86 Ibid.
87 TNA, FO 371/136337, Foot to Lennox-Boyd, 22 June 1958.
88 *Cyprus Mail*, Vol. 42, No. 4294, 14 June 1958.
89 *Hansard*, Vol. 597, p. 345.
90 Makarios quoted in *Cyprus Mail*, Vol. 42, No. 4290, 10 June 1958.
91 Grivas, *Memoirs*, p. 149.
92 Ibid., p. 145.
93 TNA, WO 216/915, Kendrew Memorandum, 19 July 1958.
94 Ibid.
95 Ibid.
96 *Hansard*, Vol. 591, Written Answers, p. 79.
97 Holland, *Britain and the Revolt in Cyprus*, p. 267.
98 TNA, CO 926/676, Special Branch Half-Monthly Intelligence Report, Vol. VI, No. 14/58, 4 August 1958.
99 Foot Papers, Box 4, Folder 2 181/11, Telegram No. 458, Foot to Higham, 30 March 1958.
100 RHL, Foot Papers, Foot to Allen, 31 January 1958.
101 TNA, FO 371/136337, Telegram No. 891, Bowker to Lennox-Boyd, 14 June 1958.
102 USNA, Records of the American Embassy, Turkey, RG 84 Box 157, Letter from Menderes to Macmillan, 14 June 1958.
103 RHL, Foot Papers, Box 2, Folder 2 181/5, Telegram No. 104, Foreign Office to POMEF. Undated, c. January 1958.
104 RHL, Foot Papers, Box 2, Folder 2 181/5, Telegram No. 137, Colonial Office to Foot, 18 January 1958.
105 RHL, Foot Papers, Box 6, Folder 1 181/6, Letter from Caccia to Foot, 20 June 1958.
106 RHL, Foot Papers, Box 6, Folder 1 181/16, Note from Sinclair to Foot, 23 June 1958.
107 RHL, Foot Papers, Box 3, Folder 3 181/8, Telegram from Foot to Lennox-Boyd, 3 October 1957.
108 *Cyprus Mail*, Vol. 42, No. 4312, 3 July 1958.
109 Seraphim-Loizou, *The Cyprus Liberation Struggle 1955–1959*, p. 279.
110 Ibid.

111 This insult played on the imagery of TMT's seal which pictured a wolf howling at a crescent moon.
112 TNA, CO 926/932, EOKA General Order, Mid-June 1958.
113 TNA, CO 926/940, TMT Leaflet, 28 May 1958.
114 TNA, CO 926/952, TMT Leaflet, 11 June 1958, emphasis in original.
115 Author's Interview with Rauf Denktaş, 10 April 2009.
116 Ibid.
117 TNA, CO 926/676, Special Branch Half-Monthly Intelligence Report, Vol. VI, No. 13/58, July 1958.
118 TNA, Co 926/676, Cyprus Local Intelligence Committee, Intelligence Assessment (3), 31 July 1958.
119 RHL, Foot Papers, Box 6, Folder 1 181/16, Telegram No. 1109, Foreign Office to Athens, 6 August 1958.
120 RHL, Foot Papers, Box 6, Folder 1 181/16, EOKA Leaflet in Telegram No. 1297, Foot to Colonial Office, 4 August 1958.
121 RHL, Foot Papers, Box 6, Folder 1 181/16, TMT Leaflet in Telegram No. 1755, Foot to Colonial Office, 5 August 1958.
122 TNA, WO 106/6020, Darling, 'Report on the Cyprus Emergency', p. 68.

Chapter 10

1 John Reddaway, *Burdened with Cyprus: The British Connection* (London: K. Rustem & Bro. and Weidenfeld & Nicolson Ltd., 1986), p. ii.
2 Makarios interview with Barbara Castle, MP, on 22 September. *The Times*, 23 September 1958, p. 10.
3 RHL, Foot Papers Box 6, Folder 2, Telegram No. 329, Macmillan to Foot, 10 August 1958.
4 Ibid.
5 Ibid.
6 Macmillan Diary, 9 August 1958, quoted in *Riding the Storm*, p. 676.
7 Ibid., p. 677.
8 Ibid., p. 678.
9 FRUS, *US Department of State, Vol. X, Part 1, FRUS, 1958-60: E. Europe Region; Soviet Union, Cyprus*, 254. Memorandum of Conversation, Athens, 9 August 1958.
10 FRUS, 265. Memorandum of Conversation, MC 16 Boston, 27 September 1958.
11 RHL, Foot Papers, Box 6, Folder 2, Telegram No. 1272, Macmillan to Lloyd, 12 August 1958.
12 Ibid.
13 FRUS, 265. Memorandum of Conversation, MC 16 Boston, 27 September 1958.
14 TNA, CAB 128/32, CC (58) 67th Conclusions, 12 August 1958.
15 Ibid.
16 Ibid.
17 RHL, Foot Papers, Box 6, Folder 2, Telegram No. 271, Foreign Office to POMEF, 15 August 1958.
18 Ibid.
19 *The Times*, Saturday, 16 August 1958; p. 6; Issue 54231; col A.
20 RHL, Foot Papers, Box 6, Folder 2, Message from Makarios to Foot, 16 August 1958.

21 Ibid.
22 TNA, CAB 128/32, CC (58) 68th Conclusions, 27 August 1958.
23 Ibid.
24 RHL, Foot Papers, Box 6, Folder 2, Telegram No. 1436, Foot to Lennox-Boyd, 23 August 1958.
25 RHL, Foot Papers, Box 6, Folder 2, Minute by the Chief of Staff (Cyprus), August 1958.
26 EOKA Leaflet, 21 August 1958, quoted in *The Times*, 22 August 1958, p. 6.
27 *The Times*, 27 August 1958, p. 8.
28 TNA, CO 926/941, EOKA Leaflet, 8 August 1958.
29 *The Times*, 16 September 1958, p. 7.
30 Darling, 'Report on the Cyprus Emergency'.
31 Ibid.
32 Vanezis, *Makarios: Pragmatism v. Idealism* (London: Abelard-Schumann Ltd., 1971), p. 83.
33 TNA, CAB 128/32, CC (58) 67th Conclusions, 12 August 1958.
34 Ἄλκιμος Νεολαία ΕΟΚΑ.
35 TNA, CO 926/941, ANE Leaflet, 15 October 1958.
36 Seneca, *Letters from a Stoic* (New York: Penguin Books, 1969), p. LXXI.
37 RHL, Foot Papers, Box 7, Folder 1, Telegram from Lennox-Boyd to Foot, 20 September 1958.
38 Ibid.
39 *The Times*, 23 September 1958, p. 10.
40 Ibid.
41 Xydis, *Cyprus, Conflict and Conciliation*, pp. 41–2.
42 TNA, FO 371/123863, Personal Letter from Lennox-Boyd to Lord Home, 6 January 1956.
43 Xydis, *Cyprus: Conflict and Conciliation*, p. 87.
44 RHL, Foot Papers, Box 1, Folder 1, Brief for Sir Hugh Foot, No. 5, 19 November 1957.
45 Drousiotis, *EOKA*, p. 213.
46 Xydis, *Cyprus: Conflict and Conciliation*, p. 186.
47 FRUS, 250. Telegram from Ambassador Houghton, (Paris) to the Department of State, Paris, 28 July 1958.
48 RHL, Foot Papers, Box 7, Folder 1, Note from Foot to Martin, 11 November 1958.
49 Ibid.
50 Averoff speech at the United Nations, 24 November 1958, quoted in Cmnd. 735, *Report on the Proceedings of the Thirteenth Session of the General Assembly of the United Nations* (London: Her Majesty's Stationery Office, May 1959), p. 30.
51 'Speech by the Minister of State for Foreign Affairs on Cyprus in the First Committee on November 25, 1958', in Cmnd. 735, *Report on the Proceedings of the Thirteenth Session of the General Assembly of the United Nations* (London: Her Majesty's Stationery Office, May 1959), p. 134.
52 Ibid., p. 137.
53 Ibid., p. 138.
54 Ibid., p. 141.
55 Zorlu speech on 25 November 1958, quoted in *Report on the Proceedings of the Thirteenth Session of the General Assembly of the United Nations* (London: Her Majesty's Stationery Office, May 1959), p. 31.

56 Cmnd. 735, *Report on the Proceedings of the Thirteenth Session of the General Assembly of the United Nations* (London: Her Majesty's Stationery Office, May 1959), p. 32.
57 Ibid., p. 33.
58 Author's Interview with Rauf Denktaş, 10 April 2009, Nicosia.
59 Ibid.
60 Dimitris Bitsios, *Cyprus: The Vulnerable Republic* (Thessaloniki: The Institute for Balkan Studies, 1975), p. 96.
61 Brendan O'Malley and Ian Craig, *The Cyprus Conspiracy: America, Espionage and the Turkish Invasion* (London: I.B. Tauris Publishers, 1999), p. 71.
62 Cmnd. 735, *Report on the Proceedings of the Thirteenth Session of the General Assembly of the United Nations*, p. 33.
63 Hatzivassiliou, *Britain and the International Status of Cyprus*, p. 153.
64 Foot Papers, Box 8, Folder 1, 181/126, Note from Lennox-Boyd to Foot, 18 December 1958.
65 Ibid.
66 Ibid.
67 Ibid.
68 FRUS, 297. Telegram from Ambassador Amory Houghton to the Department of State, 19 December 1958.
69 Ibid.
70 Bitsios, *Cyprus*, p. 101.
71 Evanthis Hatzivassiliou, 'Security and the European Option: Greek Foreign Policy, 1952-62', *Journal of Contemporary History*, Vol. 30, No. 1 (January 1995), p. 191.
72 EOKA Leaflet, 24 December 1958, quoted in *The Times*, 27 December 1958, p. 6.
73 RHL, Foot Papers, Box 8, Folder 1, 181/126, Telegram No. 911 from Allen to Foreign Office, 27 December 1958.
74 RHL, Foot Papers, Box 8, Folder 1, 181/126, Telegram No. 906, Allen to Foot, 25 December 1958.
75 RHL, Foot Papers, Box 8, Folder 1, 181/126, Telegram No. 913, Allen to Foreign Office, 28 December 1958.
76 Bitsios, *Cyprus*, p. 97.
77 RHL, Foot Papers, Box 8, Folder 1, 181/126, Telegram No. 248, Macmillan to Foot, 6 February 1959.
78 Bitsios, *Cyprus*, p. 102.
79 RHL, Foot Papers, Box 8, Folder 3, 181/28, Telegram from Lloyd to Foot, 12 February 1959.
80 Author's Interview with Rauf Denktaş, 10 April 2009, Nicosia.
81 RHL, Foot Papers, Box 8, Folder 3, 181/28, Telegram No. 279, Lennox-Boyd to Foot, 12 February 1959.
82 Bitsios, *Cyprus*, p. 108.
83 IWM, Darling Papers, GB62, General Kenneth Darling, 'Cyprus: The Final Round', pp. 26–7.
84 Bitsios, *Cyprus*, p. 109.
85 Hatzivassiliou, *Britain and the International Status of Cyprus*, p. 160.
86 Alastos, *Cyprus Guerrilla: Grivas, Makarios and the British* (London: Heinemann, 1960), pp. 2–3.
87 RHL, Foot Papers, Box 8, Folder 3, 181/28, Telegram (unnumbered), Foot to Sinclair, 19 February 1959.

88 RHL, Foot Papers, Box 8, Folder 3, 181/28, Note from Makarios to Foot [undated], emphasis in original.
89 Cmnd. 680, *Conference on Cyprus: Final Statements at the Closing Plenary Session at Lancaster House on February 19, 1959*, Miscellaneous No. 5 (1959).
90 Ibid.
91 Ibid.

Conclusion

1 Grivas, *Memoirs*, p. 203.
2 Ibid.
3 Ibid., pp. 198–9.
4 Grivas's order quoted in Seraphim-Loizou, *The Cyprus Liberation Struggle 1955–1959*, p. 335.
5 Makarios declared 'We have won!' quoting the declaration of the runner Pheidippides, who supposedly cried νενικήκαμεν on returning to Athens from the battlefield of Marathon in 490 BCE.
6 Seraphim-Loizou, *The Cyprus Liberation Struggle 1955–1959*, p. 332.
7 Darling 'Report on the Cyprus Emergency', p.68.
8 Ibid.
9 CTNA, Letter from Kütchük to Makarios, 12 September 1961.
10 Ibid.
11 Memoirs of Sir Alec Bishop, *Look Back with Pleasure* (Unpublished, from the private collection of Mrs. Juliet Campbell, Oxford), p. 265.

Bibliography

Archival sources and unpublished memoirs

The Archives of the Archbishopric of Cyprus (AAC), Nicosia
    Papers of Archbishop Leontios
    Papers of Archbishop Makarios II
    'St. Barnabas the Apostle', Monthly Periodical of the Cypriot Church, March 1954 to October 1956
    Minutes of the Ethnarchy Council Meetings

Bishop, Alec, *Look Back with Pleasure* (Unpublished, from the private collection of Mrs. Juliet Campbell, Oxford)

The Council for the History and Memory of the EOKA Struggle (SIMAE), Nicosia

The Cyprus State Archives (CSA), Nicosia

The Cyprus Turkish National Archive and Research Center (CTNA), Kyrenia

The Eisenhower Papers: http://eisenhower.press.jhu.edu/

The Imperial War Museum (IWM), London
    Papers of Field Marshal Sir John Harding
    Papers of General Sir Kenneth Darling
    Papers of Corporal Ian W.G. Martin

The MacMillan Cabinet Papers

The National Archives of the United Kingdom (TNA), Kew, London

Series: CAB 128, CAB 129, CO 926, CO 968, FO 371, PREM 11, WO 32, WO 106, WO 216

The National Archives of the United States (USNA), College Park, Maryland
    Digital Archive of the CIA
    Foreign Relations of the United States (FRUS), Vol. XXIV, 1955-1957: The Soviet Union; Eastern Mediterranean (Washington: US Department of State, 1989)
    Foreign Relations of the United States (FRUS), Vol. X, Part 1, 1958-60: E. Europe Region; Soviet Union, Cyprus (Washington: US Department of State, 1993)
    RG 59: Records of the US State Department
    RG 84: Records of the US embassies in London, Athens, and Ankara
    RG 218: Records of the US Joint Chiefs of Staff

The Archives of Rhodes House Library (RHL), Oxford
  Papers of Sir Robert Percival Armitage (Mss. Afr. S. 2204)
  Papers of Sir Hugh Foot (Mss. Medit. S. 35)
  Papers of Sir John Reddaway (Mss. Medit. S. 25, S. 32)
  Corruption of Youth in Support of Terrorism in Cyprus (Nicosia: The Government of Cyprus, August 1957)
  'Facts About the Question of Cyprus', from the Turkish Embassy, London (1955)
  Registration of the Population 1956: Report and Tables (Nicosia: Statistics Section Financial Secretary's Office, September 1958)

Printed primary sources

Archbishop Makarios III, 'Message to the People of Cyprus', *Hellenic News*, Bulletin No. 38 (Washington, DC: The Royal Greek Embassy Information Service, 1955).
Cmnd. 455, *Cyprus Statement of Policy* (London: Her Majesty's Stationery Office, June 1958).
Cmnd. 679, *Conference on Cyprus: Documents Signed and Initialled at Lancaster House on February 19, 1959*, Miscellaneous No. 4 (1959).
Cmnd. 680, *Conference on Cyprus: Final Statements at the Closing Plenary Session at Lancaster House on February 19, 1959*, Miscellaneous No. 5 (1959).
Cmnd. 735, *Report on the Proceedings of the Thirteenth Session of the General Assembly of the United Nations Held at New York*, United Nations No. 1 (1959) (London: Her Majesty's Stationery Office, May 1959).
Cmnd. 780, *The Colonial Territories: 1958-1959, Presented to Parliament by the Secretary of State for the Colonies by Command of Her Majesty*, June 1959.
'Cyprus: Background to Enosis', *Information Department Memorandum* (London: The Royal Institute of International Affairs, 1957).
Discussion on Cyprus in the North Atlantic Treaty Organisation, September-October 1958, Miscellaneous No. 14 (1958) (London: Her Majesty's Stationery Office, October 1958).
Documents and Press Comments on the Cyprus Question (Athens: Press and Information Department, Prime Minister's Office, 1954).
Economides, M., *Cyprus: The Case for Enosis* (London: Zeno Publications, 1954?).
Explanatory Memorandum in support of the Greek request for inclusion of the item of Cyprus on the agenda for the forthcoming General Assembly of the United Nations, 13 June 1956.
Harding, Field Marshal Sir John, 'The Cyprus Problem in Relation to the Middle East', *International Affairs*, Vol. 34, No. 3 (July 1958), pp. 291–6.
Kouchouk, Fazil Dr., *The Voice of Cyprus: Who Is at Fault* (Nicosia: Bozkurt Press, November 1956).
Kouchouk, Fazil Dr., *The Voice of Cyprus* (Cyprus: Turkey Republic of Northern Cyprus Ministry of Foreign Affairs and Defence, 1956).
Letter addressed to the Secretary-General by the Permanent Representative of Greece to the United Nations, 26 April 1956 (Christian X. Palamas to Drag Hammarskjold).
Loizides, Savvas, *The Cyprus Question and the Law of the United Nations* (Nicosia: Nicosia Printing Works, 1951).
Loizides, Savvas, *Άτυχη Κύπρος, Πως έζησα τους πόθους και τους καημούς της, 1910-1980* [Unfortunate Cyprus, how I lived its passions and sorrows, 1910-1980] (Athens: Bergadi, 1980).

Parliamentary Debates (Hansard) Fifth Series – Volumes 431, 434, 445, 446, 451, 476, 500, 520, 523, 535, 526, 527, 530, 531, 540, 549, 550, 556, 562, 564, 565, 589, 591, 592, 597, 601, *House of Commons: Official Report* (London: Her Majesty's Stationery Office).

Rossides, Zenon, *The Island of Cyprus and Union with Greece* (Nicosia: The Cyprus Ethnarchy Office, 1954).

Terrorism in Cyprus: The Captured Documents, trans. by authority of the Secretary of State for the Colonies (London: Her Majesty's Stationery Office, 1956).

United Nations, Official Records of the General Assembly: Plenary Meetings, 14 October 1952–28 August 1953 (New York: United Nations, 1953).

United Nations, Official Records of the General Assembly, Eighth Session: Plenary Meetings, 15 September–9 December 1953 (New York: United Nations, 1953).

United Nations, Official Records of the General Assembly, Ninth Session: General Committee, 21 September–17 December 1954 (New York: United Nations, 1954).

United Nations, Official Records of the General Assembly: Plenary Meetings, 21 September–17 December 1954 (New York: United Nations, 1954).

Newspapers

Cyprus Mail, Nicosia, 1950–1959.
Halkın Sesi [English Edition], Nicosia, 1956–1958.
The Chicago Daily Tribune, Chicago, 1947–1950.
The Cyprus Times, Nicosia, 1946–1959.
The New York Times, New York, 1946–1960.
The Times, London, 1946–1960.
The Times of Cyprus, Nicosia, 1955–59.

Published memoirs

Averoff-Tossizza, Evangelos, *Lost Opportunities: The Cyprus Question*, 1950-1963, trans. Timothy Cullen and Susan Kyriakidis (New York: Aristide D. Caratzas, 1986).

Azinas, Andreas, *50 Years of Silence: Cyprus Struggle for Freedom, My EOKA Secret File*, Vols. A&B (Nicosia: Airwaves, 2002).

Bitsios, Dimitris, *Cyprus: The Vulnerable Republic* (Thessaloniki: The Institute for Balkan Studies, 1975).

Clerides, Glafkos, *Cyprus: My Deposition* (Nicosia: Alithia Publishing, 1989).

Denktaş, Rauf R., *The Cyprus Triangle* (New York: The Office of the Turkish Republic of Northern Cyprus, 1988).

Denktaş, Rauf R., *The Cyprus Problem: What It Is – How Can It be Solved?* (Cyrep: Lefkoşa, 2004).

Durrell, Lawrence, *Bitter Lemons* (London: Faber and Faber, 1957).

Eden, Anthony, *Full Circle* (London: Cassell, 1960).

Eisenhower, Dwight D., *Mandate for Change, 1953-1956*, the White House Years (New York: Doubleday, 1963).

Eisenhower, Dwight D., *Waging Peace, 1956-1961*, the White House Years (New York: Doubleday, 1965).

Fallaci, Oriana, *Intervisa con la storia* (Milano: Biblioteca Universale Rizzoli, 1994).
Foot, Sir Hugh, *A Start in Freedom* (London: Hodder and Stoughton, 1964).
Grivas, Giorgios, *Απομνεμονευματα Αγωνοσ EOKA 1955-1959* [Memoirs of the EOKA Struggle] (Athens: Idiotiki Ekdosi, 1961).
Grivas, Giorgios, *Guerrilla Warfare and EOKA's Struggle: A Politico- Military Study*, trans. A.A. Pallis (London: Longmans, 1964).
Grivas, Giorgios, *The Memoirs of General Grivas*, ed. Charles Foley (London: Longmans, Green and Co. Ltd., 1964).
Hart, Charles, *Cyprus Crisis – 1955-56: 'B' Troop 45 Commando Royal Marines v. Dighenis* (Portsmouth: Holbrook Printers, 2003).
Kyriakides, Renos, *Ρωμανός της Πιτσιλλιάς [Romanos of Pitsillias]* (Nicosia: Livadioti, 2008).
Lloyd, Selwyn, *Suez 1956: A Personal Account* (New York: Mayflower Books, 1978).
Lyssiotis, Renos, *'My Marshal, I Surrender!' and 19 Other Stories*, trans. Susan Papas (Nicosia: MAM, 2016).
Seraphim-Loizou, Elenitsa, *The Cyprus Liberation Struggle: 1955-1959 Through the Eyes of a Woman EOKA Area Commander*, trans. John Vickers (Nicosia: Epiphaniou Publications, 2000).
Storrs, Ronald, *The Memoirs of Sir Ronald Storrs* (New York: G.P. Putnam's Sons, 1937).
Macmillan, Harold, *Tides of Fortune: 1945-1955* (New York: Harper and Row, 1969).
Macmillan, Harold, *Riding the Storm: 1956-1959* (London: Macmillan, 1971).
Noel-Baker, Francis, *My Cyprus File* (Nicosia: Zavallis Press, 1985).
Papaioannou, Ezekias, *Ενθυμήσεις από της ζωής μου [Memories From My Life]* (Nicosia: Εκδοση Πυρσος, 1988).
Reddaway, John, *Burdened with Cyprus: The British Connection* (London: K. Rustem & Bro. and Weidenfeld & Nicolson Ltd., 1986).

Interviews

Author's Interviews: Andreas Azinas, Yilmaz Bora, Andreas Chartas, Glafcos Clerides, Rauf Denktaş, Geoffrey Jukes, Yiannis Kolokasides, Renos Kyriakides, Constantinos Loizou, Vassos Lyssarides, Thassos Sophocleous.

Secondary sources

Alastos, Doros, *Cyprus in History* (London: Zeno Booksellers & Publishers, 1955).
Alastos, Doros, *Cyprus Guerrilla: Grivas, Makarios and the British* (London: Heinemann, 1960).
Anderson, David, *Histories of the Hanged: The Dirty War in Kenya and the End of Empire* (New York: W.W. Norton, 2005).
Anderson, David and David Killingray, eds, *Policing and Decolonisation: Politics, Nationalism, and the Police, 1917-65* (New York: St. Martin's Press, 1992).
Andrew, Christopher, *Defence of the Realm: The Authorized History of MI5* (London: Allen Lane, 2009).
Aydin, Mustafa, 'Determinants of Turkish Foreign Policy: Changing Patterns and Conjunctures during the Cold War', *Eastern Studies*, Vol. 36, No. 1 (January, 2000), pp. 103-9.

Bachheli, Tozun, *Greek-Turkish Relations since 1955* (Boulder: Westview Press, 1990).
Baker, Colin, *Retreat from Empire: Sir Robert Armitage in Africa and Cyprus* (London: I.B. Tauris Publishers, 1998).
Barker, Dudley, *Grivas: Portrait of a Terrorist* (London: The Cresset Press, 1959).
Bartlett, Christopher J., *A History of Postwar Britain: 1945-1974* (London: Longman, 1977).
Beckingham, Charles F., 'The Turks of Cyprus', *The Journal of the Royal Anthropological Institute of Great Britain and Ireland*, Vol. 87, No. 2 (July–December, 1957), pp. 165–74.
Bennet, Huw, *Fighting the Mau Mau: The British Army and Counter-Insurgency in the Kenya Emergency* (Cambridge: Cambridge University Press, 2012).
Blood, L. Lloyd, 'Mediterranean', *Journal of Comparative Legislation and International Law* (Oxford: Oxford University Press, 1939).
Brambilla, Elena, 'Convivencia under Muslim Rule: The Island of Cyprus after the Ottoman Conquest (1571-1640)'. Working paper. ND c. 2010. http://www.cliohworld.net/onlread/6/12.pdf
Byford-Jones, W., *Grivas and the Story of EOKA* (London: Robert Hale Limited, 1959).
Carruthers, Susan L., *Winning Hearts and Minds: British Governments, the Media, and Colonial Counter-Insurgency, 1944-1960* (London: Leicester University Press, 1995).
Carver, Michael, *Harding of Petherton, Field Marshal* (London: Weidenfeld and Nicolson, 1978).
Charters, David A., *The British Army and Jewish insurgency in Palestine, 1945-47* (Hampshire: Macmillan Press, 1989).
Chrysoloras, Nikos, 'Why Orthodoxy? Religion and Nationalism in Greek Political Culture', *LSE Symposium on Modern Greece*, 2003. http://www2.lse.ac.uk/european Institute/research/hellenicObservatory/pdf/1st_Symposium/NicosChrysoloras1stLSES ymposiumPaper.pdf
Clogg, Richard, 'The Byzantine Legacy in the Modern Greek World: The Megali Idea', in *The Byzantine Legacy in Eastern Europe*, ed. Lowell Clucas (Boulder: East European Monographs, 1988).
Close, David H., *The Greek Civil War, 1943-1950*, Studies of Polarization (London: Routledge, 1993).
Close, David H., *The Origins of the Greek Civil War* (London: Longman, 1995).
Coates, John, *Suppressing Insurgency: An Analysis of the Malayan Emergency, 1948-1954* (Boulder: Westview Press, 1992).
Corum, James S., *Training Indigenous Forces in Counterinsurgency: A Tale of Two Insurgencies* (Carlise: Strategic Studies Institute US Army War College, March 2006). www.StrategicStudiesInstitute.army.mil
Crawshaw, Nancy, *The Cyprus Revolt: An Account of the Struggle for Union with Greece* (London: George Allen & Unwin, 1978).
Crouzet, François, *Le Conflit de Chypre, 1946-1959* (Bruxelles: Bruylant, 1973).
Darwin, John, *Unfinished Empire: The Global Expansion of Britain* (New York: Bloomsburg Press, 2012).
Demetriou, Chares, 'Political Radicalization and Political Violence in Palestine (1920-1948), Ireland (1850-1921), and Cyprus (1914-1959)'. *Social Science History*, Vol. 36, No. 4 (Fall, 2012), pp. 391–420.
Dietzel, Irene and Vasilios N. Makrides, 'Ethno-Religious Coexistence and Plurality in Cyprus under British Rule (1878-1960)', *Social Compass*, Vol. 56, No. 1 (2009), pp. 69–83.
Dimaras, Konstaninos, *Ελληνικός Ρομαντισμός* [Greek Romanticism] (Athens: Ermis, 1985).

Dimitrakis, Panagiotis, 'British Intelligence and the Cyprus Insurgency, 1955-1959', *International Journal of Intelligence and CounterIntelligence*, Vol. 21, No. 2 (2008), pp. 375–94.

Dixon, Paul, '"Hearts and Minds"? British Counter-Insurgency from Malaya to Iraq', *The Journal of Strategic Studies*, Vol. 32, No. 3 (2009), pp. 353–81.

Dorril, Stephen, *MI6: Fifty Years of Special Operations* (London: Fourth Estate, 2000).

Drousiotis, Makarios, *EOKA: η σκοτεινή όψη [EOKA: The Dark Side]* (Λευυκωσία: Έκδοσης Αλφάδι, 2002).

Enloe, Cynthia H., 'Police and Military in the Resolution of Ethnic Conflict', in *Annals of the American Academy of Political and Social Science*, Vol. 433, Ethnic Conflict in the World Today (September, 1077), pp. 137–49.

Faustmann, Hubert, 'The UN and the Internationalization of the Cyprus Conflict, 1949-58', in *The Work of the UN in Cyrus: Promoting Peace and Development*, ed. Oliver P. Richmond and James Ker-Lindsay (New York: Palgrave Macmillan, 2001).

Foley, Charles, *Island in Revolt* (London: Longmans, 1962).

Foley, Charles and W. I. Scobie, *The Struggle for Cyprus* (Stanford: Hoover Institution Press, 1975).

Frazee, Charles A., *The Orthodox Church and Independent Greece 1821-1852* (Cambridge: Cambridge University Press, 1969).

French, David, *The British Way in Counter-Insurgency, 1945-1967* (Oxford: Oxford University Press, 2012).

French, David, *Fighting EOKA: The British Counter-Insurgency Campaign on Cyprus, 1955-1959* (Oxford: Oxford University Press, 2015)

Galpern, Steven G., *Money, Oil, and Empire in the Middle East* (Cambridge: Cambridge University Press, 2009).

Genevoix, Maurice, *The Greece of Karamanlis* (London: Doric Publications, 1973).

Georghallides, George S., *Cyprus and the Governorship of Sir Ronald Storrs* (Nicosia: Cyprus Research Center, 1985).

Goebel, Stefan and Derek Keene, 'Towards a Metropolitan History of Total War: An Introduction', in *Cities into Battlefields: Metropolitan Scenarios, Experiences and Commemorations of Total War*, ed. Stefan Goebel and Derek Keene (Farnham: Ashgate Publishing Limited, 2011), pp. 1–46.

Güven, Dilek, 'Riots against the Non-Muslims of Turkey: 6-7 September 1955 in the Context of Demographic Engineering', *European Journal of Turkish Studies*, Vol. 12 (2011), pp. 1–17.

Hadjipavlou, Maria, 'The Cyprus Conflict: Root Causes and Implications for Peacebuilding', *Journal of Peace Research*, Vol. 44 (May, 2007), pp. 349–65.

Hatay, Mete, 'Three Ways of Sharing the Sacred: Choreographies of Coexistence in Cyprus', in *Religion, Politics, and Conflict Resolution*, ed. Elazar Barkan and Karen Barkley (New York: Columbia University Press, 2015), pp. 69–96.

Hatzivassiliou, Evanthis, 'Security and the European Option: Greek Foreign Policy, 1952-62', *Journal of Contemporary History*, Vol. 30, No. 1 (January, 1995), pp. 187–202.

Hatzivassiliou, Evanthis, *Britain and the International Status of Cyprus, 1955-1959* (Minneapolis: University of Minnesota, 1997).

Hatzivassiliou, Evanthis, *The Cyprus Question, 1878-1960: The Constitutional Aspect* (Minneapolis: University of Minnesota, 2002).

Hatzivassiliou, Evanthis, *Στρατηγικές του Κυπριακού, Η δεκαετία του 1950 [Strategies of the Cyprus Problem]* (Athens: Patakis, 2005).

Hatzivassiliou, Evanthis, *Greece and the Cold War: Front Line State, 1952-1967* (London: Routledge, 2006).
Hitchens, Christopher, *Hostage to History: Cyprus from the Ottomans to Kissinger* (London: Verso, 1997).
Hoffman, Bruce, *The Failure of British Military Strategy within Palestine 1939-1947* (Ramat-Gan: Bar-Ilan University Press, 1983).
Hoffman, Bruce, 'The Palestinian Police Force and the Challenges of Gathering Counter-Terrorism Intelligence, 1939-1947', (2008) [Unpublished].
Holland, Robert, 'Never, Never Land: British Colonial Policy and the Roots of Violence in Cyprus, 1950-54', *The Journal of Imperial and Commonwealth History*, Vol. 21 (1993), pp. 148–76.
Holland, Robert, *Britain and the Cyprus Revolt 1954-1959* (Oxford: Clarendon Press, 1998).
Holland, Robert and Diana Markides, *The British and the Hellenes: Struggles for Mastery in the Eastern Mediterranean, 1850-1960* (Oxford: Oxford University Press, 2006).
Jackson, Ashley, 'Empire and Beyond: The Pursuit of Overseas National Interests in the Late Twentieth Century', *The English Historical Review*, Vol. CXXII, No. 409 (2007), pp. 1350–66.
Katsourides, Yiannos, *The History of the Communist Party in Cyprus: Colonialism, Class, and the Cypriot Left* (London: I.B. Tauris, 2014).
Katsourides, Yiannos, *The Greek-Cypriot Nationalist Right in the Era of British Colonialism: Emergence, Mobilisation and Transformations of Right-Wing Party Politics* (Cham: Springer, 2017).
Kelling, George Horton, *Countdown to Rebellion: British Policy in Cyprus, 1939-1955* (New York: Greenwood Press, 1990).
Kitromilides, Paschalis, 'Greek Irredentism in Asia Minor and Cyprus', *Middle Eastern Studies*, Vol. 26 (December, 2006), pp. 3–17.
Koumoulides, John T. A., *Cyprus and the War of Greek Independence, 1821-1829* (Athens: National Centre of Social Research, 1971).
Kraemer, Joseph S., 'Revolutionary Guerrilla Warfare & the Decolonization Movement', *Polity*, Vol. 4, No. 2 (Winter, 1971), pp. 137–58.
Lamb, Richard, *The Failure of the Eden Government* (London: Sidgwick and Jackson, 1987).
Landau, Jacob, *Pan-Turkish: From Irredentism to Cooperation* (Bloomington: Indiana University Press, 1995)
Le Geyt, Philip S., *Makarios in Exile* (Nicosia: Anagennesis Press, 1961).
Leventis, Yiorghos, *Cyprus: The Struggle for Self-Determination in the 1940s, Prelude to Deeper Crisis* (Frankfurt: Peter Lang, 2002).
Lewis, Bernard, 'The Ottoman Empire and its Aftermath', *Journal of Contemporary History*, Vol. 15, No. 1, Imperial Hangovers (January, 1980), pp. 27–36.
Lloyd-Blood, L. 'Mediterranean', in *Journal of Comparative Legislation and International Law* (Oxford: Oxford University Press, 1939).
Loizou, Peter, 'Notes on Future Anthropological Research in Cyprus', in *Regional Variation in Modern Greece and Cyprus: Towards a Perspective on the Ethnography of Greece*, ed. Muriel Dimen and Ernestine Friedl (New York: New York Academy of Sciences, 1976).
Mallinson, William, *Britain and Cyprus: Key Themes and Documents since World War II* (London: I.B. Tauris, 2011).

Markides, Diana W., 'Britain's "New Look" Policy for Cyprus and the Makarios-Harding Talks, January 1955-March 1956', *Journal of Imperial and Commonwealth History*, Vol. 23, Issue 3 (September, 1995), pp. 479–502.
Markides, Diana W., *Cyprus 1957-1963: From Colonial Conflict to Constitutional Crisis, the Key Role of the Municipal Issue* (Minnesota: University of Minnesota, 2001).
Markides, Kyriacos, *The Rise and Fall of the Cyprus Republic* (New Haven: Yale University Press, 1977).
Mayes, Stanley, *Makarios: A Biography* (London: The Macmillan Press, 1981).
Mockaitis, Thomas R., *British Counterinsurgency 1919-60* (London: Macmillan, 1990).
Murphy, Philip, *Alan Lennox-Boyd: A Biography* (London: I.B. Tauris, 1999).
Nevzat, Altay, *Nationalism amongst the Turks of Cyprus: The First Wave* (Oulu: Oulu University Press, 2005).
Newsinger, John, *British Counterinsurgency: From Palestine to Northern Ireland* (Houndmills: Palgrave, 2002).
Neyzi, Leyla, 'Remembering Smyrna/Izmir: Shared History, Shared Trauma', *History & Memory*, Vol. 20, No. 2 (Fall/Winter, 2008), pp. 106–27.
O'Ballance, Edgar, *The Greek Civil War 1944-1949* (London: Faber and Faber, 1966).
O'Malley, Brendan and Ian Craig, *The Cyprus Conspiracy: America, Espionage and the Turkish Invasion* (London: I.B. Tauris Publishers, 1999).
O'Shaughnessy, '"To Gain the Hearts and Subdue the Minds of America": General Sir Henry Clinton and the Conduct of the British War in America', *Proceedings of the American Philological Society*, Vol. 158, No. 3 (September, 2013), pp. 199–208.
Panourgiá, Neni, *Dangerous Citizens: The Greek Left and the Terror of the State* (New York: Fordham University Press, 2009).
Papadakis, Yiannis, 'Greek-Cypriot Narratives of History and Collective Identity: Nationalism as a Contested Process', *American Ethnologist*, Vol. 25, No. 2 (May, 1998), pp. 149–65.
Papadopoulos, Omiros, *Οργάνωσις Χ: Τρία χρόνια τρεις αιώνες* [Organisation X: Three Years Three Centuries] (Athens: Νέα Θέσις, 2000).
Paparizos, Antonis, 'Enlightenment, Religion, and Tradition in Modern Greek Society', in *Greek Political Culture Today*, ed. Nikos Demertzis, 74–115 (Athens: Odysseas, 2000).
Pericleous, Chrysostomos, *Cyprus Referendum: A Divided Island and the Challenge of the Annan Plan* (London: I.B. Tauris, 2009).
Peristiany, Jean. G, 'Anthropological Sociological, and Geographical Fieldwork in Cyprus', *Annals of the New York Academy of Sciences*, Vol. 268 (1976), pp. 345–54.
Plumer, Aytug, *Cyprus, 1963-64: The Fateful Years* (Nicosia: CYREP, 2003).
Pollis, Adamantia, 'Intergroup Conflict and British Colonial Policy: The Case of Cyprus', *Comparative Politics*, Vol. 5, No. 4 (July, 1973), pp. 575–99.
Popplewell, Richard, '"Lacking Intelligence": Some Reflections on Recent Approaches to British Counter-insurgency, 1900-1960', *Intelligence and National Security*, Vol. 10, No. 2 (April, 1995), pp. 336–52.
Rappas, Alexis, *Cyprus in the 1930s: British Colonial Rule and the Roots of the Cyprus Conflict* (London: I.B. Tauris, 2014).
Robbins, Simon, 'The British Counter-insurgency in Cyprus', *Small Wars & Insurgencies*, Vol. 23, Nos. 4–5 (2012), pp. 720–43.
Rosenbaum, Naomi, 'Success in Foreign Policy: The British in Cyprus, 1878-1960', *Canadian Journal of Political Science*, Vol. 3, No. 4 (December, 1970), pp. 605–27.
Runciman, Steven, *The Fall of Constantinople 1453* (Cambridge: Cambridge University Press, 1965).

Sanders, David, *Losing an Empire, Finding a Role: British Foreign Policy since 1945* (London: Macmillan Press, 1990).
Scherer, Joseph L., *Blocking the Sun: The Cyprus Conflict* (Minneapolis: Minnesota Mediterranean and East European Monographs, Number 5, 1997).
Smith, Michael Llewellyn, *Ionian Vision: Greece in Asia Minor, 1919-1922* (Ann Arbor: The University of Michigan Press, 1998).
Stearns, Monteagle, *Entangled Allies: US Policy toward Greece, Turkey, and Cyprus* (New York: Council on Foreign Relations Press, 1992).
Stefanidis, Ioannis D., *Isle of Discord: Nationalism, Imperialism and the Making of the Cyprus Problem* (New York: New York University Press, 1999).
Stefanidis, Ioannis D., *Stirring the Greek Nation: Political Culture, Irredentism and Anti-Americanism in Post-War Greece, 1945-1967* (Hampshire: Ashgate Publishing, 2007).
Stephens, Robert, *Cyprus, a Place of Arms: Power Politics and Ethnic Conflict in the Eastern Mediterranean* (London: Pall Mall Press, 1966).
Stern, Laurence, 'Bitter Lessons: How We Failed in Cyprus', *Foreign Policy* Vol. 19 (Summer, 1975), pp. 34–78.
Strachan, Hew, 'British Counter-Insurgency from Malaya to Iraq', *RUSI*, Vol. 152, No. 6 (December, 2007), pp. 8–11.
Stubbs, Richard, *Hearts and Minds in Guerrilla Warfare: The Malayan Emergency, 1948-1960* (New York: Oxford University Press, 1989).
Taber, Robert, *The War of the Flea: A Study of Guerrilla Warfare Theory and Practise* (New York: Lyle Stuart, 1965).
Tachau, Frank, 'The Face of Turkish Nationalism: As Reflected in the Cyprus Dispute', *Middle East Journal*, Vol. 13, No. 3 (Summer, 1959), pp. 262–72.
Tal, Lawrence, 'Britain and the Jordan Crisis of 1958', *Middle Eastern Studies*, Vol. 31, No. 1 (January, 1995), pp. 39–57.
Terlexis, Pantazis, Διπλωματία και πολιτική του κυπριακού. Ανατομία ενός λάθους [Diplomacy and Policy of the Cyprus Problem: Anatomy of an Error] (Αθήνα: Κέδρος, 1971).
Thorpe, Richard, *Eden: The Life and Times of Anthony Eden, First Earl of Avon, 1897-1977* (London: Chatto & Windus, 2003).
Tilman, Robert O., 'The Non-Lessons of the Malayan Emergency', *Asian Survey*, Vol. 6, No. 8 (August, 1966), pp. 407–19.
Townsend, Charles, *The British Campaign in Ireland, 1919-1921: The Development of Political and Military Policies* (London: Oxford University Press, 1975).
Türkmen, Füsün, 'Cyprus 1964 Revisited: Was It Humanitarian Intervention?' *Perceptions*, Winter, 2005, pp. 61–88.
Uzer, Umut, *Identity and Turkish Foreign Policy: The Kemalist Influence in Cyprus and the Caucasus* (London: I.B. Tauris, 2011).
Vanezis, P. N., *Makarios: Faith and Power* (London: Abelard-Schumann Ltd, 1971).
Vanezis, P. N., *Makarios: Pragmatism v. Idealism* (London: Abelard-Schumann Ltd, 1974).
Varnavas, Andreas, *A Brief History of the Liberation Struggle of EOKA (1955-1959)*, trans. Phillipos Stylianou (Nicosia: The Foundation of the EOKA Liberation Struggle, 2004).
Vryonis, Speros, *The Mechanism of Catastrophe: the Turkish Pogrom of September 6-7, 1955, and the Destruction of the Greek Community of Istanbul* (New York: Greekworks, 2005).
West, Nigel, *The Friends: Britain's Post-war Secret Intelligence Operations* (London: Weidenfeld and Nicolson, 1988).
Wilkinson, Paul, ed., *British Perspectives on Terrorism* (London: Allen & Unwin, 1981).

Williams, Charles, *Harold Macmillan* (London: Weidenfeld & Nicolson, 2009).
Woodhouse, Christopher M., *The Struggle for Greece: 1941-1949* (New York: Beekman/Esanu, 1979).
Woodhouse, Christopher M., *Karamanlis: The Restorer of Greek Democracy* (Oxford: Clarendon Press, 1982).
Woodhouse, Christopher M., *Apple of Discord* (London: Hutchinson, 1985).
Xydis, Stephen G., *Cyprus: Conflict and Conciliation, 1954-1958* (Columbus: The Ohio State University Press, 1967).
Xydis, Stephen G., *Cyprus; Reluctant Republic* (The Hague: Mouton, 1973).
Yesilbursa, Behcet K., 'Turkey's Participation in the Middle East Command and Its Admission to NATO, 1950-52', *Middle Eastern Studies*, Vol. 35, No. 4 (October, 1999), pp. 70–102.

PhD theses

Assos, Demetris, 'Makarios: A Study of Anti-Colonial Nationalist Leadership, 1950-1959'. PhD diss., University of London, 2009. eTHos https://ethos.bl.uk/OrderDetails.do?uin=uk.bl.ethos.53678.
Clark, David J., 'The Colonial Police and Anti-Terrorism: Bengal 1930-36, Palestine 1937-47 and Cyprus 1955-59'. PhD diss., University of Oxford, 1978.
Faustmann, Hubert, 'Divide and Quit? The History of British Colonial Rule in Cyprus, 1878-1960'. PhD diss., Mannheim, 1999.
Karyos, Andreas, 'EOKA, 1955-1959: A Study of the Military Aspects of the Cyprus Revolt'. PhD diss., University of London, 2011. eTHos https://ethos.bl.uk/OrderDetails.do?uin=uk.bl.ethos.582011.

Index

Afxentiou, Grigoris 51
   death of 107–8, 136
AKEL (Progressive Party of Working People) 53, 56, 136, 137
   attitudes toward *enosis* 32–4
   attitudes toward Winster Constitution 25
   establishment of 14
Armitage, Robert (governor of Cyprus) 53, 56, 89, 92, 95
   dismissal of 65–6
   meeting with Gerald Templer 88
Asia Minor Catastrophe 8, 13, 16, 127, 146, 168, 173 n.2
Atlee, Clement 27
auxiliary police 95–6
Averoff-Tossizza, Evangelos 41, 61, 102, 115, 116, 123, 151, 158–63
   discussions with Makarios 37–8
   and Zurich and London agreements 164–5
Azinas, Andreas 48, 50, 51, 77

Baghdad Pact 69, 115, 119, 121, 144–5, 147
Baker, George (chief of staff to Harding) 90
   report on the Cyprus Emergency 108
Bishop Kyprianos of Kyrenia 103
   deportation of 70, 83
   opposition to compromise 78–80, 163
Bowker, James (British ambassador in Turkey) 71, 79, 122, 126, 141

Churchill, Winston 9, 12, 17
Communist Party of Cyprus (CPC) 13–4
Congress of Berlin (1878) 11–12, 15
Cypriot Orthodox Church 25, 49, 50, 60, 86, 91, 103, 104
   attitudes toward *enosis* 1, 8, 10–15, 25
   attitudes toward Turkish-Cypriots 8, 121
   'Blueprint of the National Struggle' 31, 32, 48–9
   as leaders of nationalist sentiment 8, 31–8, 48, 63, 76
   relations with British administration 25, 70, 84, 86, 103, 105
Cyprus
   becomes Crown Colony 175 n.36
   demographics 24, 81, 94, 96
   independence of 2, 5, 13, 14, 33, 42, 130, 136, 149, 150, 158–62, 164–5, 171
   intercommunal violence of 1958 4, 6, 95–6, 129–30, 138–48, 149–51, 157
   partition of 18, 110, 112–23, 125–7, 129–35, 138–41, 145, 149–52, 154, 158–61, 166, 171
   riots of 1931 13, 21, 23, 24, 25, 90
   role in the Greek War of Independence 7, 11
   self-determination for 26, 29, 31, 35, 37, 38, 41, 42, 55, 58–61, 68–9, 71–5, 77, 78, 80, 81, 101, 105, 111, 113–22, 131, 133, 134, 150, 155, 159–60, 170
   and Treaty of Berlin (1878) 11–12, 15, 17, 56
Cyprus Intelligence Committee (CIC) 52, 90–1, 107, 108, 123, 139
Cyprus is Turkish Association (KTC) 61, 62, 73
Cyprus Police Force (CPF) 91–7, 170
   casualties 170
   efforts to reform 93–6
   ethnic composition of 94–6
   expansion of mobile reserve 95–6
   targeted by EOKA 92

Darling, Kenneth (director of operations in Cyprus)   95, 156, 165, 170
  Report on the Cyprus Emergency   95, 156, 170
Denktaş, Rauf   146, 147, 161, 164
  political leader of TMT   146–7
Dighenis (cryptonym), *see* Grivas, Giorgos

Eden, Anthony   38, 50, 56, 63, 66, 67, 68, 97, 98, 101, 110, 114
  opposition to *enosis*   38, 40
  resignation   106, 114
  and Suez crisis   106, 109
Eisenhower, Dwight   124, 159
EOKA (National Organization of Cypriot Fighters)
  attacks on British security forces   51–3, 66, 69, 72, 80, 89, 92–3, 97–103, 106–7, 127, 138, 143, 156–7
  attacks on Cyprus Police Force   92–6
  attacks on Greek-Cypriot leftists   85, 136–8, 155, 157, 169, 170
  attacks on 'traitors'   53, 85, 93, 101, 137, 150, 155–7, 169–70
  attacks on Turkish-Cypriots   150, 157
  casualties   99, 123, 155, 157, 170
  formation   45–51
  guerrilla teams   5, 47–9, 52, 78, 85, 93, 99, 143, 168, 171
  ideology   45–9, 170
  members, number and profile   1, 48, 52, 91, 169
    members hanged by authorities   100, 102, 170
    members tortured by authorities   5, 85, 99
  protests, strikes   5, 49, 98, 123
Ethnarchy Bureau   68, 104
Ethnarchy Council   34, 47, 78, 80, 104

Famagusta   45, 51, 52, 123, 133, 134, 138, 155
  violence against the Left in   137–8
Foot, Hugh (governor of Cyprus)   21, 22, 125, 134–8, 140–2, 154, 157, 158, 160, 163–6
  arrival in Cyprus   126, 129–31

  attitudes toward Makarios   81
  attitudes toward partition   125, 129, 145
  as Colonial Secretary and Acting Governor in Cyprus   21
  plan for Cyprus (Foot Plan)   129, 131, 133–4, 137, 139, 140
  relations with military in Cyprus   132–3, 144

Georghiades, Polykarpos   123
  accusations as British spy   196 n.69
Geunyeli incident   142, 146
Greece
  civil war   3, 8, 32, 35, 46, 49, 168
  elections of 1952   137
  elections of 1956   101
  elections of 1958   151, 162
  and NATO   5, 22, 57, 59, 89, 96, 115, 123, 129, 152, 154, 158, 162
Greek War of Independence   7, 11
  and fallout in Cyprus   11
Grivas, Giorgos   50, 52, 53, 55, 72, 73, 78, 80, 82, 84, 87, 91–3, 96–8, 100–2, 104, 106–8, 123, 133, 135, 137, 142, 143, 146, 155, 156–8, 163–5, 167, 169, 171
  anti-communism   47
  death of   172
  as 'Dighenis'   51, 90–1, 102, 106, 147, 162–4
  early life and education   45–7
  and formation of EOKA   48–9
  relations with Makarios   49–51, 90, 105, 136, 167
  role in the Greek Civil War   46–7
  and Zurich and London Agreements   167–8

Halkın Sesi (The Voice of the People)   121, 126
Harding, John (governor of Cyprus)   54, 84, 85, 86, 88, 89, 90, 92, 93, 95, 97–101, 103, 104, 108, 110, 111, 118, 119, 120, 124–5, 126, 132, 156, 165
  appointed as governor of Cyprus   65–6
  arrival in Cyprus   68

career background 66
departure from Cyprus 124–5, 127
negotiations with Makarios 67–83, 102, 109
Hellenism 9–10, 14, 51, 137
Hopkinson, Henry 50
  statement on Cyprus in Parliament 38–41

interrogation of EOKA detainees 85, 91, 98, 99, 101, 107
Istanbul pogrom 61–2, 140

Karamanlis, Constantinos 114, 116, 137, 147, 151–3
  attitudes toward *enosis* 101
  and Zurich and London Agreements 163–6
Kemal, Mustapha (Atatürk) 15–16, 49, 61, 141, 142, 166, 197 n.100
Kendrew, Douglas (chief of operations in Cyprus) 143, 144, 156
  attitudes toward Turkish base on Cyprus 132
  relations with Hugh Foot 132–3
Kenya
  British experience with counter-insurgency in 39, 91, 95–6, 142, 170
  and Mau Mau 2, 4
Kontemenos massacre 142
Kütchük, Fazil 73, 126, 140, 146, 164, 166, 171
Kyrenia 83, 119, 142, 172
Kyrillos III (archbishop of Cyprus) 9, 23–4
Kyrou, Alexis 38, 41–2, 174 n.8

Labour government 27, 36
  program of civic improvements in Cyprus 24
  and Winster Constitution 22
Larnaca 12, 51, 52, 77, 107, 131, 140
Lausanne, Treaty of 17, 60, 118
Lennox-Boyd, Alan 55, 65–7, 70–2, 77, 92, 99, 104, 111, 112, 114–17, 119–22, 124–6, 140–2, 145, 161–2
  visits to Cyprus 81–3

Leontios (archbishop of Cyprus) 24
  death of 25
  differences with Archbishop Makarios II 25
Limassol 51–3, 107
Lloyd, Selwyn 41, 42, 96, 119, 121, 122, 133, 134, 152, 158
Loizides, Savvas 47, 48
Loizides, Socrates 47, 48, 51
London Agreement 164, 165, 167, 171
London Conference of 1955, *see* Tripartite Conference

Macmillan, Harold 55, 58, 66, 71, 109–11, 119, 121, 124, 125, 129, 130, 145, 147, 149–53, 156, 163–6
  becomes prime minister 106
  tridominium plan 130–1, 158, 160
  and the Tripartite Conference (1955) 56, 59–60
Makarios II (archbishop of Cyprus) 37
  differences with Archbishop Leontios 25
Makarios III (archbishop of Cyprus) 38, 41, 55, 56, 59, 61, 90, 92, 100, 101, 103, 108, 110, 114, 124, 126, 131, 147, 149–50, 151, 153–4, 157, 158, 162, 163, 168, 171, 172
  attitudes toward Turkey and Turkish-Cypriots 34–5, 45, 58
  attitudes toward violence 47–53, 135–6, 142
  brinksmanship 81, 165
  decision to begin insurgency 50–1
  deportation to the Seychelles 66, 83–4, 85, 104, 111
  elected archbishop 37, 83
  interview with Barbara Castle 158–9
  and London and Zurich Agreements 165–6
  negotiations with Harding 67–83, 97–8, 102, 109
  relations with Grivas 45–53, 105, 167, 169
  role in organizing 1950 plebiscite 37
Malaya 65–6, 83, 86–7, 89–90, 92, 95–6, 98, 170

Martin, John (deputy undersecretary of state for the colonies) 98, 111, 118, 160
Mau Mau 2, 4
Meghali Idhea (Great Idea) 7–8, 12, 14, 25, 127
  Underpinnings 10–11
Menderes, Adnan 98, 134, 147, 152, 172
  attitudes to partition 117, 120, 122, 145
  plane crash 164
  role in Istanbul Pogrom 61, 62
  and Zurich and London Agreements 163–4

NATO 22, 57, 59, 62, 68, 69, 71–4, 77, 89, 96, 108, 115, 121, 123, 126, 129, 131, 145, 152, 154, 158, 161, 162, 164, 166
Nicosia 38, 51–3, 80, 81, 83, 101, 118, 122–3, 133, 134, 138, 140, 152, 155, 172

operations by security forces
  Black Mak 123
  Foxhunter I 98
  Foxhunter II 98
  Lucky Alphonse 101
  Matchbox 144, 154
  Pepperpot 101
  Table Lighter 144

Palestine 1, 2, 4, 21, 26, 29, 36, 91, 117, 118, 120, 126, 140, 142, 170
pan-Hellenism 9, 10, 14, 51
Papagos, Alexandros (prime minister of Greece) 47, 50, 101
Paphos 37, 72, 73, 119
Peake, Charles (British ambassador in Athens) 76, 115, 116
PEON (Pancyprian National Youth Organisation) 48, 90, 103
plebiscite of January 1950 18, 32–7, 76, 83

Q unit 91, 170, 190 n.39

Radcliffe, Cyril
  constitutional proposals 109–24, 126, 131, 151
referendum on *enosis* (1950), *see* plebiscite of January 1950

St. George (caique) 50–1
Sèvres, Treaty of 15
Sinclair, George (deputy governor of Cyprus) 90, 126, 133, 139, 140, 165
Smyrna 12, 15, 16, 127, 146
Storrs, Sir Ronald 8–9, 13
Suez crisis 105–10, 112, 114, 121, 145, 147, 171

Templer, Gerald 98
  and 'hearts and minds' 87
  as model for counter-insurgency command 66, 86, 90, 92
  visit to Cyprus 88
Tripartite Conference 54, 55–61, 63, 65–8, 71, 109, 119, 123, 152
Turkey 1–5, 12–13, 15, 22, 29, 33–7, 42, 49, 54, 69, 73–80, 87, 96, 109–11, 113, 115–16, 118–21, 126, 129, 132–4, 139–141, 144–5, 147–54, 158–60, 169, 170, 172
  and London and Zurich agreements 161–6
  opposition to *enosis* 8–10, 17–19, 24–6, 71–2, 79, 86, 89, 117, 130–1
  support for TMT 146–7
  at Tripartite Conference 55–63, 68
Turkish-Cypriots 22, 25, 27, 35, 49, 58, 69, 72, 73, 75, 78–81, 87, 100–1, 109, 113–15, 119, 121–2, 123, 124, 126, 129–36, 138–42, 144–6, 148, 150, 154, 156–8, 161, 164, 169–71
  as members of Cyprus Police Force 94–6, 143
  opposition to *enosis* 24–6, 28, 32, 35–6, 57, 86, 89, 117
  origins 10
  plebiscite of 1950 34
  relations with Turkey 17–18, 60, 68, 117

Turkish Resistance Organization
(TMT)   1, 134, 135, 140, 144, 154
- attacks against Greek-Cypriots   143, 145–8
- attacks against Turkish-Cypriot 'Leftists' and 'traitors'   138
- formation   127
- leadership   147
- training and equipment   139

United Nations   17, 33, 37–9, 49, 50, 52, 55, 56, 59, 63, 97, 106, 108, 123–4, 149–50, 153, 158–62
- debate of September 1954   41–3, 45, 76, 170

Venizelos, Eleftherios   166, 168
- and Meghali Idhea   8, 12
- at the Paris Peace Conference   12

Venizelos, Sophocles   35, 38, 159

Winster, Reginald (governor of Cyprus)   24, 28, 35
- and constitutional proposals   25, 29, 68, 69, 109, 116

Wolseley, Garnet (administrator of Cyprus)
- arrival in Cyprus   12

'X' organization   46–8
- formation by Grivas   46
- publications of Makarios III for   46

Zorlu, Fatin   134, 146, 152, 160, 164, 166, 172
- approach to Averoff   161–2
- formation of TMT   146–7
- meetings with Averoff in Paris   161–2
- at the Tripartate Conference (1955)   60–1

Zurich Agreement   150, 163, 165–7, 171

www.ingramcontent.com/pod-product-compliance
Lightning Source LLC
Chambersburg PA
CBHW072233290426
44111CB00012B/2075